ITERATURE, ENGLISH LITERATURE, AND WORLD S IN ENGLISH: AN INFORMATION GUIDE SERIES

dore Grieder, Curator, Division of Special Collections, Fales Library,
y

Duane DeVries, Associate Professor, Polytechnic Institute of New York,

erican and English literature in this series:

Y FICTION IN AMERICA AND ENGLAND, 1950-1970—*Edited by Paul A. Echholz*

A IN AMERICA AND ENGLAND, 1950-1970—*Edited by*

LETTERS AND JOURNALS—*Edited by Margaret C. Patterson*

N POETRY AND DRAMA, 1760-1975—*Edited by William P. French, mritjit Singh, and Genevieve Fabre*

LE ENGLISH POETRY TO 1500—*Edited by Walter H. Beale*

RY, 1660-1800—*Edited by Donald C. Mell*

ANTIC POETRY, 1800-1835—*Edited by Donald H. Reiman*

RY, 1900-1950—*Edited by Emily Ann Anderson*

---

s part of the
RMATION GUIDE LIBRARY

ists of a number of separate series of guides covering
e social sciences, humanities, and current affairs.

Paul Wasserman, Professor and former Dean, School
formation Services, University of Maryland

r: Denise Allard Adzigian, Gale Research Company

Contemporar
America anc
1950-1

AMERICAN L
LITERATURI

Series Editor: The
New York Univers

Associate Editor:
Brooklyn

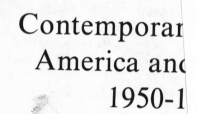

Other books on A

CONTEMPORA
Alfred F. Rosa an

MODERN DRA
Richard H. Harri

AUTHOR NEW

AFRO-AMERIC
Michel J. Fabre,

OLD AND MID

ENGLISH POE

ENGLISH ROM

ENGLISH POE

The above se
GALE IN

The Library
major areas i

General Edit
of Library a

Managing E

Contemporary Poetry in America and England 1950-1975

A GUIDE TO INFORMATION SOURCES

Volume 41 in the American Literature, English Literature, and World Literatures in English Information Guide Series

Martin E. Gingerich

Associate Professor of English
Western Michigan University
Kalamazoo

Gale Research Company
Book Tower, Detroit, Michigan 48226

Library of Congress Cataloging in Publication Data

Gingerich, Martin E.
Contemporary poetry in America and England, 1950-1975.

(Volume 41 in the American literature, English literature, and world literatures in English information guide series)
Bibliography: p.
Includes indexes.
1. American poetry—20th century—Bibliography.
2. English poetry—20th century—Bibliography. I. Title.
II. Series: Gale information guide library. American literature, English literature, and world literatures in English ; v. 41.
Z1231.P7G56 1983 [PS303] 016.811'5 73-16992
ISBN 0-8103-1221-2

VITA

Martin E. Gingerich is associate professor of English at Western Michigan University, Kalamazoo. He received his M.A. in 1961 from the University of Maine and Ph.D. in 1967 from Ohio University.

Besides writing several essays for periodicals, he has written W.H. AUDEN: A REFERENCE GUIDE (Boston: G.K. Hall, 1977), and is in the process of working on THE LOUD HILL OF WALES: GEOGRAPHICAL INFLUENCES ON DYLAN THOMAS.

CONTENTS

Contents

Contents

ACKNOWLEDGMENTS

This project has been supported in part by the Faculty Research Fund, Western Michigan University, and by the department of English, who granted me released time to work on it. I am grateful to Bettina Meyer and Joan Morin of the interlibrary loan staff of Waldo Library, Western Michigan University, and others on that staff.

I owe a special debt of gratitude to Darcy Gingerich who helped me in the early stages to find what Waldo Library held and what had to be borrowed. My friend Gilbert Bennett of University College, Swansea, Wales, sought out and sent to me necessary pieces of information. Margaret Williamson, who does not know me at all, supplied me with some information that I dare say appears in no other reference work in the United States. Let me not forget to acknowledge that when I made errors in numbering, it was my wife who did the renumbering.

And finally, I wish to thank Ted Grieder, Denise Allard Adzigian, and Pamela Dear for their careful editing of my manuscript.

INTRODUCTION

"'What is the use of a book,' thought Alice, 'without pictures or conversations?'" And while it is tempting to reply, "Not much," this work is intended to be useful to both advanced and beginning students of contemporary poetry. It attempts to specify and describe the major sources of information about the period from 1950 to 1975 and also the critical writing produced in response to the work of more than a hundred poets of the period. This flow of critical writing today quickly dates, of course, any bibliography, and one on contemporary writers is dated almost as soon as the writers are selected. At some point, nevertheless, bibliographers must stop collecting and start typing. And though lovers of poetry, they will realize then that if there are not and never can be too many poets there are at least too many poets for the book. As a consequence of this realization, bibliographers are obliged, as I have been, to omit numerous materials and writers they would have liked to include.

In addition to the obvious reasons, I particularly regret not having been able to visit England and Wales to make a more thorough search for secondary materials relating to poets, since my principal criterion for inclusion has been the amount of critical effort prompted by a poet's work. Even so, for both English and American poets, I have ignored that criterion occasionally--for example, in the case of certain older poets of the period who seemed to me to have been critically neglected. All these, I think, should receive some notice before they are lost to us in the crowd of new, young poets. In the case of the latter, I decided that if I could not add to the information already available in such biobibliographical guides as CONTEMPORARY POETS (no. 62) and CONTEMPORARY AUTHORS (no. 22), there was no point in duplication. For poets not included here, therefore, readers should search these and the other works listed in my general chapters.

Still other poets one might expect to find in a guide to contemporary poetry but not found here have already been included in other volumes of this Gale Information Guide Series. Sir John Betjeman, for example, appears in ENGLISH POETRY, 1900-1950 (Emily Ann Anderson, comp., Detroit, Gale Research Co., 1982). Canadian, Irish, Scottish, and black American are other examples of groups of writers for whom volumes exist. My one anxiety in this respect involves one of my greatest pleasures in poetry. Writers in Wales, I learned, do not consider themselves English and in some cases dispute even the label Anglo-Welsh: "What's Anglo-Welsh? I'm Welsh!" But I have included a few Welsh poets here (who write in English) because I saw no other guide planned for them in the series. I should add that in America there are very few critical studies of Welsh poets; Roland Mathias, for example, whom I omit but admire as much as the poets I have included, has received no critical attention beyond a few brief reviews. But even the lack of criticism is a necessary kind of information to convey to students of contemporary poetry.

After choosing my poets, I wished, naturally, to guide readers to everything available about them. To be thorough in their search, however, readers must be cautioned to use the general chapters of the guide and the indexes, not just the chapter on individual poets. For example, in chapter 7 will be found numerous titles naming the poets treated, all cross-referenced to other works under the name of the poet in the author index. For students who are looking for a topic rather than for a poet, the title index will also serve as a subject index, though it will require browsing rather than just looking up a word. The other chapters afford students an overview of the period and of the problems in interpretation peculiar to contemporary works. They are arranged in order of decreasing generality, leading into the chapter of specific studies on individual poets.

Unfortunately, a full treatment of any of these chapters would make a book; I have had to aim selectively at representing samples that will take students into the various areas of their libraries where larger selections of related materials will be found.

I have not included, incidentally, a source of information that could prove useful particularly to students just beginning their studies. It lies in the introductions, notes, and bibliographies in the many anthologies of contemporary poetry published today. Frequently, as in the NORTON ANTHOLOGY OF MODERN POETRY (no. 260), short biographies of the selected poets make up part of the introductory material. A large listing of such anthologies can be found in the various editions of CONTEMPORARY POETS (no. 62).

The more advanced a student is in the study of poetry, however, the more useful will be the chapter on individual poets. Looking up a poet in that chapter and the name in the author index will reveal all that has been written by and about that poet; but again, further use of the library is necessary. In the entry on Robert Lowell, for example, appear first a primary bibliography intended to suggest the range and scope of Lowell's poetic output and then a secondary bibliography listing bibliographies, critical books (some with annotated bibliographies), and critical articles (including interviews and dissertations). My selections supplement and continue the work of the editors and critics cited there. For example, Richard J. Fein's Twayne book on Lowell (no. 984) in its second edition annotates critical works on Lowell into 1979. I have supplemented Fein's list by annotating items Fein has listed without comment and continued it by including items he omitted or that appeared too late for him to include. I have also included, as Fein does not, notes on dissertations abstracted in

DISSERTATION ABSTRACTS INTERNATIONAL, which abstracts are the basis for my annotations. A student of Lowell's poetry can therefore survey a nearly complete, annotated list of writings about Lowell by using Fein's bibliography in conjunction with my entry on him.

This example of Lowell illustrates my basic pattern and practice. For each poet I have supplied a primary bibliography, which I have taken from published lists, and cited applicable bibliographies, biographies (or autobiographies) and letters, critical books, and critical articles. Except where noted and except for one or two items described in MLA ABSTRACTS, I have examined all the secondary items and described them as objectively as I could. Although I have everyman's supply of prejudices, I have tried to keep them out of my comments. Unlike bibliographers of earlier periods of literature, the criticism of which has been sifted and resifted and is of such a quantity that a student needs a guide to quality, I have not attempted to evaluate and have, instead, adopted the point of view of T.S. Eliot when he said that some day may come along a critic of genius who knows exactly what to make of Shakespeare's laundry list.

Chapter 1

BIBLIOGRAPHIES AND REFERENCE WORKS

The works listed in this chapter can be found in the reference collections of most libraries. Some of these, however, are bibliographical articles appearing in journals that may be shelved in a library's nonreference areas. I have supplemented rather than duplicated the work already done by Gershator, Nyren, Perloff, Pownall, Somer and Cooper, Tucker and Stein, and Williams (respectively, nos. 30, 61, 62, 63, 69, 72, and 78).

1 Akeroyd, Joanne Vinson, and George F. Butterick, comps. WHERE ARE THEIR PAPERS? A UNION LIST LOCATING THE PAPERS OF FORTY-TWO CONTEMPORARY AMERICAN POETS AND WRITERS. Storrs: University of Connecticut Library, 1976. 75 p.

Lists holdings of manuscript material in participating libraries.

2 ANNUAL BIBLIOGRAPHY OF ENGLISH LANGUAGE AND LITERATURE. Cambridge, Engl.: Modern Humanities Research Association, 1920--. Subject indexes and abstracts.

Similar to MLA annual bibliographies (56) in subjects and arrangement. Volume for 1975 was published in 1978.

3 Beebe, Maurice. "Selected Bibliography on Theories of Modernism and Post-Modernism." JOURNAL OF MODERN LITERATURE, 3, no. 5 (1974), 1080-84.

A list of ninety-five items on the subject.

4 Bertholf, Robert J. "The Key in the Window: Kent's Collection of Modern American Poetry." SERIF, 7, no. 3 (1970), 52-70.

Describes the holdings in contemporary American poetry at Kent State's Department of Special Collections, most of which are apparently editions of works by Black Mountain, Origin, and San Francisco poets. A few other poets are included.

5 BIBLIOGRAPHIES IN CONTEMPORARY POETRY. Potsdam, N.Y.: F.W. Crumb Memorial Library (SUNY), 1972. 68 p.

Includes primary and secondary bibliographies for Robert Creeley to 1967, Galway Kinnell to 1967, Stanley Kunitz to 1967, Lewis Turco to 1971, and five other poets. Not annotated but has a biographical sketch of each poet. Lists reviews of individual books.

6 THE BIBLIOGRAPHY OF CONTEMPORARY POETS, 1973. London: Regency Press, 1973. 195 p. Index of pseudonyms.

Issued irregularly (year included in title). A directory of hundreds of poets, all "dedicated to their craft." Includes relatively unknown poets whose poems were published in anthologies mostly of the Regency Press.

7 BOOK REVIEW DIGEST. New York: Wilson, 1905--. Monthly (not February or July).

Brief excerpts from reviews listed. Subject and title index; main entry by author of book.

8 BOOK REVIEW INDEX. Detroit: Gale Research Co., 1965--. Bimonthly.

Lists book reviews of the year. Main entry by author of book but has title index which refers the user to author entries.

9 Boos, Florence, ed. "1976 Bibliography of Literature in English by and about Women: 600-1960." WOMEN & LITERATURE, 5, No. 2 (1977), 1-167 supplement.

Not seen. Cited in 1978 MLA INTERNATIONAL BIBLIOGRAPHY, Item 892. Bibliography for 1977 appears in WOMEN & LITERATURE, 6, No. 2 (1978), supplement.

10 Borklund, Elmer. CONTEMPORARY LITERARY CRITICS. New York: St. Martin's Press, 1977. 550 p.

Biobibliographical essay on each of 115 British and American critics, including some contemporary poets as critics. JOURNAL OF MODERN LITERATURE says "a truly impressive summation of literary theory in the twentieth century."

11 Bradbury, Malcolm, Eric Mottram, and Jean Franco, eds. PENGUIN COMPANION TO AMERICAN LITERATURE. New York: McGraw-Hill, 1971. 384 p.

Biobibliographical facts on some contemporary poets (Hyam Plutzik, for example, whom other sourcebooks ignore).

12 BRITISH NATIONAL BIBLIOGRAPHY. London: Council of the British National Bibliography, 1950--.

Lists and describes new works published in Britain. Subject sections give fullest information; shorter entries appear in alphabetical listing. In 1976 began a two-volume annual issue dividing subject and alphabetical sections.

13 Bruccoli, Matthew J., and C.E. Frazer Clark, eds. FIRST PRINTINGS OF AMERICAN AUTHORS: CONTRIBUTIONS TOWARD DESCRIPTIVE CHECKLISTS. 4 vols. Detroit: Gale Research Co., 1977-78. 1,657 p.

Identifies first printings of five hundred authors, colonial to the present. "Featured" lists provide full information for British and American printings; "Standard" lists only American printings. Asterisks in Table of Contents indicate which authors are "featured." Volume 4 has cumulative index of authors.

14 BULLETIN OF BIBLIOGRAPHY, 1897--. Quarterly.

Publishes bibliographies in the humanities and social sciences. A cumulative index, 1897-1975, has been published separately.

15 Callow, James T., and Robert J. Reilly, eds. GUIDE TO AMERICAN LITERATURE FROM EMILY DICKINSON TO THE PRESENT. New York: Barnes and Noble, 1977. 272 p.

Contains secondary, critical material on seventy-two writers under headings like "Social Protest" and "Realism" and under genre headings as well. Includes a few contemporary poets in this guide, under "Modern Poets."

16 Chicorel, Marietta, ed. CHICOREL INDEX SERIES. New York: Chicorel Library, 1970--.

Volumes 4, 5, and 6 in this series have to do with poetry; 4 and 5 are most useful to students of contemporary poetry. Arranged alphabetically by title, first line, author, and performer (in the case of discs and tapes), and also with separate listings for author, title, and so on. First line entries are only for untitled poems.

17 CHRISTIANITY AND LITERATURE, 27, No. 4 (1978), 71-100.

Bibliographies in each issue of this journal supplement standard bibliographies since they include journals omitted from other lists. The number cited lists items on David Jones, Robert Lowell, Peter Porter, Stevie Smith, Gary Snyder, and Robert Penn Warren.

18 Clark, LaVerne Harrell. FOCUS 101. Chico, Calif.: Heidelberg Graphics, 1979. 145 p.

Biobibliographical accounts accompanied by photographs of 101 world poets writing in English, mostly from Britain and the United States.

19 Clark, LaVerne Harrell, and Mary MacArthur, eds. THE FACE OF POETRY: 101 POETS IN TWO DECADES--THE 60'S AND THE 70'S. Photographs by Clark. Foreword by Richard Eberhart. Arlington, Tex.: Gallimaufry, 1976. 300 p.

Not seen, but probably the same material from item 18 was used with the addition of poems. Cited in JOURNAL OF MODERN LITERATURE, 7, No. 4: 641, which describes it as "representative poems accompanied by remarkable photographs."

20 Cline, Gloria Stark, and Jeffrey A. Baker, eds. AN INDEX TO CRITICISM OF BRITISH AND AMERICAN POETRY. Metuchen, N.J.: Scarecrow Press, 1973. 318 p. Index, bibliog., pp. 267-70.

Extensive range and entries on several contemporary poets. Arranged by poet, by critic, and by poem.

21 Congdon, Kirby, ed. CONTEMPORARY POETS IN AMERICAN ANTHOLOGIES, 1960-1977. Metuchen, N.J.: Scarecrow Press, 1978. 228 p.

Part 1 lists anthologies; part 2 lists authors. Includes British and American poets living in 1960.

22 CONTEMPORARY AUTHORS: A BIO-BIBLIOGRAPHICAL GUIDE TO CURRENT AUTHORS AND THEIR WORK. Detroit: Gale Research Co., 1962--. Biannual.

Volumes in this series, under various editors, now number 1-103 and then begin a new series. Lists living authors and those who died after 1960. A cumulative index in each volume must be used since entries are not reprinted from volume to volume. Entries are arranged alphabetically within each volume.

23 "Current Bibliography." TWENTIETH CENTURY LITERATURE, 1954--. Quarterly.

Subjects in world literature listed alphabetically with a sentence or two of annotation, often a direct quotation from the work listed.

24 Daiches, David, ed. THE PENGUIN COMPANION TO ENGLISH LITERATURE. New York: McGraw-Hill, 1971. 576 p.

Encyclopedic information on writers from Anglo-Saxon times to the present (1970). Weak in contemporary writers but includes, for example, Ted Hughes, though not Jon Silkin or Charles Tomlinson.

25 Davis, Lloyd, and Robert Irwin, comps. CONTEMPORARY AMERICAN POETRY: A CHECKLIST. Metuchen, N.J.: Scarecrow Press, 1975. 184 p. Title index.

Primary bibliography of books to end of 1973 by poets active after 1950. Includes W.H. Auden, for example.

26 A DIRECTORY OF AMERICAN POETS. New York: Poets and Writers, 1973--. Irregular.

Entitled A DIRECTORY OF AMERICAN POETS AND FICTION WRITERS, in subsequent editions. Lists American writers with their addresses and phone numbers, organizations that sponsor readings and workshops, information on anthologies, films about poets, and suggestions for organizing readings and workshops. Includes both poets and fiction writers but not playwrights.

27 EXPLICATOR, 1942--.

"A Checklist of Explication" appears in each volume and always includes some contemporary writers. Items are listed by the subject of the explication. Those published in EXPLICATOR are indexed by author.

28 Fairbanks [Myers], Carol, ed. MORE WOMEN IN LITERATURE: CRITICISM OF THE SEVENTIES. Metuchen, N.J.: Scarecrow Press, 1979. 457 p.

Extends and enlarges the coverage in 1976 edition (below). Does not repeat entries, but some dissertations in the previous edition are books or articles in the second.

29 ______. WOMEN IN LITERATURE: CRITICISM OF THE SEVENTIES. Metuchen, N.J.: Scarecrow Press, 1976. 256 p.

Lists general books and articles in world literature and all genres relating to women's studies. May sometimes be cataloged under "Myers."

30 Gershator, Phillis, ed. A BIBLIOGRAPHIC GUIDE TO THE LITERATURE OF CONTEMPORARY AMERICAN POETRY, 1970-1975. Metuchen, N.J.: Scarecrow Press, 1976. 124 p. Topical guide (subject index), author index, title index.

Annotates reference works on the subject, general works in history, collections of critical essays, interviews, and criticism, anthologies, and textbooks.

31 Graham, John. "Ut Pictura Poesis." BULLETIN OF BIBLIOGRAPHY, 29, No. 1 (1972), 13-15, 18.

Mostly on precontemporary literature; lists some general studies on the relationship of literature and other arts; section on page 15 on "Concrete Poetry."

32 Greiner, Donald J., ed. DICTIONARY OF LITERARY BIOGRAPHY. Vol. 5: AMERICAN POETS SINCE WORLD WAR II. Parts 1 and 2. Detroit: Gale Research Co., 1980. Part I, A-K, 446 p.; part 2, L-Z, 449 p.

Each volume has "master entries," with extended essays on poets considered by the editor to be major influences (like Ammon, Ashbery, Lowell, Nemerov, Rich), and "standard entries," which vary in length according to the poet's "influence and the size of his canon." Part 1 has sixty-nine poets and part 2 sixty-four. The primary criterion for inclusion is that the poet had not published more than one collection of poetry before 1945. Biographical information, a critical essay, and a bibliography make up each entry.

33 GYPSY SCHOLAR. East Lansing: Michigan State University, 1973--. 3 issues per year.

Publishes a list of doctoral dissertations from British, Canadian, and U.S. universities for degrees granted in the current year.

34 Havlice, Patricia Pate, ed. INDEX TO LITERARY BIOGRAPHY. 2 vols. Metuchen, N.J.: Scarecrow Press, 1975. 1,308 p.

Covers thousands of authors from antiquity to the present (1975). Key to abbreviations is in the first volume only. For contemporary poets the reader is referred usually to CONTEMPORARY AUTHORS (no. 22) or CONTEMPORARY POETS (no. 62).

35 Hoffman, Daniel, ed. HARVARD GUIDE TO CONTEMPORARY AMERICAN WRITING. Cambridge, Mass.: Harvard University Press, 1979. 606 p.

Surveys American literature from World War II to the end of the 1970s. Poetry is discussed in the three final chapters, pp. 439-606.

36 INDEX TO BOOK REVIEWS IN THE HUMANITIES. Detroit: Phillip Thomson, 1960--. Quarterly.

Lists reviews that appeared during the year under author of book being reviewed.

37 Inge, M. Thomas, Maurice Duke, and Jackson R. Bryer, eds. RESOURCES FOR AMERICAN LITERARY STUDY. 1971--. Spring and autumn.

Accepts annotated and evaluative checklists, evaluative bibliographical essays, accounts or catalogs of collections of research material, edited correspondence, personal papers, and so on. Rarely on contemporary poets, but materials on late moderns appear more frequently.

38 Ivask, Ivar, and Gero von Wilpert. WORLD LITERATURE SINCE 1945. New York: Frederick Ungar, 1973. 724 p. Bibliogs., index.

Chapters for American and British literature contain sections on contemporary poets.

39 Johnson, Robert Owen, ed. AN INDEX TO LITERATURE IN THE NEW YORKER. 3 vols. Metuchen, N.J.: Scarecrow Press, 1969-71.

Original works and reviews from 1925 listed by title: "every poem, short story, Profile, Reporter at Large, Letter, Onward and Upward with the Arts, Around City Hall, and similar material, as well as references to literary figures taken from Talk of the Town, Letters from Paris and London, and extended discussions in book reviews." Inclusive to 1970.

40 Jones, Brynmor, ed. A BIBLIOGRAPHY OF ANGLO-WELSH LITERATURE 1900-1965. Llandysul, Wales: J.D. Lewis, 1970. 139 p. General index.

"Published by the Wales and Monmouthshire Branch of the Library Association." Primary bibliographies on Raymond Garlick, David Jones, John Ormond, Vernon Watkins, and others along with a few items of criticism on these writers.

41 Jones, Howard Mumford, and Richard M. Ludwig. GUIDE TO AMERICAN LITERATURE AND ITS BACKGROUND SINCE 1890. 4th ed. Cambridge, Mass.: Harvard University Press, 1972. 240 p.

Lists works on American history, politics, sociology, fine and popular arts, as well as works on literary history and criticism. Sections on the contemporary period.

42 JOURNAL OF MODERN LITERATURE. 1970--. Annual Review Number.

Lists general subjects in ten categories, including criticism of poetry and works by and about individual authors. Reviews books the editors deem likely to attract attention, some of which reviews are themselves critical essays. Also has information on professional conferences, library acquisitions, requests for research assistance, and so on. The term "modern" here is international and ranges from Emily Dickinson and Henry James to the present.

43 Kolb, Harold H., Jr., ed. A FIELD GUIDE TO THE STUDY OF AMERICAN LITERATURE. Charlottesville: University of Virginia Press, 1976. 136 p. Index.

A selective list to guide beginners through studies in American literature; has some entries on contemporary poetry. Sections on Bibliographies, Literary History and Criticism, Reference Works, Editions and Series, Anthologies, and Journals.

44 Kunitz, Stanley, ed. TWENTIETH CENTURY AUTHORS: FIRST SUPPLEMENT. New York: H.W. Wilson, 1955. 1,123 p.

Predecessor of Wakeman's WORLD AUTHORS (no. 74) and should be checked for older contemporary poets omitted by Wakeman.

45 Kuntz, Joseph Marshall, ed. POETRY EXPLICATION. Denver: Alan Swallow, 1962; updated, Boston: G.K. Hall, 1980. 570 p.

Lists explications on individual poems published during 1950-59, arranged alphabetically by poet and within these entries by title and within these by explicator. Poems range from Old English to contemporary.

46 Leary, Lewis, ed. ARTICLES ON AMERICAN LITERATURE, 1950-1967. Durham, N.C.: Duke University Press, 1970. 752 p.

Adds to the quarterly checklists of AMERICAN LITERATURE some items from PMLA, AMERICAN QUARTERLY, NEW ENGLAND QUARTERLY, and other journals. Includes items from bibliographies on individual authors. Listed by subject of the article (all of American literature makes up the subjects). Section on poetry as a subject, pages 690-700.

47 Leary, Paris, and Robert Kelly, eds. "Biographies and Bibliography." In their A CONTROVERSY OF POETS: AN ANTHOLOGY OF CONTEMPORARY AMERICAN POETRY. Garden City, N.Y.: Anchor, 1965, pp. 523-67.

Biobibliographical information mostly in the poets' own words or from data supplied by them.

48 Lepper, Gary M., ed. A BIBLIOGRAPHICAL INTRODUCTION TO SEVENTY-FIVE MODERN AMERICAN AUTHORS. Berkeley, Calif.: Serendipity Books, 1976. 428 p.

Descriptive primary bibliographies for a dozen or so of the poets in this present guide and for a few not included here.

49 Lewis, Jenny. POETRY IN THE MAKING: CATALOGUE OF AN EXHIBITION OF POETRY MANUSCRIPTS IN THE BRITISH MUSEUM APRIL-JUNE 1967. London: Turret Books, 1967. 68 p. Index.

Brief biographical notes on authors followed by description of manuscripts in the exhibition.

50 Lewis, Linda K., comp. "Women in Literature: A Selected Bibliography." BULLETIN OF BIBLIOGRAPHY, 35 (1978), 116-22, 131.

Unannotated list of books and articles on how women have been portrayed over the centuries and into the twentieth century.

51 McElrath, Joseph R., Jr., ed. "Interviews with Contemporary Writers." RESOURCES FOR AMERICAN LITERARY STUDIES, 6 (Spring 1976), 70-78.

Section 1 lists tapes (both audio and video) in the collection at Brockport, N.Y. (SUNY), by date, writer, and interviewer. Section 2 lists the edited texts of those printed in journals. The interviewers are most often American poets. At the time of the article twelve tapes were available for public distribution: Bly (two), Creeley, Dickey, Ferlinghetti, Ginsberg, Kinnell (two tapes but one interview), Levertov, Logan, Snyder, and Wilbur.

52 Malkoff, Karl. CROWELL'S HANDBOOK OF CONTEMPORARY AMERICAN POETRY: A CRITICAL HANDBOOK OF AMERICAN POETRY SINCE 1940. New York: Crowell, 1973. 338 p.

Guides readers through the special problems of contemporary poetry with articles on theory, schools and movements, and individual poets. Offers an overview of contemporary poetry.

53 Marcan, Peter, ed. POETRY THEMES: A BIBLIOGRAPHICAL INDEX TO SUBJECT ANTHOLOGIES AND RELATED CRITICISM IN THE ENGLISH LANGUAGE, 1875-1975. London: Bingley; Hamden, Conn.: Shoe String Press, 1977. 317 p.

Divides themes into twenty-one categories, some with subdivisions. The entries are almost exclusively anthologies on these subjects; thus this bibliography is useful only from a subject approach, as intended. It would be almost impossible, for example, to find a specific poem by a specific poet.

54 Mellown, Elgin W., ed. A DESCRIPTIVE CATALOGUE OF THE BIBLIOGRAPHIES OF 20TH CENTURY BRITISH WRITERS. Troy, N.Y.: Whitston, 1972; 446 p. 2nd ed., 1978. 414 p.

Items listed alphabetically by the subject of the bibliography or critical work. Describes contents of each work listed.

55 Mitgang, Herbert, ed. WORKING FOR THE READER: A CHRONICLE OF CULTURE, LITERATURE, WAR AND POLITICS IN BOOKS FROM THE 1950S TO THE PRESENT. New York: Horizon Press, 1970. 250 p.

Contains short reviews from newspapers and journals.

56 MLA INTERNATIONAL BIBLIOGRAPHY. New York: Modern Language Association of America, 1919--. Annual.

Has changed format over the years; issued as a separate volume since 1969. Keeps fairly well abreast of current criticism. For a specific poet, this is probably the first bibliography to check for recent work.

57 Murphy, Rosalie, ed. CONTEMPORARY POETS OF THE ENGLISH LANGUAGE. Chicago: St. James Press, 1970; New York: St. Martin's Press, 1971. 1,244 p.

See also Perloff (no. 62) for 3rd edition. Lists eleven hundred poets "now writing in the English language." Supplies biobibliographical information and for some poets a critical article or comment by the poet. Includes a list of nearly five hundred anthologies with contemporary poems from around the world.

58 Nadel, Ira Bruce, ed. JEWISH WRITERS OF NORTH AMERICA: A GUIDE TO INFORMATION SOURCES. American Studies Information Guide Series, vol. 8. Detroit: Gale Research Co, 1981. 493 p. Indexes.

Checklists of primary works and a few items of criticism on Allen Ginsberg, Anthony Hecht, John Hollander, David Ignatow, Kenneth Koch, Stanley Kunitz, Denise Levertov, Philip Levine, Howard Nemerov, Muriel Rukeyser, Delmore Schwartz, Karl Shapiro, Louis Zukofsky, and others. Most entries on individual poets are annotated elsewhere in the present guide. Nadel includes lists of general works on the subject of Jewish writing.

59 Nager, Rae Ann, ed. "A Selective Annotated Bibliography of Recent Work on English Prosody." STYLE, 11 (Spring 1977), 136-70.

Sections on individual poets as well as on general and theoretical works. Includes Bunting, Dickey, and Charles Olson.

60 Nilon, Charles H., ed. BIBLIOGRAPHY OF BIBLIOGRAPHIES IN AMERICAN LITERATURE. New York: R.R. Bowker, 1970. 483 p.

Includes a few older contemporary poets. Useful for earlier writers and as an introduction to research in American literature.

61 Nyren [Curley], Dorothy, ed. A LIBRARY OF LITERARY CRITICISM: MODERN AMERICAN LITERATURE. 4th enl. ed. 4 vols. New York: Frederick Ungar, 1969. 2,082 p.

Wide-ranging look at modern writers in America, including contemporary authors. Prints excerpts from reviews and articles. Primary bibliographies appear at end of each volume. Index of critics is in volume 3. Volume 4 is a supplement published in 1976. See previous editions for earlier works.

62 Perloff, Marjorie, ed. CONTEMPORARY POETS. 3rd ed. London: St. James Press; New York: St. Martin's Press, 1980. 1,865 p.

Similar to previous edition by James Vinson (see Murphy [no. 57] for first edition). Each poet has a biography, primary bibliography, usually a personal comment by the poet himself, a critical essay, and often a secondary bibliography. These bibliographies are fairly complete, but a student must be alert for minor errors and misprints. Third edition has an appendix listing deceased writers of the contemporary period (Plath, Roethke, etc.).

63 Pownall, David E., ed. ARTICLES ON TWENTIETH-CENTURY LITERATURE: AN ANNOTATED BIBLIOGRAPHY, 1954-1970. 7 vols. New New: Kraus-Thompson, 1973-80. 4,971 p.

Compiled from "Current Bibliography" in the first sixteen years of TWENTIETH CENTURY LITERATURE. But Pownall has corrected that list and enlarged it to include previously omitted serials and annotations of articles. Excluded are book reviews, review articles, elementary articles on teaching literature, and popular journalism. Also excluded are articles on modern literature in general. Most useful on older authors after 1900 and easiest to use for articles on a specific author.

64 Richardson, Kenneth, ed. TWENTIETH CENTURY WRITING: A READER'S GUIDE TO CONTEMPORARY LITERATURE. London: Newnes Books, Hamlyn Publishing Group, 1969. 751 p.

Of some use on older contemporary poets, but most of this information is available elsewhere.

65 Robbins, John Albert. AMERICAN LITERARY MANUSCRIPTS: A CHECKLIST OF HOLDINGS. 2nd ed. Athens: University of Georgia Press, 1977. 387 p.

Manuscripts of some contemporary poets are included. Listed by author.

66 Schwartz, Narda Lacey, ed. ARTICLES ON WOMEN WRITERS 1960-1975: A BIBLIOGRAPHY. Santa Barbara, Calif., and Oxford, Engl.: ABC-Clio Press, 1977. 256 p.

Dates in the title refer to time of publication of the articles, not to authors' works; but the list includes many contemporaries.

67 Seymour-Smith, Martin. FUNK AND WAGNALLS GUIDE TO MODERN WORLD LITERATURE. New York: Wolfe, 1973. 1,227 p.

See the entries headed "British Literature" and "American Literature." Brief notes on a dozen or so contemporaries whom Seymour-Smith evaluates in the tone of "A" levels British criticism. Mostly on earlier writers.

68 Smith, William James, ed. GRANGER'S INDEX TO POETRY, 1970-1977. New York: Columbia University Press, 1978. 635 p. First line and title index, Author index, Subject index.

An index of poems reprinted in anthologies, many by contemporary poets. Use with previous editions.

69 Somer, John, and Barbara Eck Cooper, eds. AMERICAN AND BRITISH LITERATURE 1945-1975: AN ANNOTATED BIBLIOGRAPHY OF CONTEMPORARY SCHOLARSHIP. Laurence: Regents Press of Kansas, 1980. 326 p. Index.

Sections A--General Studies, D--Poetry, E--Critical Theory are particularly useful to students of contemporary poetry. Sections A through E are annotated. Studies of individual authors are not included; only book-length studies are included--no articles. This present guide lists only a few of the books cited by Somer and Cooper; thus, readers should be sure to examine this resource.

70 Temple, Ruth Z., and Martin Tucker, eds. A LIBRARY OF LITERARY CRITICISM: MODERN BRITISH LITERATURE. 3 vols. New York: Frederick Ungar, 1966. 1,465 p.

Excerpts of critical commentary arranged to show chronological shifts in authors' reputations. Includes some contemporary poets. See supplementary volume 4 (no. 72).

71 ______. TWENTIETH CENTURY BRITISH LITERATURE: A REFERENCE GUIDE AND BIBLIOGRAPHY. New York: Frederick Ungar, 1968. 261 p.

Somewhat dated; but still useful if later guides are not available. On general literature, including some older contemporary poets and some now neglected by the most recent contemporary criticism.

72 Tucker, Martin, and Rita Stein, eds. MODERN BRITISH LITERATURE: A LIBRARY OF LITERARY CRITICISM. Vol. 4: SUPPLEMENT. New York: Frederick Ungar, 1975. 663 p.

Supplements earlier volumes (no. 70) by adding fifty new authors, not all poets, and updating the excerpts of critical commentary on the older authors.

73 Unger, Leonard, ed. AMERICAN WRITERS: A COLLECTION OF LITERARY BIOGRAPHIES. 4 vols. New York: Scribner's, 1974; SUPPLEMENT in 2 volumes, 1979. 3,172 p. Index.

Biobibliographical information and critical essays, originally published as University of Minnesota Pamphlets on American Writers Series. In the 1974 volumes are Berryman, Eberhart, Jarrell, Lowell, MacLeish, Marianne Moore, and Warren. In the SUPPLEMENT are Elizabeth Bishop, Sylvia Plath, and Adrienne Rich.

74 Wakeman, John, ed. WORLD AUTHORS, 1950-1970: A COMPANION VOLUME TO TWENTIETH CENTURY AUTHORS. New York: H.H. Wilson, 1975. 1,596 p.

General biographical information about individual authors, half of whom provided autobiographical articles. Check Kunitz (no. 44) for poets who are omitted but might be expected to be here.

75 Walcutt, Charles C., and J. Edwin Whitesell, eds. THE EXPLICATOR CYCLOPEDIA. Volume 1: MODERN POETRY. Chicago: Quadrangle Books, 1966. 366 p.

Reprints items from THE EXPLICATOR, 1-20 (1942-62).

76 Ward, A[lfred] C., ed. LONGMAN COMPANION TO TWENTIETH CENTURY LITERATURE. 2nd ed. London: Longman, 1975. 598 p.

Objective and informative but has few new poets.

77 Whittington, Jennifer, comp. LITERARY RECORDINGS: A CHECKLIST OF THE ARCHIVE OF RECORDED POETRY AND LITERATURE IN THE LIBRARY OF CONGRESS. Washington, D.C.: Library of Congress, 1981. 299 p. Author index.

This inventory of the collection is the successor of earlier lists in 1961 and 1966 and is revised through May 1975. It now includes "nearly a thousand poets reading their own work . . . and recordings of other literary events." Entries are arranged alphabetically by person or event and chronologically within the entry. Information about available copies appears on page iv. LPs are listed on pages 279-85.

78 Williams, Jerry T., et al., comps. SOUTHERN LITERATURE 1968-1975: A CHECKLIST OF SCHOLARSHIP. Boston: G.K. Hall, 1978. 287 p.

From the annual checklists in MISSISSIPPI QUARTERLY are annotated items on Ammons, Berry, Dickey, Jarrell, Miller, and Warren.

79 Woodress, James J., ed. AMERICAN LITERARY SCHOLARSHIP. Durham, N.C.: Duke University Press, 1963--. Annual.

Editorship now alternates between J. Albert Robbins and Woodress. Chapter authors vary, but since 1972 Linda Welshimer Wagner has written "Poetry: The 1930s to the Present" in which she reviews articles and books appearing during the volume year.

80 THE WRITERS DIRECTORY 1982-84. Detroit: Gale Research Co., 1981. 1,149 p.

An alphabetical listing of living writers who write in English throughout the world, with biographical details, lists of publications, and addresses for most of them. A separate section lists writers by various categories of genre or subject.

80A THE YEAR'S WORK IN ENGLISH STUDIES. London: English Association, 1919--. Index of critics, authors, subjects.

Describes and evaluates recently published journals, articles, and books relating to twentieth-century verse in Britain and America.

81 Zulauf, Sander W., and Irwin H. Weiser, eds. INDEX OF AMERICAN PERIODICAL VERSE. Metuchen, N.J.: Scarecrow Press, 1971--. Annual.

Indexes by author poems of four thousand poets published in periodicals during the year and supplies the addresses of the periodicals. The issue for 1977 appeared in 1979.

Chapter 3

STUDIES IN GENERAL AESTHETICS AND POETIC THEORY

This chapter lists books and articles more directly related to the arts and literature than the preceding, but is still fairly general in intent. Again I treat these works as Anglo-American though a reader can often tell by the title or by the annotation whether or not a work leans toward English or American viewpoints.

100 Abbs, Peter, ed. THE BLACK RAINBOW: ESSAYS ON THE PRESENT BREAKDOWN OF CULTURE. London: Heinemann, 1975. 247 p.

On nihilism in contemporary literature. Essays are by Ian Robinson on "Pop Poetry," David Holbrook on Ted Hughes, John McCabe on music, and Charles Parker on popular songs. Other essays discuss limits in art, the novel, language, architecture, and philosophy.

101 Adams, Hazard. "Contemporary Ideas of Literature: Terrible Beauty or Rough Beast?" CONTEMPORARY LITERATURE, 17 (Summer 1976), 349-77.

A survey of some current concepts of literature. Adams discusses recent theories, particularly the differences between the "structuralists" and the "phenomenologists," both of whom fail to balance their own points of view with the requirement of looking "at literature from its own point of view."

102 Alvarez, A. "The Art of Suicide." PARTISAN REVIEW, 37, No. 3 (1970), 339-58.

On the question of why many of our young artists act as if they want to die even though they do not try actual suicide.

103 Anderson, Albert A. "The Quarrel between Poetry and Philosophy." TOPIC, No. 28 (Fall 1974), pp. 18-32.

The quarrel is understandable but unnecessary. It is a lover's quarrel. Poetry and philosophy cannot live without each other.

104 Barrett, William. TIME OF NEED: FORMS OF IMAGINATION IN THE TWENTIETH CENTURY. New York: Harper, 1972. 401 p.

Nihilism and some artistic expressions of it. Barrett sees art as a concern with the meaning of life and views nihilism as "the birth pangs of a new reality struggling for expression."

105 Bayley, John. THE USES OF DIVISION: UNITY AND DISHARMONY IN LITERATURE. New York: Viking Press, 1976. 248 p.

Two sections are on contemporary poetry: "The Self as Available Reality," pages 157-71, on John Berryman and "The Importance of Elsewhere," pages 171-82, on Larkin. The first includes mention of Larkin; the second is on Larkin alone. Both are poets who "reveal without confiding."

106 Blaisdell, Gus. "Building Poems." VORT, 3, No. 3 (1976), 125-36.

On words as the medium of the poet and on the possibilities of verbal precision.

107 Bogan, Louise. A POET'S ALPHABET: REFLECTIONS ON THE LITERARY ART AND VOCATION. Ed. Robert Phelps and Ruth Limmer. New York: McGraw-Hill, 1970. 474 p. Index.

Collection of Bogan's essays and reviews, which include comments on numerous contemporary poets.

108 Brower, Reuben A., ed. TWENTIETH-CENTURY LITERATURE IN RETROSPECT. Harvard English Studies, 2. Cambridge, Mass.: Harvard University Press, 1971. 363 p.

Somewhat less useful on later writers, but Donald Wesling's "The Prosodies of Free Verse," pages 155-87, is a useful though fairly technical descriptive essay.

109 Carruth, Hayden. "The Act of Love: Poetry and Personality." SEWANEE REVIEW, 84 (Spring 1976), 305-13.

An existential view of why many modern poems fail: since a poet is a personality and is independent, his work is "a process of self-transcendence" and is an act of love, "seeking pure existence." Too many contemporary poems "are the products of objectivity [and] express no spiritual consciousness."

110 Cheadle, B.D. "A Perspective on Modernism in English Poetry." ENGLISH STUDIES IN AFRICA [Johannesburg], 19, No. 2 (1976), 65-81.

"Modernism depends on the poet's attitude toward his audience. Cheadle uses Eliot, primarily, and Pound and Yeats, to illustrate modern contrast to earlier poets, concluding with a brief comment on Larkin's "First Sight" (1964).

111 Chiari, Joseph. THE AESTHETICS OF MODERNISM. London: Vision, 1970. 224 p.

A background study and exposition of the development of modernism as an attitude in art.

112 Coppay, Frank L. "The Internal Analysis of Compression in Poetry." STYLE, 11 (Winter 1976), 19-38.

A technical linguistic discussion of poetic compression, which responds to a previous essay by Samuel R. Levin, "The Analysis of Compression in Poetry," FOUNDATIONS OF LANGUAGE, 7 (1971), 39-55.

113 Cronin, Anthony. A QUESTION OF MODERNITY. London: Secker and Warburg, 1966. 130 p.

The first four chapters are on the interpretation of literature, especially poetry; the last two chapters are on criticism. The middle two are on Joyce and Beckett. For Cronin, what a work of literature has to tell us about being alive is a clue to its worth.

114 Davidson, Donald. "What Metaphors Mean." CRITICAL INQUIRY, 5 (Autumn 1978), 31-47.

They "mean what the words, in their most literal interpretation, mean, and nothing more." Yet to interpret and elucidate metaphor is an appropriate act of literary analysis.

115 Davie, Donald. "Landscape as Poetic Focus." SOUTHERN REVIEW, n.s. 4 (Summer 1968), 685-91.

The value of focus on landscape as a corrective "upon the poet's manipulation of the historical record." Landscape in Charles Olson and Ed Dorn is discussed briefly.

116 _____. "Poetry as Taking a Stand." SHENANDOAH, 29, No. 2 (1978), 45-52.

A discussion of "affirmation" in poetry, with comments on or by Bunting, Lowell, and Ashbery.

117 Donoghue, Denis. THE ORDINARY UNIVERSE: SOUNDINGS IN MODERN LITERATURE. New York: Macmillan, 1968. 320 p.

An illustration of "formalist" criticism (as opposed to substantive") with examples mostly from earlier writers like Yeats, Eliot, and Stevens but occasional mention of Richard Wilbur and Charles Tomlinson. Donoghue balances form with substance and has a fairly lengthy commentary, pages 21-31, on Tomlinson's SEEING IS BELIEVING (1958).

118 Doyle, Esther M., and Virginia Hastings Floyd, eds. STUDIES IN INTERPRETATION. Vol. 2. Amsterdam: Rodopi, 1977. 307 p. Notes.

Essays on oral interpretation and oral aspects of poetry. See in particular: Lee Hudson, "Poetics in Performance: The Beat Generation," pages 59-76, on the emphasis the beat poets put on oral performance and their desire for a "natural" idiom; and Paul H. Gray, "American Concrete: New Poetic, New Performance," pages 77-99, on defining "concrete" poetry and its relationship to and possibilities for oral performance.

119 Eagleton, Terry. CRITICISM AND IDEOLOGY: A STUDY IN MARXIST LITERARY THEORY. Atlantic Highlands, N.J.: Humanities Press, 1976. 191 p.

A defense of Marxist literary theory as the only literary theory. No analysis of contemporary poets except brief comments.

120 Edmiston, Susan, and Linda Cirino. LITERARY NEW YORK: A HISTORY AND GUIDE. Boston: Houghton Mifflin, 1976. 409 p.

Divides the city into sections and describes the literary notables who lived there or worked and visited there. A literary history from precolonial times, it includes only a few of the older contemporary writers like Marianne Moore and Allen Ginsberg.

121 Efron, Arthur. "Criticism and Literature in the One-Dimensional Age." MINNESOTA REVIEW, 8, No. 1 (1968), 48-62.

On the ramifications for literary criticism that are suggested by Herbert Marcuse's ONE-DIMENSIONAL MAN (1964): "The creative tension between the conscious mind and the unconscious is being eliminated."

122 Eriksson, Pamela D. "British and American Poetry Since 1945." UNISA ENGLISH STUDIES, 12, No. 1 (1974), 27-41.

A survey of the poetry of the 1950s and 1960s.

123 Farwell, Marilyn R. "Feminist Criticism and the Concept of the Poetic Persona." BUCKNELL REVIEW, 24, No. 1 (1978), 139-56.

Persona as a critical tool seems inadequate to Farwell: "Feminist criticism wants a cultural context that takes into consideration the reality of the writer's experience, the psychology and socialization of the individual writer."

124 Fraser, G.S. ESSAYS ON TWENTIETH-CENTURY POETS. Leicester, Engl.: Leicester University Press; Totowa, N.J.: Rowman and Littlefield, 1977. 255 p.

The final two essays are on contemporary poets: "The Poetry of Thom Gunn," pages 233-43; (reprinted from CRITICAL QUARTERLY, 3, No. 4 [1961]), and "Philip Larkin: The Lyric Note and the Grand Style," pages 243-53, in which Fraser demonstrates the "lyrical and romantic quality" in Larkin's verse.

125 Furbank, P.N. "Do We Need the Terms 'Image' and 'Imagery.'" CRITICAL QUARTERLY, 9, No. 4 (1967), 335-45.

About poetry and criticism generally. Furbank discusses the uses and misuses of the terms in his title.

126 Galvin, Brendan. "The Mumbling of Young Werther: Angst by Blueprint in Contemporary Poetry." PLOUGHSHARES, 4, No. 3 (1978), 122-29.

On the vagueness and monotony of details in contemporary poems: "One might think that a poem is a school necktie."

127 Geertz, Clifford, ed. MYTH, SYMBOL, AND CULTURE. New York: Norton, 1974. 227 p.

This book was originally the winter 1972 issue of DAEDALUS. Eight essays relate the humanities and social sciences on the common ground of "the systematic study of meaningful forms."

128 Geiger, Don. THE DRAMATIC IMPULSE IN MODERN POETICS. Baton Rouge: Louisiana State University Press, 1968. 165 p.

On the "speaker, persona, mask" of a lyric poem and some possibilities for oral delivery. Most examples are from earlier poets.

129 _____. "Poetry as Awareness of What?" In STUDIES IN INTERPRETATION. Ed. Esther M. Doyle and Virginia Hastings Floyd. Amsterdam: Rodopi, 1972, pp. 287-307.

A study of the relationship of poetry to "fact." Geiger explores the views of several literary theorists (R.S. Crane, I.A. Richards, and Eliseo Vivas, for example) and concludes that "instances" poetic or real of a general truth are "inseparable from particular interpretations."

130 Goodman, Paul. SPEAKING AND LANGUAGE: DEFENCE OF POETRY. New York: Random House, 1971. 242 p.

Goodman's view of the nature of speaking (or not speaking) and language and of how the language of literary works is like or different from other forms of language.

131 Green, Martin. SCIENCE AND THE SHABBY CURATE OF POETRY: ESSAYS ABOUT THE TWO CULTURES. New York: Norton, 1965. 159 p.

Defends C.P. Snow's thesis about this educational and cultural split against the attacks of F.R. Leavis and Lionel Trilling and explores some of the implications of the problem.

132 Gross, Harvey Seymour. SOUND AND FORM IN MODERN POETRY: A STUDY OF PROSODY FROM THOMAS HARDY TO ROBERT LOWELL. Ann Arbor: University of Michigan Press, 1964. 334 p.

Background of modern prosody and to some extent an argument for the study of prosody. Chapter entitled "The Generation of Auden," pages 247-301, includes some contemporary poets.

133 Harding, D.W. WORDS INTO RHYTHM: ENGLISH SPEECH RHYTHM IN VERSE AND PROSE. Cambridge, Engl.: Cambridge University Press, 1976. 166 p.

In these Clark lectures of 1971-72, Harding discourses on rhythm and metrics in all their complexities as terms, using a few examples from contemporary poets.

134 Hardison, O.B., Jr., ed. THE QUEST FOR IMAGINATION: ESSAYS IN TWENTIETH CENTURY AESTHETIC CRITICISM. Cleveland, Ohio: Press of Case Western Reserve University, 1971. 301 p.

These essays range from background studies to speculation, providing a cross-section of various approaches to literary interpretation.

135 Hartman, Geoffrey H. "The Maze of Modernism: Reflections on MacNeice, Graves, Hope, Lowell, and Others." In his BEYOND FORMALISM: LITERARY ESSAYS, 1958-1970. New Haven, Conn.: Yale University Press, 1970, pp. 258-80.

Comments on contemporary poets are relatively brief. Hartman describes their difference from modernist poets as "their 'conspicuous consumption' of historical forms." Today's poets, he says, want "to get out from under . . . the burden of the past . . . . [They see] impositions, where there are merely common obligations."

136 Hertz, Peter D. "Minimal Poetry." WESTERN HUMANITIES REVIEW, 24 (Winter 1970), 31-40.

Minimal poetry (for example, a poem of two words like Aram Saroyan's "Wire air") is beginning a new age in poetry, "concerned with something real . . . . Language is once again liberated to act as language."

137 Hill, Geoffrey. "Poetry as 'Menace' and "Atonement.'" UNIVERSITY OF LEEDS REVIEW, 21 (1978), 66-68.

Hill's inaugural lecture on December 5, 1977, as Chair of English Literature. He reflects on the risks a poet runs in working at his craft of attempting to achieve "at-oneness" with himself and the world of not-self.

138 Hoffman, Steven K. "Impersonal Personalism: The Making of a Confessional Poetic." ELH, 45 (Winter 1978), 687-709.

Confessional poetry "synthesizes" the Romantic tradition of the nineteenth century with the "masking techniques and objectifications of the twentieth." Hoffman examines the poems of Lowell, Berryman, Plath, and others.

139 Howe, Irving, ed. THE IDEA OF THE MODERN IN LITERATURE AND THE ARTS. New York: Horizon, 1967. 317 p.

This book was also published in Fawcett World Library as LITERARY MODERNISM (1967), and Howe's introduction appeared in COMMENTARY, 40, No. 5 (1967), as "The Culture of Modernism." These essays attempt to define modernism. Some of them are by contemporary poets, but none are about them.

140 Hungerland, Isabel C. POETIC DISCOURSE. Berkeley: University of California Press, 1958. 177 p.

An exposition of poetry as a specialized language, how it differs from other forms of discourse, and ways to evaluate and interpret it.

141 Jones, Alan, and R.F. Churchhouse, eds. THE COMPUTER IN LITERARY AND LINGUISTIC STUDIES. Proceedings of the Third International Symposium. Cardiff: University of Wales Press, 1976. 362 p.

An overview of the uses and possibilities of computer study in literary works, although most of the papers in the collection are on older or foreign texts.

142 Jones, Evan. "Why Do You Write Poetry?" QUADRANT, 131 (June 1978), 61-62.

Jones muses on the complexity of the question and the inadequacy of short answers to it: "We need a way of talking which can render the whole living complex of thought-and-feeling if we want truly to say anything adequate at all."

143 Judson, John. "The Irradiation of the Particular: Some Thoughts on Things, Images, and a Sense of Place in Poetry." OHIO REVIEW, 19 (Fall 1978), 89-98.

Reflections on the transition of actual experiences into poems, into art.

144 Kenner, Hugh. "The Poetics of Error." TAMKANG REVIEW, 6, Nos. 2-7, (1974-76), 89-98.

Western belief "that ideograph and meaning in Chinese enjoy some intrinsic, natural connection," though false, led Western poets to learn "the pertinence of name-magic to poetry."

145 Kessler, Jascha. "National Literature and the Tribe of Poets." LITERARY REVIEW, 21 (Summber 1978), 439-55.

Poets have nothing to do with a "National Literature"; the poet is "simply the principal curator of a society's archaic linguistic artifacts." Kessler fears that the poet will disappear from society.

146 Key, Mary Ritchie. MALE/FEMALE LANGUAGE, WITH A COMPREHENSIVE BIBLIOGRAPHY. Metuchen, N.J.: Scarecrow Press, 1975. 200 p. Index.

Not about contemporary poetry but applicable to some kinds of analyses of it.

147 Kloefkorn, William. "Persona: The Problem of the Private Voice in the Public Poem." INTERDISCIPLINARY ESSAYS, 4 (Spring 1975), 14-26.

The problem is "the task of making the voice convincing at the same time that it provides an apparent disconnection, a jolt, a surprise . . .--something that takes the reader from the literal to the abstract, from the mundane to the extraordinary, from the definite to the indefinite, from this world to another." Kloefkorn illustrates with his own poems.

148 Kostelanetz, Richard, ed. ON CONTEMPORARY LITERATURE. New York: Avon, 1965 [1964]; rpt. Plainview, N.Y.: Books for Libraries, 1971. 638 p.

Anthology of critical essays, a few of which may have interest for historians of contemporary literature. Kostelanetz' introductory essay contrasts the contemporary with the modern. Leslie Fiedler and A. Alvarez survey British writing; Jonathan Cott reviews Berryman and Roethke; and Randall Jarrell and John Hollander discuss Lowell.

149 Lansdowne, Andrew. "Poetry and Woetry: Some Pernicious Trends in Modern Poetry." PACIFIC QUARTERLY (Moana), 3 (April 1978), 149-58.

Some of these trends are "to write about nothing," "to write in a completely esoteric and personal fashion," to use "the verbal enigma," to deny "spiritual and moral values," and to reject "paradox," when to do so is a rejection of truth. In addition to examples from South Pacific writers, Lansdowne uses Creeley's "Bits."

150 Meyerhoff, Hans. TIME IN LITERATURE. Berkeley and Los Angeles: University of California Press, 1955. 174 p.

Meyerhoff compares uses of time in literature and the concept of time in science. He is more philosophical than literary and uses earlier writers.

151 Moers, Ellen. LITERARY WOMEN. Garden City, N.Y.: Doubleday, 1976. 352 p.

Numerous though brief comments on older writers and some poets like Plath.

152 Morrison, Blake. "In Defence of Minimalism." CRITICAL QUARTERLY, 18, No. 2 (1976), 43-51.

Defines "minimalism" and justifies it in contemporary poets as an "advance into new territory."

153 Morse, J[osiah] Mitchell. PREJUDICE AND LITERATURE. Philadelphia: Temple University Press, 1976. 206 p.

On the obstacles to understanding literal and metaphorical meanings.

154 Mphahlele, Ezekiel. "The Function of Literature at the Present Time: The Ethnic Imperative." DENVER QUARTERLY, 9 (Winter 1975), 16-45.

Black poets and their struggles, but also a theoretical essay on the tensions between individual and social demands on art.

155 Nathan, Leonard. "The Private 'I' in Contemporary Poetry." SHENANDOAH, 22 (Summer 1971), 80-99.

Romanticism continues into the contemporary period as the dominant mode, though modified by today's poets.

156 Navero, William Anthony. "The Rediscovery of the Usages of the Utensils and the Services (The Emergence of Mythopoeic Post-Modern Image and the Poetics of Charles Olson)." Dissertation, SUNY, Buffalo, 1977 (DAI 38: 1393).

Theoretical examination of imagery, from imagism to Olson's projective verse, and its relation to "the process of mythology and ritual initiation," followed by a close textual analysis of

APOLLONIUS OF TYANA (1951) to show the transition to postmodern form.

157 Olson, Elder. ON VALUE JUDGMENTS IN THE ARTS AND OTHER ESSAYS. Chicago: University of Chicago Press, 1976. 365 p.

Essays on making aesthetic judgments with older writers as examples, but has an essay contrasting Louise Bogan and Leonie Adams.

158 Poggioli, Renato. THE THEORY OF THE AVANT-GARDE. Cambridge, Mass.: Belknap Press of Harvard University, 1968. 267 p.

Attemps to define the essence of the avant-garde and investigate its relationship to other human affairs, examining first avant-garde as a "mythology," then "from the viewpoint of psychology and sociology," and finally "as the object and subject of its own theory."

159 Polleta, Gregory T., ed. ISSUES IN CONTEMPORARY LITERARY CRITICISM. Boston: Little, Brown, 1973. 833 p.

Anthology of critical essays making up a history of modern criticism. Reprints essay on "Skunk Hour" in Ostroff (no. 208) and Alvarez' talk with Donald Davie in THE MODERN POET (no. 195).

160 Proffitt, Edward. "The Epic Lyric: The Long Poem in the Twentieth Century." RESEARCH STUDIES, 46 (March 1978), 20-27.

Uses Wordsworth's PRELUDE (1850) to illustrate the modern lyricist's ontological struggle to write long poems.

161 Raban, Jonathan. THE SOCIETY OF THE POEM. London: Harrap, 1971. 191 p.

Looks at contemporary poetry in the society producing the poets and at the society figured in the poetry. Three pages of acknowledgments suggest the range of Raban's study of British and American poets. Unfortunately, this wide-ranging work has no index.

162 Rosenthal, M.L. "Dynamics of Form and Motive in Some Representative Twentieth-Century Lyric Poems." ELH, 37 (March 1970), 136-51.

Using a musical analogy and examples from Duncan and Levertov, Rosenthal discusses the reciprocity of traditional forms and the newer, more open forms. Numerous other poets are briefly mentioned.

163 _____. POETRY AND THE COMMON LIFE. New York: Oxford University Press, 1974. 148 p.

Rosenthal believes that "people have been kept from their poetry." Thus, the poets discussed celebrate the ordinary experiences of life, common to all. He cites W.C. Williams who thought other poets wrote too learnedly.

164 Scheer-Schaetzler, Brigitte. "Language at the Vanishing Point: Some Notes on the Use of Language in Recent American Literature." REVUE DES LANGUES VIVANTES, 42 (1976), 497-508.

A partial explanation of the distrust of language shown by contemporary writers, mostly novelists, but includes a brief comment on Patchen.

165 Scully, James, ed. MODERN POETICS. New York: McGraw-Hill, 1965. 251 p. Also, in England, as MODERN POETS ON MODERN POETRY. London: Collins and Fontana, 1966.

These essays are all available elsewhere but for convenience, see "Idiosyncrasy and Technique" by Marianne Moore, pages 105-18; "The Preface to THE ANATHEMETA" by David Jones, pages 193-222; and Frederick Seidel's interview with Robert Lowell, pages 223-51. A biographical headnote appears before each selection.

166 Skelton, Robin. POETIC TRUTH. New York: Barnes and Noble; London: Heinemann, 1978. 131 p.

Third in a series on the "art and craft of poetry." The first two, THE PRACTICE OF POETRY (1971) and THE POET'S CALLING (1975), Skelton meant to be practical books; this one is speculative and theoretical (albeit Skelton denies that it is learned). Despite Skelton's modesty, his book will interest anyone, learned or not, who wonders about the relationship of poetry to reality.

167 _____. THE POET'S CALLING. New York: Barnes and Noble; London: Heinemann, 1975. 214 p.

A description of the poet's way of life. For, Skelton believes, the poet has to "discipline his life in ways which non-poets may think peculiar." Skelton includes his conversations with other poets as illustrative detail for his obviously highly personal account. This is the second of a series. The first, THE PRACTICE OF POETRY (1971), is advice to would-be-poets; the third, POETIC TRUTH (no. 166), is speculative and theoretical.

168 Spender, Stephen. "Form and Pressure in Poetry." TIMES LITERARY SUPPLEMENT, 23 October 1970, pp. 1226-28.

A poet's work relates to his time and to the criticism of that time. Modern poets are the examples, but Spender pleads for tolerance of different "tendencies" and the abandonment of the belief "that the period of history in which we live is so unprecedented that only form which reflects a correspondingly unprecedented awareness of the external situation can be good."

169 Stafford, William. WRITING THE AUSTRALIAN CRAWL: VIEWS ON THE WRITER'S VOCATION. Ann Arbor: University of Michigan Press, 1978. 161 p.

Comments on writing poetry. Some of these pieces were articles; some "remarks put together for conferences"; and some interviews.

170 Strier, Richard. "The Poetics of Surrender: An Exposition and Critique of New Critical Poetics." CRITICAL INQUIRY, 2 (Autumn 1975), 171-89.

Describes and assesses the strengths and weaknesses of the "New Criticism." Hart Crane's poem "At Melville's Tomb" and his "Voyages" sequence serve as principal illustrations.

171 Thompson, Denys. THE USES OF POETRY. Cambridge, Engl.: Cambridge University Press, 1978. 238 p. Index.

Chapters on why we should make or read poems with some scattered comments on contemporary poets.

172 Tissot, Roland. "The Ideology of Super-Realism." In MYTH AND IDEOLOGY IN AMERICAN CULTURE. Ed. Régis Durand. Villeneuve-d'Ascq, France: Universite de Lille III, 1976. pp. 129-43.

An artist's ideology creeps into his work despite his efforts to reject "the contingency and originality of personal style."

173 Viereck, Peter. "Strict Form in Poetry: Would Jacob Wrestle with a Flabby Angel?" CRITICAL INQUIRY, 5 (Winter 1978), 203-22.

Viereck muses, with some harrangueing and namecalling, on the virtues of strict forms over freer forms.

174 Vroon, Ronald, trans. 20TH CENTURY AMERICAN LITERATURE: A SOVIET VIEW. Moscow: Progress, 1976. 528 p.

Aleksei Zverev's "Opening the Doors of Association: On Contemporary American Poetry," pp. 160-80, and essays on fiction may interest readers on what Soviet scholars and critics think of American literature. Of interest also is a list of American writers translated fairly regularly into the various languages of USSR, pp. 503-11.

175 Warren, Robert Penn. DEMOCRACY AND POETRY. London and Cambridge, Mass.: Harvard University Press, 1975. 118 p.

The relationship of the "self" to democracy and poetry. Emphasis is placed more on apprehending the concept of the self; the other terms are used generally.

176 White, Hayden. "The Absurdist Moment in Contemporary Literary Theory." CONTEMPORARY LITERATURE, 17 (Summer 1976), 378-403.

"Absurdist critics . . . criticize endlessly in defense of the notion that criticism is impossible."

177 Wilson, Edmund. LETTERS ON LITERATURE AND POLITICS, 1912-1972. New York: Farrar, Straus and Giroux, 1977. 806 p. Index.

Mostly modern American and British, but by use of the index, pages 743-68, readers can find numerous letters written to and about poets like Berryman, Bogan, and Lowell.

Chapter 4
GENERAL STUDIES OF POETRY AND POETS

Works listed in this chapter are more specifically about contemporary poetry and poets than those in the previous two sections but still general enough to be treated as introductions, surveys, or broad studies of schools and trends. Many are concerned with themes, subjects, or techniques in recent poetry.

178 Banerjee, Jacqueline. "The Ultimate Response: Some Encounters with Death in Modern Poetry." LITERARY HALF-YEARLY, 17, No. 2 (1976), 45-57.

> Modern poets attempt "to 'place' death--to appreciate, in relation to it, the value that can and should attach to life; and to confront the actual face of our mortality with a new directness."

179 Beebe, Maurice. "Introduction: What Modernism Was." JOURNAL OF MODERN LITERATURE, 3, No. 5 (1974), 1065-84.

> Beebe defines "modernism" as a term applicable to a period of time commencing with Impressionism and not really ending but blending with the contemporary period (since some writers are still modernist) and to a kind of writing style having four characteristics: formalism, irony, use of myth as a way of ordering art, and a concern with its own creation.

180 Berryman, John. THE FREEDOM OF THE POET. New York: Farrar, Straus and Giroux, 1976. 390 p.

> A collection of essays, reviews, and stories. "Robert Lowell and Others," pages 286-96, is a slightly revised reprint of "Lowell, Thomas, & Co.," PARTISAN REVIEW, 14 (January-February 1947), 73-85. "Poetry Chronicle, 1948: Waiting for the End, Boys" was originally a review of ten books of poems for PARTISAN REVIEW, 15 (February 1948), 254-67, that represented Berryman's view of the poetic "climate at that time." And an essay on Lowell's "Skunk Hour" had already been reprinted in Ostroff (no. 208). Other chapters

are on older writers with only occasional mention of younger poets.

181 Bloom, Harold. FIGURES OF CAPABLE IMAGINATION. New York: Seabury Press, 1976. 274 p.

A collection of Bloom's essays on Geoffrey Hill, American-Jewish poetry, John Hollander, W.S. Merwin, John Ashbery, A.R. Ammons, and Mark Strand. I have annotated those not already annotated in individual bibliographies and cross-referenced them at the appropriate individual entries, in chapter 8.

182 Breslin, Paul. "How to Read the New Contemporary Poem." AMERICAN SCHOLAR, 47 (Summer 1978), 357-70.

Though talented, many contemporary poets "have followed the zeitgeist down a blind alley." Breslin sees their work as a kind of surgery of the ego, and once a reader recognizes this "solipsistic ideology," many of the answers to the puzzles in their poems become clear.

183 Brown, Merle. "Poetic Listening." NEW LITERARY HISTORY, 10 (1978), 125-39.

Poetry is difficult because it is "twice told." It is being written as the poet listens to what he is writing, to what he is speaking; and the listening becomes part of the poem. The reader must similarly listen to himself. Brown uses Frank O'Hara's "A Step Away from Them" and John Ashbery's "Self Portrait in a Convex Mirror" to illustrate.

184 Clausen, Christopher. "The Decline of Anglo-American Poetry." VIRGINIA QUARTERLY REVIEW, 54 (1978), 73-86.

Explores the causes of "the present situation, in which serious poetry has virtually no audience at all outside the English departments."

185 Collins, Michael J. "Formal Allusion in Modern Poetry." CONCERNING POETRY, 9 (Spring 1976), 5-12.

Collins treats modern poets like Frost, Eliot, and Cummings but leads into the application to contemporary verse of his point that form gives meaning not only in conventional ways but "by alluding to other poems written in the same form and asking us to see the poem in hand in relationship to them." John Ormond's "To a Nun" affords a brief example.

186 CONTEMPORARY LITERATURE, 18 (Summer 1977).

This special issue collects general essays on postwar poetry in

England and America: Marjorie Perloff (comparison-contrast), Charles Tomlinson (himself among others), Michael Wood (English poetry), Lawrence Kramer (Ashbery and Hughes), Bernard Bergonzi (Davie and Larkin), Merle Brown (Silkin), Catherine R. Stimpson (Gunn), Paul Mariani (Tomlinson), and M.L. Rosenthal (poetic sequences). Annotations for these articles appear at their separate entries in this guide.

187 Cummins, Paul. "The Sestina in the 20th Century." CONCERNING POETRY, 11, No. 1 (1978), 15-23.

On the attractions of the sestina form for modern and contemporary poets. Included on pages 22-23 is a brief bibliography of modern and contemporary sestinas.

188 Dickey, William. "Public and Private Poetry." HUDSON REVIEW, 25 (Summer 1972), 295-308.

For the presentation of a public or private voice (or any relationship between the two), Dickey lists the only possibilities as ritual, irony, or confession [my word for Dickey's making the private self public].

189 Fraser, Kathleen. "On Being a West Coast Woman Poet." WOMEN'S STUDIES, 5 (1977), 153-60.

Fraser describes her personal experience of the Pacific coast life and of dealing with "patriarchal influence--male writers, critics and editors."

190 Friebart, Stuart, and David Young, eds. A FIELD GUIDE TO CONTEMPORARY POETRY AND POETICS. New York and London: Longman, 1980. 320 p.

A collection of essays by poets on poets and on the craft, art, and criticism of poetry taken from the journal FIELD. Pieces are by Stafford, Levertov, Hall, Bly, James Wright, Simpson, Simic, Snyder, Kinnell, Charles Wright, Francis, Benedikt, and others.

191 Gierasch, Walter. "Reading Modern Poetry." COLLEGE ENGLISH, 2, No. 1 (1940), 26-36.

Intended to be helpful to those not used to reading modern verse. Examples are Rukeyser's "Boy with His Hair Cut Short" and Gregory's "VI" from CHORUS FOR SURVIVAL. Gierasch tells us to "define the subject [and then] the poet's point of view."

192 Gilbert, Sandra M. "'My Name Is Darkness': The Poetry of Self-Definition." CONTEMPORARY LITERATURE, 18 (1977), 443-57.

Gilbert speculates "that the self-defining confessional genre, with its persistent assertions of identity and its emphasis on a central mythology of the self, may be (at least for our own time) a distinctively female poetic mode." She explores this speculation in poems by Plath, Wakoski, Rich, Sexton, Levertov, and others.

193 Grubb, Frederick. A VISION OF REALITY: A STUDY OF LIBERALISM IN TWENTIETH-CENTURY VERSE. London: Chatto and Windus, 1965. 246 p.

On earlier writers, usually with the view of what is wrong with their kind of liberalism and how their work could have been better with the right kind of political bent; but a last chapter in the same vein, "The Wintry Dawn," has sections on Peter Porter, Thom Gunn, Ted Hughes, and Philip Larkin.

194 Hall, Donald. GOATFOOT, MILKTONGUE, TWINBIRD: INTERVIEWS, ESSAYS, AND NOTES ON POETRY, 1970-1976. Ann Arbor: University of Michigan Press, 1978. 208 p.

A collection of Hall's comments on himself and on British and American poetry, all previously published except for a transcript of an interview at SUNY-Brockport, April 1972. The title essay is reprinted in Friebart and Young (no. 190).

195 Hamilton, Ian, ed. THE MODERN POET: ESSAYS FROM THE REVIEW. London: MacDonald, 1968; New York: Horizon Press, 1969. 200 p.

"A selection of essays from the first fifteen issues of THE REVIEW (London)" from 1962. Most are of interest to students of contemporary poetry, for they are on Gunn, Fuller, Lowell, Plath, Bernard Spencer, Larkin, Berryman, and Jarrell. There are also interviews and essays on general concerns.

196 Harrington, Jane Gouwens. "Animal Imagery in Modern American and British Poetry." Dissertation, University of Notre Dame, 1978 (DAI, 39: 1549).

Poems used to illustrate modern ways of using animal imagery include some by Eberhart, Dickey, Berry, Nemerov, Merwin, Silkin, Roethke, Hughes, and Kinnell.

197 Homberger, Eric. THE ART OF THE REAL: POETRY IN ENGLAND AND AMERICA SINCE 1939. London: Dent; Totowa, N.J.: Rowman and Littlefield, 1977. 246 p. Index, bibliog.

A literary history of contemporary poetry beginning with Louis

MacNeice and ending with Ted Hughes. It attempts to show a stimulus-response relationship in the course of the years discussed. Each section is preceded by a chronology of works in the decade.

198 Janik, Del Ivan. "Poetry in the Ecosphere." CENTENNIAL REVIEW, 20 (Fall 1976), 395-408.

In addition to Williams, Lawrence, and Jeffers, Janik discusses Roethke, Hughes, and Snyder as poets with a biocentric view.

199 Juhasz, Suzanne. "The Critic as Feminist: Reflections on Women's Poetry, Feminism, and the Art of Criticism." WOMEN'S STUDIES, 5 (1977), 113-27.

Feminist critics differ from traditional critics in that they do not "readily accept any tradition." The critic is then freer to respond to the poem's own terms.

200 Levertov, Denise. "On the Edge of Darkness." LAMAR JOURNAL OF THE HUMANITIES, 4 (1978), 3-14.

On the history and nature of political poetry, which "does not obey special laws but must be subject to those which govern every kind of poetry."

201 Luytens, David Bulwer. THE CREATIVE ENCOUNTER. London: Secker and Warburg, 1960. 200 p.

The "creative encounter" is an existential one. Luytens considers older poets but a long chapter, "Robert Lowell: Poet of Reconciliation," pages 128-200, surveys Lowell's poety as "his straining will to conquer experience, to stake out a new and personal sphere of values."

202 Malkoff, Karl. ESCAPE FROM THE SELF: A STUDY IN CONTEMPORARY POETRY AND POETICS. New York: Columbia University Press, 1977. 195 p. Index.

One concern unifies contemporary poetry: "the challenge to the integrity of the self." Malkoff argues that traditional views of the self are no longer valid for criticism of today's poetry which requires either a nonrational or an arational view.

203 Martin, Graham, and P.N. Furbank, eds. TWENTIETH-CENTURY POETRY: CRITICAL ESSAYS AND DOCUMENTS. Atlantic Highlands, N.J.: Open University Press, 1975. 464 p.

An anthology designed for an Open University course on

twentieth-century poetry with essays on Larkin, Lowell, Hughes, and Plath. In the chapter entitled "Modernism" are Ian Hamilton's interviews with Larkin and Christopher Middleton, reprinted from LONDON MAGAZINE, 4, No. 6 (1964), 71-82.

204 Molesworth, Charles. "Contemporary Poetry and the Metaphors for the Poem." GEORGIA REVIEW, 32 (Summer 1978), 319-31.

Examines the results of the shift from the metaphor of the poem as, in John Ciardi's words, "a machine for making choices," a metaphor representing the view of new critics, to new metaphors of the late fifties and sixties: "the poem as a force-field"; "the poem as a 'leaping' or associatively linked cluster of nondiscursive images"; or "the poem as commentary on some unspoken myth." Reprinted in no. 275 below.

205 NATIONAL POETRY FESTIVAL HELD IN THE LIBRARY OF CONGRESS, OCTOBER 22-24, 1962--PROCEEDINGS. Washington, D.C.: Library of Congress, 1964. 367 p.

The poetry readings printed here include the comments between poems. Some of the poets, like Robert Frost, have been writing long enough to be in a guide to modern poets; but most of the poets are contemporary. The discussions after the presentation of papers show lively disagreements; at one, Lewis Turco moved (page 175) "that all writers, critics, and others who are interested in the question of what is real American poetry be banished to Kokomo, there to fight it out among themselves and leave the rest of the poets, who simply want to write poetry, to the craft of their art." There was no second.

206 Osing, Gordon. "Integrity and Images in Contemporary Poetry." INTERPRETATIONS: STUDIES IN LANGUAGE AND LITERATURE, 6 (1974), 70-77.

Although contemporary poets dispute most things and denigrate one another, "all agree that an image must be important and right." Osing attempts a kind of peace-making: "The poems we end up honoring . . . are those which present the poet's special experiences, the language's integrity represented in the submerged analogies and symbols of the culture, and a conscious tribute to other language properties and forms."

207 Ostriker, Alicia. "The Nerves of a Midwife: Contemporary American Women's Poetry." PARNASSUS, 6, No. 1 (1977), 69-87.

The term "women's poetry" may be justified on the same grounds as the term "American poetry." Four elements in women's poetry that are "original, important, and organically connected" are "the quest for autonomous self-definition; the intimate treatment of the body; the release of anger; and . . . the contact imperative." This last element refers to the need for "mutuality" as opposed to roles of dominance and submission.

208 Ostroff, Anthony, ed. THE CONTEMPORARY POET AS ARTIST AND CRITIC. Boston: Little, Brown, 1964. 236 p.

Poets comment on poems by other poets. Three poets' interpretations are thus compared to the author's original intentions in each symposia. Representing contemporary poets are Wilbur, Roethke, Kunitz, Lowell, Eberhart, and Shapiro.

209 Pinsky, Robert. THE SITUATION OF POETRY: CONTEMPORARY POETRY AND ITS TRADITIONS. Princeton, N.J.: Princeton University Press, 1976. 187 p. Index.

Pinsky's thesis is that "contemporary poetry is by and large traditional." He postulates and traces "affinities" rather than influences and comments on numerous poets like Lowell, Berryman, Bogan, O'Hara, Cunningham, and Ammons. Includes notes and a bibliography of the sources of the poems quoted.

210 Poulin, A., Jr. "Contemporary American Poetry: The Radical Tradition." CONCERNING POETRY, 3 (Fall 1970), 5-21.

Contemporary poetry is not so extreme a departure from modern traditions in verse as is sometimes thought. Reprinted in his CONTEMPORARY AMERICAN POETRY (3rd ed., Boston: Houghton Mifflin, 1980, pp. 577-95).

211 Quasha, George. "Dialogos: Between the Written and the Oral in Contemporary Poetry." NEW LITERARY HISTORY, 8 (Spring 1977), 485-506.

Effects and counter-effects of oral on written poetry and written on oral poetry. Along with theoretical discussions of the subject are comments on the theorizing statements of poets like Charles Olson and Robert Duncan. After Quasha's essay are three responses to it by Dennis Tedlock, Monroe C. Beardsley, and Robert Kellogg.

212 Replogle, Justin. "Vernacular Poetry: Frost to Frank O' Hara." TWENTIETH CENTURY LITERATURE, 24 (Summer 1978), 137-53.

With more discussion of Frost than O'Hara, Replogle contrasts "poetry's familiar 'music'" with "the sound of sense" in order to define vernacular poetry.

213 Sisson, C.H. "Some Reflections on American Poetry." PARNASSUS, 6, No. 2 (1978), 55-62.

Sisson's comments reflect his notion of continuity: "A literature may, for historical reasons, bear the name of a national state . . . . But a literature is a literature of the language."

214 Stewart, David H. "The Poetry of Protest." MICHIGAN QUARTERLY REVIEW, 10 (Winter 1971), 1-4.

Introductory to an issue devoted to protest poetry, this essay suggests questions to be asked and focuses on the question of "the role of the individual in a mass world."

215 Tallman, Warren. "Wonder Merchants: Modernist Poetry in Vancouver during the 1960's." OPEN LETTER, 3rd Series, No. 6 (Winter 1976), pp. 175-207.

An account of "visitations" in Vancouver by some American poets, particularly Creeley and Duncan, and their influence on Canadian poets. Tallman also comments on Olson's "proprioception."

216 Thompson, Susan. "The Vast Thin Line: Poems by a Schizophrenic Author." MICHIGAN QUARTERLY REVIEW, 17 (Summer 1978), 348-63.

The poems illustrated here are by persons whom a physician has diagnosed schizophrenic. Thompson believes that these poems and their like can supply "words for our ambivalence about the intangible boundaries that we continuously redefine."

217 Vernon, John. "Fresh Air: Humor in Contemporary American Poetry." In COMIC RELIEF: HUMOR IN CONTEMPORARY AMERICAN LITERATURE. Ed. Sarah Blacher Cohen. Urbana: University of Illinois Press, 1978, pp. 304-23.

Vernon sees two kinds of humor in verse since "the great and not-so-great moderns": one that "hovers between surrealism and a kind of epistemological skepticism, a refusal to mean or to respect meaning"; and another that is "not the end of the poem but a means to the end."

Chapter 5

GENERAL STUDIES OF AMERICAN POETS AND LITERATURE

This chapter has studies similar to those in the previous chapter except these are all related to the poets and literature of the United States.

218 Altieri, Charles. ENLARGING THE TEMPLE: NEW DIRECTIONS IN AMERICAN POETRY DURING THE 1960'S. Lewisburg, Pa.: Bucknell University Press, 1979. 258 p.

Studies the shift from modernism to postmodernism.

219 AMERICAN LITERATURE IN THE 1950'S: ANNUAL REPORT 1976. Tokyo: American Literature Society of Japan, 1977. 285 p.

"Symposium: Beat Literature," pages 269-79, surveys the "movement" and its worldwide influence. Shozo Tokunaga, "Introduction: Poetry of the 1950's," pages 99-104, traces the "break" with "Modernist aesthetic theories and practice" from Charles Olson's essay "Projective Verse" in POETRY NEW YORK (1950). Hisao Kanaseki, "The Education of Charles Olson," pages 111-24, describes not only Olson's education but also America's education by Olson.

220 Asarnow, Herman. "Contemporary Poets and the Responsibilities of the Small Press." DENVER QUARTERLY, 12, No. 4 (1978), 90-94.

Contrasts two small press books of poems and finds that their strengths and weaknesses are "as much the responsibility of the publisher as of the poet."

221 Bloom, Harold. "The Sorrows of American-Jewish Poetry." COMMENTARY, 53 (March 1972), 69-74.

Discusses why there are no modern Jewish poets of major importance. Reprinted in no. 181.

222 Bluestein, Gene. "Folk Tradition, Individual Talent: A Note on the Poetry of Rock." MASSACHUSETTS REVIEW, 11 (Spring 1970), 373-84.

Begins with a discussion of T.S. Eliot as folk bard and ends with Bob Dylan, making "bare the waste land and qualities of American life."

223 Boyers, Robert, ed. CONTEMPORARY POETRY IN AMERICA: ESSAY AND INTERVIEWS. New York: Schocken Books, 1975. 370 p.

A reprint of most of nos. 22-23 of SALMAGUNDI. Three general essays and twenty on individual poets include most well-known poets and some "not universally admired."

224 _____. EXCURSIONS: SELECTED LITERARY ESSAYS. Port Washington, N.Y.: Kennikat Press, 1977. 244 p.

"The American Poetry Scene" in part 2 has essays on Roethke, Lowell, Plath, Belitt, Rich, and Nemerov. All these have been collected from various journals.

225 Brown, Cheryl, and Karen Olson, eds. FEMINIST CRITICISM: ESSAYS ON THEORY, POETRY, AND PROSE. Metuchen, N.J.: Scarecrow Press, 1978. 383 p.

The following essays are on contemporary poets: Suzanne Juhasz, "'The Blood Jet': The Poetry of Sylvia Plath" (reprinted from no. 259), and "The Feminist Poet: Alta and Adrienne Rich"; Rise B. Axelrod on Anne Sexton; R.L. Widmann on Cynthia MacDonald; and Dianne Sadoff on Levertov, Nancy Willard, and Wakoski.

226 Cambon, Glauco. RECENT AMERICAN POETRY. University of Minnesota Pamphlets on American Writers, no. 16. Minneapolis: University of Minnesota Press, 1962. 46 p. Bibliog.

Mentions numerous poets but has extended comments on Wilbur, Merwin, Snodgrass, James Wright, Kinnell, and Logan.

227 Cantrell, Carol Helmstetter. "Self and Tradition in Recent Poetry." MIDWEST QUARTERLY, 18 (July 1977), 343-60.

Examines the poems of several confessional poets (Ginsberg, Lowell, Plath, et al.) in relation to Eliot's principles about the poet and personality.

228 Charters, Ann, ed. SCENES ALONG THE ROAD: PHOTOGRAPHS OF THE DESOLATION ANGELS, 1944-1960. New York: Portents, Gotham Book Mart, 1970. 56 p.

Snapshots of beat writers.

229 Charters, Samuel. SOME POEMS/POETS: STUDIES IN AMERICAN UNDERGROUND POETRY SINCE 1945. Photographs by Ann Charters. Berkeley, Calif.: Oyez, 1971. 118 p.

Charters reflects on his reading poems by Olson, Spicer, Duncan, Snyder, Welch, Ginsberg, Ferlinghetti, Creeley, Everson, and Larry Eigner. He decries the word "studies," but these essays contain a good deal of analyses and statement about "trends and impacts and the influence of somebody on somebody else."

230 Chassman, Neil A., et al. POETS OF THE CITIES NEW YORK AND SAN FRANCISCO 1950-1965. New York: E.P. Dutton, 1974. 175 p. Bio. notes on artists.

Essays by various artists: one by Creeley, which is partly autobiographical; and one by John Clellon Holmes on the beats.

231 Chung [Odell], Ling. "The Reception of Cold Mountain's Poetry in the Far East and the United States." NEW ASIA ACADEMIC BULLETIN, 1 (1978), 85-96.

On Han Shan, or Cold Mountain, and his adoption as a hero by the beats. Although his cult among the beat generation has faded away, ironically "Cold Mountain poems have found their way into many anthologies of Chinese literature in English" and gained him a stature in the United States never achieved in China.

232 Clausen, Christopher. "Grecian Thoughts in the Home Field: Reflections on Southern Poetry." GEORGIA REVIEW, 32 (Summer 1978), 283-305.

Contemporary poets treated here are Warren and Dickey along with older poets like Ransom and Tate. Of the poems he inspects, Clausen asks "how their authors have given poetic form to the wealth of identifiably regional materials and attitudes." He wonders what will happen to southern regional poetry as the South's salient features disappear. Warren's "The Ballad of Billie Potts" and Dickey's "May Day Sermon" are examined.

233 Cooperman, Stanley. "Poetry of Dissent in the United States." MICHIGAN QUARTERLY REVIEW, 10 (Winter 1971), 23-28.

"'Demanding his own destruction,' with increasing shrillness, has indeed become a moral imperative--almost a conditioned response--for many poets and critics of our time, and teachers as well." Cooperman argues against propagandistic poetry; he sees, however, some hope for poetry because a number of poets like Wakoski and Kinnell "have refused to limit poetic action to any fixed recipe."

234 Corman, Cid. Introduction. In his THE GIST OF ORIGIN. New York: Grossman, 1975, pp. xv-xxxvii.

Creeley and Olson figure most in Corman's account of meeting many of the poets whose work appeared in ORIGIN and of the beginnings of the magazine.

235 _____. WORD FOR WORD: ESSAYS ON THE ARTS OF LANGUAGE. Santa Barbara, Calif.: Black Sparrow Press, 1977. 174 p.

This volume has general essays on poetry and a section on oral poetry. AT THEIR WORD, the sequel (Black Sparrow, 1978, 222 pp.), has reviews of Creeley, Whalen, Snyder, and others and essays on Zukofsky and Warren.

236 Creeley, Robert. "The BLACK MOUNTAIN REVIEW." WORKS, 2 (Spring 1971), 45-54.

Origin, nature, and people involved with this review in an ancedotal account by one of the founding editors and contributors.

237 Davie, Donald. TRYING TO EXPLAIN. Poets on Poetry. Ann Arbor: University of Michigan Press, 1979. 213 p.

Contains a review of Berryman's FREEDOM OF THE POET (no. 180), in which Davie describes Berryman the man, and a review of Lowell's SELECTED POEMS, in which he quarrels with the inclusion of poems that express views no longer held by Lowell. An article on American literature tries to distinguish where and when this literature became distinct from the British.

238 Dickstein, Morris. GATES OF EDEN: AMERICAN CULTURE IN THE SIXTIES. New York: Basic Books, 1977. 300 p.

"What happened in the sixties was no one's deliberate choice, but one of those deep-seated shifts of sensibility that alters the whole moral terrain." Dickstein examines Ginsberg's influence and comments on numerous contemporary writers.

239 Donoghue, Denis, ed. SEVEN AMERICAN POETS FROM MacLEISH TO NEMEROV: AN INTRODUCTION. Minneapolis: University of Minnesota Press, 1975. 330 p.

These essays appeared separately as University of Minnesota Pamphlets on American Writers. Donoghue's introduction notes that the poets here "demonstrate seven different ways of being American" and gives a few observations on each. Then the following essays appear in order: MacLeish, by Grover Smith; Eberhart, by Ralph Mills, Jr.; Roethke, also by Mills; Jarrell, by M.L. Rosenthal; Berryman, by William J. Martz; Lowell, by Jay Martin; and Nemerov, by Peter Meinke.

240 Duncan, Erika. "Portrait of the Artist as a Young Woman: Choral Voices of Contemporary Women Writers." BOOK FORUM, 3, No. 1 (1977), 59-80. Photos., bibliogs.

The characteristic problems of women writers and brief descriptions of the writing and subjects of ten writers.

241 Duncan, Robert. AS TESTIMONY: THE POEM AND THE SCENE. San Francisco: White Rabbit Press, 1964. 20 p.

Duncan comments on the meaning of two poems, one by Harold Dull and one by Joanne Kyger, and also on the personalities of other poets.

242 Easy, Peter. "The Treatment of American Indian Materials in Contemporary American Poetry." JOURNAL OF AMERICAN STUDIES, 12 (April 1978), 81-98.

The ramifications of "ethnopoetics." Easy categorizes the kinds of uses Amerindian material receives from contemporary poets like Gary Snyder and Jerome Rothenberg.

243 Edson, Russell. "The Prose Poem in America." PARNASSUS, 5, No. 1 (1976), 321-25.

The characteristics of the American prose poem do not derive from Baudelaire. It is not a form and may even be antiform; it is not "poetic prose" and "must be no more than prose"; and it exists now because "something that needs expression is not being fully released."

244 Ellert, JoAnn C. "The Bauhaus and Black Mountain College." JOURNAL OF GENERAL EDUCATION, 24, No. 3 (1972), 144-52.

Ellert examines the influence of the Bauhaus in Weimar, Germany, on Black Mountain College, North Carolina, through the sixteen-year tenure of Josef Albers and his wife, Anni. Both institutions had been originally "established as a protest against what their founders considered 'the false values' of existing institutions."

245 Faas, Ekbert. TOWARDS A NEW AMERICAN POETICS: ESSAYS AND INTERVIEWS. Santa Barbara, Calif.: Black Sparrow Press, 1978. 296 p.

Essays by Faas on Olson, Snyder, Creeley, Bly, and Ginsberg, each of the last four followed by an interview with the poet.

Faas also interviews Robert Duncan. Preceding these is a Preamble, a general essay on modern and contemporary poetry delineating various lines of reaction.

246 Felstiner, John. "Bearing the War in Mind." PARNASSUS, 6, No. 2 (1978), 30-37.

In contrast to stateside protest poets, American poets in Vietnam were denied "a poignant distance from the scene, a vicarious agony, a time-lag for shame or anger to develop, and a freedom to move between jargon and sane speech."

247 Fiedler, Leslie. "A Kind of Solution: The Situation of Poetry Now." KENYON REVIEW, 26 (Winter 1964), 54-79.

Presumably the solution to the sad situation of poetry in 1963 is the sad situation itself. Fiedler mentions Wilbur and Lowell but talks principally of the beats and their progeny.

248 Fischer, John. THE STUPIDITY PROBLEM AND OTHER HARRASSMENTS. New York: Harper and Row, 1964. 275 p.

An appraisal of American society during a ten-year period when Fischer wrote articles on various topics for HARPER'S "The Editor's Easy Chair." The collection is not strictly chronological, but grouped by subject.

249 Friedman, Norman. "The Wesleyan Poets I-IV." CHICAGO REVIEW, 18, Nos. 3-14 (1966), 53-73; 19, No. 1 (1966), 55-72; 19, No. 2 (1967), 52-73; 19, No. 3 (1967), 64-90.

The four essays review the work of twenty-three poets published by the Wesleyan University Press at the beginning of its Wesleyan Poets Series.

250 Goodin, Gayle. "Contemporary Deep South Poetry: A Classification of Subjects." Dissertation, University of Mississippi, 1978 (DAI, 39: 1566).

Classifies prevalent subjects of these poets and finds that they write about what concerns most people: home and family, religion, themselves, sex, love, and society.

251 Gruen, John. THE PARTY'S OVER NOW: REMINISCENCES OF THE FIFTIES--NEW YORK'S ARTISTS, WRITERS, MUSICIANS, AND THEIR FRIENDS. New York: Viking, 1972. 282 p.

Arty anecdotes about painters, musicians, and others, but also about a few contemporary poets among whom are Kenneth Koch, Frank O'Hara, and John Ashbery.

252 Habe, Hans [pseud.]. THE WOUNDED LAND: JOURNEY THROUGH A DIVIDED AMERICA. New York: Coward-McCann, 1964. 310 p.

A view of America and Americans by a European during the months before the assassination of John F. Kennedy. Even Habe's misinterpretations provide food for thought.

253 Hassan, Ihab. "Since 1954." In LITERARY HISTORY OF THE UNITED STATES. Ed. Robert E. Spiller et al. 3rd ed. New York: Macmillan, 1969, pp. 1412-41.

Section 4, pages 1427-35, surveys the verse of the period. Hassan discusses formalists and antiformalists as groups or movements. Lowell and Wilbur are examples of the first and the beat poets examples of the second. He also makes some attempt to delineate differences of individual poets within the groups.

254 Hazo, Samuel. "Poetry and the American Public." AMERICAN SCHOLAR, 45 (Spring 1976), 278-90.

On the difficulties "real" poets who are also beginners face in publishing their poems or otherwise bringing their work before the public.

255 ______. "The Poets of Retreat." CATHOLIC WORLD, 198 (October 1963), 33-39.

Assesses the possibilities for beat poets. They may be "the Shelleys and Wordsworths of midcentury."

256 Heyen, William, ed. AMERICAN POETS IN 1976. Indianapolis: Bobbs-Merrill, 1976. 496 p.

Twenty-nine essays by contemporary poets on their own and others' work. Anne Sexton's contribution is the text of an interview taped by Heyen and Al Poulin at Brockport the morning after a poetry reading, September 11, 1973. Part 2 of the selected bibliography is an extensive list of reviews and commentary by contemporary writers on one another and also general critical works on the period.

257 Howard, Richard. ALONE WITH AMERICA: ESSAYS ON THE ART OF POETRY IN THE UNITED STATES SINCE 1950. New York: Atheneum, 1969; enl. ed., 1980. 688 p.

Essays on forty-one poets from A.R. Ammons to James Wright. In the enlarged edition, Howard has not added poets, only made additions to the essays, "not with the intention of rectifying, merely of extending the account."

258 Hungerford, Edward Buell, ed. POETS IN PROGRESS: CRITICAL PREFACES TO TEN CONTEMPORARY AMERICANS. Evanston, Ill.: Northwestern University Press, 1962, 213 p.; augmented rpt., 1967, 298 p.

The augmented version adds essays on Levertov, Simpson, and Sexton. The essays, or versions of them, were first published in TRI-QUARTERLY from fall 1958 to 1967. The earlier edition is annotated in Somer and Cooper (no. 69), page 191; annotations are in the individual poets chapter of this present guide.

259 Juhasz, Suzanne. NAKED AND FIERY FORMS: MODERN AMERICAN POETRY BY WOMEN: A NEW TRADITION. New York: Harper Colophon Books, 1976. 212 p.

Juhasz says she has tried neither to explain away, glorify, nor ignore the sex of the poets discussed. Her introductory chapter is entitled "The Double Bind of the Woman Poet." Essays are on Levertov, Plath, Sexton, Rich, and others.

260 Kalstone, David. "Contemporary American Poetry, 1945--." In THE NORTON ANTHOLOGY OF AMERICAN LITERATURE. Ed. Ronald Gottesman et al. New York: Norton, 1979. Vol. 2, pp. 2251-57.

As an introduction to this section of the Norton anthology, Kalstone describes the differences between modern and contemporary American poetry and lists and discusses what he considers to have been some particularly influential books during the period.

261 Kazin, Alfred. NEW YORK JEW. New York: Alfred A. Knopf, 1978. 308 p.

Kazin's autobiography from 1942 on, in which he remembers Plath, Jarrell, Lowell, and Schwartz, with a few pages on each.

262 Knisley, Patrick Allen. "The Interior Diamond: Baseball in Twentieth Century American Poetry and Fiction." Dissertation, University of Colorado, Boulder, 1978 (DAI, 39: 2939).

The game of baseball as myth, metaphor, and ritual in various works of literature.

263 Kostelanetz, Richard. MASTER MINDS: PORTRAITS OF CONTEMPORARY AMERICAN ARTISTS AND INTELLECTUALS. New York: Macmillan, 1969. 383 p.

The fourteen portraits of men in various professions afford a fairly broad view of American culture and society. Ginsberg's profile appears on pages 183-209. He is the only poet represented.

264 _____. THE YOUNG AMERICAN WRITERS: FICTION, POETRY, ETC. New York: Funk and Wagnalls, 1968. 395 p.

Kostelanetz' introduction and essay "New American Arts" (reprinted from his book of that title) offer general surveys of the search for "the new" in contemporary arts.

265 Kronenberger, Louis. "A Taste of Money: On 'Upper Bohemia,' or the Writer in America Today." ENCOUNTER, 22, No. 5 (1964), 14-21.

Writers today have been more "infected" by the life around them than they have affected it. They live nowadays pretty much like everyone else, unlike the bohemian writers of yesteryear.

266 Kunitz, Stanley. A KIND OF ORDER, A KIND OF FOLLY: ESSAYS AND CONVERSATIONS. Boston: Little, Brown, 1975. 320 p. Index.

Reviews and reminiscences of various poets, some modern and some contemporary.

267 Lacey, Paul A. THE INNER WAR: FORMS AND THEMES IN RECENT AMERICAN POETRY. Philadelphia: Fortress, 1972. 132 p.

Discusses poets whose "inner war" has produced poems that "may help us discover how to reach the right resolution" of our own inner struggles. For Lacey this war seems a spiritual struggle and thus supplies chapter titles like "Witnesses to the Spiritual," "The Sacrament of Confession," and "The Sacred Truth of Wretchedness." The poets are Everson, Levertov, James Wright, and Bly.

268 Lento, Takako U. "The Deathwish and the Self in Contemporary American Poetry." KYUSHU AMERICAN LITERATURE, 19 (1978), 17-27.

Merwin, Kinnell, Sexton, and Berryman are studied to understand "why some American poets have to kill themselves." Since the relationship of the self to its world "determines the kind of freedom the self aspires for," a poet's self-destructive impulse is a desire for liberation from the conditions of his existence.

269 Lieberman, Laurence. UNASSIGNED FREQUENCIES: AMERICAN POETRY IN REVIEW, 1964-1977. Urbana: University of Illinois Press, 1977. 296 p.

A collection of Lieberman's reviews and critical essays, which, he says, are "representative of the remarkable variety and sweep of poetry in the United States today."

270 Lincoln, Kenneth. "(Native) American Poetries." SOUTHWEST REVIEW, 63 (Autumn 1978), 367-84.

On cultural differences between American and Native American poetry. Their conflicts "can be dealt with once they are acknowledged."

271 McGovern, Ann, ed. "Voices from Within: The Poetry of Women in Prison." RADICAL TEACHER, 6 (1977), 45-47.

Three columns of introductory comments on her visits to Bedford Hills Correctional Facility precede McGovern's account of "writing nights" and samples of the women's poems.

272 Martin, Robert K. THE HOMOSEXUAL TRADITION IN AMERICAN POETRY. Austin: University of Texas Press, 1979. 259 p.

Studies how much a poet's awareness of himself as a homosexual affects his work. Failure of critics to observe this aspect of a poet's identity, Martin believes, has led to misinterpretation of numerous texts. Poets included are Ginsberg, Duncan, Gunn, Howard, Merrill, Edward Field, and Alfred Corn, on pages 164-217.

273 Mazzaro, Jerome. POSTMODERN AMERICAN POETRY. Urbana: University of Illinois Press, 1980. 203 p.

A collection of Mazzaro's essays, many of them revised by extension. They support the view that postmodernism is the opposite of modernism, which is exemplified by Eliot's remark that poetry "is not the expression of personality, but an escape from personality." Chapters on Jarrell, Roethke, Ignatow, Berryman, Plath, and Elizabeth Bishop.

274 Mersmann, James F. OUT OF THE VIETNAM VORTEX: A STUDY OF POETS AND POETRY AGAINST THE WAR. Lawrence: University Press of Kansas, 1974. 277 p.

Compares these poems with poems of other wars, and studies the protests of Ginsberg, Levertov, Bly, Duncan, and others, concluding that society ("life as we have known it") must change or perish.

275 Molesworth, Charles. THE FIERCE EMBRACE: A STUDY OF CONTEMPORARY AMERICAN POETRY. Columbia and London: University of Missouri Press, 1979. 214 p.

A collection of Molesworth's essays, almost all of which appeared elsewhere in various journals. Presumably new are his first interchapter, third interchapter, and chapter 10, "Reflections in Place of a Conclusion," pages 196-204.

Other chapters are on Roethke; Lowell and Ginsberg; Plath, Sexton, and Berryman; O'Hara; Kinnell; Bly; Levine; and Ashbery.

276 ______. "'We Have Come This Far': Audience and Form in Contemporary American Poetry." SOUNDINGS, 59 (Summer 1976), 204-25; rpt. in THE FIERCE EMBRACE (no. 275), pp. 1-21.

> Surveys postwar poetry and its small audiences of students and other poets, still further diminished by government and commercial language pollution. Now, with the end of the anthology "wars," perhaps poetry can "find the audience it so deeply, though often confusingly, desires." A new audience may be "an important force in shaping the new ideas of form."

277 Moran, Ronald, and George Lensing. "The Emotive Imagination: A New Departure in American Poetry." SOUTHERN REVIEW, 3 (Winter 1967), 51-67.

> Lensing and Moran use Donald Hall's words to define their term: "This new imagination reveals through images a subjective life which is <u>general,</u> and which corresponds to an old objective life of shared experience and knowledge." They call it a school comprising Bly, Simpson, Stafford, and James Wright, which uses a kind of noncerebral imagination that is apprehended by feeling. They discuss the successes and excesses of the resulting poetry. Reprinted in no. 375.

278 Oppen, Mary. MEANING: A LIFE. Santa Barbara, Calif.: Black Sparrow Press, 1978. 213 p.

> This is Mary Oppen's life, of course, but the Oppens knew numerous artists, literary and other kinds, from all over the world. Her recollections, particularly of older writers like Zukofsky and Reznikoff, in the last half of the book may prove useful as a picture of publishing and literary life from the thirties to the fifties.

279 Packard, William, ed. THE CRAFT OF POETRY: INTERVIEWS FROM <u>THE NEW YORK QUARTERLY</u>. Garden City, N.Y.: Doubleday, 1974. 354 p. Bibliog.

> Interviews with seventeen American poets. Interviewers are listed for each poet but no date is given. Copyright date suggests 1970-74.

280 Parkinson, Thomas, ed. A CASE BOOK ON THE BEAT. New York: Thomas Y. Crowell, 1961. 326 p. Bibliog.

"Criticism and Commentary," pages 179-310, is a collection of twelve comments, both partisan and nonpartisan, intended as an overview. A few are on fiction writers, a few on verse writers, but most on the group.

281 Paul, Sherman. REPOSSESSING AND RENEWING: ESSAYS IN THE GREEN AMERICAN TRADITION. Baton Rouge: Louisiana State University Press, 1976. 311 p.

On the Emersonian tradition from Thoreau to Gary Snyder. "From Lookout to Ashram: The Way of Gary Snyder," pages 195-235, is on Snyder's espousal of "the wild" and applies biographical materials to the interpretation of poems.

282 "Poetry Today in the United States and Canada." NEW: AMERICAN AND CANADIAN POETRY, No. 15 (April-May 1971).

A series of comments by poets and poet-editors on poetry in North America. Some are general; some are reviews of specific volumes of poems, like Victor Contoski's of Charles Simic's SOMEWHERE AMONG US A STONE IS TAKING NOTES, pages 23-26; some are assessments of individuals like Dave Etter's "John Woods: America's Best Poet," pages 26-30.

283 Reid, Alfred S. "Modern American Poetry beyond Modernism." FURMAN STUDIES, 24, No. 1 (1976), 1-12.

Lists three characteristics of modernism--"its mythmaking approach to reality; its political conservatism; and its loss of faith"--and goes on to elaborate these. The move away from such features replaces them with "personal immediacy, political . . . liberalism, and . . . faith."

284 Rosenberger, Francis Coleman, ed. WASHINGTON AND THE POET. Charlottesville: University Press of Virginia, 1977. 79 p.

An anthology of poems about Washington, D.C., and the U.S. government. Its brief biographical notes, pages 69-76, include some poets one may not otherwise read.

285 Rubin, Louis D., Jr., and Robert D. Jacobs, eds. SOUTH: MODERN SOUTHERN LITERATURE IN ITS CULTURAL SETTING. Garden City, N.Y.: Doubleday, 1961; rpt., Westport, Conn.: Greenwood, 1974. 433 p.

A background study but not specifically about poetry. It has an essay by Louise Cowan on the difference between southern poetry and modern poetry in the South, pages 95-114, and one by Ellington White on R.P. Warren, pages 198-209. There is also a "Checklist for Further Reading" compiled by James Meriwether.

286 SALMAGUNDI, Nos. 22-23 (Spring-Summer 1973).

Boyers' CONTEMPORARY POETRY IN AMERICA (no. 223) reprinted most of the contents of this special issue, excluding a few poems. Most well-known and some less-known poets are included in both the journal and the book. Mazzaro's essay on David Ignatow, omitted from the book, has been reprinted in no. 273.

287 Shapcott, Thomas, ed. CONTEMPORARY AMERICAN AND AUSTRALIAN POETRY. Brisbane: University of Queensland Press, 1976. 513 p.

An anthology of verse from the two countries. Shapcott's introduction explains similarities that justify the comparison and may give Americans and Australians a somewhat different view of their own poets.

288 Shaw, Robert B. AMERICAN POETRY SINCE 1960: SOME CRITICAL PERSPECTIVES. Cheadle, Engl.: Carcanet Press, 1973. 220 p.

The individual critics represented support "the prevalent view of 'sixties poetry as a poetry of revolt," but each has his own unique enthusiasms. In addition to general essays and essays on groups or movements are essays on individual poets: Lowell, Berryman, Merwin, Ashbery, Rich, O'Hara, Dickey, Plath, and Strand. The interview with Mark Strand, incidentally, is a revised version of an earlier printing in OHIO REVIEW, 13, No. 2 (1972), 54-71; and Bloom's essay on Ashbery is reprinted in no. 181.

289 Simpson, Louis. "California Poets." LONDON MAGAZINE, 11 (February-March 1972), 56-63.

Simpson's experiences among these poets led him to see them as chauvinistic and pretty much all cut from the same pattern.

290 Stessel, Harry. "Confessional Poetry: A Guide to Marriage in America." MODERNA SPRAK, 72, No. 4 (1978), 337-55.

Stessel sees a correlation between the attitudes of confessional poets and the state of matrimony.

291 "Supplement: On Rhythm from America." AGENDA, 11 (Spring-Summer 1973), 37-66.

Responses to questions about poetic technique from Davie, Eberhart, Hall, Daryl Hine, Lowell, Middleton, George Oppen, Snodgrass, and Stafford.

292 TRI QUARTERLY, 43 (Fall 1978).

A special issue on little magazines giving an overview of

this aspect of American culture. On pages 666-750 appears Peter Martin's "An Annotated Bibliography of Selected Little Magazines."

293 Tytell, John. NAKED ANGELS: LIVES AND LITERATURE OF THE BEAT GENERATION. New York: McGraw-Hill, 1976. 273 p.

Background of the "beat" movement and its relation to other movements. The poet represented is Ginsberg in "Allen Ginsberg and the Messianic Tradition," pages 212-57, which surveys his poetic career and his contribution to literature.

294 Vendler, Helen. PART OF NATURE, PART OF US: MODERN AMERICAN POETS. Cambridge, Mass.: Harvard University Press, 1980. 376 p.

A collection of Vendler's reviews and essays, most of which are on specific works by contemporary poets. See her Table of Contents or List of Books Discussed.

295 Vincent, Sybil Korff. "'An Old Man Called Me Darling': The Diction of the Love Poetry of Some Contemporary Poets during the Period 1945 through 1975." Dissertation, University of Toledo, 1977 (DAI, 38: 2797).

A word study of ten poets of this thirty-one year period to discover changes in "the sensibility of the poets and of contemporary American society regarding love and sexuality."

296 Wagner, Linda W. AMERICAN MODERN: ESSAYS IN FICTION AND POETRY. Port Washington, N.Y.: Kennikat Press, 1979. 263 p.

Chapters on contemporary poetry begin on page 95 with chapter 9. I have annotated these essays in the individual poets chapter or in the appropriate general chapters. Almost all poets discussed by Wagner are related to William Carlos Williams in aims and techniques.

297 _____. "Modern American Literature: The Poetics of the Individual Voice." CENTENNIAL REVIEW, 21 (1977), 333-54.

Treats the matter of personal expression first in fiction and then turns to poetry, pages 343-54, where the poems of Plath, Wakoski, Sexton, Merwin, Rich, Kinnell, and Olson are discussed. Reprinted in no. 296.

298 Weatherhead, A. Kingsley. THE EDGE OF THE IMAGE: MARIANNE MOORE, WILLIAM CARLOS WILLIAMS, AND SOME OTHER POETS. Seattle: University of Washington Press, 1967. 251 p.

Part of the chapter entitled "Literary Relationships," pages 186 ff., discusses the influence of Williams and Moore on such later poets as Ginsberg, Olson, Creeley, Wilbur, Levertov, and Duncan.

299 Williams, Mary C. "The Poetic Knife: Poetry by Recent Southern Women Poets." SOUTH CAROLINA REVIEW, 11, No. 1 (1978), 44-59.

Of the poets discussed here as feminine and feminist, only Vassar Miller has a separate entry in this present guide. Williams sees her as somewhat set apart from the others and gives her the longest discussion: "Pain is the justification and source for her poetry as for her life." Williams does not, however, focus on Miller's physical disability, something that could explain some aspects of her being different. Williams concludes her comments on all of the poets by stating that "As long as there are differences between men and women, there will not be unisex poetry."

300 Williams, Miller. "Intuition, Spontaneity, Organic Wholeness and the Redemptive Wilderness: Some (Old) Currents in Contemporary Poetry." THE SMITH, No. 18 (December 1975), 141-51.

Groups a number of writers together under the name of poets of intuition or antirationalists and explains and justifies such a classification: Bly, Snyder, Wagoner, Roethke, Ammons, Kinnell, Merwin, James Wright, and Larry Lieberman. He sees James Dickey as "nearly" in the group.

301 "Yale's Younger Poets: Interview with Chester Kerr, Stanley Kunitz, Carolyn Forché." BOOK FORUM, 2 (1976), 367-68, 370, 386.

A report of an interview (with generous quotations). Apparently, but not necessarily, the poets were interviewed separately. Kerr talks about the Yale series and the competition; Kunitz talks about Forché and the task of selecting a winner; and Forché (with biographical comments by the editor) talks about her verse.

Chapter 6

GENERAL STUDIES OF ENGLISH POETS AND LITERATURE

Though "English" refers to England and Wales for the purposes of this guide, this general chapter naturally includes statements about poets and literature from other parts of the British Commonwealth. Additional works that give a general view of British culture may be found in the previous chapters; titles listed here are specifically concerned with Britain.

302 Burnham, Richard. "THE DUBLIN MAGAZINE's Welsh Poets." ANGLO-WELSH REVIEW, No. 60 (1978), pp. 49-63.

On the debt of encouragement owed by several Welsh poets (including R. S. Thomas) to Seamus O'Sullivan for printing their work when English journals proved less than hospitable.

303 Collins, Michael J. "The Rhetorical Double in Modern British Poetry." MODERN BRITISH LITERATURE, 2 (1977), 176-81.

The image of the double is as important in many poems as in drama and fiction. The double here discussed is not so much "of the author" as of another figure in the poem." Contemporary examples are in poems by Larkin ("Mr. Bleaney") and Hill ("September Song").

304 Cox, C.B., and A.E. Dyson. MODERN POETRY: STUDIES IN PRACTICAL CRITICISM. London: Edward Arnold, 1963. 168 p.

The commentary is intended to show us how to criticize a poem in a formal and traditional way. The poems begin with Hardy, Georgian poets, and modern poets like Yeats and Eliot and are followed by comment on individual poems by R.S. Thomas, Philip Larkin, Ted Hughes, Thom Gunn, and John Wain. Each receives three or four pages of comment.

305 Cozens, Andrew. "Poets in Cambridge: An Introduction." WINDLESS ORCHARD, 24 (1975-76), 4-5.

A collection of poems to illustrate the variety of poetry being written in England, with comment by Cozens and Robert Novak, who continues the discussion, pages 25, 35, and 47-48.

306 Davie, Donald. "Letter from England." PARNASSUS, 6, No. 1 (1977), 129-37.

Davie describes the political situation and points out the need to trust poets rather than politicians. He comments on C.H. Sisson; the POETRY NATION REVIEW; and Elaine Feinstein, "a very important and serious poet, unsettling most preconceptions about what British poets are like."

307 _____. THE POET IN THE IMAGINARY MUSEUM: ESSAYS OF TWO DECADES. Ed. Barry Alpert. New York: Persea Books, 1977. 343 p.

Alpert's introduction explores the relationship of Davie's criticism to his art. Davie's essays are often reviews of specific books, especially his essays on contemporaries. I have listed and annotated many of these under individual poets.

308 _____. THOMAS HARDY AND BRITISH POETRY. New York: Oxford University Press, 1972. 192 p.

On Hardy and the Hardyesque in modern and contemporary poets. Many comparisons and illustrations appear throughout, but see "Landscapes of Larkin," pages 63-82; "Roy Fisher: An Appreciation," pages 152-72; and "An Afterword for the American Reader," pages 183-88.

309 ENGLISH STUDIES (Amsterdam), 1919--. 6 issues per year.

An annual section, "Current Literature," has illuminating comments on the previous year's publications. Published in Lisse since 1979.

310 Fraser, G.S. "English Poetry, 1930-1960." In THE TWENTIETH CENTURY. HISTORY OF LITERATURE IN THE ENGLISH LANGUAGE. Ed. Bernard Bergonzi. London: Barrie and Jenkins, 1970. Vol. 7, pp. 277-309.

Fraser's chapter emphasizes the 1930s and thus treats a few of the earlier writers of the contemporary period. The later sections of the chapter, however, as might be expected, include a general survey of younger poets.

311 Fuller, Roy. "Poetry in My Time." ESSAYS BY DIVERS HANDS. London: Oxford University Press, 1969. Vol 35, pp. 67-84.

Fuller acknowledges his literary debts to Geoffrey Grigson and John Davenport. He talks briefly of later poets from the point of view of one brought up on Eliot, Pound, Yeats, and Auden.

312 Gitzen, Julian. "British Nature Poetry Now." MIDWEST QUARTERLY, 15, No. 4 (1974), 323-37.

"British nature poetry has returned to prominence, and with themes and images which would have offended earlier poets." Gitzen elaborates this statement by citing poets R.S. Thomas, Seamus Heaney, Ted Walker, Peter Redgrove, Ted Hughes, and Charles Tomlinson and characterizing their differences from one another and the difference of all of them from traditional nature poets.

313 Hamilton, Ian. "Context." LONDON MAGAZINE, 1 (February 1962), 27-53.

Twenty-six poets reply to an inquiry of six questions about poetry, public issues, uses of poetry, influences on themselves by living writers, poetic language, and the contemporary social and cultural milieu.

314 Hobsbaum, Philip. "The Present Condition of British Poetry." HUDSON REVIEW, 26 (Autumn 1973), 598-608.

The American view that British poetry is anemic applies only to pop poets and metropolitan poets. A third group, represented by such poets as Peter Redgrove, belies this criticism.

315 Holbrook, David. LOST BEARINGS IN ENGLISH POETRY. New York: Barnes and Noble, 1977. 255 p.

Explains why present-day poetry is in the pathetic state it is and what is needed for improvement. In essence, Holbrook believes, an existential sense of self has been lost by poets writing now.

316 Johnson, Abby Ann Arthur. "THE POETRY REVIEW: Poetic Conservatism in an Age of Experimentation, 1909-1968." Dissertation, University of Illinois, 1969 (DAI, 31: 762).

The beginnings, ideologies, and practices of the Poetry Society in Britain as revealed in its journal, POETRY REVIEW.

317 ______. "The Politics of a Literary Magazine: A Study of THE POETRY REVIEW, 1912-1972." JOURNAL OF MODERN LITERATURE, 3, No. 4 (1974), 951-64.

After pointing out the contemporaneity of the journal's recent issues, Johnson describes its nature at inception and its subsequent history.

318 King, P.R. NINE CONTEMPORARY POETS: A CRITICAL INTRODUCTION. London: Methuen, 1979. 256 p. Primary and secondary bibliogs., index of poems.

A chapter of thirty to forty pages is devoted to each of the following: Larkin, Hughes, Tomlinson, Plath, Gunn, and Heaney. Douglas Dunn, Tom Paulin, and Paul Mills are treated in a separate chapter.

319 Kuna, F.M. "A New Myth-Consciousness in Contemporary English Poetry." ENGLISH STUDIES, 51 (June 1970), 214-28.

On the revival of an interest in myth and the mythic among young poets and its effect on today's poetry.

320 Miller, Karl. Introduction. In his WRITING IN ENGLAND TODAY: THE LAST FIFTEEN YEARS. Harmondsworth, Engl.: Penguin Books, 1968, pp. 13-28.

Miller surveys the movements and schools, trends and influences, and economics and politics of the fifties and sixties.

321 "Modern British Poetry." CONTEMPORARY LITERATURE, 12, No. 4 (1971).

The articles on contemporaries, most of which are annotated in the individual poets chapter of this present guide, are on George Barker, David Jones, Charles Tomlinson, Christopher Middleton, Geoffrey Hill, David Gascoyne, and Basil Bunting.

322 Morrison, Blake. "The Movement: A Reassessment." PN REVIEW, 4, No. 1 (1977), 26-29; and No. 2 (1977), 43-48.

Morrison shows that, yes, there was a poetic group called The Movement despite cries of "Fraud" and "PR job." Though publicity had played some role, it did not create The Movement; "friendship, mutual influence, and common belief" did that.

323 _____. THE MOVEMENT: ENGLISH POETRY AND FICTION OF THE 1950S. Oxford, Engl.: Oxford University Press, 1980. 326 p. Bibliog., index.

The origin, beliefs, attitudes, and techniques of a postwar literary group who opposed the New Critical stance prevalent in the 1930s. Larkin, Davie, and Amis are most discussed, but similar "elements" are examined in the work of Gunn, Jennings, and Enright.

324 Press, John, ed. A MAP OF ENGLISH VERSE. London: Oxford University Press, 1969. 282 p.

The final chapter has Introduction, Criticism, Poems, and Select Bibliography on the poets of the fifties.

325 Ries, Lawrence Robert. "The Response to Violence in Contemporary British Poetry." Dissertation, Southern Illinois University, 1971 (DAI, 32: 5243).

Examines the responses to two kinds of violence, natural and social, by Plath, Hughes, Gunn, Wain, Porter, Redgrove, and George MacBeth. Ries admires the stance advocated by Gunn and Hughes.

326 Schmidt, Michael. A READER'S GUIDE TO FIFTY MODERN BRITISH POETS. London: Heinemann; New York: Barnes and Noble, 1979. 432 p.

Brief essays, about thirty of which are on contemporary poets. Schmidt's judgments are highly personal, but he gives a good bit of factual information. The book is better viewed as a sourcebook than as a guide; the original title in the Pan Literature Series was AN INTRODUCTION TO FIFTY MODERN BRITISH POETS.

327 Schmidt, Michael, and Grevel Lindop, eds. BRITISH POETRY SINCE 1960: A CRITICAL SURVEY. Oxford, Engl.: Carcanet Press, 1972. 289 p.

Includes the following essays, reprinted from various journals: Ian Hamilton, "The Making of the Movement"; Calvin Bedient, "On Charles Tomlinson"; Jon Silkin, "The Poetry of Geoffrey Hill"; Michael Schmidt, "A Defence"; Alan Brownjohn, "A View of English Poetry in the Seventies"; and Terry Eagleton, "Myth and History in Recent Poetry." A list of awards and prizes won by British poets during the 1960s is on pages 253-59. A bibliography compiled by Barbara Atkinson lists poets and their books to 1971.

328 Schoon, Sarah Legg. "The Idea of Pastoral in Modern British Poetry." Dissertation, St. Louis University, 1978 (DAI, 39: 1601).

Tests the modern use of pastoralism against the classical use and divides the poets into traditional and antipastoral. Chapters 4 and 5 treat contemporary poets, among whom are Barker, Hughes, Tomlinson, Davie, Larkin, and R.S. Thomas.

329 Sergeant, Howard. "British Poetry, 1952-1977." CONTEMPORARY REVIEW, 231 (October 1977), 196-201.

An account of the various schools, movements, and groups in reaction to the past and to one another along with comment on individual poets. The two broad groups now are "academic and pop." During the period the market for poetry has moved from slow to brisk.

330 Skelton, Robin. "Britannia's Muse." MASSACHUSETTS REVIEW, 5 (Summer 1964), 725-37.

Reviews the year's books of poems by older poets and some

of the younger, including brief comment on Lehmann, Larkin, Tomlinson, Hughes, and others.

331 Stanford, Derek. INSIDE THE FORTIES: LITERARY MEMOIRS 1937-1957. London: Sidgwick and Jackson, 1977. 242 p. Index.

Stanford reminisces on meeting David Gascoyne and comments on his personality and his poems, pages 106-11. Index lists other comments. More prominent in his memoirs is Muriel Spark, better known as a novelist, who appears as subject in two chapters: "Polishing the Church Silver" and "Ordeals and Comforters," pages 176-205. Numerous other contemporary poets are mentioned.

332 Swinden, Patrick. "English Poetry." In THE TWENTIETH CENTURY MIND: HISTORY, IDEAS, AND LITERATURE IN BRITAIN. Ed. C.B. Cox and A.E. Dyson. London: Oxford University Press, 1972. Vol. 3, pp. 386-413.

Survey of English poetry from the 1950s to the 1970s: Movement poets John Wain, Ted Hughes, Thom Gunn, and Donald Davies; and Charles Tomlinson and others. Swinden attempts to show relationships, influences, and affinities among these poets.

333 Tomlinson, Charles. "Poetry Today." In THE MODERN AGE. Pelican Guide to English Literature. Baltimore: Penguin Books, 1961. Vol. 7, pp. 458-74.

No contemporary poet has used, let alone advanced, the "finer awareness of the community of European values" created by Pound, Yeats, and Eliot. Instead, "poetic culture in Britain would seem to be living on an overdraft, the overdraft being the work of the writers of the older generation who are still with us."

334 Wollman, Maurice, ed. TEN CONTEMPORARY POETS. Harrap's English Classics. London: George G. Harrap, 1963; rpt., 1973. 176 p.

Ten or so poems each and brief biobibliographical notes aimed at students in senior schools in Britain. Poets are Thomas Blackburn, Enright, Graves, Gunn, Hughes, Patrick Kavanagh, MacNeice, Vernon Scannell, Hal Summers, and R.S. Thomas.

335 Young, Alan. "Twentieth Century Poetry: An Open University Course." CRITICAL QUARTERLY, 19 (Spring 1977), 57-62.

Describes and evaluates the use of texts, radio, television, and phonograph in the Open University course. Young's main objection is to "the American presence in and supposed influence on English poetry" in the course which excludes many "strongly distinctive and unclassifiable British voices."

Chapter 7

STUDIES OF TWO OR MORE POETS

These studies are usually comparative by intention, although I have also listed some in which the overall effect is comparative. Only those studies comparing two or more contemporary poets are here. Where the comparison of a single poet is with an older writer, obviously the intent is comparative; but I have listed such books and articles only in the individual poets chapter. All studies are fully cross-referenced in the Author Index.

336 Abbs, Peter. "The Revival of the Mythopoeic Imagination--A Study of R.S. Thomas and Ted Hughes." POETRY WALES, 10, No. 4 (1975), 10-27.

Abbs is impressed by the attempts of these two poets "to fashion a new style of poetry"--Thomas in H'M and Hughes in CROW. He traces "the development of each poet in the light cast by their latest volumes." He notes finally a few of their weaknesses, which may have been caused by the strengths of their "new poetry, broad, free-ranging, essentially mythopoeic."

337 Allen, Donald, ed. ON BREAD AND POETRY: A PANEL DISCUSSION WITH GARY SNYDER, LEW WELCH, AND PHILIP WHALEN. Bolinas, Calif.: Grey Fox, 1977. 62 p.

Held in early June 1965, the interviews give accounts of the poets, opinions of writing poems as a profession, and comments on the "hip-square" conflict.

338 André, Kenneth Michael. "Levertov, Creeley, Wright, Auden, Ginsberg, Corso, Dickey: Essays and Interviews with Contemporary American Poets." Dissertation, Columbia University, 1974 (DAI, 36: 3681).

Most of these, perhaps all, have been published and are either annotated in this present guide in the chapter on individual poets or in the bibliographies cited in the same chapters.

339 August, Bonne Tymorski. "The Poetic Use of Womanhood in Five Modern

American Poets: Moore, Millay, Rukeyser, Levertov, and Plath." Dissertation, New York University, 1978 (DAI, 39: 3576).

Although each of these poets is naturally distinct from the others, their work "demonstrates their preoccupation with power in all its forms" and "the parallel sense of alienation . . . from men, male-dominated institutions, and . . . male definitions of power."

340 Axelrod, Steven. "Colonel Shaw in American Poetry: 'For the Union Dead' and Its Precursors." AMERICAN QUARTERLY, 24 (October 1972), 523-37.

A background study of Colonel Robert Shaw and his treatment in poems by Berryman and Lowell.

341 ______. "Plath's and Lowell's Last Words." PACIFIC COAST PHILOLOGY, 11 (1976), 5-14.

A close look at Plath's "Words" and Lowell's "Skunk Hour" will show "the danger and the opportunity inherent" in confessional poems: "Lowell transcends the romantic dilemmas that consumed Plath, transcends solipsism, transcends even rebellion."

342 Bedient, Calvin. "Absentist Poetry: Kinsella, Hill, Graham, Hughes." PN REVIEW, 4, No. 1 (1976), 18-24.

History and characteristics of "absentist poetry" and its manifestations in the work of the poets mentioned in the title.

343 Behm, Richard H. "A Study of the Function of Myth in the Work of Four Contemporary Poets: Charles Simic, Galway Kinnell, Gary Snyder, and Robert Duncan." Dissertation, Bowling Green State University, 1976 (DAI, 37, 5118).

Describes the principal myths used by these poets and identifies the functions served by these and all other myths: "the arational process of knowing an 'inexpressible' truth and the embodiment of the revelation of that truth in a form."

344 Blaydes, Sophia B. "Metaphors of Life and Death in the Poetry of Denise Levertov and Sylvia Plath." DALHOUSIE REVIEW, 57 (Autumn 1977), 494-506.

Both poets "question the nature and value of man's life, and they convey their contrasting visions of reality in clear, vigorous images and metaphors."

345 Bloxham, Laura Jean. "William Blake and Visionary Poetry in the Twentieth Century." Dissertation, Washington State University, 1975 (DAI, 36: 5275).

Studies the influence of Blake on Roethke, Snyder, and Ginsberg and describes their "concepts of the visionary."

346 Bobbitt, Joan. "Lowell and Plath: Objectivity and the Confessional Mode." ARIZONA QUARTERLY, 33 (Winter 1977), 311-18.

Despite the obvious personal material of these poets, "their attitude towards it and treatment of it are frequently detached and impersonal." Bobbitt analyzes tone in numerous poems.

347 Bold, Alan Norman. GUNN & HUGHES: THOM GUNN AND TED HUGHES. New York: Barnes and Noble, 1976. 136 p. Bibliog.

Bold lays to rest the notion of Hughes and Gunn as "poets of violence" and contends that they "do not have much in common either in motivation or achievement." He elaborates and specifies their chief differences to counteract the early confusion of critics who treated them as one poet.

348 Bowles, Gloria Lee. "Suppression and Expression in Poetry by American Women: Louise Bogan, Denise Levertov, and Adrienne Rich." Dissertation, University of California, Berkeley, 1976 (DAI, 37: 5822).

These poets are examples of women poets who first followed the "masculinist tradition" and then found their own voices.

349 Brown, Robert C. "The Far End of Solitude: Poets Who Wait." INNISFREE, 4 (1977), 27-36.

Poets who have used the verb "to wait" illustrate "the central issue of our culture, . . . the conflict between secular and spiritual concerns." Brown examines, among others, poems by Anne Sexton, Howard Nemerov, William Stafford, and Robert Penn Warren.

350 Caruso, Barbara Ann. "Circle without Boundaries: Feminist Criticism and the Contemporary Woman Poet." Dissertation, Bowling Green State University, 1977 (DAI, 38: 5455).

Shows us how to read a poem by a woman "within a Feminist context."

351 Cloud, Jeraldine Neifer. "Robert Lowell, Sylvia Plath, and the Confessional Mode in Contemporary Poetry." Dissertation, Emory University, 1976 (DAI, 37: 2858).

Studies the poetry of Lowell and Plath, the chief representatives of the confessional mode, in order to define and justify the mode. Both these poets "transcend" the self through their art.

352 Combs, Maxine S. "A Study of the Black Mountain Poets." Dissertation, University of Oregon, 1967 (DA, 28: 3666).

Considers three poets on the staff of the Black Mountain College (Olson, Duncan, and Creeley) and four students there (Jonathan Williams, Edward Dorn, John Wieners, and Joel Oppenheimer), with a chapter on each of the former and one on the younger poets. A final chapter defines critical theory.

353 Cramer, Mark Jonathan. "Neruda and Vallejo in Contemporary United States Poetry." Dissertation, University of Illinois, Urbana-Champaign, 1976 (DAI, 37: 354).

The influence of Neruda and Vallejo has been chiefly on Bly, James Wright, and Merwin through their editing and translating and has in turn been transmitted by them to other poets like Simic and Levine. This study concentrates on the first three named.

354 Davey, Frankland W. "Theory and Practice in the Black Mountain Poets: Duncan, Olson, and Creeley." Dissertation, University of Southern California, 1968 (DA, 29: 256).

Gathers various statements by these poets to make a smooth, organized declaration about poetry and reality and then tests it on their poems.

355 Di Piero, W.S. "Lowell and Ashbery." SOUTHERN REVIEW, 14 (April 1978), 359-67.

A review of Lowell's DAY BY DAY and Ashbery's RIVERS AND MOUNTAINS, DOUBLE DREAM OF SPRING, and HOUSEBOAT DAYS. Lowell's "suffers generally from the hazards of remembrance" and Ashbery's show us "the poetry of a man writing at the height of his powers." In the latter's work, Di Piero likes "the unanticipated idea, the quick jungle of possibility that one line can create."

356 Dullea, Gerard J. "Ginsberg and Corso: Image and Imagination." THOTH, 11, No. 2 (1971), 17-27.

As romantics and revolutionaries, beat poets had to find a voice consistent with their anticonventional, antitraditional philosophy and consequently turned to free verse as the most open form available despite its respectability; but since poetry requires language and language meaning, beat poetry "seems radically flawed."

357 Duplessis, Rachel Blau. "Lyric Documents: The Critique of Personal Consciousness in Levertov, Rich and Rukeyser." In MYTH AND IDEOLOGY IN AMERICAN CULTURE. Ed. Régis Durand. Villeneuve d'Ascq,

France: University de Lille III, 1976, pp. 65-80.

Revised and shortened from her article in FEMINIST STUDIES (no. 358). These three poets "enact a personal awakening to political and social life . . . and situate their consciousness and its formation at a specific historical moment." They represent women writers who adopt "the critique of personal consciousness . . . as a motif" and who struggle with the question of womanhood and personhood.

358 _____. The Critique of Consciousness and Myth in Levertov, Rich, and Rukeyser." FEMINIST STUDIES, 3, Nos. 1-2 (1975), 199-221.

Revised and shortened for no. 357. Examines several poems as analyses of womanhood and roles of individuals in effecting social change. Still another version, which I have not seen, or a third part, appeared in the journal of the North Eastern Modern Language Association for April 1975 or--the note in FEMINIST STUDIES is unclear--was read at the convention of that date.

359 Elliott, David Lindsey. "The Deep Image: Radical Subjectivity in the Poetry of Robert Bly, James Wright, Galway Kinnell, James Dickey, and W.S. Merwin." Dissertation, Syracuse University, 1978 (DAI, 39: 3577).

"Their poetry is neither impersonal nor personal, but <u>trans-personal</u>, for [these poets] do not attempt to rise above <u>the personality</u> or to stay within it, but instead plunge down through it to reach the deepest levels of the psyche."

360 Elliott, William D. "Poets of the Moving Frontier: Bly, Whittemore, Wright, Berryman, McGrath and Minnesota North Country Poetry." MID-AMERICA, 3 (1976), 17-38.

Attempts to define midwestern poetry, which seems not only a geographically slippery term but one which may be applied by different persons to something that is fading away or to something experiencing a rebirth.

361 Engel, Bernard F. "From Here We Speak." OLD NORTHWEST, 2, No. 1 (1976), 37-44.

Uses William Stafford, James Wright, and Thomas McGrath as examples of midwestern poets who have transcended regionalism.

362 Folsom, Lowell Edwin. "America, the Metaphor: Place as Person as Poem as Poet." Dissertation, University of Rochester, 1976 (DAI, 37: 4352).

At the end of this study, Roethke, Snyder, and Merwin are

placed in a historical perspective and seen to "relive the discovery and expansion of America within their imaginations; . . . the continent becomes a metaphor of the poet's self."

363 Gustafson, Richard. "'Time Is a Waiting Woman': New Poetic Icons." MIDWEST QUARTERLY, 16, No. 3 (1975), 318-27.

Describes "new images of time, and hence of wisdom" in present-day women's poetry: Rich, Plath, Wakoski, and Robin Morgan.

364 Hall, Donald. "Two Poets Named Robert." OHIO REVIEW, 18, No. 3 (1977), 110-25.

Hall reviews 1976 collections of verse by Lowell and Francis "to talk about the perversity of literary reputations." He talks mostly about the unjust neglect of Francis by readers of poetry and the unearned praise given to Lowell.

365 Harris, Victoria Frenkel. "The Incorporative Consciousness: A Study of Denise Levertov and Robert Bly." Dissertation, University of Illinois, Urbana-Champaign, 1977 (DAI, 38: 6119).

On the relationship of the poet to the world and of the reader to the poem.

366 Heaney, Seamus. "Now and in England." CRITICAL INQUIRY, 3 (Spring 1977), 471-88.

Concerned with the poetry of Hughes, Hill, and Larkin, who "are aware of their Englishness as deposits in the descending storeys of the literary and historical past." Heaney differentiates their individual attitudes and techniques as expressive of those attitudes. He thinks their "sense of an ending [has made them] look in, rather than up, to England."

367 Hill, Robert White. "Nature Imagery in the Poetry of Theodore Roethke and James Dickey." University of Illinois, Urbana-Champaign, 1972 (DAI, 34: 773).

Contrasts Roethke's "basically passive" view of nature to Dickey's "active" view. Roethke "discovers" and Dickey "makes."

368 Janssens, G.A.M. "The Present State of American Poetry." ENGLISH STUDIES, 51 (April 1970), 112-37.

Summarizes briefly the condition of poetry and criticism in the fifties and sixties and then presents a temperate view of the achievements of Bly and Wright.

369 Kalstone, David. FIVE TEMPERAMENTS: ELIZABETH BISHOP, ROBERT LOWELL, JAMES MERRILL, ADRIENNE RICH, JOHN ASHBERY. New York: Oxford University Press, 1977. 212 p.

Tells us how these five poets handle autobiography, how their personalities are revealed in their work, and how their inner landscapes are delineated.

370 Kammer, Jeanne Henry. "Repression, Compression and Power: Six Women Poets in America, 1860-1960." Dissertation, Carnegie-Mellon University, 1976 (DAI, 37: 2182).

The poets discussed (Dickinson, HD, Moore, Bishop, Plath, and Levertov) write in the compressed form of the lyric because of the conditions under which women have lived in a male dominated society.

371 Kazin, Alfred. "Robert Lowell and John Ashbery: The Difference between Poets." ESQUIRE, 89 (January 1978), 20-22.

Not seen. Cited in JOURNAL OF MODERN LITERATURE, 7, No. 4 (1979), 617.

372 Kenner, Hugh. A HOMEMADE WORLD: THE AMERICAN MODERNIST WRITERS. New York: Knopf, 1975. 254 p. Index.

On modern writers but has sections on Charles Olson and Louis Zukofsky.

373 Kherdian, David. SIX POETS OF THE SAN FRANCISCO RENAISSANCE: PORTRAITS AND CHECKLISTS. Fresno, Calif.: Giligia Press, 1965. 196 p. Bibliogs.

Photographs or drawings and biographical essays on each of the six--Ferlinghetti, Snyder, Whalen, Meltzer, McClure, and Everson. Primary bibliographies. Secondary bibliography lists early reviews and other commentary.

374 _____. SIX SAN FRANCISCO POETS. Fresno, Calif.: Giligia Press, 1969. 61 p.

The essays and interviews in no. 373 without the bibliographies. Introduction by Kherdian.

375 Lensing, George S., and Ronald Moran. FOUR POETS AND THE EMOTIVE IMAGINATION: ROBERT BLY, JAMES WRIGHT, LOUIS SIMPSON, AND WILLIAM STAFFORD. Baton Rouge: Louisiana State University Press, 1976. 238 p.

Defines "emotive imagination"--chapter 1 is a revised version of no. 277--and then examines each poet separately, arguing that together they represent a school or movement. The authors also discuss poems that do not illustrate the traits of this "movement."

376 Levertov, Denise. THE POET IN THE WORLD. New York: New Directions, 1973. 275 p.

A collection of Levertov's views and reviews, primarily about art and artists (including literary artists), from about 1960 to 1973.

377 Levine, Ellen Sue. "From Water to Land: The Poetry of Sylvia Plath, James Wright, and W.S. Merwin." Dissertation, University of Washington, 1974 (DAI, 35: 4532).

Studies the use of landscape by these poets and finds that their earlier poems are dominated by water and sea imagery and their later poems by land imagery. Levine relates this phenomenon to their ideas of the self.

378 Lewis, Peter Elfed. "Robert Creeley and Gary Snyder: A British Assessment." STAND, 3, No. 4 (1972), 42-47.

Contrasts the later work of Creeley and Snyder to their earlier work. The two poets are treated separately, although a transitional paragraph opposes Creeley's "exquisiteness" to Snyder's "robustness." In sum, Lewis thinks of them as, while gifted, both "lightweights."

379 Libby, Anthony. "Fire and Light, Four Poets to the End and Beyond." IOWA REVIEW, 4 (Spring 1973), 111-26.

Bly, Dickey, Hughes, and Merwin "seem to form a dominant contemporary pattern not only because of intersecting vision but because of similar styles created to cope with these visions." Without denying them their individualities, Libby finds in their work "lines that could be attributed to one or more of the others." He discusses each poet separately but with references to the others.

380 ______. "God's Lioness and the Priest of Sycorax: Plath and Hughes." CONTEMPORARY LITERATURE, 15, No. 3 (1974), 386-405.

On the influences, psychological and others, these two poets ("the Scott and Zelda of our time") had on each other. Libby replies to assertions by various critics and produces a general survey of the criticism on Plath and Hughes.

381 Liberthson, Daniel. THE QUEST FOR BEING: THEODORE ROETHKE, W.S. MERWIN, AND TED HUGHES. New York: Gordon Press, 1977.

Not seen. Cited in 1977 MLA INTERNATIONAL BIBLIOGRAPHY, p. 185. I could not locate the book, but it was originally a dissertation at SUNY Buffalo, 1976. In that form, according to DAI, 37: 3613, it is three separate essays bound thematically by the idea of "Orphism." Each of these poets in confronting being and nonbeing must express that confrontation in poetry and thereby redeem their lives by communing with their dead pasts through poetic work. Orpheus is the prototype of such poets.

382 McClave, Heather. "Situations of the Mind: Studies of Center and Periphery in Dickinson, Stevens, Ammons, and Plath." Dissertation, Yale University, 1975 (DAI, 36: 3715).

Ways of looking at the self and the world by the poets mentioned.

383 McMillen, Barbara Fialkowski. "A Study of the Formal and Thematic Uses of Film in the Poetry of Parker Tyler, Frank O'Hara and Adrienne Rich." Dissertation, Ohio University, 1976 (DAI, 37: 1549).

Defines the term "cinematic" and relates it to the poets named, who use film as form and theme.

384 Martin, Wallace D. "Beyond Modernism: Christopher Middleton and Geoffrey Hill." CONTEMPORARY LITERATURE, 12, No. 4 (1971), 420-36.

Emphasizes similarities in these two dissimilar poets. Martin is interested in "the aspects of modernism that serve as the context of their achievements." He describes the modernist tradition, first in Middleton and then in Hill.

385 Mazzaro, Jerome. "Integrities." KENYON REVIEW, 32, No. 1 (1970), 163-68.

Review of PIECES by Creeley and THE ZIGZAG WALK by Logan. Mazzaro develops the theme of honesty in these poets' self-explorations. Creeley and Logan live "in a fallen world where self and the other have become separate."

386 Meeker, Michael William. "The Influence of the Personal Element on Language, Form, and Theme in the Poetry of James Dickey and Galway Kinnell." Dissertation, University of Wisconsin, Madison, 1975 (DAI, 37: 312).

Despite similarities in subject, tone, and point of view, Dickey and Kinnell have different assumptions about language and form that have moved them in different directions.

387 Meltzer, David, ed. THE SAN FRANCISCO POETS. New York: Ballantine, 1971. 339 p.

Interviews with Rexroth, Everson, Ferlinghetti, Welch, McClure, and Richard Brautigan. A checklist of titles by these six. "S F Poetry Chronology," pages 309-18, lists the work of many other writers of the area.

388 Menides, Laura Jehn. "The Uses of the Past in Modern American Poetry: Eliot, Pound, Williams, Crane, Berryman, Olson, Lowell." Dissertation, New York University, 1978 (DAI, 39: 3583).

Berryman's HOMAGE TO MISTRESS BRADSTREET, Olson's MAXIMUS POEMS, and Lowell's early poems, LIFE STUDIES, HISTORY, and DAY BY DAY attempt "to discover or create an American past that is usable for the present." Lowell first rejects his American past and then in later volumes returns to it.

389 Minock, Daniel William. "Conceptions of Death in the Modern Elegy and Related Poems." Dissertation, Ohio State University, 1975 (DAI, 36: 1496).

Contemporary poems discussed are Lowell's "Quaker Graveyard in Nantucket" and "For the Union Dead," Roethke's "Meditations of an Old Woman" and "North American Sequence," Plath's "Daddy," and Ginsberg's KADDISH. Poems by modern writers are also considered.

390 Mizejewski, Linda. "Sappho to Sexton: Woman Uncontained." COLLEGE ENGLISH, 35, No. 3 (1973), 340-45.

Plath and Sexton belong to a tradition in literature that employs the metaphor of "woman broken off, flying into night, swept into air, running over earth like a thunderstorm."

391 Molesworth, Charles. "'With Your Own Face On': Origins and Consequences of Confessional Poetry." TWENTIETH CENTURY LITERATURE, 22 (May 1976), 163-78.

On the strengths and weaknesses of the confessional mode. Molesworth thinks Berryman, Lowell, Snodgrass, Sexton, and others, have not been strict enough with themselves. Revised reprint in no. 275.

392 Moramarco, Fred. "John Ashbery and Frank O'Hara: The Painterly Poets." JOURNAL OF MODERN LITERATURE, 5, No. 3 (1976), 436-62.

Because paintings, especially hyperrealistic and surrealistic as well as expressionistic, have influenced Ashbery and O'Hara, "We need to look at a great many paintings to read them well."

393 Nadel, Alan. "Roethke, Wilbur, and the Vision of the Child: Romantic and Augustan in Modern Verse." LION AND THE UNICORN, 2, No. 1 (1978), 94-113.

The desire of poets to simplify and the desire to "manifest the complex" blend in the writing of children's verse where are united also Romanticism and Neo-Classicism. Despite differences in their view of childhood, both Roethke and Wilbur love children, believe "poetry can be written for children," and "use poetry as a simplifying device, to instruct through delighting."

394 Northouse, Cameron, and Thomas P. Walsh, eds. SYLVIA PLATH AND ANNE SEXTON: A REFERENCE GUIDE. Boston: G.K. Hall, 1975. 152 p. Bibliogs.

Separate bibliographies of secondary works, annotated to and into 1973. See listing in individual poets chapter.

395 Oberg, Arthur. MODERN AMERICAN LYRIC: LOWELL, BERRYMAN, CREELEY, AND PLATH. New Brunswick: Rutgers University Press, 1978. 195 p.

Oberg has separate chapters on each, since he sees these poets, although of the same company, as uniquely different, each "playing and working out his life and death on paper." He contrasts their variety of lyric by way of introduction with those of Donald Justice and Charles Wright. The poets discussed here "intend their poems to terrify and comfort, in the service of love."

395A Paul, Sherman. THE LOST AMERICA OF LOVE: REREADING ROBERT CREELEY, EDWARD DORN, AND ROBERT DUNCAN. Baton Rouge: Louisiana State University Press, 1982. 232 p.

Not seen; advertisement from the publisher calls it "a meditative book."

396 Pearson, Sheryl Sherman. "The Confessional Mode and Two Recent Poets." RACKHAM LITERARY STUDIES, 2 (1972), 1-10.

Because the term "confessional," if it has meaning at all, must "derive from literary confessions of the past," Pearson outlines its history and tests its applicability to the poems of Lowell and Plath.

397 Perloff, Marjorie. "'Transparent Selves': The Poetry of John Ashbery and Frank O'Hara." YEARBOOK OF ENGLISH STUDIES, 8 (1978), 171-96.

Parallels the careers of Ashbery and O'Hara: "To compare and contrast the achievement of these two poets is to get some sense of the excitement and diversity characteristic of 'New York Poetry' in the fifties and sixties." Perloff comments on specific poems as well as on general characteristics.

398 Phillips, Robert S. THE CONFESSIONAL POETS. Crosscurrents/Modern Critiques. Carbondale: Southern Illinois University Press, 1973. 173 p.

Treats Snodgrass, Sexton, Berryman, Plath, Lowell, and Roethke in separate chapters. Mostly these are previously published essays and have been annotated in bibliographies listed under these individual poets. Only two chapters appear to be new: that on Roethke and the introductory chapter on the nature of confessional poetry, which is viewed as any poetry wherein the poet does not disguise himself and speaks openly, honestly, and directly to the reader.

399 Quinn, Sister Bernetta. "Warren and Jarrell: The Remembered Child." SOUTHERN LITERARY JOURNAL, 8 (Spring 1976), 24-40.

Warren's and Jarrell's uses of childhood amount to "a celebration of childhood" and a search for "heroism."

400 Rao, Vimala C. "Oriental Influence on the Writings of Jack Kerouac, Allen Ginsberg, and Gary Snyder." Dissertation, University of Wisconsin, Milwaukee, 1974 (DAI, 35: 6677).

Rao establishes a link to earlier transcendentalists, studies each writer separately, and then describes problems arising out of "the East-West synthesis."

401 Ries, Lawrence. WOLF MASKS: VIOLENCE IN CONTEMPORARY POETRY. Port Washington, N.Y.: Kennikat Press, 1977. 162 p. Notes, bibliog.

Studies the reactions to violence by Plath, Gunn, Hughes, and Wain.

402 Rodman, Selden. TONGUES OF FALLEN ANGELS. New York: New Directions, 1974. 271 p.

Conversations with twelve men of letters, including Ginsberg and Kunitz. Ginsberg's contribution covers a period of about eight years, parts of which are descriptions of beat performances (pages 183-99). Kunitz' has biographical and autobiographical talk and some talk about poetry (pages 93-111).

403 Rollins, J. Barton. "Robert Lowell and Richard Eberhart: The Birth of a Poet." AMERICAN NOTES AND QUERIES, 17 (October 1978), 24-26.

On the acquaintance of Eberhart and Lowell at St. Mark's school in Boston and afterward and what it meant to Lowell's verse.

404 Romano, John. "The New Laureates." COMMENTARY, 60, No. 4 (1975), 54-58.

Questions why laurels have been heaped on Ammons and Ashbery. Romano sees them as a product of a "Williams-Stevens controversy" with, at present, Stevens in the ascendancy. Ammons and Ashbery, according to Romano, share "a profound indifference toward the lived human life."

405 Rosenblatt, Jon. "The Limits of the 'Confessional Mode' in Recent American Poetry." GENRE, 9 (Summer 1976), 153-60.

Definitions of "confessional poetry" are inadequate for distinguishing such lyrics from other contemporary lyrics, and poets like Lowell, Berryman, and Plath are better read "in the larger context of Romantic and modern concerns with self in relation to the modern world and nature."

406 Saltman, Benjamin. "The Descent to God: Religious Language in Several Contemporary Poets." Dissertation, Claremont Graduate School, 1967 (DAI, 29: 272).

Everson, Roethke, Ginsberg, and Lowell "see religious progress as the result of an effort to unify the values of the spirit and the flesh."

407 Schulman, Grace. "To Create the Self." TWENTIETH CENTURY LITERATURE, 23 (October 1977), 299-313.

John Ashbery, along with Arthur Gregor and Jean Garrigue, "has developed a method of meditation through which the soul may strive toward unity of being." Schulman describes the style and method for presenting "visionary experience."

408 Schwartz, Marilyn Meritt. "From Beat to Beatific: Religious Ideas in the Writings of Kerouac, Ginsberg, and Corso." Dissertation, University of California, Davis, 1976 (DAI, 37: 5833).

On the religous view of art imparted by these writers; the subject is treated historically in the early chapters followed by separate chapters for each poet.

409 Spiegelman, Willard. "Alphabeting the Void: Poetic Diction and Poetic Classicism." SALMAGUNDI, No. 42 (Spring 1978), pp. 132-45.

Review of Ammons' SELECTED POEMS: 1951-1977 and Nemerov's COLLECTED POEMS (also Allen Tate's COLLECTED POEMS 1919-1976). Spiegelman enumerates how much is "shared" by these disparate works; he is especially interested in their styles.

410 Swinden, Patrick. "Old Lines, New Lines: The Movement Ten Years After." CRITICAL QUARTERLY, 9 (1968), 347-59.

Compares and contrasts the work of Larkin and Gunn in respect to technique and meanings; then compares and contrasts Davie to both of them. Swinden believes that Gunn and Davie have "outgrown or transformed whatever was provincial and limiting" in the aims of The Movement.

411 Tanenhaus, Beverly. "Politics of Suicide and Survival: The Poetry of Anne Sexton and Adrienne Rich." BUCKNELL REVIEW, 24, No. 1 (1978), 106-18.

Compares and contrasts Sexton and Rich in respect to their attitudes toward being women.

412 Thompson, Susan. "Boundaries of the Self: Poetry by Frost, Roethke, and Berryman, Considered in the Light of the Language of Schizophrenia." Dissertation, University of Texas, Austin, 1974 (DAI, 35: 5430).

The language of the schizophrenic, which contains many elements commonly construed to be poetic, can help us understand the language of the poet.

413 Tomlinson, Charles. "The Middlebrow Muse." ESSAYS IN CRITICISM, 7 (April 1957), 208-17.

Review of NEW LINES, an anthology edited by Robert Conquest. Tomlinson's title expresses his opinion of this anthology of "The Movement" verse. He comments briefly on each poet represented: Amis, Larkin, Wain, Enright, Davie, Gunn, Conquest, Jennings, and others. But he thinks it all lacks "genuineness."

414 Uroff, Margaret Dickie. SYLVIA PLATH AND TED HUGHES. Urbana: University of Illinois Press, 1979. 235 p.

Studies the influence of each of these two poets on the other's poetic development and tries to correct some of the extravagances of critics who have studied the two separately. There are separate chapters on the poets (where "the muse visited each in turn"), an introductory essay on the kind of critical treatment each has received, and a chapter on their essays about themselves.

415 Wagner, Linda W. "Levertov and Rich: The Later Poems." SOUTH CAROLINA REVIEW, 11, No. 2 (1978), 18-27.

The later poems of these two poets show them "exploring full ranges of consciousness and psyche [resulting in] a poetry of engagement." Reprinted in no. 296.

416 Walker, Cheryl Lawson. "The Women's Tradition in American Poetry." Dissertation, Brandeis University, 1973 (DAI, 34: 4295).

Louise Bogan ("the classic women's tradition poet") and Sylvia Plath ("a modern instance") exemplify the tradition. Other poets, "who no longer seem to be drawn to renunciation" and whose "commitment to life reflects . . . the breaking down of the women's tradition," are Elizabeth Bishop, Gwendolyn Brooks, Denise Levertov, Adrienne Rich, Anne Sexton, and Maxine Kumin.

417 Wilkinson, Robert Taylor. "The Way into the Self: Contemporary American Poets and the Re-Discovery of a Tradition." Dissertation, Washington State University, 1978 (DAI, 39: 2946).

Examines the main elements of the "alternative Tradition" as represented in the poetry of Bly, Snyder, and Ignatow.

418 Williams, Jay Robert. "Three Postwar American Poets: W.D. Snodgrass, Sylvia Plath, and Robert Lowell." Dissertation, University of Oregon, 1976 (DAI, 37: 5835).

Williams believes "confessional" is now a useless critical term and studies the imagery, form, and themes of these three poets "without necessarily referring to the poet's biography."

419 Wilson, Matthew Thomas. "A.R. Ammons, Theodore Roethke, and American Nature Poetry." Dissertation, Rutgers University, 1978 (DAI, 39: 889).

In early poems Ammons desires to transcend nature but in later poems "moves toward shared experience." Roethke throughout maintains his desire for transcendence but adapts it to his changing perceptions. Wendell Berry (included though unnamed in the title) exploits the "metaphor of penetration" pervasive in male nature poets including, presumably, Roethke as well as Ammons.

420 Wosk, Julie Helen. "Prophecies for America: Social Criticism in the Recent Poetry of Bly, Levertov, Corso, and Ginsberg." Dissertation, University of Wisconsin, Madison, 1974 (DAI, 35: 6169).

Treats poetry for social comment as a genre, describes and interprets works of these poets as part of that genre, and assesses their attempts "to transcend the genre's tensions and limitations."

421 Zollman, Sol. "Criticism, Self-Criticism, No Transformation: The Poetry of Robert Lowell and Anne Sexton." LITERATURE AND IDEOLOGY, 9 (1971), 29-36.

"If poets trusted their experience and related their own conflicts to the antagonistic contradictions of imperialist society, they would see the connection between their problems and the struggle against imperialism." Lowell and Sexton are examples of the plight of poets "in a decadent and parasitic society."

422 Zweig, Paul. "Making and Unmaking." PARTISAN REVIEW, 40, No. 2 (1973), 269-79.

James Wright, George Oppen, and Anne Sexton are reviewed separately with Wright receiving most of the comment. The careers of both Wright and Oppen (along with their reputations) are summarized and evaluated. Sexton's attempt at putting Grimm's tales into verse (TRANSFORMATIONS) has "impoverished" the tales.

Chapter 8

INDIVIDUAL POETS

Primary bibliographies for the individual poets are meant to suggest the extent and availability of their work. In the following, only monographs of poetry are listed, even though many authors have also written fiction and criticism. The listings are meant to be comprehensive and representative but not exhaustive. Fuller primary bibliographies can be found in CONTEMPORARY POETS (no. 62), in DICTIONARY OF LITERARY BIOGRAPHY (no.32), and in bibliographies and reference guides cited for individual poets.

The list of secondary materials is as complete as I could make it up to 1978, although I have included some titles that came to my attention as late as 1981. I have tried not to duplicate work already done in individual guides and bibliographies and instead have tried to extend and supplement them. To find everything included by and about a specific poet, readers should use the author index, since I have placed all cross-references there. I have included no cross-references to standard reference works noted previously in this guide because serious students will check such resources as a routine research procedure.

After the checklist of primary works, my listings are as follows: bibliographies published as books or articles; biographical and autobiographical books (letters but not interviews); critical books or individually published pamphlets; and, finally, chapters in books, dissertations, and articles in journals.

DANNIE ABSE

(Welsh; September 22, 1923--)

POEMS

AFTER EVERY GREEN THING. London: Hutchinson, 1949.
WALKING UNDER WATER. London: Hutchinson, 1952.
TENANTS OF THE HOUSE. London: Hutchinson, 1957; New York: Criterion, 1958.
POEMS, GOLDERS GREEN. London: Hutchinson, 1962.
D. ABSE: A SELECTION. London: Studio Vista, 1963.
A SMALL DESPERATION. London: Hutchinson, 1968.
SELECTED POEMS. London: Hutchinson; New York: Oxford University Press, 1970.
FUNLAND, AND OTHER POEMS. London: Hutchinson; New York: Oxford University Press, 1973.
COLLECTED POEMS, 1948-1976. London: Hutchinson; Pittsburgh: University of Pittsburgh Press, 1977.

BIOGRAPHY

423 Abse, Dannie. A POET IN THE FAMILY. London: Hutchinson, 1974. 198 p.

Abse's life as a boy in Cardiff, as a medical student in London, and as a doctor in South Wales and the RAF. He tells of his struggles to become a poet, but less than might perhaps be expected.

CRITICAL ARTICLES

424 Boada, Mark. "An Interview with Dannie Abse at Princeton University." ANGLO-WELSH REVIEW, 25, No. 54 (1975), 128-46.

Abse talks about his life as poet and medical doctor, about his Jewishness, and about modern British and American poetry (from 1975 MLA ABSTRACTS, page 141).

425 Mathias, Roland. "The Poetry of Dannie Abse." ANGLO-WELSH REVIEW, 16, No. 38 (1967), 84-98.

Commentary on and evaluation of poems from TENANTS OF THE HOUSE and POEMS, GOLDERS GREEN. The first Mathias thinks "the high plateau of Abse's achievement" and the second less high; for in this latter book he lacked "the energy and the discernment to cut the secondary material and carry through the intended theme unobscured to its conclusion." Mathias outlines Abse's strengths and weaknesses.

See also excerpts of articles on Dannie Abse in no. 72.

A.R. AMMONS

(American; February 18, 1926--)

POEMS

OMMATEUM. Philadelphia: Dorrance, 1955.
EXPRESSIONS OF SEA LEVEL. Columbus: Ohio State University Press, 1964.
CORSONS INLET. Ithaca, N.Y.: Cornell University Press, 1965.
TAPE FOR THE TURN OF THE YEAR. Ithaca, N.Y.: Cornell University Press; London: Oxford University Press, 1965.
NORTHFIELD POEMS. Ithaca, N.Y.: Cornell University Press, 1966; London: Oxford University Press, 1967.
SELECTED POEMS. Ithaca, N.Y.: Cornell University Press, 1968.
UPLANDS. New York: Norton, 1970.
BRIEFINGS. New York: Norton, 1971.
COLLECTED POEMS, 1951-1971. New York: Norton, 1972.
SPHERE: THE FORM OF A MOTION. New York: Norton, 1974.
DIVERSIFICATIONS: POEMS. New York: Norton, 1975.
THE SNOW POEMS. New York: Norton, 1977.
THE SELECTED POEMS, 1951-1977. New York: Norton; London: Oxford University Press, 1977.
HIGHGATE ROAD. Ithaca, N.Y.: Inkling Press, 1978.
SIX-PIECE SUITE. Ithaca, N.Y.: Palaemon Press, 1979.

BIBLIOGRAPHY

See Jerry T. Williams (no. 78).

CRITICAL BOOK

426 Holder, Alan. A.R. AMMONS. Boston: Twayne, 1978. 179 p. Bibliog., notes, index.

Treats poems, up to but not including THE SNOW POEMS (1977), thematically rather than strictly chronologically.

A biographical introductory chapter and a concluding summarizing chapter frame six chapters of analysis.

CRITICAL ARTICLES

427 Buell, Frederick. "'To Be Quiet in the Hands of the Marvelous': The Poetry of A.R. Ammons." IOWA REVIEW, 8, No. 1 (1977), 67-85.

In Ammons' early work speaks the voice of a seer who is "a presence of more than ordinary awareness and longing." The later poems from about 1956 have "a great variety of voices and lyric selves." By this change he joins "the mainstream of American visionary poetry." The poem for Ammons is a computer into which he feeds information and waits for, or "produces," the unified data.

428 DeRosa, Janet. "Occurrences of Promise and Terror: The Poetry of A.R. Ammons." Dissertation, Brown University, 1978.

Not seen; cited in GYPSY SCHOLAR, 5, No. 3 (1978), 153.

429 Flint, R.W. "The Natural Man." PARNASSUS, 4, No. 2 (1976), 49-56.

Review of DIVERSIFICATIONS. Fitting this collection into the corpus of Ammons' work, Flint says that with it Ammons has returned "to the Frost or Hardy model" of nature poetry. Flint also compares Ammons to Dickey and comments on some individual poems.

430 Fogel, Daniel. "Toward an Ideal Raggedness: The Design of A.R. Ammons' HIBERNACULUM." CONTEMPORARY POETRY, 3, No. 1 (1978), 25-37.

Fogel sees this poem as "a symbol for the poet's inner being" and describes the form and content. He compares the poem with Ammons' other long poems and traces influences from Coleridge and Wordsworth in addition to the usually acknowledged ones of Emerson and Whitman.

431 Lynen, John F. "A Contemporary Transcendentalist: The Poetry of A.R. Ammons." QUEEN'S QUARTERLY, 81 (Spring 1974), 111-16.

Review of COLLECTED POEMS. "Ammons is most at home in the long, rambling discursive poems." Lynen finds him too "bossy" on occasion and too constricting. Ammons often talks <u>at</u> the reader rather than <u>to</u> him.

432 Rotella, Guy. "'Ghostlier Demarcations, Keener Sounds': A.R. Ammons' 'Corsons Inlet.'" CONCERNING POETRY, 10, No. 2 (1977), 25-33.

"Corsons Inlet" narrates a meditative walk and reveals in this meditation Ammons' major themes: "man's search for and discovery of order and disorder and of the possibilities and limits of his perceptions and conceptions."

433 Sitter, John E. "About Ammons' SPHERE." MASSACHUSETTS REVIEW, 19 (Summer 1978), 201-12.

SPHERE illustrates a "fresh fluency" in poetry that contradicts the postwar truism that poetry is difficult and criticism easier. Harold Bloom is Sitter's idea of a complex critic.

434 Wolf, Thomas J. "A.R. Ammons and William Carlos Williams: A Study in Style and Meaning." CONTEMPORARY POETRY, 2, No. 3 (1977), 1-16.

A metrical analysis of Ammons' elegy "WCW" to show the influence of Williams on Ammons.

JOHN ASHBERY

(American; July 28, 1927--)

POEMS

TURANDOT AND OTHER POEMS. New York: Tibor de Nagy, 1953.
SOME TREES. New Haven, Conn.: Yale University Press, 1956.
THE POEMS. New York: Tibor de Nagy, 1960.
THE TENNIS COURT OATH. Middletown, Conn.: Wesleyan University Press, 1962.
RIVERS AND MOUNTAINS. New York: Holt, Rinehart, and Winston, 1966.
SELECTED POEMS. London: Jonathan Cape, 1967.
FRAGMENT. Los Angeles: Black Sparrow Press, 1969.
THE DOUBLE DREAM OF SPRING. New York: Dutton, 1970.
THREE POEMS. New York: Viking, 1972.
SELF-PORTRAIT IN A CONVEX MIRROR. New York: Viking, 1975.
HOUSEBOAT DAYS. New York: Viking, Penguin, 1977.
AS WE KNOW. New York: Viking, Penguin, 1979.

BIBLIOGRAPHY

435 Kermani, David K. JOHN ASHBERY: A COMPREHENSIVE BIBLIOGRAPHY (INCLUDING HIS ART CRITICISM AND WITH SELECTED NOTES FROM UNPUBLISHED MATERIALS). New York: Garland, 1976. 244 p.

Complete descriptive primary bibliography through July 1975. Kermani also lists reviews and discussions of Ashbery's work "which," he says, "are NOT included in the standard indexes under 'Ashbery, John.'"

CRITICAL BOOKS

436 Lehman, David, ed. BEYOND AMAZEMENT: NEW ESSAYS ON JOHN ASHBERY. Ithaca, N.Y.: Cornell University Press, 1980. 294 p. Index, bibliog.

Lehman says he asked for responses to questions like "Is there a method by which to extract the sense and flavor of an Ashbery poem? How 'private' a poet is he?" The essays are by Douglas Crase, Marjorie Perloff, John Koethe, Lehman, Keith Cohen, Fred Moramarco, Charles Berger, David Rigsbee, Leslie Wolf, and Lawrence Kramer.

437 Shapiro, David. JOHN ASHBERY: AN INTRODUCTION TO THE POETRY. Columbia Introductions to Twentieth-Century American Poetry. New York: Columbia University Press, 1979. 193 p. Index.

Introductory general survey of Ashbery; a chapter on "The Early Work"; and chapters on individual monographs. Shapiro says he has tried to treat the poems as poems but has included what he knows about Ashbery's temperament.

CRITICAL ARTICLES

438 Altieri, Charles. "Motives in Metaphor: John Ashbery and the Modernist Long Poem." GENRE, 11 (Winter 1978), 653-87.

Ashbery is different from other writers of long poems. Witness his "diffidence and somewhat self-indulgent self-contempt with which he poses the problems," along with his "ambitious cultural questioning of his modernist predecessors." Altieri also defines what he thinks the contemporary long poem must be and do.

439 Bedient, Calvin. "The Tactfully Folded-Over Bill." PARNASSUS, 6, No. 1 (1977), 161-69.

Review of HOUSEBOAT DAYS. "The language itself is the 'content,' the difficulty we find in getting hold of the matter is the poetry." One danger for Ashbery lies in a particular characteristic of his work: "In one form or another, his manner thus threatens to be all to him." Bedient analyzes parts of several poems.

440 Bloom, Harold. "John Ashbery: The Charity of the Hard Moments." SALMAGUNDI, 22-23 (Spring-Summer 1973), 103-31.

"Ashbery goes back through Stevens to Whitman." Bloom reviews Ashbery's work, comparing him with Stevens' Whitmanesque and Emersonian echoes. Reprinted in nos. 181, 223, and 288.

441 Boyers, Robert. "A Quest without an Object." TIMES LITERARY SUPPLEMENT, 1 September 1978, pp. 962-63.

Review of HOUSEBOAT DAYS. "Meaning . . . is often left out of an Ashbery poem not to deprive readers of what they expect but to insure the continuity of a quest for which ends are necessarily threatening." Boyers comments also on Lieberman's discussion of Ashbery in UNASSIGNED FREQUENCIES (no. 269).

442 Corn, Alfred. "A Magma of Interiors." PARNASSUS, 4, No. 1 (1975), 223-33.

Review of SELF-PORTRAIT IN A CONVEX MIRROR. "The poems seem to be imitations of consciousness, 'meditations' about the present, including the moment of writing." They want "to render as much of psychic life as will go onto the page . . .--'a magma of interiors,' one of the poems puts it."

443 Di Piero, W.S. "John Ashbery: The Romantic as Problem Solver." AMERICAN POETRY REVIEW, 2, No. 4 (1973), 39-42.

Ashbery's DOUBLE DREAM OF SPRING confronts the problems of awareness of the real and knowledge of it through art--problems raised by his earlier work.

444 Engel, Bernard F. "On John Ashbery's 'Self-Portrait in a Convex Mirror.'" NOTES ON MODERN AMERICAN LITERATURE, 2 (Winter 1977), Item 4.

Ashbery's style, his relation to other poets, and his difficulty for readers.

445 Jackson, Richard. "Writing as Transgression: Ashbery's Archeology of the Moment: A Review Essay." SOUTHERN HUMANITIES REVIEW, [12] (Summer 1978), 279-84 [Mistakenly marked XIII; it is bound with Vol. XII as the third number].

On the French influence on Ashbery, especially Derrida and Foucault; on language; and on temporal perspective. "Communication and interpretation become not attempts to recover some 'meaning' that serves as a center governing a stable structure, but rather the attempt to observe the play of possible meanings a text might allow."

446 Johnson, Rosemary. "Paper Boats: Notes on HOUSEBOAT DAYS." PARNASSUS, 6, No. 2 (1978), 118-24.

Johnson thinks Ashbery "a poet of high moral seriousness, an epistemological poet no less, whose work explores the modes, limits, and grounds of true knowledge." She concludes that he is "a Restoration man."

447 Kalstone, David. "Reading John Ashbery's Poems." DENVER QUARTERLY, 10 (Winter 1976), 6-34.

Ashbery's technique derives from his view of the present as his "point of departure." His sense of "thwarted nature" and of the "discontinuity between present and past" has made him develop a method that "would make these feelings fully and fluidly available." Reprinted in no. 369.

448 Lyons, Neva Gibson. "The Poetry of John Ashbery." Dissertation, University of Oklahoma, 1977 (DAI, 38: 2113).

Studies Ashbery's work chronologically, finding its difficulty resides "in its combination of allusive and nonreferential qualities." Lyons also discusses Ashbery's uses of surrealism, his themes, and his subjects.

449 Molesworth, Charles. "'This Leaving-Out Business': The Poetry of John Ashbery." SALMAGUNDI, Nos. 38-39 (Spring-Summer 1977), pp. 20-41.

Discusses Ashbery's poems from SOME TREES to SELF-PORTRAIT IN A CONVEX MIRROR. "The absence of sustaining warmth and integrating knowledge will always be Ashbery's true subject, his lasting concern; for him nothing is more fundamental."

450 Revell, Donald. "John Ashbery's Tangram." NOTES ON MODERN AMERICAN LITERATURE, 1 (1977), item 12.

"Applying only to itself and its verbal forebears, an Ashbery poem exemplifies the creation of art in art, of the true phrase in a world of words." Revell illustrates by examining "Farm Implements and Rutabagas in a Landscape," a sestina employing the techniques of a Chinese puzzle.

451 Shapiro, David Joel. "The Meaning of Meaninglessness: The Poetry of John Ashbery." Dissertation, Columbia University, 1973 (DAI, 35: 4557).

This is also the title of his first chapter in no. 437. The study is an account of Ashbery's work as it changes in style chronologically from book to book. Ashbery's techniques seem "a sensible exploration of a universe of moral and physical uncertainty."

GEORGE BARKER

(English; February 26, 1913--)

POEMS

THIRTY PRELIMINARY POEMS. London: David Archer, 1933.
POEMS. London: Faber and Faber, 1935.
CALAMITERROR. London: Faber and Faber, 1937.
LAMENT AND TRIUMPH. London: Faber and Faber, 1940.
EROS IN DOGMA. London: Faber and Faber, 1944.
NEWS OF THE WORLD. London: Faber and Faber, 1950.
THE TRUE CONFESSIONS OF GEORGE BARKER. London: Fore Publications, 1950; London: Parton Press, 1957; enl. ed., London: MacGibbon and Kee, 1965.
A VISION OF BEASTS AND GODS. London: Faber and Faber, 1954.
COLLECTED POEMS, 1930-1955. London: Faber and Faber, 1957.
THE VIEW FROM A BLIND I. London: Faber and Faber, 1962.
COLLECTED POEMS, 1930-1965. New York: October House, 1965.
DREAMS OF A SUMMER NIGHT. London: Faber and Faber, 1966.
THE GOLDEN CHAINS. London: Faber and Faber, 1968.
AT THURGATON CHURCH. London: Trigram Press, 1969.
TO AYLSHAM FAIR. London: Faber and Faber, 1970.
POEMS OF PLACES AND PEOPLE. London: Faber and Faber, 1971.
IN MEMORIAM DAVID ARCHER. [London: Faber and Faber], 1973.
DIALOGUES, ETC. London: [Faber and Faber], 1976.

CRITICAL BOOKS

452 Fodaski, Martha. GEORGE BARKER. New York: Twayne, 1969. 190 p. List of important dates, bibliog., list of secondary items, index of names and titles.

> Eight chapters on such subjects as Barker's "esthetic," early work, specific collections, the fifties and sixties, and a final chapter entitled "The English Bard and the Scotching Reviewers." Fodaski says all his work "manifests Romantic faith in the individual."

453 Heath-Stubbs, John, and Martin Green, eds. HOMAGE TO GEORGE BARKER ON HIS SIXTIETH BIRTHDAY. London: Martin Brian and O'Keeffe, 1973. 94 p.

Some memorial poems, essays, and reviews: Paul Potts, "Many Happy Returns," pages 11-20; David Wright, "Memories of 23A," pages 29-35; Maurice Carpenter, "Memories of George Barker," pages 41-45 (a rebel in the thirties); Karl Miller, "Rome's Rake," pages 50-54; Patrick Swift, "Prolegomenon to George Barker," pages 57-75; Anthony Thwaite, "A Few Memories: In Homage," pages 78-82; C.H. Sisson, "For the Sixtieth Birthday of George Barker," pages 83-88.

CRITICAL ARTICLES

454 Pondrom, Cyrena N. "An Interview with George Barker." CONTEMPORARY LITERATURE, 12 (Autumn 1971), 375-401.

Held September 9, 1970, in Aylsham, England. Barker answers questions on the nature of poetry, his own work, his friends, and himself.

455 Verbieren, Dianne Rochelle. "Moral Motives and Manner in the Poetry of George Barker." Dissertation, University of New Brunswick, 1972 (DAI, 33: 1746).

Examines Barker's "poetic orientation, his moral vision and world view, and his place in the literary and intellectual climate of his time." Verbieren has an entire chapter on THE TRUE CONFESSIONS OF GEORGE BARKER.

BEN BELITT

(American; May 2, 1911--)

POEMS

THE FIVE-FOLD MESH. New York: Knopf, 1938.
WILDERNESS STAIR. New York: Grove Press, 1955.
THE ENEMY JOY: NEW AND SELECTED POEMS. Chicago: University of Chicago Press, 1964.
NOWHERE BUT LIGHT: POEMS 1964-1969. Chicago: University of Chicago Press, 1970.
THE DOUBLE WITNESS: POEMS 1970-1976. Princeton: Princeton University Press, 1978.

BIBLIOGRAPHY

455A VOYAGES, 1 (Fall 1967). A Belitt special issue, not seen. Cited in no. 62.

SPECIAL ISSUE

456 MODERN POETRY STUDIES, 7, No. 1 (Spring 1976).

This special issue contains in sequence the items cited below. Jerome Mazzaro, "Some Versions of Self: The Poetry of Ben Belitt," pp. 3-25, traces through his work various stages of the struggle introduced in FIVE-FOLD MESH in the form of modern man's "second fall from innocence." Willard Spiegelman, "'In the Mash of the Upper and Nether': Ben Belitt's Places," pp. 26-41, discusses "the basic foreigness" in the places of Belitt's landscape poems because of his distancing the scenes. Robert Weisberg, "Ben Belitt: Speaking Words against the Word," pp. 43-61, considers Belitt's contribution to the notion of "meaning lost to language." And Richard Vine, "Death and the Eye," pp. 61-80, examines Belitt's ideas about death as they appear in his work.

CRITICAL ARTICLES

457 Boyers, Robert. "To Confront Nullity: The Poetry of Ben Belitt." SEWANEE REVIEW, 81 (Autumn 1973), 553-73.

Belitt's work exemplifies the pleasures of reading "difficult" language in poems, language that is necessary to his verse because it "evokes a complex state of consciousness." Boyers fears that, as Henry Rago said, Belitt's art "is rich in ways . . . lost to most of his contemporaries." Reprinted in no. 224.

458 Honig, Edwin. "'Just Bring Me Back Alive': Translation as Adam's Dream." MODERN POETRY STUDIES, 7 (Autumn 1976), 88-104.

Honig talks to Belitt about the experience of translating. This is part of an interview that appeared later in MODERN LANGUAGE NOTES (Autumn 1976).

459 Hutton [Landis], Joan. "Antipodal Man: An Interview with Ben Belitt." MIDWAY, 10, No. 3 (1970), 19-40.

Belitt answers questions about his personal life, specific images in specific poems, ways of working, and other poets.

460 Landis, Joan Hutton. "A 'Wild Severity': Toward a Reading of Ben Belitt." SALMAGUNDI, Nos. 22-23 (Spring-Summer 1973), pp. 187-205.

Examines Belitt's themes and concerns and therefore his craftsmanship. In addition to short analyses of several poems, Landis takes a close look at "Soundings: Block Island." Reprinted in no. 223.

MARVIN BELL

(American; August 3, 1937--)

POEMS

THINGS WE DREAMT WE DIED FOR. Iowa City: Stonewall Press, 1966.
POEMS FOR NATHAN AND SAUL. Mt. Vernon, Iowa: Hillside Press, 1966.
A PROBABLE VOLUME OF DREAMS. New York: Atheneum, 1969.
THE ESCAPE INTO YOU. New York: Atheneum, 1971.
WOO HAVOC. Somerville, Mass.: Barn Dream Press, 1971.
RESIDUE OF SONG. New York: Atheneum, 1974.
STARS WHICH SEE, STARS WHICH DO NOT SEE. New York: Atheneum, 1977.

CRITICAL ARTICLES

461 Dodd, Wayne, and Stanley Plumly. "A Conversation with Marvin Bell." OHIO REVIEW, 17, No. 3 (1976), 40-62.

Held November 14, 1975, in Athens, Ohio. Bell talks about influences, beliefs, hopes, techniques, writing programs for students, and his life.

462 Lewis, Peter Elfed. "The Poetry of Marvin Bell." STAND, 13, No. 4 (1972), 34-40.

What impresses Lewis is Bell's versatility in subjects and tone, though he finds him occasionally too incomprehensibly personal and his use of puns, although effective at times, frequently irritating. "But what is certain is that Bell possesses a powerful, original and mature poetic voice."

463 Oberg, Arthur. "Marvin Bell: 'Time's Determinant./Once I Knew You.'" AMERICAN POETRY REVIEW, 5, No. 3 (1976), 4.

Explores the changes in Bell's life and art, noting "lines of continuity as well as lines of departure." Oberg discusses each collection chronologically.

MICHAEL BENEDIKT

(American; May 26, 1935--)

POEMS

CHANGES. Detroit: New Fresco, 1961.
THE BODY. Middletown, Conn.: Wesleyan University Press, 1968.
SKY. Middletown, Conn.: Wesleyan University Press, 1970.
MOLE NOTES. Middletown, Conn.: Wesleyan University Press, 1971.
NIGHT CRIES. Middletown, Conn.: Wesleyan University Press, 1976.

CRITICAL ARTICLES

464 Blais, W.A. "Divagations on Contemporary Poetry: An Interview with Michael Benedikt." FALCON, No. 5 (Winter 1972), pp. 5-21.

Held at Mansfield State College, Pennsylvania. Benedikt discusses prose poems, theories of form, language, surrealism, and some specific poems of his own.

465 Gallo, Louis. "A Note on MOLE'S NOTES: Michael Benedikt and the Idea of Transformation." MODERN POETRY STUDIES, 8, No. 1 (1977), 22-29.

On the persona of MOLE NOTES, who liberates from "false consciousness," which liberation "portends an actual transformation of consciousness."

WENDELL BERRY

(American; August 5, 1934--)

POEMS

THE BROKEN GROUND. New York: Harcourt, Brace, 1964.
OPENINGS: POEMS. New York: Harcourt, Brace, 1968.
FINDINGS. Iowa City: Prairie Press, 1969.
FARMING: A HANDBOOK. New York: Harcourt, Brace, 1970.
THE COUNTRY OF MARRIAGE. New York: Harcourt, Brace, 1970.
THE EASTWARD LOOK. Berkeley, Calif.: Sand Dollar Press, 1974.
HORSES. Monterey, Ky.: Larkspur Press, 1975.
TO WHAT LISTENS. Crete, Nebr.: Best Cellar Press, 1975.
THE KENTUCKY RIVER: TWO POEMS. Monterey, Ky.: Larkspur Press, 1976.
CLEARING. New York: Harcourt, Brace, 1977.
THREE MEMORIAL POEMS. Berkeley, Calif.: Sand Dollar Press, 1977.

BIBLIOGRAPHY

See Lepper(no. 48) and Williams (no. 78).

CRITICAL ARTICLE

466 Collins, Robert Joseph. "A Secular Pilgrimage: Nature, Place and Morality in the Poetry of Wendell Berry." Dissertation, Ohio State University, 1978 (DAI, 39: 4935).

Traces the theme of art versus nature in Berry's novels, essays, and, especially, poems.

JOHN BERRYMAN

(American; October 25, 1914-January 7, 1972)

POEMS

POEMS. Norfolk, Conn.: New Directions, 1942.
THE DISPOSSESSED. New York: William Sloane, 1948.
HOMAGE TO MISTRESS BRADSTREET. New York: Farrar, Straus and Cudahy, 1956.
HIS THOUGHTS MADE POCKETS & THE PLANE BUCKT. Pawlett, Vt.: Claude Fredericks, 1958.
77 DREAM SONGS. New York: Farrar, Straus and Giroux, 1964.
BERRYMAN'S SONNETS. New York: Farrar, Straus and Giroux, 1967.
HIS TOY, HIS DREAM, HIS REST. New York: Farrar, Straus and Giroux, 1967.
HIS TOY, HIS DREAM, HIS REST. New York: Farrar, Straus and Giroux, 1968.
THE DREAM SONGS. New York: Farrar, Straus and Giroux, 1969.
LOVE & FAME. New York: Farrar, Straus and Giroux, 1970.
DELUSIONS, ETC. New York: Farrar, Straus and Giroux, 1972.
HENRY'S FATE AND OTHER POEMS. New York: Farrar, Straus and Giroux, 1972.
SELECTED POEMS 1938-1968. London: Faber and Faber, 1972.

BIBLIOGRAPHY

467 Arpin, Gary Q. JOHN BERRYMAN: A REFERENCE GUIDE. Boston: G.K. Hall, 1976. 158 p.

Annotated secondary bibliography through July 1975. The listing below in this guide supplements and continues Arpin.

See also Lepper (no. 48) and Williams (no. 78).

CRITICAL BOOKS

468 Arpin, Gary Q. MASTER OF THE BAFFLED HOUSE: "THE DREAM SONGS" OF JOHN BERRYMAN. Rook Critical Monographs 1. Derry, Pa.: Rook Society, 1976. 60 p. Notes, bibliog.

An introduction to THE DREAM SONGS. Arpin discusses origins, influences, style, technique, and specific poems. Arpin reprints this in part in no. 469.

469 ______. THE POETRY OF JOHN BERRYMAN. Port Washington, N.Y.: Kennikat Press, 1978. 111 p. Bibliog., index.

Arpin's introduction reviews the critical opinions on Berryman; the remaining chapters treat his work chronologically.

470 Berndt, Susan G. BERRYMAN'S BAEDEKER: THE EPIGRAPHS TO "THE DREAM SONGS." Rook Critical Monographs 2. Derry, Pa.: Rook Society, 1976. 46 p.

Identifies and elaborates the eight epigraphs as aids to interpret THE DREAM SONGS.

471 Conarroe, Joel. JOHN BERRYMAN: AN INTRODUCTION TO THE POETRY. Columbia Introductions to Twentieth-Century American Poetry. New York: Columbia University Press, 1977. 215 p.

Conarroe's introductory chapter is a compact biography of Berryman, because, he says, "I do not want to shy away from biographical questions." In ensuing chapters he relates the life very directly to the poems as he describes and interprets them.

472 Haffenden, John. JOHN BERRYMAN: A CRITICAL COMMENTARY. New York: New York University Press, 1980. 216 p. Notes, bibliog., index.

A study of Berryman's mature work: HOMAGE TO MISTRESS BRADSTREET, THE DREAM SONGS, and LOVE & FAME. His "poetry may be regarded as the mythopoeic recomposition of his own experience."

473 JOHN BERRYMAN STUDIES: A SCHOLARLY AND CRITICAL JOURNAL. January 1975-- . Quarterly.

Issues have a running bibliography of current criticism and articles and essays on Berryman and other American poets.

CRITICAL ARTICLES

474 Barbera, Jack Vincent. "Shape and Flow in THE DREAM SONGS."

TWENTIETH CENTURY LITERATURE, 22 (May 1976), 146-62.

DREAM SONGS receives its pattern from Berryman's life and thus is open-ended (stopped by an act of his will) and local (having no overall pattern but "structured . . . within Songs and the grouping of Songs").

475 _____. "Under the Influence." JOHN BERRYMAN STUDIES, 2, No. 2 (1976), 56-65.

Barbera discusses the influence of alcohol on Berryman's work and then goes on to consider other influences of a literary vintage.

476 Barza, Steven. "About John Berryman." COLORADO QUARTERLY, 26, No. 3 (1977), 51-72.

Reflections on Berryman's suicide take Barza to Bellow's HUMBOLDT'S GIFT, to confessional poets, to Berryman's poems.

477 Colson, William Redmond. "Berryman's Henry: The Making of a Character." Dissertation, Indiana University, 1976 (DAI, 37: 5119).

Henry is an "independent hero," although obviously related to Berryman. Colson compares and contrasts the two and relates them to the protagonist of Berryman's novel, RECOVERY.

478 Conarroe, Joel. "After Mr. Bones: John Berryman's Last Poems." HOLLINS CRITIC, 13, No. 4 (1976), 1-12.

On LOVE & FAME and DELUSIONS, ETC. Conarroe defends the first as "a work that strives for direct, unambiguous communication, and that more often than not achieves its goal." The second he thinks an "honorable failure" because it lacks the "control required if desperate emotion is to be translated into formal art." Passages have been reprinted in no. 471.

479 Finney, Kathe Davis. "Obscurity in John Berryman's DREAM SONGS." Dissertation, Brown University, 1977 (DAI, 38: 5475).

Attempts to isolate and explain the causes of the obscurity.

480 Haffenden, John. "The Beginning of the End: John Berryman, December 1970 to January 1971." CRITICAL QUARTERLY, 18, No. 3 (1976), 81-90.

This and the next few items are parts extracted from Haffenden's biography of Berryman to be published by Farrar, Straus and Giroux (and Faber and Faber). Here Haffenden reveals Berryman's state of mind in reflecting on "for him the related topics of fatherhood, suicide, death, and immortality" up to the year before his death.

481 _____. "Berryman in the Forties: A Biographical Passage, I and II." NEW REVIEW, 3 (September-October 1976), 25-34.

The first section goes to summer 1943; the second continues to spring 1947. Haffenden recounts numerous details about Berryman's teaching, writing, and relations with friends and acquaintances.

482 _____. "Drink as Disease: John Berryman." PARTISAN REVIEW, 44, No. 4 (1977), 565-83.

Explores the periods of elation and confidence followed by depression and self-doubt experienced by Berryman in 1969 and 1970, his drinking, and his experiences in Alcoholics Anonymous and in various hospitals.

483 _____. "Politics in the Later Thought of John Berryman." STAND, 18, No. 3 (1977), 10-13.

In 1971, Berryman's work showed "an expansion of sympathies," and as evidence Haffenden cites his poem on Guevara and his public notice of Vietnam.

484 _____. "A Year on the East Coast: John Berryman, 1962-63." TWENTIETH CENTURY LITERATURE, 22 (May 1976), 129-45.

An account of Berryman's year at Breadloaf and Brown University while writing DREAM SONGS.

485 Hyde, Lewis. "Alcohol and Poetry: John Berryman and the Booze Talking." AMERICAN POETRY REVIEW, 4, No. 4 (1975), 7-12.

The relationship of Berryman's alcoholism to his poetry. Hyde describes in some detail the nature of alcoholism, the AA program, and past poets who had problems. Then he diagnoses Berryman.

486 Kameen, Paul John. "John Berryman's Dream Songs: A Critical Introduction." Dissertation, SUNY, Albany, 1976 (DAI, 37: 969).

Attempts "to make the process of exegesis easier for the nonspecialist" by examining the comic elements, the protagonist, the narrative, and the language of DREAM SONGS.

487 McClatchy, J.D. "John Berryman: The Impediments to Salvation." MODERN POETRY STUDIES, 6, No. 3 (1975), 246-77.

Argues that Berryman's comments about Hart Crane apply to Berryman himself who "seems to have been exploring there his own possibilities as well as Crane's." McClatchy pursues this theme in Berryman's life and work.

488 Middleton, Elizabeth Ann. "Vision of the Whiskey Priest: Cohesive Forces in THE DREAM SONGS by John Berryman." Dissertation, University of Massachusetts, 1975 (DAI, 36: 891).

Berryman creates unity in his long poem by means of the structure of the minstrel show and the quest journey.

489 O'Grady, Tom. "Henry in the 'Naturul' World: A Study of Pastoral Imagery in John Berryman's THE DREAM SONGS." NEW LAUREL REVIEW, 7, No. 1 (1977), 5-16.

Since the imagery in THE DREAM SONGS reflects Henry's feelings and needs at the moment, O'Grady analyzes some pastoral images which "create the appearance of a man of instincts close to the soil and the animals and brimming with a natural wisdom."

490 Shaw, Robert B. "An Interview with John Berryman." ANTAEUS, No. 8 (Winter 1973), pp. 7-19.

This interview is Item 1969 .B37 in Arpin's REFERENCE GUIDE (no. 467), entered under McClelland, David, et al. Originally it was published in the HARVARD ADVOCATE along with other tributes, all annotated by Arpin under the names of the contributors. Shaw in this reprinting includes a brief framing statement about drinking and talking with Berryman. Other critics cite this interview under John Plotz et al.

491 Simons, John L. "Henry on Bogie: Reality and Romance in 'Dream Song No. 9' and HIGH SIERRA." LITERATURE/FILM QUARTERLY, 5 (1977), 269-72.

Simons elaborates the "close, nearly parallel, relationship to the Raoul Walsh-Humphrey Bogart film."

492 Stitt, Peter. "John Berryman's Literary Criticism." SOUTHERN REVIEW, 14 (Spring 1978), 368-74.

Review of Berryman's FREEDOM OF THE POET. Stitt is impressed by Berryman's seriousness, authority, wit, and enthusiasm but thinks his editors "have not been serving him well" since his death: for example he notes that this book has placed the most interesting essays at the end of the book when they should have been placed first "to put his best foot forward."

493 Thornbury, Charles W. "The Significance of Dreams in THE DREAM SONGS." LITERATURE AND PSYCHOLOGY, 25, No. 3 (1975), 93-107.

The SONGS, like dreams, have a logic of indirection. Thus they are not haphazard. Article is abstracted in 1975 MLA ABSTRACTS, vol. 1, 209.

494 Wardzinski, Paul D. "Berryman's THE DREAM SONGS." EXPLICATOR, 34, No. 9 (1976), Item 70.

A possible source for "Henry House" is in the poetry of Julia Moore.

495 Warner, Anne Bradford. "Literary Tradition and Psychoanalytic Technique in Berryman's DREAM SONGS." Dissertation, Emory University, 1977 (DAI, 38: 3505).

Applying these two "different attentions" shows that seemingly "indiscriminate and eccentric combinations" are really Berryman's "rendering of the creative mind."

496 Waterman, Andrew. "John Berryman: The Poet as Critic." PN REVIEW, 5, No. 1 (1978), 27-30.

Some of the "agitations" of Berryman's life enter the essays in THE FREEDOM OF THE POET "but not self indulgently." Waterman appreciates the kind of knowledge as poet Berryman brings to his practice as critic: "Each essay involves him in an intellectual and imaginative venture, a risk-taking with values and skills organically related to his poetic enterprise."

ELIZABETH BISHOP

(American; February 8, 1911-October 6, 1979)

POEMS

NORTH AND SOUTH. Boston: Houghton Mifflin, 1946.
POEMS: NORTH AND SOUTH--A COLD SPRING. Boston: Houghton Mifflin, 1955.
QUESTIONS OF TRAVEL. New York: Farrar, Straus and Giroux, 1965.
SELECTED POEMS. London: Chatto and Windus, 1967.
THE BALLAD OF THE BURGLAR OF BABYLON. New York: Farrar, Straus and Giroux, 1968.
THE COMPLETE POEMS. New York: Farrar, Straus and Giroux, 1969.
GEOGRAPHY III. New York: Farrar, Straus and Giroux, 1976.

BIBLIOGRAPHY

497 MacMahon, Candace W. ELIZABETH BISHOP: A BIBLIOGRAPHY 1927-1979. Charlottesville: University Press of Virginia, 1980. 246 p.

Full descriptive bibliography of primary materials including photocopies of book covers, dust jackets, title pages, and copyright pages. The secondary items are not annotated, but MacMahon lists tables of contents and notes the nature of comments in "Works Which Mention Elizabeth Bishop."

CRITICAL BOOK

498 Stevenson, Anne. ELIZABETH BISHOP. New York: Twayne, 1966. 144 p.

MacMahon (no. 497) describes the contents, p. 169.

SPECIAL ISSUE

499 "Homage to Elizabeth Bishop, Our 1976 Laureate." WORLD LITERATURE TODAY, 51 (Winter 1977), 1-52.

This special issue contains in sequence the items listed below:

Ivar Ivask, "World Literature Today, or Books Abroad II and GEOGRAPHY III," pages 5-6, explains the new format of BOOKS ABROAD and why it is honoring Elizabeth Bishop. Marie-Claire Blais, "Presentation of Elizabeth Bishop to the Jury," page 7, explains that Bishop concerns herself with the "struggle for accommodation with what is intolerable in life."

John Ashbery, "Second Presentation of Elizabeth Bishop," pages 8-11, calls Bishop a "writer's writer" and reviews her career and his responses at different times to her work. "Chronology," pages 12-14, lists various events of Bishop's life. Octabio Paz, "Elizabeth Bishop, or The Power of Reticence," pages 15-16, advises listening to Bishop's silences: "[P]oetry is not in what words say but in what is said between them." Celia Bertin, "A Novelist's Poet," pages 16-17, notes that Bishop is "endlessly interested in any story about people."

Penelope Mortimer, "Elizabeth Bishop's Prose," pages 17-18, says Bishop uses "the same eyes and ears" and the same voice as in her poetry. Frank Bidart, "On Elizabeth Bishop," page 19, likes "her sense of the cost as well as the pleasures of observing." Helen Vendler, "Domestication, Domesticity and the Otherworldly," pages 23-28, argues that Bishop's work "vibrates [between] the domestic and the strange." Howard Moss, "The Canada-Brazil Connection," pages 29-33, says Bishop is "excited by new places, or old ones that become new by the switch in viewpoint which great distances provide." Candace Slater, "Brazil in the Poetry of Elizabeth Bishop," pages 33-36, reminds us that Brazil has changed profoundly since Bishop's residence there.

Anne R. Newman, "Elizabeth Bishop's 'Songs for a Colored Singer,'" pages 37-40, discusses the musical quality of Bishop's poems, themes, and rhythms. Lloyd Schwartz, "The Mechanical Horse and the Indian Princess: Two Poems from NORTH AND SOUTH," pages 41-44, points out that "Cirque d'Hiver" and "Florida" illustrate "coming to terms with alternatives" and are Bishop's statement about what it means to live in our kind of world. Eleanor Ross Taylor, "A Note on Elizabeth Bishop," pages 44-46, believes Bishop is imbued with the spirit of the explorer.

Jerome Mazzaro, "Elizabeth Bishop's Particulars," pages 46-49, says, "More can be learned about how to write poetry from Elizabeth Bishop than from reading the writing of most other poets." And Sybil Estess, "Toward the Interior: Epiphany in 'Cape Breton' as Representative Poem," pages 49-52, applies Joyce's term to the poem to show Bishop "is not simply an objective poet."

CRITICAL ARTICLES

500 Brown, Ashley. "Elizabeth Bishop in Brazil." SOUTHERN REVIEW, 13 (Autumn 1977), 688-704.

Biographical essay with a reminiscence and a commentary on the poems relating to Brazil.

501 Bryan, Nancy L. "A Place for the Genuine: Elizabeth Bishop and the Factual Tradition in Modern American Poetry." Dissertation, Claremont Graduate School, 1973 (DAI, 34: 4245).

Fits Bishop's work into "the search for factuality" as practiced by Williams, Moore, and Stevens and sees her emigration to Brazil in 1952 as "the discovery of a New World."

502 Estess, Sybil Pittman. "Discoveries of Travel: Elizabeth Bishop and the Poetry of Process." Dissertation, Syracuse University, 1976 (DAI, 38: 2786).

"Discovery . . . is inseparable from the processes" of discovery.

503 ______. "Elizabeth Bishop: The Delicate Art of Map Making." SOUTHERN REVIEW, 13 (Autumn 1977), 705-27.

"Bishop has made extraordinary description the most salient characteristic of her poetry and prose." But this characteristic is not just enumeration or naming; rather it is "personalized perception" that combines imagination and "realistic description."

504 ______. "Shelters for 'What Is Within': Meditation and Epiphany in the Poetry of Elizabeth Bishop." MODERN POETRY STUDIES, 8 (Spring 1977), 50-59.

By "a process of meditation and epiphanic perception," Bishop's imagery, though descriptive and related objectively, allows the world to appear "radiant."

505 Gordon, Jan B. "Days and Distances: The Cartographic Imagination of Elizabeth Bishop." SALMAGUNDI, Nos. 22-23 (Spring-Summer 1973), pp. 294-305.

As "containment" seems important in the world of Bishop's fiction, so the world of the poems is "a world where the poet charts--which is to say, that scale and perspective become primary considerations." Reprinted in no. 223.

506 Hopkins, Crale D. "Inspiration as Theme: Art and Nature in the Poetry of Elizabeth Bishop." ARIZONA QUARTERLY, 32 (Autumn 1976), 197-212.

In Bishop's poetry "the relationship between art and nature is both the theme of individual poems and the framework or source of inspiration that affects nearly all her work." Hopkins incorporates biographical details to reinforce this thesis.

507 Kalstone, David. "Questions of Memory: New Poems by Elizabeth Bishop." PLOUGHSHARES, 2, No. 4 (1975), 173-81.

Later poems by Bishop "refigure" the early ones. The later ones are "less geological, less historical, less vastly natural; her poems are more openly inner landscapes than ever." Reprinted in no. 369.

508 Ludwigson, Carl Raymond. "Fire Buried in the Mirror: The Poetry of Elizabeth Bishop." Dissertation, Northern Illinois University, 1978 (DAI, 39: 4939). Bibliog.

Bishop's poetry is always searching for identity through images of "the reality of the self" and "the reality of the other." Bibliography of 138 primary items and 49 secondary items.

509 McClatchy, J.D. "The Other Bishop." CANTO, 1 (Winter 1977), 165-74.

A critical review of GEOGRAPHY III. McClatchy shows us what is distinctive about these poems and how they differ from her earlier work, for other reviewers spoke of the books as "identical" to her other verse. This book makes her previous poems seem like singing out of fear of "the burying ground."

510 Marcus, Leonard S. "Elizabeth Bishop: The Poet as Mapmaker." MICHIGAN QUARTERLY REVIEW, 17 (Winter 1978), 108-18.

Review of GEOGRAPHY III. Bishop has become calmer and "more terrible and beautiful." The strength and sympathy of her work derives from her "ability to see aesthetic and human concerns as nearly equal aspects of a whole."

511 Mazzaro, Jerome. "Elizabeth Bishop and the Poetics of Impediment." SALMAGUNDI, 27 (Summer-Fall 1974), 118-44.

Bishop is "willing to see life as a dialectical process involving man and his environment rather than a process of man's will being imposed upon his surroundings." Mazzaro uses Ransom's idea of "precious objects" for his interpretation. Reprinted with additions in no. 273.

512 Mullen, Kathleen Ruth. "Manipulation of Perspective in the Poetry of

Elizabeth Bishop." Dissertation, University of Texas, Austin, 1977 (DAI, 38: 2793).

Studies the techniques used for "manipulation of perspective on the physical world, on the perceiver, and on value."

513 Mullen, Richard Francis. "The Map-Maker's Colors: A Study of the Form and Language of Elizabeth Bishop's Poetry." Dissertation, Columbia University, 1979 (DAI, 40: 2666).

Bishop's poems "fuse contradictory dualities": "ironic self-awareness with a childlike quizzical wonder"; "literal observation [with] dreamlike incomprehensibility"; "importance of self [with] the problematical conditions of conscious knowledge"; and "the rational [with] the irrational."

514 Newman, Anne Royall. "Elizabeth Bishop: A Study of Form and Theme." Dissertation, University of South Carolina, 1974 (DAI, 36: 891).

Weaknesses that others have seen in Bishop's poetry are really her strengths. Contrary to the view "that over-control has inhibited her poetry," she reveals "her passionate response to life." Instead of an "over-concern with the ordinary," she has carefully attended "to small details of objective reality" and thereby achieved "intense moments of exaltation."

515 Perloff, Marjorie. "Elizabeth Bishop: The Course of a Particular." MODERN POETRY STUDIES, 8 (Winter 1977), 177-92.

Relates the point of view in Bishop's story "In the Village" to her perceptions in her verse. Perloff treats poems from throughout Bishop's COMPLETE POEMS.

516 Robinson, Patricia Lancaster. "The Textures of Reality: A Study of the Poetry of Elizabeth Bishop." Dissertation, Rutgers University, 1978 (DAI, 39: 4261).

Nature is her great subject and "water, which symbolizes death . . . her most important natural image."

517 Schwartz, Lloyd. "One Art: The Poetry of Elizabeth Bishop, 1971-1976." PLOUGHSHARES, 3, Nos. 3-4 (1977), 30-52.

Bishop's work is unified by showing us the need for constant readjustment of vision. Her poems dramatize how complex are even the most apparently simple things, "how isolation may be as necessary as communication, how looking back may be as comforting--or as terrible--as looking ahead or around." Moreover, her last books make us resee her first books.

518 Smith, William Jay. "Geographical Questions: The Recent Poetry of Elizabeth Bishop." HOLLINS CRITIC, 14, No. 1 (1977), 1-11.

"It is with the location, both factual and spiritual, of places that her poems often begin. It is with journeys, real and imaginary, to these places that they develop." Smith illustrates his judgments by a close look at "In the Waiting Room," "Crusoe in England," and "The Moose."

519 Spiegelman, Willard. "Elizabeth Bishop's 'Natural Heroism.'" CENTENNIAL REVIEW, 22 (Winter 1978), 28-44.

Defines the term "natural heroism" by reference to Wordsworth and by reference to three types of poems he finds in Bishop: poems tracing the "outline of heroic situations" only to "undercut them"; poems "internalizing" conflicts and making the "act of learning itself a heroic process"; and poems implying "positive values" by "the via negativa of denial."

520 _____. "Landscape and Knowledge: The Poetry of Elizabeth Bishop." MODERN POETRY STUDIES, 6 (Winter 1975), 203-24.

Spiegelman compares Bishop's techniques, subjects, and themes to those of Wordsworth and Coleridge to show how she "passes from statement or elegant description to re-enactments of the processes of discovering and learning."

521 Starbuck, George. "'The Work': A Conversation with Elizabeth Bishop." PLOUGHSHARES, 3, Nos. 3-4 (1977), 11-29.

Starbuck has reproduced the flavor of a conversation rather than an interview--not a question-and-answer session. Bishop talks about her work, some writers she has met, and people and things in Brazil.

522 Wallace-Crabbe, Chris. "Matters of Style: Judith Wright and Elizabeth Bishop." WESTERLY: A QUARTERLY REVIEW, 1 (1978), 53-57.

Not seen; cited in 1978 MLA INTERNATIONAL BIBLIOGRAPHY, Item 2483. The date and number citation may be erroneous.

523 Wood, Michael. "RSVP." NEW YORK REVIEW OF BOOKS, 24 (June 9, 1977), 29-30.

Review of GEOGRAPHY III. It is a book of "invitations," asking us to do things: look; watch; think; listen; sometimes enjoy. Wood describes the poems he enjoys most from the book and those he enjoys least.

524 Wyllie, Diana Elizabeth. "A Critical Study of Elizabeth Bishop's Poetry." Dissertation, Bowling Green State University, 1977 (DAI, 38: 6732).

Concentrates on "the speaking voice in the poems."

PAUL BLACKBURN

(American; November 24, 1926-September 13, 1971)

POEMS

THE DISSOLVING FABRIC. Palma, Mallorca: Divers Press, 1955.
BROOKLYN-MANHATTAN TRANSIT: A BANQUET FOR FLATBUSH. New York: Totem Press, 1960.
SING-SONG. Cleveland: Asphodel Bookshop, 1966.
SIXTEEN SLOPPY HAIKU AND A LYRIC FOR ROBERT REARDON. Cleveland: 400 Rabbit Press, 1966.
THE CITIES. New York: Grove Press, 1967.
THE REARDON POEMS. Madison, Wis.: Perishable Press, 1967.
IN, ON, OR ABOUT THE PREMISES: BEING A SMALL BOOK OF POEMS. New York: Grossman, 1968.
TWO NEW POEMS. Mt. Horeb, Wis.: Perishable Press, 1969.
THREE DREAMS AND AN OLD POEM. Buffalo, N.Y.: University Press of Buffalo, 1970.
THE JOURNALS: BLUE MOUNDS ENTRIES. Mt. Horeb, Wis.: Perishable Press, 1971.
EARLY SELECTED Y MAS: POEMS 1949-1966. Los Angeles: Black Sparrow Press, 1972.
THE JOURNALS. Ed. Robert Kelly. Los Angeles: Black Sparrow Press, 1975.
HALFWAY DOWN THE COAST: POEMS AND SNAPSHOTS. Northampton, Mass.: Mulch Press, 1975.

CRITICAL ARTICLE

525 Feld, Ross. "It May Even All Be Alright." PARNASSUS, 2, No. 2 (1974), 73-86.

> An assessment of Blackburn's poetry and also of the man. Feld "can personally attest" that he was "a wonderfully and beautifully generous poet." Feld points out weaknesses as well as strengths and some of the reasons why Blackburn is not better appreciated.

ROBERT BLY

(American; December 23, 1926--)

POEMS

SILENCE IN THE SNOWY FIELDS. Middletown, Conn.: Wesleyan University Press, 1962.
THE LIGHT AROUND THE BODY. New York: Harper and Row, 1967.
THE MORNING GLORY. Santa Cruz, Calif.: Kayak Press, 1969.
THE TEETH MOTHER NAKED AT LAST. Madison, Minn.: American Writers against Vietnam War; San Francisco: City Lights Press, 1970.
THE SHADOW-MOTHERS. New York: Harper and Row, 1970.
JUMPING OUT OF BED. Barre, Mass.: Barre, 1972.
SLEEPERS JOINING HANDS. New York: Harper and Row, 1973.
THE DEAD SEAL NEAR McCLURE'S BEACH. Rushden, Engl.: Sceptre Press, 1973.
POINT REYES POEMS. Half Moon Bay, Calif.: Mudra, 1974.
LEAPING POETRY. Boston: Beacon Press, 1975.
THIS BODY IS MADE OF CAMPHOR AND GOPHER WOOD. New York: Harper and Row, 1977.
THIS TREE WILL BE HERE FOR A THOUSAND YEARS. New York: Harper and Row, 1979.

CRITICAL BOOK

526 Friberg, Ingegerd. MOVING INWARD: A STUDY OF ROBERT BLY'S POETRY. Goteberg, Sweden: Acta U Gothoburgensis, 1977. 225 p.

On Bly's imagery, which includes "descriptive elements, metaphors, symbols, archetypes, and myths." His "poetry originates in his material surroundings but develops into an expression of an inner experience which he conveys in a subjective choice of imagery."

CRITICAL ARTICLES

527 Alexander, Franklyn. "Robert Bly." GREAT LAKES REVIEW, 3, No. 1 (1976), 66-69.

Checklist with biographical comments. Bly's work to 1973 and eighteen essays and reviews.

528 Atkinson, Michael. "Robert Bly's SLEEPERS JOINING HANDS: Shadow and Self." IOWA REVIEW, 7, No. 4 (1976), 135-53.

Jungian archetypes are "the key to the book's integrity."

529 Dodd, Wayne. "Robert Bly: An Interview." OHIO REVIEW, 19, No. 3 (1978), 32-48.

Discussion of current poetry and criticism.

530 Faas, Ekbert. "An Interview with Robert Bly." BOUNDARY 2, 4 (Spring 1976), 677-700.

Bly talks about influences, surrealism, other poets, and his poetic techniques.

531 ______. "Robert Bly." BOUNDARY 2, 4 (Spring 1976), 707-26.

On Bly as surrealist and as one who will be known as the "poet who helped relate American open form poetics back to some of its European origins."

532 Gitzen, Julian. "Floating on Solitude: The Poetry of Robert Bly." MODERN POETRY STUDIES, 7, No. 3 (1976), 231-41.

Bly is concerned with "not the objective portrayal of external nature but, rather, the presentation of various states of mind." He is a subjective poet and also a social critic.

533 Libby, Anthony. "Robert Bly Alive in Darkness." IOWA REVIEW, 3, No. 3 (1972), 78-79.

Bly's "associative and implicitly irrationalist poetry depends not on form but on imagery" and paradoxically, says Libby, we can best appreciate his "irrational evocations" by trying "to explain them logically." This Libby proceeds to try.

534 Lockwood, William J. "Robert Bly: The Point Reyes Poems." In WHERE THE WEST BEGINS: ESSAYS ON MIDDLE BORDER AND SIOUXLAND WRITING, IN HONOR OF HERBERT KRAUSE. Ed. Arthur R. Huseboe and William Geyer. Sioux Falls, S. Dak.: Center for Western Studies, Augustana College, 1978, pp. 128-34.

These poems, representative of Bly's recent work, derive from his "increased sense of the connectedness of things not only in nature but, to some extent, also in history" and mark a new stage in his career.

535 Molesworth, Charles. "Domesticating the Sublime: Bly's Latest Poems." OHIO REVIEW, 19, No. 3 (1978), 56-66.

Attempts to understand Bly's change to a "religious poetry," to find middle ground between "the dismissive and the obsequious" responses to this poetry. This shift in subject, while continuing his "idiom," is Bly's way of reaffirming "the value of spontaneity" and reviving the sacredness of the body. "Ecstasy now manifests what daily existence hides, the true nature of the body."

536 _____. "Thrashing in the Depths: The Poetry of Robert Bly." ROCKY MOUNTAIN REVIEW OF LANGUAGE AND LITERATURE, 29 (1975), 95-117.

Bly's polemics are essential to his poetry.

537 Nelson, Howard. "Welcoming Shadows: Robert Bly's Recent Poetry." HOLLINS CRITIC, 12 (April 1975), 1-15.

Bly's recent poems offer detailed observations of the natural world and at the same time "highly 'subjective' intuitions about the visible and invisible worlds."

538 Piccione, Anthony. "Robert Bly and the Deep Image." Dissertation, Ohio University, 1969 (DA, 31: 1286).

On the "aesthetic of 'deep image' poetry" as a way into Bly's poetry and on Bly's place "in the continuum of contemporary American poetry."

539 Power, Kevin. "Conversation with Robert Bly." TEXAS QUARTERLY, 19, No. 3 (1976), 80-94.

Bly talks about his work, his beliefs, his likes and dislikes. Power has structured a fairly tight question-and-answer session that allows Bly to do most of the talking.

540 Sage, Frances Kellogg. "Robert Bly: His Poetry and Literary Criticism." Dissertation, University of Texas, Austin, 1974 (DAI, 35: 5423).

All Bly's poetry and prose "reflect his interest in deep image and the inner life." His "solitude poetry" and his "social protest poetry" seem to Sage a contradiction not yet "integrated fully in Bly's critical theories."

541 Till, David Kelland. "The Work of Robert Bly: The Great Mother and the New Father." Dissertation, University of New Mexico, 1978.

Not seen; cited in COMPREHENSIVE DISSERTATION INDEX, 1978 SUPPLEMENT, Vol. 4, p. 411.

LOUISE BOGAN

(American; September 11, 1897-February 4, 1970)

POEMS

BODY OF THIS DEATH. New York: R.M. McBride, 1923.
DARK SUMMER. New York: Scribner's, 1929.
THE SLEEPING FURY. New York: Scribner's, 1929.
POEMS AND NEW POEMS. New York: Scribner's, 1941.
COLLECTED POEMS 1923-53. New York: Noonday, 1954.
THE BLUE ESTUARIES. New York: Farrar, Straus and Giroux, 1968.

BIBLIOGRAPHY

542 Couchman, Jane. "Louise Bogan: A Bibliography of Primary and Secondary Materials, 1915-1975: Parts I-III." BULLETIN OF BIBLIOGRAPHY, 33, No. 2 (1976), 73-77, 104; No. 3 (1976), 111-26; No. 4 (1976), 178-81.

Numbers 2 and 3 are primary bibliographies and 4 is secondary, mostly reviews. Couchman includes only material not in Smith (no. 544).

BIOGRAPHY

543 Limmer, Ruth, ed. WHAT THE WOMAN LIVED: SELECTED LETTERS OF LOUISE BOGAN, 1920-1970. New York: Harcourt, Brace and Jovanovich, 1973. 402 p.

Limmer's introduction defends publishing letters of one who "stood for public reticence." The letters are arranged chronologically and, because they are often to major figures in the literary world, give a general view of the time and an occasional close look at other writers.

544 Smith, William Jay. LOUISE BOGAN: A WOMAN'S WORDS. Washington, D.C.: Library of Congress, 1971. 82 p. Bibliog.

Literary biography of Bogan with Smith's reminiscences of acquaintance with her and his comments on her work. Primary bibliography includes a list of records and tapes. Smith's comments are a transcript of his lecture at the Library of Congress, May 4, 1970.

CRITICAL ARTICLES

545 Bowles, Gloria. "Louise Bogan: To Be (or Not to Be?) Woman Poet." WOMEN'S STUDIES, 5 (1977), 131-35.

Women poets in Bogan's time were in competition and jealous of one another.

546 Perlmutter, Elizabeth F. "A Doll's Heart: The Girl in the Poetry of Edna St. Vincent Millay and Louise Bogan." TWENTIETH CENTURY LITERATURE, 23, No. 2 (1977), 157-79.

Millay looks back to make sure her lyrics "measure up" to tradition, and Bogan looks forward to the modernist mode of "reducing the lyric to its essentials, and to redefining its sources in emotion." All the same, both are "adepts in the craft of lyric versification."

547 Ridgeway, Jaqueline. "The Necessity of Form to the Poetry of Louise Bogan." WOMEN'S STUDIES, 5 (1977), 137-49.

Bogan's poetry requires conventional form, although poets all around her were abandoning it, because "her poetry deals with a struggle for meaning in a life bound by form." Ridgeway points out biographical details that relate to Bogan's work.

548 _____. "The Poetry of Louise Bogan." Dissertation, University of California, Riverside, 1977 (DAI, 38: 3503).

Ridgeway discerns "the concept of a universal pattern that dwarfs human aspiration and understanding."

549 Roethke, Theodore. "The Poetry of Louise Bogan." CRITICAL QUARTERLY, 3, No. 2 (1961), 142-50.

Roethke praises Bogan's poems for their "range, both emotional and geographical"; "brilliant (and exact) imagery"; "great economy, with the exact sense of diction"; and "music rich and subtle." Rpt. in TO THE YOUNG WRITER. Ed. A.L. Bader. Ann Arbor: University of Michigan Press, 1965, pp. 122-35.

RICHARD EMIL BRAUN

(American; November 22, 1934--)

POEMS

COMPANIONS TO YOUR DOOM. Detroit: New Fresco, 1961.
CHILDREN PASSING. Austin: University of Texas, 1962.
BAD LAND. Penland, N.C.: Jargon Society, 1971.
THE FORECLOSURE. Urbana: University of Illinois Press, 1972.

CRITICAL ARTICLES

550 Mazzaro, Jerome. "Putting It Together: The Poetry of Richard Emil Braun." MODERN POETRY STUDIES, 5, No. 3 (1974), 251-69.

Braun's poetry has been neglected because it is not moralistic even in the best sense. Braun insists "that the American dream cannot be separated from an American nightmare." He describes the whole experience of America.

551 _____. "'We're All Doctors Here': An Interview with Richard Emil Braun." MODERN POETRY STUDIES, 7, No. 3 (1976), 178-95.

Held at Braun's cabin in British Columbia, August 17, 1976. Braun talks about how he began to write poetry, influences on him, his interest in the classics, his verse techniques, and the benefits derived from translating.

552 Swanson, Roy Arthur. "Deceptive Symmetry: Classical Echoes in the Poetry of Richard Emil Braun." MODERN POETRY STUDIES, 7, No. 3 (1976), 195-218.

The echoes "range from the immediate reverberations of reference and allusion to the greater and increasingly indefinite resonances of structure and themes."

553 Turco, Lewis. "Richard Emil Braun: A Narrator of Enigma." MODERN POETRY STUDIES, 7, No. 3 (1976), 170-78.

The major elements of Braun's poetry are two: "a narrative of ordinary events that coagulate to terror, and thematic discussion that refuses to settle into blunt statement."

BASIL BUNTING

(English; March 1, 1900--)

POEMS

REDMICULUM MATELLARUM. Milan: Matellarum, 1930.
POEMS: 1950. Galveston, Tex.: Cleaner's Press, 1950.
THE FIRST BOOK OF ODES. London: Fulcrum Press, 1965.
LOQUITUR. London: Fulcrum Press, 1965.
THE SPOILS. Newcastle-upon-Tyne, Engl.: Migrant Press, 1965.
BRIGGFLATTS. London: Fulcrum Press, 1966.
TWO POEMS. Santa Barbara, Calif.: Unicorn Press, 1967.
WHAT THE CHAIRMAN TOLD TOM. Cambridge, Mass.: Pym-Randall Press, 1967.
COLLECTED POEMS. London: Fulcrum Press, 1968; rpt. 1970; rev. ed., London: Oxford University Press, 1978.
VERSION OF HORACE. London: Holborn, 1972.

BIBLIOGRAPHY

554 Guedalla, Roger. BASIL BUNTING: A BIBLIOGRAPHY OF WORKS AND CRITICISM. Norwood, Pa.: Norwood Editions, 1973. 183 p. Index.

Descriptive primary bibliography including books and periodicals with contributions by Bunting. Secondary bibliography of reviews and articles, unannotated, includes one section of readings and recordings with notes on some of the occasions and contents and another section that lists critical and biographical studies by anyone who mentions Bunting.

SPECIAL ISSUE

555 AGENDA, 16, No. 1 (1978).

This special issue contains in sequence the items listed below:

"Basil Bunting Talks about BRIGGFLATTS," pages 8-19 (reprinted from WRITING, No. 6 [1970]; Kenneth Cox, "A Commentary on Bunting's 'VILLON,'" pages 20-36; Jeffrey Wainwright, "William Wordsworth at BRIGGFLATTS," pages 37-45; Anthony Suter, "Musical Structure in the Poetry of Basil Bunting," pages 46-54; Peter Dale, "Basil Bunting and the Quonk and Groggle School of Poetry," pages 55-65; Peter Makin, "Bunting and Sound," pages 66-81; Anthony Suter, "Imagery and Symbolism in Basil Bunting's Poetry," pages 82-98; Michael Hamburger, "Gratulatory Variation for Basil Bunting with an Inaudible Ground-Bass, Growled," pages 99-100; Roland John, "Basil Bunting: A Note," pages 101-05.

CRITICAL ARTICLES

556 Cole Thomas. "Bunting: Formal Aspects." POETRY, 78, No. 4 (1951), 366-69.

Review of POEMS: 1950. "Bunting is more concerned with overall structure (i.e., as we use the word in music) than with stanzaic forms." He has achieved a "bare" kind of beauty, the result of "his concern with the concrete image, his clarity of thought, and his simplicity of language."

557 Dodsworth, Martin. "Sea-Town Records." LISTENER, 81 (27 March 1969), 432-33.

A paragraph of four or five luke-warm sentences about COLLECTED POEMS: "The diction . . . commands respect, but rhythmically he is very monotonous."

558 Forde, Sister Victoria Marie. "Music and Meaning in the Poetry of Basil Bunting." Dissertation, University of Notre Dame, 1973 (DAI, 34: 1905).

On various influences of composers and poets in Bunting's work and on themes and technical aspects relating to music in the poems.

559 Fraser, G.S. "A Craftsman." NINE, 3, No. 8 (1952), 273-77.

Review of POEMS: 1950. After debunking the Preface to this collection, Fraser tests Bunting's technique as to "tone-leading of vowels, duration of syllables, and melodic coherence" and judges Bunting a minor poet but "a major craftsman in verse."

560 Johnson, Carol. "Poetics of Disregard: Homage to Basil Bunting." ART INTERNATIONAL, 14, No. 8 (20 October 1970), 21-22.

Laments Bunting's lack of recognition and praises COLLECTED POEMS AND BRIGGFLATTS. Johnson advises buying the record of Bunting reading from BRIGGFLATTS (Stream Records, 10 Bramley Road, London W 10). "Indeed, form and content have perhaps never been more consubstantial."

561 Kenner, Hugh. "The Chisel: A Resurrected Poet." POETRY, 78, No. 6 (1951), 361-65.

Review of POEMS: 1950. Kenner praises Bunting's sonority, realistic detail, concentration of thought and words; but sometimes finds him too ironically pat. "Bunting's subjects and treatment have an interest outlasting the area in which they were conceived."

562 Kramer, Jane. [On Bunting]. In her ALLEN GINSBERG IN AMERICA. New York: Random House, 1969, pp. 141-45.

Ginsberg and Bunting converse in a taxi in 1967, returning from a poetry reading by Bunting. Bunting thinks himself personally not interesting, and Ginsberg is distressed to learn he has destroyed manuscript pages of lines left out of BRIGGFLATTS and also numerous letters to him from Ezra Pound.

563 Lesch, Barbara E. "Basil Bunting: A Major British Modernist." Dissertation, University of Wisconsin, Madison, 1979 (DAI, 40: 2663).

A detailed analysis of Bunting's work to assess his participation in the modernist tradition and his rank among modern poets.

564 Porter, Peter. [Review of COLLECTED POEMS]. LONDON MAGAZINE, NS 9, No. 3 (1969), 76-80.

On Pound's influence on Bunting, citing specific poems and lines.

565 Read, Herbert. "Basil Bunting: Music or Meaning?" AGENDA, 4, Nos. 5-6 (1966), 4-10.

Read accepts Bunting's assertion that poems must be read aloud and must not be read silently for meaning. He then discusses the sounds of BRIGGFLATTS.

566 Suter, Anthony. "Basil Bunting, Poet of Modern Times." ARIEL, 3, No. 4 (1972), 25-32.

Considers Bunting's social concerns. Despite his emphasis of aesthetic over social matters, Bunting has ideas about "a perfect life" but no "political programme for the achievement of this form of society."

567 _____. "Time and the Literary Past in the Poetry of Basil Bunting." CONTEMPORARY LITERATURE, 12, No. 4 (1971), 510-26.

Bunting's awareness of literature and its past developed from his home life, education, travel, and Ezra Pound. Suter points out how Bunting uses these and other influences in his work and transcends them as Eliot had. By means of its musical structure BRIGGFLATTS "succeeds with the form" Bunting had all along been seeking, the form in which he "states his theme of time directly."

568 Tomlinson, Charles. "Experience into Music: The Poetry of Basil Bunting." AGENDA, 4, Nos. 4-5 (1966), 11-17.

From LOQUITUR through THE SPOILS, Bunting has arrived at "a music that combines strength and delicacy." This "music" in his later poems, specifically BRIGGFLATTS, is not just a matter of tone, rhyme, and syntax "but in the use throughout of current motifs."

569 Woof, R.S. "Basil Bunting's Poetry." STAND, 8, No. 2 (1966), 28-34.

Woof looks briefly at LOQUITUR to prepare us for his comments on BRIGGFLATTS, which take up the remainder of the essay. He explicates the narrative and some of the important images in the poem and interprets Bunting's attitudes toward people and the world.

570 Zukofsky, Louis. "'London or Troy?' 'Adest.'" POETRY, 38, No. 3 (June 1931), 160-62.

Review of REDMICULUM MATELLARUM. "Mr. Bunting would not be among the isolate instances of Englishmen concerned with poetry in this time, were his content only the product of a classical ear directing a polished manner. All his poems . . . are grounded in an experience, though the accompanying tones of the words are their own experience."

CHARLES CAUSLEY

(English; August 24, 1917--)

POEMS

FAREWELL, AGGIE WESTON. Aldington, Engl.: Hand and Flower Press, 1951.
SURV.IVOR'S LEAVE. Aldington, Engl.: Hand and Flower Press, 1953.
UNION STREET. London: Hart-Davis, 1957; Boston: Houghton Mifflin, 1958.
JOHNNY ALLELUIA. London: Hart-Davis, 1961.
UNDERNEATH THE WATER. London: Macmillan, 1968.
FIGURE OF EIGHT. London: Macmillan, 1969.
COLLECTED POEMS 1951-1975. London: Macmillan; Boston: Godine, 1975.
THE ANIMALS' CAROL. London: Macmillan, 1978.
ST. MARTHA AND THE DRAGON. London: Oxford University Press, 1978.

CRITICAL ARTICLE

571 Levy, Edward. "The Poetry of Charles Causley." PN REVIEW, 5, No. 2 (1978), 46-48.

Causley is concerned with "lovelessness, violence, indifference, and disappointments" as real forces in the world; and Levy says Causley makes poetry "a weapon against these forces." "A Ballad for Katherine of Aragon" and "A Wedding Portrait" represent the kind of "truth" Causley knows.

JOHN CIARDI

(American; June 24, 1916--)

POEMS

HOMEWARD TO AMERICA. New York: Henry Holt, 1940.
OTHER SKIES. Boston: Little, Brown, 1947.
LIVE ANOTHER DAY. New York: Twayne, 1950.
FROM TIME TO TIME. New York: Twayne, 1951.
AS IF: POEMS NEW AND SELECTED. New Brunswick, N.J.: Rutgers University Press, 1955.
I MARRY YOU. New Brunswick, N.J.: Rutgers University Press, 1958.
39 POEMS. New Brunswick, N.J.: Rutgers University Press, 1959.
IN THE STONEWORKS. New Brunswick, N.J.: Rutgers University Press, 1961.
IN FACT. New Brunswick, N.J.: Rutgers University Press, 1962.
PERSON TO PERSON. New Brunswick, N.J.: Rutgers University Press, 1964.
THIS STRANGEST EVERYTHING. New Brunswick, N.J.: Rutgers University Press, 1966.

BIBLIOGRAPHY

572 White, William, comp. JOHN CIARDI: A BIBLIOGRAPHY. Detroit: Wayne State University Press, 1959. 65 p.

Descriptive primary bibliography. The secondary materials included are brief reviews and commentary.

CRITICAL BOOKS

573 Krickel, Edward. JOHN CIARDI. Boston: Twayne, 1980. 189 p. Annotated bibliog., index.

Biographical chapter, several chapters on Ciardi's verse, a chapter on his translations, and a chapter on his place among poets.

574 Williams, Miller. THE ACHIEVEMENT OF JOHN CIARDI: A COMPREHENSIVE SELECTION OF HIS POEMS WITH A CRITICAL INTRODUCTION. Glenview, Ill.: Scott, Foresman, 1969. 86 p.

The man who is Ciardi is also the poet and the subject of his poems. "The self-conscious presence of the poet in John Ciardi's poems is the condition from which all their qualities arise." The poems selected are from OTHER SKIES through THIS STRANGEST EVERYTHING.

GREGORY CORSO

(American; March 26, 1930--)

POEMS

THE VESTAL LADY ON BRATTLE. Cambridge, Mass.: Richard Brukenfeld, 1955; rpt., San Francisco: City Lights, 1969.
GASOLINE. San Francisco: City Lights, 1958.
BOMB. San Francisco: City Lights, 1958.
THE HAPPY BIRTHDAY OF DEATH. New York: New Directions, 1960.
SELECTED POEMS. London: Eyre and Spottiswoode, 1962.
THE MUTATION OF THE SPIRIT. New York: Death Press, 1964.
THERE IS YET TIME TO RUN BACK THROUGH LIFE AND EXPIATE ALL THAT'S BEEN SADLY DONE. New York: New Directions, 1965.
ELEGIAC FEELINGS AMERICAN. New York: New Directions, 1970.
EGYPTIAN CROSS. New York: Phoenix Book Shop, 1971.
THE NIGHT LAST NIGHT WAS AT ITS NIGHTEST. New York: Phoenix Book Shop, 1972.
EARTH EGG. New York: Unmuzzled Ox, 1974.

BIBLIOGRAPHY

575 Wilson, Robert A., comp. A BIBLIOGRAPHY OF WORKS BY GREGORY CORSO. New York: Phoenix Book Shop, 1966.

Not seen; cited in 1968 MLA INTERNATIONAL BIBLIOGRAPHY, Item 9870.

CRITICAL ARTICLES

575A Gaiser, Carolyn. "Gregory Corso: A Poet, The Beat Way." In no. 280, pp. 266-75.

On Corso's life and way of life, his relationship with beat writers, and his poem "In the Fleeting Hand of Time."

576 Grunes, Dennis. "The Mythifying Memory: Corso's 'Elegiac Feelings American.'" CONTEMPORARY POETRY, 2, No. 3 (1977), 51-61.

A close reading of Corso's elegy on the death of Jack Kerouac, particularly of tree and ground images. Kerouac's death brought "to subdued fruition the Beat cycle which first came of age in the mid-fifties."

ROBERT CREELEY

(American; May 21, 1916--)

POEMS

LE FOU. Columbus, Ohio: Golden Goose Press, 1952.
THE KIND OF ACT OF. Palma, Mallorca: Divers Press, 1953.
FOR LOVE: POEMS 1950-1960. New York: Scribner's, 1962.
POEMS 1950-1965. London: J. Calder, 1966.
THE CHARM: EARLY AND UNCOLLECTED POEMS. Mt. Horeb, Wis.: Perishable Press, 1968.
PIECES. Los Angeles: Black Sparrow Press, 1968; New York: Scribner's 1969.
DIVISIONS AND OTHER EARLY POEMS. Mt. Horeb, Wis.: Perishable Press, 1969.
A DAY BOOK. New York: Scribner's 1972.
SELECTED POEMS. New York: Scribner's, 1972.
LATER: NEW POEMS. New York: New Directions, 1979.

See nos. 62 and 580 for fuller primary bibliographies.

BIBLIOGRAPHY

577 Calhoun, Douglas. [Robert Creeley: Checklist of Criticism.] WEST COAST REVIEW, 6, No. 3 (January 1972), 64-71.

Cited in Novik (no. 580), page 169. Novik says she used this checklist in compiling her bibliography.

578 Johnson, Lee Ann. "Robert Creeley. A Checklist 1946-1970." TWENTIETH CENTURY LITERATURE, 17, No. 3 (1971), 181-98.

Primary descriptive bibliography of 325 items and an unannotated list of 132 secondary items. Novik (no. 580) says she borrowed from this.

579 Locke, Jo Ellen. "Robert Creeley: An Annotated Bibliography." M.A. Thesis, Kent State University, 1970.

Not seen. Cited in Novik (no. 580).

580 Novik, Mary. ROBERT CREELEY: AN INVENTORY, 1945-1970. Kent, Ohio: Kent State University Press, 1973. 210 p.

Novik divides the secondary materials of her list into Books, Periodicals, Dissertations, Audio-Visual materials, and Dedications. These are further subdivided into such sections as essays, or notes and comments. Novik also includes a list of manuscripts and their locations. The listing of primary materials is extensive.

BIOGRAPHY

581 Butterick, George F., ed. CHARLES OLSON AND ROBERT CREELEY: THE COMPLETE CORRESPONDENCE. 2 vols. Santa Barbara, Calif.: Black Sparrow Press, 1980. 360 p.

Letters reveal the personalities and thought of both writers. Butterick says the letters continue to 1970 just before Olson died. Volume 2 ends September 1950.

CRITICAL BOOKS

582 Allen, Donald, ed. CONTEXTS OF POETRY: INTERVIEWS 1961-1971. Bolinas, Calif.: Four Seasons, 1973. 214 p.

Transcriptions of interviews with Creeley by David Ossman, Charles Tomlinson, John Sinclair and Robin Eichele, Linda Wagner, Brendan O' Regan and Tony Allan, Lewis MacAdams, Douglas Flaherty and James Bradford, and Michael André. Two others are talks or symposia by Creeley and other writers. Creeley describes the occasions for all these in his introduction or in headnotes. He talks about himself and other poets and writers.

583 Edelberg, Cynthia Dubin. ROBERT CREELEY'S POETRY: A CRITICAL INTRODUCTION. Albuquerque: University of New Mexico Press, 1978. 186 p.

After an introductory biographical chapter in which problems of studying Creeley are explained, Edelberg treats each of his major collections of verse in separate chapters. She includes transcripts of two tapes, pages 158-72: one, Edelberg's conversation with Creeley in May 1975; the other, answers to questions she "meant to ask him."

584 Ford, Arthur L. ROBERT CREELEY. Boston: Twayne, 1978. 159 p. Bibliog., index.

Ford claims a highly personal view ("If you are interested in how I read Creeley, then proceed"); in treating the poetry he moves from PIECES back to FOR LOVE and then to the fiction and later poems. Primary checklist and annotated secondary bibliography.

SPECIAL ISSUE

585 BOUNDARY 2, 6, No. 3 (1978) and 7, No. 1 (1978).

Not seen; cited (and contents listed) 1979 MLA INTERNATIONAL BIBLIOGRAPHY, Item 10477 ff.

CRITICAL ARTICLES

586 André, Michael. "Robert Creeley: An Interview." UNMUZZLED OX, 1 (November 1971), 22-45.

André keeps mostly on the subject of Creeley's poems, particularly PIECES, his latest at the time; but toward the end the focus moves to other poets. Reprinted in no. 582.

587 Bacon, Terry R. "Closure in Robert Creeley's Poetry." MODERN POETRY STUDIES, 8, No. 3 (1977), 227-47.

Studying "closure" in Creeley's poems reveals not only his "development as a poet but the essence of projectivism as well." Bacon illustrates from a wide range of poems.

588 ______. "How He Knows When to Stop: Creeley on Closure: A Conversation with the Poet." AMERICAN POETRY REVIEW, 5, No. 6 (1976), 5-7.

Creeley talks about what he tries to do in poems, which does not involve having a conclusion in mind when he starts. He describes the various ways he knows when to stop.

589 Cameron, Allen Barry. "'Love Comes Quietly': The Poetry of Robert Creeley." CHICAGO REVIEW, 19, No. 2 (1967), 92-103.

Review of FOR LOVE. Cameron attempts to describe "some of the most significant aspects" of Creeley's highly subjective and personal poetry: "What really matters, Creeley seems to be saying, is people." He discusses Creeley's techniques, forms, and themes.

590 Edelberg, Cynthia Dubin. "The Poetry of Robert Creeley." Dissertation,

New York University, 1977 (DAI, 38: 6131).

This work developed into no. 583.

591 Fortunato, Mary Jane. "Craft Interview with Robert Creeley." NEW YORK QUARTERLY, No. 13 (Winter 1973), pp. 17-47.

Creeley answers direct questions about himself, his work, and his opinions about poetry and other poets.

592 Hammond, John Greer. "Robert Creeley's Art and Its Background." Dissertation, Brandeis University, 1973 (DAI, 34: 4261).

Studies the philosophical literary theory that forms the background to the poet's art and focuses on the relation of theme to style.

593 Hayes, Frederick Philip. "The Broken World of Robert Creeley." Dissertation, University of Denver, 1978 (DAI, 39: 2273).

On Creeley's background and work, but Hayes says, "The focus of the study demonstrates the poet's search for the 'place' where communication with Another is lasting."

594 Kaufman, Robert F. "The Poetry of Robert Creeley." THOTH, 9, No. 2 (1971), 28-36.

Kaufman employs a good many metaphors from the fields of science and technology ("electrons, highly charged particles, kinetic motion, capacitor, high energy construct") but also says, "No poet wrestles more with words than Creeley; he falters, struggles, falls, and begins again in each poem." He illustrates this careful use of words in poems from 1962-67.

595 Leed, Jacob. "Robert Creeley and THE LITITZ REVIEW: A Recollection with Letters." JOURNAL OF MODERN LITERATURE, 5, No. 2 (1976), 243-59.

Narrative of a struggle to publish a "little magazine" that through mischance, poverty, and various other reasons failed before the first number. Out of it, however, Leed says, came Cid Corman's ORIGIN and Creeley's BLACK MOUNTAIN REVIEW.

596 Milner, Philip. "Life at All Its Points: An Interview with Robert Creeley." ANTIGONISH REVIEW, No. 26 (Summer 1976), pp. 37-47.

Held in Halifax, 14 February 1976. Milner keeps the flavor of a conversation in his transcription of this interview. Creeley has a long response on Canada and the writing climate there. His last observation in the interview is in part: "I am fascinated by life at all its points. I am interested in the event of being a man whose next birthday will be his 50th, what the reality of that place is and how it can be used as material for poetry or prose."

597 Oberg, Arthur. "Robert Creeley: And the Power to Tell Is Glory." OHIO REVIEW, 18, No. 1 (1977), 79-97.

Responds to Berryman's dislike of Creeley's poems, which Berryman found dull. Oberg explores what is unattractive and attractive about Creeley as he is revealed in his poems. Reprinted in no. 395 as part of chapter on Creeley.

598 Potts, Charles. "PIECES: The Decline of Creeley." WEST COAST REVIEW, 5, No. 4 (1971), 3-5.

Potts does not care for PIECES but does not believe it "diminishes or enlarges Creeley's overall reputation."

599 Rosenthal, M.L. "Problems of Robert Creeley." PARNASSUS, 2, No. 1 (1973), 205-14.

Review of A DAY BOOK, LISTEN, and CONTEXTS OF POETRY. Rosenthal thinks A DAY BOOK, despite its occasionally good passages, promises more than it delivers. His discussion of it takes up most of this review.

600 Sheffler, Ronald Anthony. "The Development of Robert Creeley's Poetry." Dissertation, University of Massachusetts, 1971 (DAI, 32: 2104).

Studies Olson's influence on Creeley and what Creeley thinks poetry is for.

601 Tallman, Warren. "Robert Creeley's Tales and Poems." OPEN LETTER, 3rd Series, No. 6 (Winter 1976), pp. 93-118.

Discusses tales from THE GOLD DIGGERS (1965) and argues that Creeley's poems are similar to his stories. Tallman analyzes individual poems from FOR LOVE, noting especially Creeley's choices and arrangements of words and lines.

602 Wagner, Linda W. "Creeley's Late Poems: Contexts." BOUNDARY 2, 6, No. 3 (1978), 309-27.

Creeley's poems "speak primarily about the poet's problems of identifying and describing, [and] . . . are epistemological both in content and method." Reprinted in no. 296.

603 ____. "The Latest Creeley." AMERICAN POETRY REVIEW, 4, No. 3 (1975), 42-44.

A long review of A DAY BOOK: "it provides the resolution" to Creeley's earlier, more puzzling period. Reprinted in no. 296.

J.V. CUNNINGHAM

(American; August 23, 1911--)

POEMS

THE HELMSMAN. San Francisco: Colt Press, 1942.
THE JUDGE IS FURY. New York: Swallow Press-Morrow, 1947.
DOCTOR DRINK. Cummington, Mass.: Cummington Press, 1950.
THE EXCLUSIONS OF A RHYME: POEMS AND EPIGRAMS. Denver: Swallow Press, 1960 [contains the three earlier books].
TO WHAT STRANGERS, WHAT WELCOME. Denver: Swallow Press, 1964.
SOME SALT. Madison, Wis.: Perishable Press, 1967.
COLLECTED POEMS AND EPIGRAMS. Chicago: Swallow Press; London: Faber and Faber, 1971.
SELECTED POEMS. Mt. Horeb, Wis.: Perishable Press, 1971.

CRITICAL BOOK

604 Winters, Yvor. THE POETRY OF J. V. CUNNINGHAM. Denver: Swallow Press, 1961. 15 p.

In this pamphlet, Winters tests Cunningham's prose assertions against his poetic practice, demonstrates Cunningham's skill as an epigrammatic poet, and corrects misstatements about influences.

CRITICAL ARTICLES

605 Baxter, John. "The Province of the Plain Style." COMPASS: A PROVINCIAL REVIEW, 3 (1978), 15-37.

Baxter praises the use of the plain style in Cunningham's COLLECTED ESSAYS (1977) and sees therein an example for those Canadians who "overlook . . . the most basic issue in Canadian unity and in Canadian independence: the continuity and integrity of the majority culture, whose language is English."

606 Carruth, Hayden. "A Location of J.V. Cunningham." MICHIGAN QUARTERLY REVIEW, 11 (Spring 1972), 75-83.

On the influence (or "congruence") of Cunningham and Yvor Winters. Pointing out their differences, Carruth says Cunningham "deserves to be considered on his own terms."

607 Powell, Grosvenor E. "The Poetry of J.V. Cunningham." TRI-QUARTERLY, 3 (Winter 1961), 20-26.

Cunningham is a Renaissance man in the twentieth century, the literary tendencies of which he has "considered and rejected." On THE HELMSMAN and THE JUDGE IS FURY. Reprinted in no. 258.

608 Stall, Lindon. "The Trivial, Vulgar, and Exalted: The Poems of J.V. Cunningham." SOUTHERN REVIEW, 9 (Autumn 1973), 1044-48.

Review of COLLECTED POEMS AND EPIGRAMS. On style and subject in Cunningham's verse, particularly his epigrams.

609 Stein, Robert A. "THE COLLECTED POEMS AND EPIGRAMS of J.V. Cunningham." WESTERN HUMANITIES REVIEW, 27, No. 1 (1973), 1-12.

Surveys the kind of recognition Cunningham has received and then illustrates from his poems the marriage of "the circumstances of modernity and worn yet persistent traditions."

PETER DALE

(English; August 21, 1938--)

POEMS

WALK FROM THE HOUSE. Oxford: Fantasy Press, 1962.
THE STORMS. London: Macmillan, 1968.
MORTAL FIRE. London: Macmillan, 1970. Reissued as MORTAL FIRE: SELECTED POEMS. London: Agenda Editions; Columbus: Ohio State University Press, 1976.
ONE ANOTHER: A SONNET SEQUENCE. London: Agenda Editions, 1978.

CRITICAL ARTICLES

610 Eagleton, Terry. "The Poetry of Peter Dale." AGENDA, 13 (Autumn 1975), 85-91.

Dale's "actual diction is often enough colourless and prosaic, just and uncluttered but excessively bleak, so a poem is frequently thrown back for its impact on a terseness of movement which from time to time threatens its emotional authenticity."

611 Gowrie, Grey. "Peter Dale." AGENDA, 13 (Autumn 1975), 74-84.

A description and an assessment of MORTAL FIRE, which Dale revised and expanded from its original appearance in 1970. Gowrie outlines the "narrative" of the sequence. He admires Dale's confronting the problems caused by "the limitations of lyricism." Dale realizes that literary problems "are welded to the ordinary difficulties of living."

DONALD DAVIE

(English; July 17, 1922--)

POEMS

BRIDES OF REASON. Oxford: Fantasy Press, 1955.
A WINTER TALENT AND OTHER POEMS. London: Routledge and Kegan Paul, 1957.
THE FORESTS OF LITHUANIA. Hessle, Engl.: Marvell Press, 1959.
NEW AND SELECTED POEMS. Middletown, Conn.: Wesleyan University Press, 1961.
EVENTS AND WISDOMS: POEMS 1957-1963. London: Routledge and Kegan Paul; Middletown, Conn.: Wesleyan University Press, 1964.
ESSEX POEMS 1963-1967. London: Routledge and Kegan Paul, 1969.
COLLECTED POEMS 1950-1970. London: Routledge and Kegan Paul; New York: Oxford University Press, 1972.
THE SHIRES. London: Routledge and Kegan Paul, 1974; New York: Oxford University Press, 1975.
IN THE STOPPING TRAIN AND OTHER POEMS. Manchester: Carcanet Press, 1977.

BIBLIOGRAPHY

See no. 62 for fuller primary bibliography.

CRITICAL ARTICLES

612 Bayley, John. "A Late Augustan. . . ." AGENDA, 10-11 (Autumn 1972-Winter 1973), 148-52.

Review of COLLECTED POEMS. Bayley contrasts Davie's verse to a kind that "we know has not got where it has without the exercise of complex acts of ruthlessness"--the work of Frost, Lowell, Berryman, for example. But Davie's "harmlessness" is "the positive innocence and natural grace of some wild creature, replacing aggression with articulation, not aiming at us but playing before us."

613 Bedient, Calvin. "On Donald Davie." IOWA REVIEW, 2, No. 2 (1971), 66-90.

On the characteristics of Davie's verse that make him seem like the Augustans. Bedient points out both strengths and weaknesses resulting from Davie's style.

614 Dekker, George. "Donald Davie: New and Divergent Lines in English Poetry." AGENDA, 14 (Summer 1976), 45-57.

Dekker compares Davie's Englishness with Larkin's to make clear the special nostalgia and "yes, old-fashioned inclusiveness of design in this expatriate's attempt to gather up the whole of his well-remembered England in one sequence of short poems [THE SHIRES]." "Dorset" receives several pages of comment.

615 Dodsworth, Martin. "Donald Davie." AGENDA, 14 (Summer 1976), 15-32.

Davie's work and attitude toward life changed between publication of WINTER TALENT and FORESTS OF LITHUANIA in which he had turned from the self-conscious stance of "The Movement" poets and had written poems as if poetry were "a way of knowing the world we are in."

616 Dunn, Douglas. "Moral Dandies." ENCOUNTER, 40 (March 1973), 68-69.

Review of COLLECTED POEMS. Davie "wants to be a Late Augustan, not just write like one."

617 Greene, Donald. "A Breakthrough into Spaciousness: The COLLECTED POEMS of Donald Davie." QUEEN'S QUARTERLY, 80 (Winter 1973), 601-15.

Part 1 of this essay discusses Canada as "a kind of bridge for Davie between his old and new homes" because of the large part that country has in COLLECTED POEMS. Part 2 tries to show a development in Davie from earliest to latest poems.

618 Pinsky, Robert. "'Us Too He Harrows.'" PARNASSUS, 6, No. 2 (1978), 185-92.

Review of IN THE STOPPING TRAIN AND OTHER POEMS. On tone, language, and subject in Davie's poems. "The best poems in this volume, particularly the impressive title poem, show how much force Davie's passionate testing and questioning of his art can exert."

619 Schmidt, Michael. "The Poetry of Donald Davie." CRITICAL QUARTERLY, 15, No. 1 (1973), 81-88.

Schmidt sees in COLLECTED POEMS "a process of increasing approximation" and describes the impression "a vast and substantially complete oeuvre" by a poet like Davie leaves on the reader.

620 ______. "'Time and Again': The Recent Poetry of Donald Davie." AGENDA, 14 (Summer 1976), 33-44.

Davie's earlier poems were "symptoms of formal and ethical changes in the poet, while 'In the Stopping Train' . . . is a consolidation, a fusion of Davie's public and private voices in a puzzling but resonant parable."

621 Von Hallberg, Robert. "Two Poet Critics: Donald Davie's THE POET IN THE IMAGINARY MUSEUM and Robert Pinsky's THE SITUATION OF POETRY." CHICAGO REVIEW, 30, No. 1 (1978), 108-15.

On the nature of the poet-critics and what is required of them beyond being either poets or critics. The two books are reviewed separately.

622 Weiss, Theodore. "Between Two Worlds or On the Move." PARNASSUS, 3, No. 1 (1974), 113-40.

Review of COLLECTED POEMS. Weiss relates Davie's criticism to his work and explains and assesses Davie's point of view in that criticism. Davie is conservative, always in defense of civility, but also always "on the move."

JAMES DICKEY

(American; February 2, 1923--)

POEMS

DROWNING WITH OTHERS. Middletown, Conn.: Wesleyan University Press, 1962.
HELMETS. Middletown, Conn.: Wesleyan University Press, 1964.
BUCKDANCER'S CHOICE. Middletown, Conn.: Wesleyan University Press, 1965.
POEMS 1957-1967. Middletown, Conn.: Wesleyan University Press, 1967.
THE EYE-BEATERS, BLOOD, VICTORY, MADNESS, BUCKHEAD, AND MERCY. Garden City, N.Y.: Doubleday, 1970.
EXCHANGES. Bloomfield Hills, Mich.: Bruccoli-Clark, 1971.
THE ZODIAC. Garden City, N.Y.: Doubleday, 1976.
THE STRENGTH OF FIELDS. Garden City, N.Y.: Doubleday, 1979.

BIBLIOGRAPHY

623 Elledge, Jim. JAMES DICKEY: A BIBLIOGRAPHY, 1947-1974. Metuchen, N.J.: Scarecrow Press, 1979. 306 p. Author index.

Elledge's Preface explains the advantages of his book over earlier bibliographies. He includes works by and about Dickey in separate sections, the first fully described and the second annotated. Poems treated in each book or article, and so on, are listed at the end of the entry.

624 ______. "James Dickey: A Supplementary Bibliography, 1975-1980, Part I." BULLETIN OF BIBLIOGRAPHY, 38, No. 2 (1981), 92-100, 104. [To be continued in No. 3]

Updates no. 623.

CRITICAL BOOKS

625 De La Fuente, Patricia, Jan Searle, and Donald Fritz, eds. JAMES DICKEY: SPLINTERED SUNLIGHT. Living Authors Series, no. 2. Edinburg, Tex.: Pan American University, 1979. 80 p.

Not seen; brochure from Pan American University says it includes an updated checklist of scholarship and five essays.

626 Ashley, Franklin. "The Art of Poetry--XX: James Dickey." PARIS REVIEW, No. 65 (Spring 1976), pp. 52-88.

Held in Columbia, South Carolina, May 1972, and again in May 1974. Dickey talks very bluntly about his writing, the poets he likes or dislikes, the role of the poet in society, and the fame brought by his novel DELIVERANCE (1969).

627 Barnwell, W.C. "James Dickey on Yeats: An Interview." SOUTHERN REVIEW, 13, No. 2 (April 1977), 311-16.

Barnwell asks Dickey about the use of Yeats's system, about how he reacts to "Yeats's attitudes toward sexuality, experience, and closed forms in writing," and about Yeats's rank as a poet among the most important four or five moderns.

628 Baughman, Ronald Claude. "The Poetry of James Dickey: Variations on Estrangement." Dissertation, University of South Carolina, 1975 (DAI, 36: 7416).

"The event that most clearly marks his view of life is World War II." Dickey from that point undergoes successive kinds of estrangements, turning "at last to a reliance on the Self." His verse "removes the psychological layers of the self to discover and confront the harrowing realities of his emotional truths."

629 Bobbitt, Joan. "Unnatural Order in the Poetry of James Dickey." CONCERNING POETRY, 11, No. 1 (1978), 39-44.

"Dickey employs shockingly bizarre or ludicrous images to communicate the alien position of nature in the 'civilized' world. Indeed, the juxtaposition of the world of nature and the world of man often leads to grotesque incongruities." The poems "Kudzu," "The Sheep Child," and "The Fiend" serve as examples.

630 Brookes, Philip James. "Mythic Continuities in the Poetry of James Dickey." Dissertation, University of Kansas, 1975 (DAI, 37: 305).

Studies how Dickey discovers "the extraordinary in the midst of the ordinary" by his use of myth.

631 Calhoun, Richard J. "After a Long Silence: James Dickey as South Carolina Writer." SOUTH CAROLINA REVIEW, 9, No. 1 (1976), 12-20.

Defends Dickey's reputation as a writer of note and assesses the Southernness in his work. The silence, real or imagined, Calhoun says, is about to end with Dickey's poem THE ZODIAC.

632 Ely, Robert. "Rising and Overcoming: James Dickey's 'The Driver.'" NOTES ON MODERN AMERICAN LITERATURE, 2 (Spring 1978), Item 12.

Almost any Dickey poem can illustrate that "rising" is what Dickey thinks important and worthwhile as a subject for poetry. Ely chooses "The Driver" as an example that combines "universal symbolism with a curious but engaging narrative."

633 Hollingsworth, Mary. "Four Writers at De Kalb." DE KALB LITERARY ARTS JOURNAL, 4, No. 4 (1970), 40-49.

A brief account of Dickey's visit to De Kalb College, Atlanta, in November 1969. The other three writers, though they have written in various genres, are novelists.

634 McGinnis, Wayne D. "Mysticism in the Poetry of James Dickey." NEW LAUREL REVIEW, 5, Nos. 1-2 (1975), 5-10.

Dickey's later poems describe a mythic relation with nature which is "a transcendence of death."

635 Mesic, Michael. "A Note on James Dickey." In no. 288, pages 145-53.

Dickey seems never to have questioned "the values of the cult of masculinity: physical strength and health, unswerving determination, and above all success, be it sexual, financial, or otherwise." Mesic thinks Dickey's talent as a poet has deteriorated.

636 Mizejewski, Linda. "Shamanism toward Confessionalism: James Dickey, Poet." GEORGIA REVIEW, 32, No. 2 (1978), 409-19.

Dickey is a poet-performer who fails in his book, THE ZODIAC. Mizejewski details the nature of this failure.

637 Passey, Joel Craig. "An Interpretive Analysis of the Interaction of Illusion and Reality in Selected Verse of James Dickey from 1951 to 1971." Dissertation, University of Illinois, Urbana-Champaign, 1975 (DAI, 36: 5638).

Passey groups the poems thematically and relates style and technique to "the poet's thematic interests."

638 Pierce, Constance. "Dickey's 'Adultery': A Ritual of Renewal." CONCERNING POETRY, 9 (Fall 1976), 67-69.

The poem shows survival "in the wilderness of inescapable watch-ticking, deadened options, and futile lives." The affair of the couple described "restores them" and allows "a renewal of hope."

639 Rose, Maxine S. "On Being Born Again: James Dickey's 'May Day Sermon to the Women of Gilmer County, Georgia, by a Woman Preacher Leaving the Baptist Church.'" RESEARCH STUDIES, 46, No. 4 (1978), 254-58.

Dickey's perception in this poem "transcends gender but . . . leaves a powerful impression at once sympathetic and empathetic toward women in society and their subjugation at masculine hands, particularly those of the Church."

640 Tucker, Charles C. "Knowledge Up, Down, and Beyond: Dickey's 'The Driver' and 'Falling.'" CEA CRITIC, 38, No. 4 (1976), 4-10.

To refute the charge of an easy optimism and gullible affirmation in Dickey's poems, Tucker analyzes these two poems and shows that their personae "push their quests for mystical knowledge [under] stringent and exacting conditions."

EDWARD DORN

(American; April 2, 1929--)

POEMS

THE NEWLY FALLEN. New York: Totem Press, 1961.
FROM GLOUCESTER OUT. London: Matrix Press, 1964.
HANDS UP! New York: Totem Press, 1964.
IDAHO OUT. London: Fulcrum Press, 1965.
GEOGRAPHY. London: Fulcrum Press, 1966.
THE NORTH ATLANTIC TURBINE. London: Fulcrum Press, 1967.
GUNSLINGER, PART I. Los Angeles: Black Sparrow Press, 1968.
GUNSLINGER, PART II. Los Angeles: Black Sparrow Press, 1969.
24 LOVE SONGS. San Francisco: Frontier Press, 1969.
THE COLLECTED POEMS, 1956-1974. Bolinas, Calif.: Grey Fox Press, 1975.
SLINGER. Berkeley, Calif.: Winglow Press, 1975.
SELECTED POEMS. Bolinas, Calif.: Grey Fox Press, 1978.

BIBLIOGRAPHY

See no. 32.

CRITICAL ARTICLES

641 Lockwood, William J. "Ed Dorn's Mystique of the Real: His Poems for North America." CONTEMPORARY LITERATURE, 19, No. 1 (1978), 58-79.

> Lockwood examines prose works by Dorn to find out "what kinds of new materials constitute the 'real' for Dorn" and then applies these statements to his study of "Idaho Out." He also comments on GEOGRAPHY and SLINGER.

642 Okada, Roy K. "An Interview with Ed Dorn." CONTEMPORARY LITERATURE, 15, No. 3 (1974), 297-314.

Edward Dorn

Conducted by Okada, 2 May 1973, Madison, Wisconsin. Edited by Ed Dorn. Dorn supplies information about his life, experiences at Black Mountain College and in Idaho, and about his work, GUNSLINGER in particular.

ALAN DUGAN

(American; February 12, 1923--)

POEMS

POEMS. New Haven, Conn.: Yale University Press, 1961.
POEMS 2. New Haven, Conn.: Yale University Press, 1963.
POEMS 3. New Haven, Conn.: Yale University Press, 1967.
COLLECTED POEMS. New Haven, Conn.: Yale University Press, 1969.
POEMS 4. Boston: Atlantic-Little, Brown, 1974.
SEQUENCE. Cambridge, Mass.: Dolphin Editions, 1976.

CRITICAL ARTICLE

643 Boyers, Robert. "Alan Dugan: The Poetry of Survival." In no. 223, pages 339-47.

An evaluation of Dugan's work to date. Boyers does not find his verse exciting but "returns to it with increasing regularity." Despite his "narrow range" and "confining style" Dugan manages to communicate "what most of us perennially feel--that even genuine commitment to a life of inconsequence fails to silence the persistent anxiety that we might be somehow less human than even we agreed to be."

ROBERT DUNCAN

(American; January 7, 1919--)

POEMS

HEAVENLY CITY, EARTHLY CITY. Berkeley, Calif.: Bern Porter, 1947.
POEMS 1948-1949. Berkeley, Calif.: Berkeley Miscellany, 1949.
MEDIEVAL SCENES. San Francisco: Centaur Press, 1950.
SONG OF THE BORDERGUARD. Black Mountain, N.C.: Black Mountain College, 1952.
CAESAR'S GATE. Palma, Mallorca: Divers Press, 1955.
LETTERS: POEMS 1953-1956. Highlands, N.C.: Jargon Press, 1958.
SELECTED POEMS 1942-1950. San Francisco: City Lights Press, 1959.
THE OPENING OF THE FIELD. New York: Grove Press, 1960.
ROOTS AND BRANCHES. New York: Scribner's, 1964; New Directions, 1969.
THE YEARS AS CATCHES: FIRST POEMS 1939-46. Berkeley, Calif.: Oyez, 1966.
BENDING THE BOW. New York: New Directions, 1968; London: Jonathan Cape, 1971.
THE FIRST DECADE: SELECTED POEMS 1940-1950. New York: Horizon Press; London: Fulcrum Press, 1968.
DERIVATIONS: SELECTED POEMS 1950-1956. New York: Horizon Press; London: Fulcrum Press, 1968.
TRIBUNALS: PASSAGES 31-35. Los Angeles: Black Sparrow Press, 1970.
THE TRUTH AND LIFE OF MYRTLE. Fremont, Mich.: Sumac Press, 1972.

CRITICAL BOOKS

644 Bertholf, Robert J., and Ian W. Reid, eds. ROBERT DUNCAN: SCALES OF THE MARVELLOUS. New York: New Directions, 1979. 245 p.

Not seen; cited in CONTEMPORARY AMERICAN POETRY (3rd ed. A. Poulin, Jr., Boston: Houghton Mifflin, 1980), page 532.

645 Bowering, George, and Robert Hogg. ROBERT DUNCAN: AN INTERVIEW. Beaver Cosmos Folio. Toronto: Coach House Press, 1971. 32 p.

Duncan talks about his technique and craft, influences on him and his work, and his beliefs. This interview also furnishes information about Olson, Creeley, and a number of other poets in their circle.

CRITICAL ARTICLES

646 Altieri, Charles. "The Book of the World: Robert Duncan's Poetics of Presence." SUN & MOON, 1 (1976), 66-94.

Duncan's view of the world is an elaboration of the myth that the world is the book of God. Altieri describes Duncan's various departures from the traditional myth and the ways in which a poet is involved in the world. "The particular myths are less statements of truth than themselves expressions of a numinous awareness for which they are only one expression."

647 Bowering, George. "Robert Duncan in Canada." ESSAYS ON CANADIAN WRITING, 4 (1976), 16-18.

On the ecstatic enthusiasm with which Robert Duncan was greeted in Vancouver in the early sixties and the influence he exerted on young poets of Canada.

648 Brien, Dolores Elise. "Robert Duncan: A Poet in the Emerson-Whitman Tradition." CENTENNIAL REVIEW, 19 (Fall 1975), 308-16.

Like Emerson and Whitman, Duncan studies the relationship of the self to the cosmos.

649 Cooley, Dennis Orin. "Keeping the Green: The Vegetative Myth of Renewal in Robert Duncan's Poetry." Dissertation, University of Rochester, 1971 (DAI, 33: 302).

Combining archetypal and formalistic approaches, Cooley explores the myth of seasonal renewal in individual poems, with special attention to "A Poem Beginning with a Line by Pindar" and "The Fire."

650 Davidson, Robert Michael. "Disorders of the Net: The Poetry of Robert Duncan." Dissertation, SUNY, Buffalo, 1973 (DAI, 34: 765).

Intended as an introduction to Duncan's verse, the study covers biography, meaning of poems, poetics, language, and form. It has a poem-by-poem commentary on THE OPENING OF THE FIELD.

651 Huybensz, Joanne. "The Mind Dance (Wherein Thot Shows Its Pattern): An Approach to the Poetry of Robert Duncan." Dissertation, SUNY, Stonybrook, 1977 (DAI, 38: 1380).

To be understood, Duncan's poetry must be seen whole because the multiplicity of themes and images are "filtered through the mythopoeic imagination." Studies biographical and literary influences on Duncan.

652 Mesch, Howard. "Robert Duncan's Interview." UNMUZZLED OX, 4, No. 1 (1976), 78-96.

Duncan, in a 1974 interview, talks about his work--style, theory, and the nature of poems. He stresses the "making" of poems.

653 Tallman, Warren. "The Eternal Mood: Robert Duncan's Devotion to Language." OPEN LETTER, 3rd Series, No. 6 (Winter 1976), pp. 70-74.

On Duncan's growth as a poet and praise for the virtues of his early poems as represented by THE FIRST DECADE, DERIVATIONS, and LETTERS.

654 Weatherhead, A.K. "Robert Duncan and the Lyric." CONTEMPORARY LITERATURE, 16 (Spring 1975), 163-74.

Duncan's poems are like collages in detail and in intent.

655 Weber, Robert C. "Robert Duncan and the Poem of Resonance." CONCERNING POETRY, 11, No. 1 (1978), 67-73.

In a poem of resonance, "each element is charged with meaning reinforcing and extending each other in an ever-widening gestalt." Thus Duncan's "collage" poems must be comprehended in totality rather than in parts. Weber examines "The Fire" from this vantage point, relating the parts to the whole pattern.

656 _____. "Roots of Language: The Major Poetry of Robert Duncan." Dissertation, University of Wisconsin, 1972 (DAI, 33: 4437).

Weber analyzes poems from THE OPENING OF THE FIELD, ROOTS AND BRANCHES, and THE BENDING OF THE BOW, applying Duncan's poetic theories to his poetic practice.

RICHARD EBERHART

(American; April 5, 1904--)

POEMS

A BRAVERY OF EARTH. New York: Jonathan Cape and Harrison Smith, 1930.
READING THE SPIRIT. London: Chatto and Windus, 1936; New York: Oxford University Press, 1937.
SONG AND IDEA. London: Chatto and Windus, 1940; New York: Oxford University Press, 1942.
POEMS: NEW AND SELECTED. Norfolk, Conn.: New Directions, 1945.
BURR OAKS. London: Chatto and Windus; New York: Oxford University Press, 1947.
BROTHERHOOD OF MEN. Pawlet, Vt.: Banyan Press, 1949.
AN HERB BASKET. Cummington, Mass.: Cummington Press, 1950.
SELECTED POEMS. New York: Oxford University Press, 1951.
UNDERCLIFF: POEMS 1946-1953. New York: Oxford University Press, 1953.
GREAT PRAISES. New York: Oxford University Press, 1957.
COLLECTED POEMS 1930-1960. New York: Oxford University Press, 1960.
THE QUARRY. New York: Oxford University Press, 1964.
SELECTED POEMS. New York: New Directions, 1965.
THIRTY-ONE SONNETS. New York: Eakins Press, 1967.
SHIFTS OF BEING. New York: Oxford University Press, 1968.
FIELDS OF GRACE. New York: Oxford University Press, 1972.

CRITICAL BOOKS

657 Engel, Bernard F. RICHARD EBERHART. New York: Twayne, 1971. 184 p. Bibliog., index.

Describes Eberhart's views on the function of poetry, his career in three stages (to 1942, to 1953, and from 1957), and his place among poets.

658 Roache, Joel H. RICHARD EBERHART: THE PROGRESS OF AN AMERICAN POET. New York: Oxford University Press, 1971. 299 p. Illus., primary bibliog., secondary checklist, index.

A chronological account of Eberhart's career, which, says Roache, "reflects the history of poetry, perhaps of serious literature in general, in America in the twentieth century."

CRITICAL ARTICLES

659 Bauerle, Richard F. "Eberhart's 'Throwing the Apple.'" EXPLICATOR, 27 (1968), Item 21.

On the rebelliousness of Adam in the Garden of Eden as it appears in the poem.

660 Bradham, Jo Allen. "Eberhart's 'The Fury of Aerial Bombardment.'" EXPLICATOR, 22 (1964), Item 71.

Explains "belt feed lever" and "belt holding pawl" and their contribution to the poem.

661 Broughton, Irving. "An Interview." AMERICAN POETRY REVIEW, 6, No. 3 (1977), 30-36. Rpt. in Richard Eberhart, OF POETRY AND POETS (Urbana: University of Illinois Press, 1979), pp. 264-301.

Eberhart talks about values in and of poems, about evaluating poets, and about some of his own poems. Questions and comments are varied and include autobiographical information and personal what-I-believe kinds of answers.

662 Cargas, Henry James. "At the Central Core of Life: An Interview with Richard Eberhart." WEBSTER REVIEW, 2, No. 1 (1975), 67-68.

Eberhart's comments seem somewhat humorous in their brevity: "Q. Is your work being understood? A. It is being understood by those who understand it." Eberhart defines poetry in mostly metaphorical assertions.

663 Clark, William Bedford. "The Walls of Wisdom: The Rational Faculty as Fortress and Prison in Eberhart's 'The Groundhog.'" CONTEMPORARY POETRY, 2, No. 2 (1977), 34-37.

More than "a meditation on mortality," Eberhart's "Groundhog" is "a troubled critique of the role intellectual objectivity plays in the contemporary sensibility."

664 Eberhart, Richard. "Eberhart's GRAVE PIECE." EXPLICATOR, 6 (1948), Item 23.

Eberhart explains the origin, the word choice, and his intentions in the poem.

665 _____. "Eberhart's THE YOUNG HUNTER." EXPLICATOR, 6 (1948), Item 24.

Eberhart rewrites this poem in prose.

666 Gerstenberger, Donna. "Three Verse Playwrights and the American Fifties." In MODERN AMERICAN DRAMA: ESSAYS IN CRITICISM. Ed. William E. Taylor. Deland, Fla.: Everett Edwards, 1968, pp. 117-28.

Eberhart's VISIONARY FARMS (1952) is seen in context with Djuna Barnes's ANTIPHON (1958) and MacLeish's J.B. (1958), but is distinctive because "its subject is typically American." Gerstenberger describes subjects and themes and laments the occasional "failure of language."

667 Mills, Ralph J., Jr. "Reflections on Richard Eberhart." CHICAGO REVIEW, 15, No. 4 (1962), 81-99.

Eberhart's intention is to present the immediacy of an action and the directness of a statement. Mills explores the ramifications of this manner in Eberhart's poems and literary career.

668 Packard, William. "Craft Interview with Richard Eberhart." NEW YORK QUARTERLY, No. 20 (1978), pp. 16-27. Rpt. in Richard Eberhart, OF POETRY AND POETS (Urbana: University of Illinois Press, 1979), pp. 302-08.

Eberhart tells us his manner of writing from physical conditions to ideas about form and content and also explains his beliefs about the writer in his time.

669 Perkins, David. "Auden and Eberhart: COLLECTED POEMS." SOUTHERN REVIEW, 13 (Autumn 1977), 728-38.

Mostly a review of Auden, but Perkins compares and contrasts the two poets.

published manuscripts. Appendix 2 lists criticism, unannotated and arranged chronologically.

BIOGRAPHY

673 Everson, William. "The Regional Incentive: Reflections on the Power of Place in Contemporary Literature." SAN JOSE STUDIES, 2, No. 3 (1976), 51-59.

Everson speaks of his own "discovery of . . . poetic vocation" as related to his identification with region but treats the attitude as a romantic one struggling against modernism. It is a general essay as well on the importance of place or region to human beings, but I list it here because of its autobiographical-biographical elements.

CRITICAL BOOK

674 Bartlett, Lee, ed. BENCHMARK & BLAZE: THE EMERGENCE OF WILLIAM EVERSON. Metuchen, N.J.: Scarecrow Press, 1979. 274 p.

Bartlett includes most of the important articles from about 1958 on as well as some reviews; a headnote for each selection serves as a guide to contents. Readers should check this collection of essays for anything published in or before 1978. Bartlett's Foreword to Everson's BIRTH OF A POET is also included.

LAWRENCE FERLINGHETTI

(American; March 24, 1919--)

POEMS

PICTURES OF THE GONE WORLD. San Francisco: City Lights Press, 1955.
A CONEY ISLAND OF THE MIND. New York: New Directions, 1958.
STARTING FROM SAN FRANCISCO. New York: New Directions, 1961.
WHERE IS VIETNAM? San Francisco: City Lights Press, 1965.
AN EYE ON THE WORLD: SELECTED POEMS. London: MacGibbon and Kee, 1967.
THE SECRET MEANING OF THINGS. New York: New Directions, 1968.
BACK ROADS TO FAR TOWNS. San Francisco: City Lights Press, 1970.
BACK ROADS TO FAR PLACES. New York: New Directions, 1971.
OPEN EYE, OPEN HEART. New York: New Directions, 1973.
DIRECTOR OF ALIENATION. Clinton, N.J.: Main Street Press, 1976.
NORTHWEST ECOLOG. San Francisco: City Lights Press, 1978.
LANDSCAPE OF LIVING AND DYING. New York: New Directions, 1979.

BIOGRAPHY

675 Cherkovski, Neeli. FERLINGHETTI: A BIOGRAPHY. Garden City, N.Y.: Doubleday, 1979. 245 p. Index.

Cherkovski bases this biography on interviews with Ferlinghetti. He supplies notes on his other sources of information and lists books containing chapters or comments on Ferlinghetti. Numerous writers of "the beat generation" receive considerable attention.

CRITICAL ARTICLES

675a Ianni, L.A. "Lawrence Ferlinghetti Fourth Person Singular and the Theory of Relativity." WISCONSIN STUDIES IN CONTEMPORARY LITERATURE, 8, No. 3 (1967), 392-406.

Ferlinghetti's work is "in general a view of life based on the philosophical implications of the theory of relativity."

676 Novak, Robert. "Ferlinghetti's Dog or Contemporary Poetry has Gone to the Dogs." WINDLESS ORCHARD, 23 (1976), 7-9, 20-22.

More on why dogs have become important images in contemporary poetry than on Ferlinghetti.

676a Skau, Michael. "Toward Underivative Creation: Lawrence Ferlinghetti's HER." CRITIQUE: STUDIES IN MODERN FICTION, 19, No. 3 (1978), 40-46.

Ferlinghetti's novel (1960) is a study of a person's relation to his creator. "The relationship between the author, frustrated in his attempt at autobiography, and his created character, prevented from asserting a measure of autonomous independence, symbolizes Ferlinghetti's view of the human predicament."

ROY FISHER

(English; June 11, 1930--)

POEMS

CITY. Worcester, Engl.: Migrant Press, 1961.
TEN INTERIORS WITH VARIOUS FIGURES. Nottingham, Engl.: Tarasque Press, 1967.
THE MEMORIAL FOUNTAIN. Newcastle-upon-Tyne, Engl.: Northern House, 1967.
COLLECTED POEMS 1969: THE GHOST OF A PAPER BAG. London: Fulcrum Press, 1969.
CORRESPONDENCE. London: Tetrad Press, 1970.
THE CUT PAGES. London: Fulcrum Press, 1971.
MATRIX. London: Fulcrum Press, 1971.
ALSO THERE. London: Tetrad Press, 1972.
BLUEBEARD'S CASTLE. Guildford, Engl.: Circle Press, 1972.
CULTURES. London: Tetrad Press, 1975.
NEIGHBOURS: Guildford, Engl.: Circle Press, 1976.
NINETEEN POEMS AND AN INTERVIEW. Pensnette, Engl.: Grosseteste, 1975.
BARNARDINE'S REPLY. Knotting, Engl.: Sceptre Press, 1977.
SCENES FROM THE ALPHABET. Guildford, Engl.: Circle Press, 1978.
THE THING ABOUT JOE SULLIVAN: POEMS 1971-1977. Manchester: Carcanet Press, 1978.

CRITICAL ARTICLES

677 Davie, Donald. "Roy Fisher: An Appreciation." In no. 308, pages 152-72.

Though not apparently directly influenced by Hardy, Fisher has a similar "sensibility." He takes "pathos and compassion as his objectives."

678 Mottram, Eric. "Roy Fisher's Work." STAND (Newcastle-upon-Tyne), 11, No. 1 (1969), 9-19.

Mottram concentrates first on "City," which he calls "the first major work Fisher composed," and describes the imagery ("continuous in Fisher's work"); he then uses SHIP'S ORCHESTRA to illustrate his musical prose: "Like listening to jazz change, reading SHIP'S ORCHESTRA you have to be alert to variants."

679 Rasula, Jed, and Mike Erwin. "An Interview with Roy Fisher." In NINETEEN POEMS AND AN INTERVIEW by Roy Fisher. Pensnette, Engl.: Grosseteste, 1975, pp. 12-38.

Fisher replies to questions about his work in general and about specific poems: how he works, what he feels in relation to his audience, the relation of poetry to the other arts, and the uses of poetry. [A note in this book says this interview also appeared in GROSSETESTE REVIEW, 8 (1973), but I could not find it.]

ROBERT FRANCIS

(American; August 12, 1901--)

POEMS

STAND WITH ME HERE. New York: Macmillan, 1936.
VALHALLA AND OTHER POEMS. New York: Macmillan, 1938.
THE SOUND I LISTENED FOR. New York: Macmillan, 1944.
THE FACE AGAINST THE GLASS. Amherst, Mass.: Privately printed, 1950.
COME OUT INTO THE SUN: POEMS NEW AND SELECTED. Amherst: University of Massachusetts Press, 1965.
LIKE GHOSTS OF EAGLES. Amherst: University of Massachusetts Press, 1974.
COLLECTED POEMS 1936-1976. Amherst: University of Massachusetts Press, 1976.

BIOGRAPHY

680 Francis, Robert. ROBERT FROST: A TIME TO TALK: CONVERSATIONS AND INDISCRETIONS RECORDED BY ROBERT FRANCIS. Amherst: University of Massachusetts Press, 1972. 100 p.

> What Francis remembers about Frost and what Frost said reveal the personalities of both men. First appear the conversations held at Fort Juniper, Francis' house outside Amherst, during the fifties; and then follow those from about twenty years earlier at Frost's house in Amherst during the thirties.

681 _____. THE TROUBLE WITH FRANCIS: AN AUTOBIOGRAPHY. Amherst: University of Massachusetts Press, 1971. 246 p.

> Francis characterizes his life as one of happy pessimism. That is, he has been growing happier and healthier; yet when he looks around him he is "more impressed with the ills of life, the injustices, frustrations, and agonies, than with anything else."

CRITICAL ARTICLES

682 Abbe, George. "Glimpses of Robert Francis." In THE OLD CENTURY AND THE NEW: ESSAYS IN HONOR OF CHARLES ANGOFF. Ed. Alfred Rosa. Rutherford, N.J.: Fairleigh Dickinson University Press, 1978, pp. 152-85.

Chatty, anecdotal picture of Robert Francis at home and away along with a glimpse of Archibald MacLeish and one or two of Abbe himself.

683 Beaulieu, Linda H. "Robert Francis on Henry Thoreau." THOREAU SOCIETY BULLETIN, No. 139 (1977), pp. 3-4.

Draws parallels between Francis and Thoreau and includes a checklist of Francis' writings on Thoreau.

684 Nelson, Howard. "Moving Unnoticed: Notes on Robert Francis's Poetry." HOLLINS CRITIC, 14, No. 4 (1977), 1-12.

Francis' style of poetry like his style of living is "governed by a spirit of independence and radical common sense." Nelson finds his best qualities are clarity, "crispness," wit, and "wholeness."

685 Sherman, Carl E. "'Man Working': Profile of Robert Francis." BOOK FORUM, 3, No. 3 (1977), 436-41. Bibliog.

Sherman describes a visit to Francis and conversation with him, from which he learns about the poet's way of life and writing. Bibliography of Francis' works.

ROY FULLER

(English; February 11, 1912--)

POEMS

POEMS. London: Fortune Press, 1940.
THE MIDDLE OF A WAR. London: Hogarth Press, 1942.
A LOST SEASON. London: Hogarth Press, 1944.
EPITAPHS AND OCCASIONS. London: John Lehmann, 1949.
COUNTERPARTS. London: Verschoyle, 1954.
BRUTUS'S ORCHARD. London: Andre Deutsch, 1957; New York: Macmillan, 1958.
COLLECTED POEMS. London: Andre Deutsch; Chester Springs, Pa.: Dufour, 1962.
BUFF. London: Andre Deutsch, 1965.
NEW POEMS. London: Andre Deutsch; Chester Springs, Pa.: Dufour, 1968.
OFF COURSE. London: Turret Books, 1969.
TINY TEARS. London: Andre Deutsch, 1973.
AN OLD WAR. Edinburgh: Tragara Press, 1974.
FROM THE JOKE SHOP. London: Andre Deutsch, 1975.
AN ILL-GOVERNED COAST: POEMS. Sunderland, Engl.: Ceolfrith Press, 1976.
RE-TREADS. Edinburgh: Tragara Press, 1979.

CRITICAL BOOK

686 Austin, Allan E. ROY FULLER. Boston: Twayne, 1979. 146 p. Bibliogs., index.

A biographical chapter, three chapters on his verse, one on his novels, one on his Oxford lectures, and an evaluative conclusion. Austin is impressed by the "homogeneity" of Fuller's work but tries to show his complexity as well.

CRITICAL ARTICLES

687 Conlon, Michael Paul. "Roy Fuller's Poetry." Dissertation, Marquette University, 1977 (DAI, 38: 7342).

A chronological consideration of Fuller's verse to show his themes, which are social, and his aesthetics, which are traditional.

688 Gitzen, Julian. "The Evolution of Roy Fuller." CONTEMPORARY POETRY, 3, No. 1 (1978), 56-69.

On the change in thematic emphasis and tone in NEW POEMS and TINY TEARS after thirty years of rather formal poems. Perhaps it is prompted by his recognition of "the oppressing prospect of his own death and the wholesale extinction of the race."

689 M[itchell], R[oger]. "Roy Fuller: An Interview." MINNESOTA REVIEW, 10 (1978), 87-94.

Fuller's answers to R.M.'s questions were received by mail on 22 April 1977. He describes his early experience with socialism and the Communist party of Great Britain, the influence or lack of it of Marxist critics, his drifting away from politics, his reaction to World War II, and his feelings now that he is "growing old and (I won't say 'respectable'--I've always been that) testy."

690 Skelton, Robin. "Five Poets and Their Stances." POETRY, 114, No. 6 (September 1969), 397-98.

Two paragraphs on the style and poetic stance of Fuller in NEW POEMS.

ISABELLA GARDNER

(American; September 7, 1915--)

POEMS

BIRTHDAYS FROM THE OCEAN. Boston: Houghton Mifflin, 1955.
THE LOOKING GLASS. Chicago: University of Chicago Press, 1961.
WEST OF CHILDHOOD. Boston: Houghton Mifflin, 1965.

CRITICAL ARTICLE

691 Logan, John. "The Celebration of Birthdays." SEWANEE REVIEW, 64 (1956), 161-63.

Review of BIRTHDAYS FROM THE OCEAN. Logan finds in Gardner's first book an "uncommon mastery of the ways of verse and which at the same time restored to verse the concern of Poetry: the inviolable beauty of truth." He singles out for special comment "When a Warlock Dies," the final poem of this collection.

JEAN GARRIGUE

(American; December 8, 1914-December 27, 1972)

POEMS

THE EGO AND THE CENTAUR. Norfolk, Conn.: New Directions, 1947; rpt., Westport, Conn.: Greenwood Press, 1972.
THE MONUMENT ROSE. New York: Noonday Press, 1953.
A WATER WALK BY VILLA D'ESTE. New York: St. Martin's Press, 1959.
COUNTRY WITHOUT MAPS. New York: Macmillan, 1964.
NEW AND SELECTED POEMS. New York: Macmillan, 1967.
STUDIES FOR AN ACTRESS AND OTHER POEMS. New York: Macmillan, 1973.

CRITICAL ARTICLE

692 Sewell, Elizabeth. "Jean Garrigue." PARNASSUS, 4, No. 1 (1975), 29-40.

Sewell recounts her difficulties with Garrigue's verse and tries to account for the feelings of claustrophobia and "the sense of loss" in it.

DAVID GASCOYNE

(English; October 10, 1916--)

POEMS

ROMAN BALCONY. London: Lincoln Williams, 1932.
MAN'S LIFE IS THIS MEAT. London: Parton Press, 1936.
HOLDERLIN'S MADNESS. London: J.M. Dent, 1938.
POEMS 1937-1942. London: Poetry London, 1943.
A VAGRANT AND OTHER POEMS. London: John Lehmann, 1951.
NIGHT THOUGHTS. London: Andre Deutsch, 1956.
COLLECTED POEMS. London: Andre Deutsch; New York: Oxford University Press, 1965.
SUN AT MIDNIGHT. London: Enitharmon Press, 1970.
COLLECTED VERSE TRANSLATIONS. London: Oxford University Press, Andre Deutsch, 1970.
THREE POEMS. London: Enitharmon Press, 1976.

BIBLIOGRAPHY

693 Atkinson, Ann. "David Gascoyne: A Check-List." TWENTIETH CENTURY LITERATURE, 6, No. 4 (1961), 180-92.

Divided into books by and books translated by, contributions to periodicals, anthologies with poems by, miscellaneous (the only item a poem, "Requiem," printed for a musical concert presented at Victoria and Albert Museum, 15 April 1956), and articles about Gascoyne. This last includes reviews and articles, some with brief descriptive notes, from 1933 to 1952.

CRITICAL ARTICLES

694 Cronin, Anthony. "Poetry & Ideas--II: David Gascoyne." LONDON MAGAZINE, 4, No. 7 (1957), 49-55.

On Gascoyne as a moral poet and the dangers and contradictions inherent in being so. Cronin believes that in his best verse as, for example, in "The Vagrant," Gascoyne makes "a perfect fusion of the impulse deriving from a superior moral vision and the impulse deriving from the poet's own circumstances, between in fact condemnation and compassion."

695 Ewart, Gavin. "A Voice from the Darkness." LONDON MAGAZINE, NS 5, No. 8 (1965), 88-94.

Review of COLLECTED POEMS. Ewart describes and evaluates the various selections representing different stages in Gascoyne's career. He reprints "An Unsagacious Animal" (not included in COLLECTED POEMS) as an example of a poem in which "Victorian phrases, used as parody, seem absolutely right."

696 Jackaman, Rob. "View from the White Cliffs: A Close Look at One Manifestation of English Surrealism." TWENTIETH CENTURY LITERATURE, 21 (1975), 72-80.

Gascoyne's poem "The Diabolical Principle" illustrates conscious artistry rather than "automatic writing."

697 Quinn, Sister Bernetta. "Symbolic Landscape in David Gascoyne." CONTEMPORARY LITERATURE, 12, No. 4 (1971), 466-94.

A close analysis and description of poems omitted from COLLECTED POEMS, mostly those from ROMAN BALCONY. Quinn stresses Gascoyne's "search for some 'landscape of delight.'"

698 Raine, Kathleen. "The Poetry of David Gascoyne: David Gascoyne and the Prophetic Role." In her DEFENDING ANCIENT SPRINGS. London: Oxford University Press, 1967, pp. 35-65.

Raine sympathetically surveys Gascoyne's entire poetic career.

699 Skelton, Robin. Introduction, COLLECTED POEMS, by David Gascoyne. London: Oxford University Press, 1965, pp. ix-xviii.

In his biobibliographical account of Gascoyne, Skelton argues that his surrealism, unlike that of other poets, grows out of moral concerns and is not merely a shock tactic and in any case points out a development towards a quieter tone and more economical yet vigorous use of language. Skelton believes that NIGHT THOUGHTS places Gascoyne in the company of "Yeats, Eliot, Auden, and MacNeice as one of the select company of British poets who have attempted, and achieved, the construction of a major new form."

700 Stanford, Derek. "David Gascoyne." In his THE FREEDOM OF POETRY: STUDIES IN CONTEMPORARY VERSE. London: Falcon Press, 1947, pp. 40-73.

Not seen; cited in no. 693, whose note reads, "a full study and commentary of the poet's work . . .; a photograph of Gascoyne is included."

ALLEN GINSBERG

(American; June 3, 1926--)

POEMS

HOWL. San Francisco: City Lights Press, 1956.
EMPTY MIRROR: EARLY POEMS. New York: Corinth Books, 1961.
KADDISH AND OTHER POEMS, 1958-1960. San Francisco: City Lights Press, 1961.
REALITY SANDWICHES. San Francisco: City Lights Press, 1963.
WICHITA VORTEX SUTRA. San Francisco: Coyote Press, 1966.
T.V. BABY POEM New York: Grossman, 1968.
ANKOR-WAT. New York: Horizon Press, 1968.
PLANET NEWS: 1961-1967. San Francisco: City Lights Press, 1968.
AIRPLANE DREAMS. Toronto: Anansi, 1968.
THE FALL OF AMERICA: POEMS OF THESE STATES. San Francisco: City Lights Press, 1972.
IRON HORSE. San Francisco: City Lights Press, 1974.
MIND BREATHS: POEMS 1972-1977. San Francisco: City Lights Press, 1977.
MOSTLY SITTING HAIKU. Patterson, N.J.: From Here Press, 1979.

BIBLIOGRAPHY

701 Kraus, Michelle P., comp. ALLEN GINSBERG: AN ANNOTATED BIBLIOGRAPHY 1969-1977. Metuchen, N.J.: Scarecrow Press, 1980. 329 p. Indexes.

> Divided into primary and secondary sections, both descriptive and evaluative, each further divided into books and the various forms of shorter pieces. The easiest way to use this work is through its appropriate indexes.

See also no. 58, pages 67-70.

CRITICAL BOOK

702 Portugés, Paul. THE VISIONARY POETICS OF ALLEN GINSBERG. Santa Barbara, Calif.: Ross-Erikson, 1978. 181 p.

Portugés explores "as factually as possible" the nature of Ginsberg's visions of William Blake, whose voice he heard speaking to him in 1948, and the effect of this visionary experience on his work. Portugés talks with Ginsberg about "other important elements of his visionary quest."

CRITICAL ARTICLES

703 Aguilar, Mary Karen. "Allen Ginsberg and the Development of Popular Poetry." Dissertation, Temple University, 1974 (DAI, 35: 4493).

Ginsberg's most effective works are those that are grounded in "social reality," dealing "concretely with the cultural and political life of his time." Aguilar treats HOWL and KADDISH and a few later poems.

704 Breslin, James. "Allen Ginsberg: The Origins of 'Howl' and 'Kaddish.'" IOWA REVIEW, 8, No. 2 (1977), 82-108.

Ginsberg's literary talents have been obscured by his public personality, but Breslin thinks that occasionally he "breaks through to new orders in the poem [one is reading] and in self-understanding." Because "Howl" and "Kaddish" seem especially apropos of such breakthrough, Breslin studies the biographical background prompting the writing of these poems.

705 Gertmenian, Donald. "Remembering and Rereading HOWL." PLOUGHSHARES, 2, No. 4 (1975), 151-63.

Gertmenian is prompted to reread HOWL by hearing Ginsberg read it at Wellesley College. He then evaluates its strengths and weaknesses and considers it "a moving and important poem."

706 Johnson, Mark Andrew. "American Visions, American Forms: A Study of Four Long Poems." Dissertation, Ohio University, 1977 (DAI, 38: 4828).

Defines the "long poem" in its forms and themes and includes Ginsberg's FALL OF AMERICA for analysis along with poems by Joel Barlow, Walt Whitman, and Hart Crane. Johnson believes from his reading of Ginsberg and Hart Crane that the "possibility of attaining the visionary experience" now generates the long poem when earlier it was the "vehicle."

707 Penglase, John Dolf. "Allen Ginsberg: The Flowering Vision of the Heart." Dissertation, University of Wisconsin, Milwaukee, 1975 (DAI, 36: 5302).

Considers Ginsberg's "growth as a visionary poet" through EMPTY MIRROR, KADDISH, PLANET NEWS, and THE FALL OF AMERICA.

708 Smits, Ronald Francis. "Self-Exploration and Ecological Consciousness in the Poetry of Allen Ginsberg." Dissertation, Ball State University, 1978 (DAI, 39: 2798).

Includes Ginsberg's essays and interviews along with poems for this study to determine the nature of an "ecological consciousness" and how Ginsberg brings it about.

709 Tallman, Warren. "Mad Song: Allen Ginsberg's San Francisco Poems." OPEN LETTER, 3rd Series, No. 6 (Winter 1976), pp. 37-47.

Sees "Howl" and other of Ginsberg's poems as incomplete "sunflowers" and as absurd (not in the existential sense) but, for all that, noble and authentic--new Declarations of Independence.

LOUISE GLÜCK

(American; April 22, 1943--)

POEMS

FIRSTBORN. New York: New American Library, 1968; London: Anvil Press, 1969.

THE HOUSE OF MARSHLAND. New York: Ecco Press, 1975; London: Anvil Press, 1976.

TEH. New York: Antaeus Editions, 1976.

CRITICAL ARTICLES

710 Bedient, Calvin. "Four American Poets." SEWANEE REVIEW, 84 (Spring 1976), 351-54.

Review of THE HOUSE OF MARSHLAND. This collection is an advance on earlier poems; it is more mature, less crowded and tense, rhythmically sure. Glück has "a romantic nostalgia for the absolute."

711 Landis, Joan Hutton. "Poems of Louise Glück." SALMAGUNDI, 36 (Winter 1977), 140-48.

Review of THE HOUSE OF MARSHLAND. In Glück's world as presented in these poems, the fall of man acts "like some perverse principle of universal harmony [;] it pervades objects, seasons, relationships, expectations; it is the paradigm most often imitated by the course of events, by human feeling." Landis also looks back at FIRSTBORN.

712 Wooten, Anna. "Louise Glück's HOUSE ON MARSHLAND." AMERICAN POETRY REVIEW, 4, No. 4 (1975), 5-6.

Glück's second book lacks some of the verve of FIRSTBORN but makes up for it in calmness and surehandedness; "she manages to be conversational and lyrical at the same time."

PATRICIA GOEDICKE

(American; June 21, 1931--)

POEMS

BETWEEN OCEANS. New York: Harcourt, Brace, 1968.
FOR THE FOUR CORNERS. Ithaca, N.Y.: Ithaca House, 1976.
THE TRAIL THAT TURNS ON ITSELF. Ithaca, N.Y.: Ithaca House, 1978.
THE DOG THAT WAS BARKING YESTERDAY. Amherst, Mass.: Lynx House Press, 1979.

CRITICAL ARTICLES

713 Gemmett, Robert J., and Philip Gerber, eds. "Myth of the Self: A Conversation with Patricia Goedicke." SOUTHERN HUMANITIES REVIEW, 5, No. 4 (1971), 319-32.

For SUNY-Brockport WRITERS FORUM, 4 December 1968. Goedicke discusses her craft and responds at some length to a question about autobiographical or "confessional" poetry. She believes that all poetry is in a sense autobiographical. She comments also on other poets, poems, and the value of poetry.

714 O'Grady, Tom, and Shirley Bossert. "The Fruit of Her Orchard." NEW LETTERS, 44, No. 1 (1977), 121-24.

Two reviews of FOR THE FOUR CORNERS arranged as a dialog by the editor, David Ray. O'Grady's thesis is that Goedicke is a philosophical poet, "a poet of real vision, a mystic, a true philosopher"; Bossert's thesis is that the theme of the book is the longevity, if not the immortality, of human relationships. Since they are considering the same poems, they do occasionally touch the same base.

715 Slate, Ron. "The Desperate Tongue: Notes on the Poetry of Patricia Goedicke." THREE RIVERS POETRY JOURNAL, 13-14 (March 1979), 9-14.

Slate elaborates Goedicke's treatment of the "excesses and dangers" of self-interest, using examples from her four collections.

HORACE GREGORY

(American; April 10, 1898--)

POEMS

CHELSEA ROOMING HOUSE. New York: Covici Friede, 1930; as ROOMING HOUSE, London: Faber and Faber, 1932.
NO RETREAT. New York: Harcourt, Brace, 1933.
A WREATH FOR MARGERY. New York: Modern Editions Press, 1933.
CHORUS FOR SURVIVAL. New York: Covici Friede, 1935.
POEMS 1930-1940. New York: Harcourt, Brace, 1941.
SELECTED POEMS. New York: Viking Press, 1951.
MEDUSA IN GRAMERCY PARK. New York: Macmillan, 1961.
COLLECTED POEMS. New York: Holt, Rinehart, 1964.
ANOTHER LOOK. New York: Holt, Rinehart, 1976.

BIOGRAPHY

716 Gregory, Horace. THE HOUSE ON JEFFERSON STREET: A CYCLE OF MEMORIES. New York: Holt, Rinehart and Winston, 1971. 276 p.

The title refers to a house in Milwaukee owned by his grandfather, whose presence--Gregory never knew him alive--pervaded and influenced the affairs of the whole family.

SPECIAL ISSUE

717 MODERN POETRY STUDIES, 4, No. 1 (1973).

This special issue contains in sequence essays by David H. Zucker, Linda Wagner, Daniel Stern, Arthur Gregor, Victor A. Kramer, M.L. Rosenthal, William V. Davis, Robert Phillips, and Robert K. Morris. Each essay is annotated below.

CRITICAL ARTICLES

718 Davis, William V. "Figures of Nightmare." MODERN POETRY STUDIES, 4, No. 1 (1973), 55-59.

Studies the personae of CHELSEA ROOMING HOUSE, who, as Gregory wrote, seem "to find cheerful pride in their distress." Davis says they are "all of us . . . people coming apart in the midst of a world coming apart."

719 Gregor, Arthur. "Props of the Western Theatre: The Later Poems of Horace Gregory." MODERN POETRY STUDIES, 4, No. 1 (1973), 28-30.

The outstanding characteristic of the later work is the quality of the "mysterious." For Gregor the world created in these poems "is a decorative wasteland, ornate and baroque."

720 Kramer, Victor A. "Contemplative Need in Horace Gregory's Poetry." MODERN POETRY STUDIES, 4, No. 1 (1973), 34-44.

"The specific need which Gregory treats is man's need to meditate about his limitations and aspirations within a society that rewards him for action not for thinking." Kramer studies the nature of the "speakers" in the poems to show what Gregory believes is required of man for living well.

721 Morris, Robert K. "The Resurrected Vision: Horace Gregory's Thirties Poems." MODERN POETRY STUDIES, 4, No. 1 (1973), 74-99.

These early poems through CHORUS FOR SURVIVAL "foreshadow, then elaborate the mythic patterns later forming or underlying the poems of Gregory's next thirty years, as well as mark his maturing as social critic and poet." Morris describes the nature of Gregory's "waste land."

722 Phillips, Robert. "The Quick-Change Artist: Notes on Horace Gregory's Poetic Imagery." MODERN POETRY STUDIES, 4, No. 1 (1973), 60-74.

The myths that fascinated Gregory and upon which he drew for his poems are "those involving transformations." Phillips says, "As in Ovid's masterpiece, Gregory's poems abound in miraculous events, quick changes." Such use of the archetype gives them universality.

723 Rosenthal, M.L. "The 'Pure' Poetry of Horace Gregory." MODERN POETRY STUDIES, 4, No. 1 (1973), 44-55.

The same "truthfulness to his material" that characterized Gregory's translations of Ovid and Catullus is carried over into his own work. Rosenthal demonstrates a "successful"

Gregory poem by comments on seven poems: "Longface Mahoney Discusses Heaven"; "Interior: The Suburbs"; "Five"; "Four Monologues from THE PASSION OF M'PHAIL"; "Elizabeth at the Piano"; "Opera, Opera!"; and "Flight to the Hebrides."

724 Stern, Daniel. "Politics and Protest in the Earlier Poems of Horace Gregory." MODERN POETRY STUDIES, 4, No. 1 (1973), 22-28.

In Gregory's POEMS 1930-1940, "the proletarian decade was encapsulated in one collection." Stern points out the "dangers" of writing political verse and how Gregory overcame them.

725 Wagner, Linda W. "Horace Gregory: Voice in Action." MODERN POETRY STUDIES, 4, No. 1 (1973), 13-22.

Looks at Gregory's poems from the 1930s to the 1950s and praises his technical skill and ear for the spoken word. Reprinted in no. 296.

726 Zucker, David H. "An American Elegist: The Poetry of Horace Gregory." MODERN POETRY STUDIES, 4, No. 1 (1973), 1-13.

Zucker takes up each book of poems as represented in Gregory's COLLECTED POEMS and discusses his changing concerns, consistent skill, historical sense, and reflective temperament.

GEOFFREY GRIGSON

(English; March 12, 1905--)

POEMS

SEVERAL OBSERVATIONS: THIRTY-FIVE POEMS. London: Cresset Press, 1939.
UNDER THE CLIFF AND OTHER POEMS. London: Routledge, 1943.
THE COLLECTED POEMS OF GEOFFREY GRIGSON 1924-1962. London: Phoenix House, 1963.
A SKULL IN SALOP. London: Macmillan, 1967.
DISCOVERIES OF BONES AND STONES. London: Macmillan, 1971.
SAD GRAVE OF AN IMPERIAL MONGOOSE. London: Macmillan, 1973.
ANGLES AND CIRCLES AND OTHER POEMS. London: Gollancz, 1974.
THE FIESTA AND OTHER POEMS. London: Secker and Warburg, 1978.

CRITICAL ARTICLES

727 Clucas, Humphrey. "An Odd Angle: The Poetry of Geoffrey Grigson." AGENDA, 14, No. 4 and 15, No. 1 (1977), 110-17.

Assessing Grigson's verse, Clucas finds it very uneven but likes the poems in which the tone is angry and irreverent and a few which purge anger that is "the product of too much certainty."

728 Fuller, Roy. "Ripeness." LISTENER, 3 September 1970, pp. 315-16.

Review of NOTES FROM AN ODD COUNTRY (essays, 1970). Fuller finds in these "notes" not only a display of "character" and learning, observation of nature and people, and personal intimacy but also the constant evaluation of these by "a true poet."

729 Mott, Michael. "Seen in Clear." POETRY, 116, No. 1 (1970), 46-50.

On Grigson's career as "editor, critic . . . controversialist" as well as poet, though ostensibly a review of A SKULL IN

SALOP. Because Mott thinks the key to Grigson's work is understanding the kind of observer Grigson is, he directs us to the essays in Grigson's POEMS & POETS (1969).

THOM GUNN

(English; August 29, 1929--)

POEMS

POEMS. Oxford: Oxford University Poetry Society, 1953.
FIGHTING TERMS. Swinford, Engl.: Fantasy Press, 1954; rpt., New York: Hawk's Well Press; rev. London: Faber and Faber, 1962.
THE SENSE OF MOVEMENT. London: Faber and Faber, 1957; Chicago: University of Chicago Press, 1959.
MY SAD CAPTAINS. London: Faber and Faber; Chicago: University of Chicago Press, 1961.
SELECTED POEMS. London: Faber and Faber, 1962.
POSITIVES. London: Faber and Faber; Chicago: University of Chicago Press, 1966.
TOUCH. London: Faber and Faber; Chicago: University of Chicago Press, 1967.
POEMS 1950-1966: A SELECTION. London: Faber and Faber, 1969.
MOLY. London: Faber and Faber, 1971.
MOLY AND MY SAD CAPTAINS. New York: Farrar, Straus and Giroux, 1973.
MANDRAKES. London: Rainbow Press, 1973.
TO THE AIR. Boston: Godine, 1974.
JACK STRAW'S CASTLE. London: Faber and Faber; New York: Farrar, Straus and Giroux, 1976.
GAMES OF CHANCE. Omaha: Abattoir Press, 1979.
SELECTED POEMS 1950-1975. London: Faber and Faber; New York: Farrar, Straus and Giroux, 1979.

CRITICAL BOOK

See no. 347.

CRITICAL ARTICLES

730 Bayley, John. "Castles and Communes." TIMES LITERARY SUPPLEMENT, 24 September 1976, p. 1194.

Review of JACK STRAW'S CASTLE. In this book Gunn seems "his most conventional yet," but he sometimes gives us a poem that "develops in the reader a slightly uneasy feeling that he has been confronted--for what purpose?--with the simulacrum of a good poem."

731 Brown, Merle E. "A Critical Performance of Thom Gunn's 'Misanthropos.'" IOWA REVIEW, 4 (Winter 1973), 73-87.

A close reading of some parts of "misanthropos" (a poem in TOUCH) with acknowledgments of Gunn's own reading of the poem and his comments about it and about poetry. Brown attempts also in his essay a criticism of criticism, which seems to him chiefly "critical maneuvers."

732 Cox, C. B., and A. E. Dyson. "Thom Gunn: 'Considering the Snail.'" In their MODERN POETRY. London: Edward Arnold, 1963, pp. 147-52.

Examines Gunn's "syllabic metre," which gives the poem its meaning.

733 Dodsworth, Martin. "Thom Gunn: Poetry as Action and Submission." In his SURVIVAL OF POETRY. London: Faber and Faber, 1970, pp. 193-215.

Like Byron, Gunn "thinks of the poet *as one who acts.*" Dodsworth sustains the comparison-contrast with Byron but always with the purpose of interpreting Gunn's poems. He thinks, for example, that Gunn in his poems is less a *poseur* than Byron was in poetry or life.

734 Fraser, G. S. "The Poetry of Thom Gunn." CRITICAL QUARTERLY, 3, No. 4 (1961), 359-67.

Fraser contrasts Gunn with Larkin in order "to bring out some of his central qualities," which Fraser lists as "range of curiosity, an undefeatedness of spirit, and a swift readiness to make choices, without any hesitant bother about how the choices will be socially taken." He considers poems through MY SAD CAPTAINS. Reprinted in no. 124.

735 Miller, John. "The Stipulative Imagination of Thom Gunn." IOWA REVIEW, 4 (Winter 1973), 54-72.

Miller's thesis is that Gunn's "attitudes, derived from a consistently existential outlook, relate very closely to the kind of metaphor he develops in his poems: to the situations and persons he uses in these poems, and especially to the way he assigns value to or derives significance from them." Miller responds also to Brown's reading of "Misanthropos" included in the same issue.

736 Powell, Neil. "The Abstract Joy: Thom Gunn's Early Poetry." CRITICAL QUARTERLY, 13, No. 3 (1971), 219-27.

Powell analyzes a poem from Greville's CAELICA ("In night when colours all to black are cast") to explain "Gunn's interest in Greville and at the same time indicate possible approaches to Gunn's own poetry." After pointing out some parallel features, he concludes, "Though an interest in abstraction remains a feature of Gunn's poetry, the abstract joy, the careful manipulation of ideas and patterns, has gone."

737 Ross, Alan. Review of POSITIVES by Thom and Ander Gunn. LONDON MAGAZINE, NS 6 (March 1967), 113-14.

"Muzzy," but given the task of writing poems in response to photographs (taken by Thom's brother Ander), Gunn "has done a good job."

738 Stimpson, Catherine R. "Thom Gunn: The Redefinition of Place." CONTEMPORARY LITERATURE, 18 (Summer 1977), 391-404.

On the expatriation of Thom Gunn and the sense of place in his poetry.

739 Swinden, Patrick. "Thom Gunn's Castle." CRITICAL QUARTERLY, 19, No. 3 (1977), 43-61.

On Gunn's poetic output to date. Pointing out that most readers have noticed "Gunn's exercise of the existential choice . . . thrust upon him," Swinden observes "another aspect of his poetic personality that seems to want to regress, to get back to the less clearly defined, and therefore less limiting and less strenuous state of being that existed before the commitment to choice presented itself." Gunn seems to have written himself into a dilemma by trying "to get beyond the power of speech."

RAMON GUTHRIE

(American; January 14, 1896-November 22, 1973)

POEMS

GRAFFITI. New York: Macmillan, 1959.
ASBESTOS PHOENIX. New York: Funk and Wagnalls, 1968.
MAXIMUM SECURITY WARD, 1964-1970. New York: Farrar, Straus and Giroux, 1970; London: Sidgwick and Jackson, 1971.

CRITICAL BOOK

740 Diller, G[eorge] E., and S[tephen] G. Nichols, Jr., eds. RAMON GUTHRIE KALEIDOSCOPE. Lunenburg, Vt.: Stinehour Press, 1963. 149 p.

Not seen; cited in no. 743. Includes "An Attempt on Ramon Guthrie's Bibliography," by Alan Cooke, pp. 143-49.

CRITICAL ARTICLES

741 Gall, Sally Moore. "The Poetry of Ramon Guthrie." Dissertation, New York University, 1976 (DAI, 37: 5828).

Examines all of Guthrie's work (1923-70) with emphasis "on Guthrie's growth as a poet and on the achievement of his late work, particularly the poems of the 1960s."

742 _____. "Ramon Guthrie's Forgotten Book." MODERN POETRY STUDIES, 9, No. 1 (1978), 55-78.

Gall imparts her enthusiasm for MAXIMUM SECURITY WARD: 1964-1970, discussing its structure, rhythms, and theme as representative of the modern lyrical sequence.

743 Laing, Alexander. "Pain, Memory, and Glory: The Poetry of Ramon Guthrie." CARLETON MISCELLANY, 11, No. 3 (1970), 2-11.

On the occasion of the appearance of MAXIMUM SECURITY WARD, Laing surveys Guthrie's career as poet and teacher and tries to explain but not excuse "the paucity of recognition."

DONALD HALL

(American; September 20, 1928--)

POEMS

POEMS. Oxford: Fantasy Press, 1952.
TO THE LOUD WIND AND OTHER POEMS. Cambridge, Mass.: Harvard Advocate, 1955.
EXILES AND MARRIAGES. New York: Viking Press, 1955.
THE DARK HOUSES. New York: Viking Press, 1958.
A ROOF OF TIGER LILIES: POEMS. New York: Viking Press, 1964.
THE ALLIGATOR BRIDE: POEMS NEW AND SELECTED. New York: Harper and Row, 1969.
THE YELLOW ROOM: LOVE POEMS. New York: Harper and Row, 1971.
THE TOWN OF HILL. Boston: David R. Godine, 1975.
KICKING THE LEAVES. New York: Harper and Row, 1978.
THE TOY BONE. Brockport, N.Y.: BOA Editions, 1979.

SPECIAL ISSUE

744 TENNESSEE POETRY JOURNAL, 4, No. 2 (1971).

This special issue contains in sequence the items listed below: Poems by Hall, pages 3-14. Ralph Mills, "Poems of the Deep Mind," pages 16-25, discusses Hall's themes and style. Scott Chisholm, "An Interview with Donald Hall," pages 26-48, talks with Hall about his poems and modern poetry. William Matthews, "Some Notes on THE ALLIGATOR BRIDE, POEMS NEW AND SELECTED," pages 49-55, analyzes Hall's search for identity. Donald Hall, "Waking up a Giant," pages 56-60, describes what is released by writing a poem.

CRITICAL ARTICLE

745 Mills, Ralph J., Jr. "Donald Hall's Poetry." IOWA REVIEW, 2 (Winter 1971), 82-125.

A survey of Hall's work, which Mills claims is representative of the course of poetry since about 1955 when the poets rebelled against the "new criticism" and "delivered poetry back into the hands of poets." Reprinted in Mills's CRY OF THE HUMAN (Urbana: University of Illinois Press, 1975), pages 192-250.

MICHAEL HAMBURGER

(English; March 22, 1924--)

POEMS

FLOWERING CACTUS. Aldington, Engl.: Hand and Flower Press, 1950.
POEMS 1950-1951. Aldington, Engl.: Hand and Flower Press, 1952.
THE DUAL SITE. London: Routledge and Kegan Paul, 1958.
WEATHER AND SEASON. London: Longmans, Green, 1963.
IN FLASHLIGHT. Leeds, Engl.: Northern House, 1965.
FEEDING THE CHICKADEES. London: Turret Books, 1968.
TRAVELLING. London: Fulcrum Press, 1969.
OWNERLESS EARTH: NEW AND SELECTED POEMS. Cheadle, Engl.: Carcanet Press; New York: Dutton, 1973.

CRITICAL ARTICLES

746 Beckmann, Gerhard. "The Poetry of Michael Hamburger." AGENDA, 9, No. 1 (1971), 16-21.

Review of TRAVELLING. Beckmann thinks it shows an increase in scope and intensity over his previous books. Hamburger may be somewhat "hampered by his links with traditional English poetry, [but he confronts] themes and realities which are as universal as they are personal."

747 Griffin, Jonathan. "Michael Hamburger, Poet and Poets' Critic." AGENDA, 9, No. 1 (1971), 8-15.

Review of TRAVELLING and THE TRUTH OF POETRY. The first underscores the consistency of Hamburger's skill, and the second attempts to define modernity. Griffin is impressed by the "integrity of Michael Hamburger's poems."

748 Warner, Val. "'Loyal to Water': A Reading of the Poetry of Michael Hamburger." AGENDA, 13 (Autumn 1975), 47-69.

Michael Hamburger

Throughout his career Hamburger has been concerned with language, its misuse, its unreality, and therefore with the need to be "conscientious over the deployment of words."

JOHN HEATH-STUBBS

(English; July 9, 1918--)

POEMS

WOUNDED THAMMUZ. London: Routledge and Kegan Paul, 1942.
BEAUTY AND THE BEAST. London: Routledge and Kegan Paul, 1943.
THE DIVIDED WAYS. London: Routledge and Kegan Paul, 1946.
THE CHARITY OF THE STARS. New York: Sloane, 1949.
THE SWARMING OF THE BEES. London: Eyre and Spottiswoode, 1950.
A CHARM AGAINST THE TOOTHACHE. London: Methuen, 1954.
THE TRIUMPH OF THE MUSE AND OTHER POEMS. London: Oxford University Press, 1958.
THE BLUE-FLY IN HIS HEAD. London: Oxford University Press, 1962.
SELECTED POEMS. London: Oxford University Press, 1965.
SATIRES AND EPIGRAMS. London: Turret Books, 1968.
ARTORIUS. London: Enitharmon Press, 1973.
FOUR POEMS IN MEASURE. New York: Helikon Press, 1973.
THE WATCHMAN'S FLUTE: NEW POEMS. Manchester: Carcanet Press, 1975.
THE MOUSE, THE BIRD, AND THE SAUSAGE. Sunderland, Engl.: Ceolfrith Press, 1978.

SPECIAL ISSUE

749 "In Honour of John Heath-Stubbs." AQUARIUS, no. 10 (1978).

This special issue contains poems for Heath-Stubbs by such poets as George Barker, Roy Fuller, and David Wright; numerous but brief reminiscences by close friends and casual acquaintances; an interview conducted by G. H. B. Wightman; and a few short critical notes. Sebastian Barker as editor evaluates the poet's "rhythm, vocabulary, authority, and humour."

ANTHONY HECHT

(American; January 16, 1923--)

POEMS

A SUMMONING OF STONES. New York: Macmillan, 1954.
THE SEVEN DEADLY SINS. Northampton, Mass.: Gehenna Press, 1958.
AESOPIC. Northampton, Mass.: Gehenna Press, 1967.
MILLIONS OF STRANGE SHADOWS. London: Oxford University Press; New York: Atheneum, 1977.
THE VENETIAN VESPERS. London: Oxford University Press; New York: Atheneum, 1979.

BIBLIOGRAPHY

See no. 58, pages 79-80.

CRITICAL ARTICLE

750 Brown, Ashley. "The Poetry of Anthony Hecht." PLOUGHSHARES, 4, No. 3 (1978), 9-24.

A brief biobiblio-historio-introduction to Hecht and an overview of his work. "He has dealt with the terrible divisiveness of the age with an extraordinary honesty and grace."

WILLIAM HEYEN

(American; November 1, 1940--)

POEMS

DEPTH OF FIELD. Baton Rouge: Louisiana State University Press, 1970.
NOISE IN THE TREES: POEMS AND A MEMOIR. New York: Vanguard Press, 1974.
THE SWASTIKA POEMS. New York: Vanguard Press, 1977.
LONG ISLAND LIGHT: POEMS AND A MEMOIR. [Revised and expanded version of NOISE IN THE TREES] New York: Vanguard Press, 1979.

BIBLIOGRAPHY

751 Stefanik, Ernest. "William Heyen: A Descriptive Checklist." BULLETIN OF BIBLIOGRAPHY, 36, No. 4 (1979), 157-76.

Descriptive primary bibliography and briefly annotated secondary bibliography of reviews, interviews, and critical articles through July 1979.

SPECIAL ISSUE

752 MANASSAS REVIEW, 1, Nos. 3 & 4 (1978).

This special issue contains an anthology of Heyen's poems and the items listed below:

William Heyen, "A Note on the Salesman," pages 3-4, characterizes Heyen's attitude toward his own poems. "THE SWASTIKA POEMS: A Conversation," pages 34-39, edited by Heyen and Stanley Rubin from a videotape for SUNY Brockport Writers Forum, March 1978, discusses the origin and development of Heyen's book, some specific poems in it, and the general subject of the Holocaust.

Cis Stefanik, "From Sight to Silence: The Process of William Heyen's Poetry," pages 52-54, studies the persona of "The

Mill," a poem representing "poetry that begins in observation and ends in silence." Vince Clemente, "William Heyen: The Pure Serene of Memory in One Man," pages 55-69, muses on Heyen as friend and poet with comments on places important to Heyen and on characteristics of his poems.

Kenneth MacLean, "Animate Mystique: The Dialectic of William Heyen's Poems," pages 70-79, describes Heyen's idea of nature and the "conflict between it and his sense of a moral identity in the human self." Ernest Stefanik, "William Heyen's 'Boys of Piston, Girls of Gear': A Field Guide to the Human in XVII MACHINES," pages 80-96, explores "man's responsibility for his own humanity" in a "machine-driven society."

Hayden Carruth, "THE SWASTIKA POEMS," pages 97-98, believes Heyen's book proves that history can serve us, that "the death camps can keep us human." Ernest Stefanik, "William Heyen: A Handlist," pages 105-15, lists separate publications and first appearances (preliminary work for no. 751).

CRITICAL ARTICLES

753 Elkins, Bill J. Review of DEPTH OF FIELD. SOUTHERN HUMANITIES REVIEW, 5, No. 3 (1971), 293-97.

Heyen's book satisfies Elkins' requirements for a first book of poems to be recommended to a friend: it is interesting and perceptive, shows insight and skill, and contains a few mature and impressive poems. Elkins discusses technique and theme in various poems.

754 Gerber, Philip L., and Robert J. Gemmet, eds. "The Individual Voice: A Conversation with William Heyen." WESTERN HUMANITIES REVIEW, 23, No. 3 (1968), 222-23.

Held at Brockport, New York, 1968. Heyen talks about his poems, poets he likes, various influences on his work, and the responsibilities of the poet.

755 McPherson, Sandra. "The Swastika Poems." AMERICAN POETRY REVIEW, 6, No. 6 (1977), 30-32.

McPherson describes and evaluates numerous poems, studying the how and why of them. Heyen's book ranges "from the predictable to the heretofore unexpressed, from history book information to the personally unique experience."

GEOFFREY HILL

(English; June 18, 1932--)

POEMS

POEMS. Oxford: Fantasy Press, 1952.
FOR THE UNFALLEN. London: Andre Deutsch, 1959; Chester Springs, Pa.: Dufour Editions, 1960.
PREGHIERE. Leeds, Engl.: Northern House, 1964.
KING LOG. London: Andre Deutsch; Chester Springs, Pa.: Dufour Editions, 1968.
MERCIAN HYMNS. London: Andre Deutsch, 1971.
SOMEWHERE IS SUCH A KINGDOM: POEMS 1952-71. Boston: Houghton Mifflin, 1975.
TENEBRAE. London: Andre Deutsch, 1978; Boston: Houghton Mifflin, 1979.

CRITICAL ARTICLES

756 Alexander, Michael. "Mercian Hymns." AGENDA, 13, No. 3 (1975), 29-30.

> Alexander praises MERCIAN HYMNS for its English subjects, its range of tone, simple manner, and "its successful incorporation of learning into the modern and every day." He is convinced that "it celebrates an important and delicate effort of understanding--understanding that crucial relationship of our imaginative life with that of the past."

757 Bloom, Harold. "The Survival of Strong Poetry." In SOMEWHERE IS SUCH A KINGDOM. By Geoffrey Hill. Boston: Houghton Mifflin, 1975, pp. xiii-xxv.

> Bloom directs our attention to the influences and resistances in Hill that make his poems difficult and "a war of poetry against poetry." He demonstrates Hill's concerns and techniques as represented by "Annunciations," which for Bloom seems a kind of test poem. Readers who can interpret it

can learn to interpret the rest of Hill." Reprinted in no. 181 and AMERICAN POETRY REVIEW, 4, No. 4 (1975), 17-20.

758 Milne, William S. "'Creative Tact': Geoffrey Hill's KING LOG." CRITICAL QUARTERLY, 20, No. 4 (1978), 39-45.

Hill's "tact" is "the testing of his powers of moral and aesthetic discrimination through the selection and deployment of his poetic diction, without being insincere to the truth of his own imagination or the objective world which resides all around him."

759 Morgan, Robert. "The Reign of King Stork." PARNASSUS, 4, No. 2 (1976), 31-48.

Describes and praises the poems in SOMEWHERE IS SUCH A KINGDOM, paying special attention to Hill's craftsmanship and themes. In "From the Latin," Morgan says, "Hill's best talents come together at once, with none of his worst."

760 Ricks, Christopher. "Geoffrey Hill and 'The Tongue's Atrocities.'" TIMES LITERARY SUPPLEMENT, 30 June 1978, pp. 743-47.

A close analysis of Hill's poems on Nazis and Jews during World War II, both philosophical and technical (including such fine points as Hill's use of brackets).

761 Silkin, Jon. "The Poetry of Geoffrey Hill." In no. 327, pages 143-64.

Discusses Hill's use of irony in word, image, structure, and themes--chiefly in poems from KING LOG.

762 Sisson, C.H. "Geoffrey Hill." AGENDA, 13, No. 3 (1975), 23-28.

Hill's propensity for allusion and meticulous reference hinders as much as helps his poems, but it is a "release" for him and more than "technical"; it seems part of his "peculiar cast of mind."

763 Utz, Stephen. "The Realism of Geoffrey Hill." SOUTHERN REVIEW, 12, No. 2 (Spring 1976), 426-33.

Review of SOMEWHERE IS SUCH A KINGDOM. Since this collection includes three earlier collections, Utz is able to study Hill's development, which he finds "so striking and unexpected that it may exhaust who follows it at one sitting through the whole volume." He sees a movement from naturalism to realism and describes Hill's contributions to poetry as a self-reflecting poetry that produces a strong sense of the world.

764 Wainwright, Jeffrey. "Geoffrey Hill's 'Lachrimae.'" AGENDA, 13, No. 3 (1975), 31-38.

The theme of this sonnet sequence is that "purest transcendence is lapped by some part of sensuous life." In these poems Hill treats the paradox of martyrdom.

765 Weatherhead, A.K. "Geoffrey Hill." IOWA REVIEW, 8, No. 4 (1977), 104-16.

Hill's poems are difficult because they are "closed" poems quite different from the postmodernists' which move "toward openness"; behind a "single word in Hill [lies] a whole landscape."

JOHN HOLLANDER

(American; October 28, 1929--)

POEMS

A CRACKLING OF THORNS. New Haven, Conn.: Yale University Press, 1958.
MOVIE-GOING AND OTHER POEMS. New York: Atheneum, 1962.
VISIONS FROM THE RAMBLE. New York: Atheneum, 1965.
PHILOMEL. London: Turret Books, 1968.
TYPES OF SHAPE. New York: Atheneum, 1969.
THE NIGHT MIRROR. New York: Atheneum, 1971.
THE HEAD OF THE BED. Boston: David Godine, 1974.
TALES TOLD OF THE FATHERS. New York: Atheneum, 1975.
SPECTRAL EMANATIONS: NEW AND SELECTED POEMS. New York: Atheneum, 1978.
BLUE WINE AND OTHER POEMS. Baltimore: Johns Hopkins University Press, 1979.

BIBLIOGRAPHY

See no. 58, pages 81-82.

CRITICAL ARTICLES

766 Bloom, Harold. "Nebuchadnezzar's Dream: Hollander's THE HEAD OF THE BED." In no. 181, pages 263-73.

On the ramifications of Lilith, "the true muse of all poets necessarily afflicted with a sense of latecoming." THE HEAD OF THE BED, Bloom says, is "haunted by an implicit psychology of belatedness." This essay is also printed as the Introduction to THE HEAD OF THE BED.

767 ______. "The White Light of Trope: An Essay on John Hollander's

'Spectral Emanations.'" KENYON REVIEW, NS 1, No. 1 (1979), 95-13.

Explains the difficulties and praises the achievement of "Poem in Seven Branches in Lieu of a Lamp" as it is subtitled.

768 Gerber, Philip L., and Robert J. Gemmett. "The Poem as Silhouette: A Conversation with John Hollander." MICHIGAN QUARTERLY REVIEW, 9, No. 4 (Fall 1970), 253-60.

For the SUNY Brockport WRITERS FORUM, 12-13 February 1969. Hollander discusses his "emblem" poems and his interest in shapes and boundaries. He concludes with comments about music and poetry.

RICHARD HOWARD

(American; October 13, 1929--)

POEMS

QUANTITIES. Middletown, Conn.: Wesleyan University Press, 1962.
THE DAMAGES. Middletown, Conn.: Wesleyan University Press, 1967.
UNTITLED SUBJECTS. New York: Atheneum, 1969.
FINDINGS. New York: Atheneum, 1971.
TWO-PART INVENTIONS. New York: Atheneum, 1974.
FELLOW FEELINGS. New York: Atheneum, 1976.
MISGIVINGS. New York: Atheneum, 1979.

CRITICAL ARTICLES

769 Friedman, Sanford. An Interview with Richard Howard." SHENANDOAH, 24, No. 1 (1972), 5-31.

Howard describes his early reading, which began about age three, and his early writing, which began somewhat later; his education at Columbia, Friedman prompting all along with connections to Howard's poems; and finally his poems and the "voices" in his poems.

770 Lynch, Michael. "Richard Howard's Finishes." AMERICAN POETRY REVIEW, 4, No. 6 (1975), 5-11.

In an age that deprecates the superficial, Howard's "poems have accepted and explored surfaces without seeking forthwith their abolition." Lynch elaborates the meanings of words like <u>surfaces</u> and <u>finishes</u> in Howard.

771 "Made Things: An Interview with Richard Howard." OHIO REVIEW, 16, No. 1 (1974), 42-58.

In Athens, Ohio, 4 October 1973. The talk centers on Howard's essays in ALONE WITH AMERICA (1969) and radiates from there: a thrust outward on Auden and Pound and what Howard has learned from them; then back to the center and outward on voices in poems; then on translating; and finally on technique, particularly an exercise on enjambment. (The interviewer is anonymous but sounds like Wayne Dodd.)

772 Martin, Robert K. "The Unconsummated Word." PARNASSUS, 4, No. 1 (1975), 109-15.

Review of TWO-PART INVENTIONS. Martin likes Howard's elegance, taste, and erudition. He describes the poems (or some of the persons and episodes) and concludes that "Howard sees civilization as the last barrier against encroaching madness and death."

773 Reed, John R. "Richard Howard's UNTITLED SUBJECTS." MODERN POETRY STUDIES, 4, No. 3 (1973), 247-59.

On Howard's move toward "confessional" poetry and what in his method is different from those of other confessional poets and even from the usual confessions. Reed compares Howard with Browning in techniques and attitude.

774 Sloss, Henry. "Cleaving and Burning: An Essay on Richard Howard's Poetry." SHENANDOAH, 29, No. 1 (1977), 85-103.

Survey of Howard's work based on an idea that his nature is two-sided: his good angel, "genial and generous," and his bad angel, whose name is "will." Sloss classifies Howard's books accordingly, with the first two, QUANTITIES and DAMAGES, as the groundwork of both categories.

775 Woll, Thomas. "Stasis within Flux: Richard Howard's FINDINGS." MODERN POETRY STUDIES, 4, No. 3 (1973), 259-71.

Woll examines the use Howard makes of the dramatic monologue. Though a dreamer, Howard is nonetheless "greatly concerned with structure and form, meaning, and language itself."

TED HUGHES

(English; August 17, 1930--)

POEMS

THE HAWK IN THE RAIN. London: Faber and Faber, 1957.
LUPERCAL. London: Faber and Faber, 1960.
SELECTED POEMS. [With Thom Gunn] London: Faber and Faber, 1962.
THE BURNING OF THE BROTHEL. London: Turret Books, 1966.
WODWO. London: Faber and Faber, 1967.
CROW. London: Faber and Faber, 1970; New York: Harper and Row, 1971.
SELECTED POEMS 1957-1967. London: Faber and Faber; New York: Harper and Row, 1972.
SPRING SUMMER AUTUMN WINTER. London: Rainbow Press, 1974; rpt. as SEASON SONGS. New York: Viking Press, 1975; London: Faber and Faber, 1976.
GAUDETE. London: Faber and Faber; New York: Harper and Row, 1977.
CAVE BIRDS. London: Faber and Faber, 1978.
REMAINS OF ELMET. London: Faber and Faber, 1979.

BIBLIOGRAPHY

776 Pocock, Janet H. "An Addition to the Ted Hughes Bibliography." BULLETIN OF BIBLIOGRAPHY, 35, No. 1 (1978), 15-18.

Supplements Sagar's list in no. 778 to 1977. General essays and critical essays on specific works along with a list of Hughes's newest poems. The second edition of Sagar's book updates the list through 1978. Neither of Sagar's nor this bibliography by Pocock is annotated.

CRITICAL BOOKS

777 Faas, Ekbert. TED HUGHES: THE UNACCOMMODATED UNIVERSE. Santa Barbara, Calif.: Black Sparrow Press, 1980. 229 p.

Faas's text runs to page 144 excluding notes, and so on. Appendixes, notes, index, and other guides for the reader round off the book. Faas claims some authority from Hughes for this book through correspondence and personal discussion. He also fits Hughes into his chart of a "new aesthetic" marked "by its departure from the mainstream Western Tradition." Thus he introduces Hughes's work in the context "of this new global tradition" and then on the basis of his acquaintance treats it from a "semi-biographical perspective." Includes appendixes on Hughes's own criticism and two interviews between Faas and Hughes.

778 Sagar, Keith. THE ART OF TED HUGHES. London: Cambridge University Press, 1975. 214 p; 2nd ed., 1978, 277 p.

Introductory biographical chapter followed by chapters on each of Hughes's major collections. Second edition adds chapters on SEASON SONGS, GAUDETE, and CAVE BIRDS. Fully descriptive primary bibliography notes differences in British and American editions; checklist of secondary works has been updated by second edition to 1978.

779 _____. TED HUGHES. Writers and Their Work, no. 227. London: Longmans for the British Council, 1972. 50 p. Bibliog.

On Hughes's other writing as well as his poetry, with special attention to CROW. Biographical information.

CRITICAL ARTICLES

780 Bedient, Calvin. "On Ted Hughes." CRITICAL QUARTERLY, 14, No. 2 (1972), 103-21.

Elaborates the thesis that Hughes is the "poet of the will to live, . . . the last stop, waterless and exposed, before nothingness."

781 Bell, Vereen. "Prometheus Bound?" SEWANEE REVIEW, 84, No. 3 (1976), xciii-xcvi.

Review of SEASON SONGS, SELECTED POEMS 1957-1967, and THE ART OF TED HUGHES by Keith Sagar. To appreciate Hughes, readers must "forget everything, moral value included (and moral and intellectual temporizing especially)." Bell also points out strengths and weaknesses in Sagar's book.

782 Bouson, J. Brooks. "A Reading of Ted Hughes's CROW." CONCERNING POETRY, 7, No. 1 (1974), 21-32.

Hughes replaces Judeo-Christian myths with "a Crow-mythology."

783 Cox, C.B., and A.E. Dyson. "Ted Hughes: 'The Casualty.'" In their MODERN POETRY. London: Edward Arnold, 1963, pp. 142-46.

The poem has "no explicit moral, but we are made to see, and therefore to judge"; "its observation, both of humans and animals, has the force of unanswerable truth."

784 Davies, Norman F. "The Poetry of Ted Hughes." MODERNA SPRAK, 71 (1977), 121-27.

On Hughes's contribution to the "animal poem." Of the Crow poems Davies says, "Hughes voices most strongly the agony of modern man, his existential despair, his feeling of helplessness in the face of the irrational forces of life and death, his inability to believe in divine Providence and personal salvation, his awareness of cruelty, his sense of doom."

785 Dyson, A.E. "Featuring . . . Ted Hughes." CRITICAL QUARTERLY, 1, No. 3 (1959), 219-26.

"The major theme in the poems is power; and power thought of not morally, or in time, but absolutely--in a present which is often violent and self destructive, but isolated from motive or consequence, and so unmodified by the irony which time confers." Dyson sees, nevertheless, in the poems "a constant striving towards moments of significance."

786 Faas, Ekbert. "An Interview with Ted Hughes." SYDNEY STUDIES IN ENGLISH, 2 (1976-77), 83-97.

Earliest printing was entitled "Ted Hughes and Crow." Hughes talks about his work, his beliefs and intentions, and about what critics call his "violence." A second interview held in 1977 appears in Faas's book (no. 777), pages 208-15. There Hughes discusses his style in later books and comments briefly on Sylvia Plath. Reprinted from WORKS IN PROGRESS, No. 5 (1972), pp. 369-88; reprinted from LONDON MAGAZINE, NS 10 (January 1971), 5-20.

787 Fernandez, Charles V. "Crow: A Mythology of the Demonic." MODERN POETRY STUDIES, 6, No. 2 (1975), 144-56.

"Demonic" is Hughes's word for a force invoked in his jaguar poems. Fernandez explores origins and myths and describes Hughes's brand of the demonic as irrational, violent, intrinsic, and creative. In CROW Hughes constructs "a new mythology, one which will adequately contain the demonic" because, according to Fernandez, "the demonic cannot be defined, destroyed, examined, or explained."

788 Gibson, John. "A Thematic Analysis of the Poetry in Ted Hughes's Major Works." Dissertation, University of Northern Colorado, 1974 (DAI, 35: 2988).

Traces recurrent themes through four of Hughes's collections: THE HAWK IN THE RAIN, LUPERCAL, WODWO, and CROW.

789 Gitzen, Julian. "Ted Hughes and Elemental Energy." DISCOURSE: A REVIEW OF THE LIBERAL ARTS, 13, No. 4 (1970), 476-92.

Gitzen argues that "dynamism (the principle that transferred and conserved energy is the vital source of all life) . . . is the touchstone for understanding [Hughes]." The violence so frequently noted in his poetry is only the "manifestation of this principle."

790 _____. "Ted Hughes and the Triumph of Energy." SOUTHERN HUMANITIES REVIEW, 7, No. 1 (1973), 67-73.

Energy is the dominating theme of Hughes's poetry, energy that eventually may annihilate everything but itself. "Hughes's vision offers . . . hope by centering not upon erring humanity but upon the chief agency of life itself."

791 Hahn, Claire. "CROW and the Biblical Creation Narratives." CRITICAL QUARTERLY, 19, No. 1 (1977), 43-52.

Hughes's "poetry is not a celebration; it is a magic or religious ritual to control the amoral power of energy." Hahn clarifies and illustrates this thesis.

792 Hainsworth, J.D. "Ted Hughes and Violence." ESSAYS IN CRITICISM, 15, No. 3 (1965), 356-59.

Disagrees with Rawson's interpretation of violence in Hughes's poems (no. 813), pointing out that violence "is often only one element, or even a subordinate element, in a poem's meaning."

793 Hirschberg, Stuart. "An Encounter with the Irrational in Ted Hughes's 'Pike.'" CONCERNING POETRY, 9, No. 1 (1976), 63-64.

The pike represents "the presence of dark, irrational forces at the edge of man's awareness." Hirschberg notes that the rhythms are evocative of "a hostile universe of brute power."

794 _____. "Hughes's New 'Rough Beast': The Malevolent New Order in

'Song of a Rat.'" CONCERNING POETRY, 11, No. 1 (1978), 59-63.

Describes the process in Hughes's poems whereby a rat is transformed into a new order of being made possible by man's "murderous disregard for the consequences of his actions."

795 Hoffman, Daniel. "Talking Beasts: The 'Single Adventure' in the Poems of Ted Hughes." SHENANDOAH, 19, No. 4 (1968), 49-68.

Discusses Hughes's work against the background of English poetry of the 1950s leading into WODWO, the unity of which is the real question of Hoffman's study. "In Hughes's poems a sensibility of extreme aloneness confronts the ultimate abstractions--Life, Energy, Instinct, Death--in the discrete concretions by which they may be known."

796 Holbrook, David. "Ted Hughes's CROW and the Longing for Non-Being." In no. 100, pages 32-54.

Holbrook details what is "bad" about CROW. "There is nothing in CROW for which to have respect or for which to feel care or concern."

797 Hughes, Geoffrey. "Crow: Myth or Trickster?" THEORIA, 48 (May 1977), 25-36.

Shows the strengths and weaknesses in Hughes's work by setting CROW in a context of his earlier poems.

798 John, Brian. "Ted Hughes: Poet at the Master-Fulcrum of Violence." ARIZONA QUARTERLY, 23, No. 1 (1967), 5-15.

John draws examples from THE HAWK IN THE RAIN and LUPERCAL to show the characteristics of the world as Hughes perceives it. "Hughes offers man the possibility of a limited heroism within the confines of an absurd existence."

799 Keutsch, Wilfried. "A Reading of Ted Hughes's 'Thrushes.'" LITERATUR IN WISSENSCHAFT UND UNTERRICHT (Kiel), 9 (1976), 115-21.

Keutsch's analysis leads him to believe the thrush demonstrates "the remorselessness of nature" while man "is only half removed from animal ferocity . . . surrendering to an unanalyzable situation."

800 Law, Pamela. "Poetry as Ritual: Ted Hughes." SYDNEY STUDIES IN ENGLISH, 2 (1976-77), 72-82.

Hughes's poems "have a real respect for violence and try to treat it as a religious force." Law looks at his poems as rituals partly because Hughes seems himself "so concerned with language as magic and with poems as rituals" and partly because poetry itself "is the most powerful ritual we have, both for calling up the primitive forces and for controlling them for good, not for evil."

801 Lodge, David. "'Crow' and the Cartoons." CRITICAL QUARTERLY, 13, No. 1 (1971), 37-42, 68.

Hughes in CROW mixes biblical and classical mythology with topical allusions to automobiles, pollution, modern warfare, and nuclear destruction, meeting thereby "Eliot's definition of poetic originality." The different effect (i.e., from that of THE WASTE LAND), Lodge thinks, "derives from Hughes's assimilation of cartoon techniques."

802 May, Derwent. "Ted Hughes." In THE SURVIVAL OF POETRY. Ed. Martin Dodsworth. London: Faber and Faber, 1970, pp. 133-63.

Hughes's best poems are "the ones that . . . reveal clues to possible joys and satisfactions for man in the life of nature." May comments on most of Hughes's books to date.

803 Megerle, Brenda. "Ted Hughes: His Monsters and Critics." SOUTHERN HUMANITIES REVIEW, 11, No. 2 (1977), 184-94.

Megerle tries to show that Hughes has a "consistent vision" throughout his work, and it "is far greater than the sum of the parts." What previous critics have been too obtuse to see is "the emphasis he gives the idea of heroism in this world which takes nihilism as a given."

804 Mollema, A. "Mythical Elements in the Poetry of Ted Hughes." DUTCH QUARTERLY REVIEW, 2 (1972), 2-14.

Access to Hughes's poetry comes through discerning the "structure provided by mythical elements" although this way of seeing requires us to look at the whole of his work. In his Crow myth, for example, Hughes has found "an objective form to comment in an almost demotic way on the phenomena of modern life."

805 Moyle, Geraldine. "Hughes' GAUDETE: A Poem Subverted by Its Plot." PARNASSUS, 6, No. 2 (1978), 199-204.

Moyle, who has faith in Hughes's skill and integrity, feels betrayed by GAUDETE because in it "Hughes has debased his art to the level of his material--exploitative sexuality, gratuitous violence, lewd occultism--and prostituted his profound talents to the creation of a whorish nightmare work." She does find some "pearls" in it.

806 Newton, J.M. "Some Notes on--CROW." CAMBRIDGE QUARTERLY, 5 (Summer-Autumn 1971), 376-84.

What impresses Newton is that, though he hears Hughes's voice sounding clearly in the poems, Hughes "doesn't seem to be there at all, making a fuss or an effort . . . . It comes over as the nature of things, the zest of life itself."

807 Novak, Robert. "Ted Hughes' Crow: Incarnation of the Universe." WINDLESS ORCHARD, 21 (1975), 40-42.

Musings on the meaning of "Crow Hears Fate Knock on the Door" by one who thinks it the antithesis of Tennyson's "flower in the crannied wall" (or at least some lines of it).

808 Peel, Marie. "Black Rainbow." BOOKS AND BOOKMEN, 16, (February 1971), 16-17.

"In CROW," Peel says, "we have our epic. Whether we are ready for it is another matter." She elaborates Crow as persona, the kind of seeing he represents, and what he sees.

809 Porter, David. "Ted Hughes." AMERICAN POETRY REVIEW, 4, No. 5 (1975), 13-18.

On a new aesthetic and the death of the old, "a new idea of poetry involving an enormous acceleration of intake . . . and aggressively reconciled to a post-literate culture."

810 Ramsey, Jarold. "CROW: or the Trickster Transformed." MASSACHUSETTS REVIEW, 19 (Spring 1978), 111-27.

"Hughes has skillfully fashioned Crow out of bits and pieces of some very ancient traditions." He has continued what Eliot says Joyce is doing in ULYSSES--"manipulating a continuous parallel between contemporaneity and antiquity"--and what Eliot does in THE WASTE LAND: namely, he uses myth "for its inherent imaginative sanity." Ramsey gathers up those bits and pieces to see from what Hughes made his Crow.

811 Rawson, C.J. "Some Sources or Parallels to Poems by Ted Hughes." NOTES & QUERIES, 15, No. 2 (1968), 62-63.

Parallels to "Hawk in the Rain" may be found in Hopkins' "Windhover" and "Hurrahing in Harvest"; in Stevens' "Auroras of Autumn"; in Dylan Thomas' "Over Sir John's Hill"; and A.C. Benson's "Hawk." Another for "Egg-head" is in Benson's "My Poet."

812 _____. "Ted Hughes and Violence." ESSAYS IN CRITICISM, 16, No. 1 (1966), 124-49.

Replies to Hainsworth (no. 792) point by point, defending but qualifying his original assertions on the violence in several poems. The two seem more at odds over the meaning of the term "romantic." See also no. 813.

813 _____. "Ted Hughes: A Reappraisal." ESSAYS IN CRITICISM, 15, No. 1 (1965), 77-94.

If Hughes's subject is the violence in the world, his code is "one of heroic confrontation." Rawson cites numerous examples and contrasts Hughes's stance with that of Thom Gunn.

814 Richards, Jean. "An Interview with British Poet, Ted Hughes, Inventor of Orghast Language." DRAMA AND THEATRE, 10 (Fall 1971), 4.

Hughes wants a language "precise in itself" but open, he says, "to the lost, hidden world we want to explore."

815 Rife, David. "Rectifying Illusion in the Poetry of Ted Hughes." MINNESOTA REVIEW, 10, Nos. 3-4 (1970), 95-99.

Granting that violence is a subject in Hughes's poetry, Rife argues that it is mostly a motif to "a larger, more significant theme . . .; namely, of man's need to prevail over the more intransigent horrors of existence by creating protective illusions." His examples are "Hawk Roosting," "The Jaguar," "The Hawk in the Rain," and "Acrobats."

816 Roberts, Neil. "Ted Hughes: Encounters with Death." DUTCH QUARTERLY REVIEW, 8 (1978), 2-17.

The reader can imaginatively experience his own death in Hughes's poems, for they make him "experience another's death as his own." Hughes only does what any self-respecting poet must do, Roberts says,--"convey knowledge of death."

817 Scigaj, Leonard Michael. "Myth and Psychology in the Poetry of Ted Hughes." Dissertation, University of Wisconsin, Madison, 1977 (DAI, 38: 4819).

Studies Hughes's interest in "primitive, pre-Christian man" as a way into his poetry and also Oriental influences and Hughes's association with drama through Peter Brook.

818 Sinnige-Breed, Afra. "Plucking Bark: An Interpretation of Hughes's 'Wodwo.'" DUTCH QUARTERLY REVIEW, 2, No. 1 (1972), 15-20.

A close-reading analysis of "Wodwo," which shows us a "transformation from 'what' into 'who.'"

819 Weatherhead, A. K. "Come on Home, Ted, We've Kept Your Room the Way It Was." NORTHWEST REVIEW, 15, No. 3 (1976), 85-89.

Review of SEASON SONGS. Although his style in this volume is not completely a return to his earlier work, Hughes "has superbly repossessed and applied those techniques that make poetry an artifact." Weatherhead had thought that after ORGHAST (1971 play) the next step was silence.

820 _____. "Ted Hughes, 'Crow,' and Pain." TEXAS QUARTERLY, 19, No. 3 (1976), 95-108.

On the changes in style and attitude of Hughes since THE HAWK IN THE RAIN. Weatherhead concludes that Hughes's "development has led to a point where the acceptance of pain in a painful universe becomes an increasingly significant obligation."

RICHARD HUGO

(American; December 21, 1923--)

POEMS

A RUN OF JACKS. Minneapolis: University of Minnesota Press, 1961.
DEATH OF THE KAPOWSIN TAVERN. New York: Harcourt, Brace, 1965.
GOOD LUCK IN CRACKED ITALIAN. Cleveland: World, 1969.
THE LADY IN KICKING HORSE RESERVOIR. New York: Norton, 1973.
WHAT THOU LOVEST WELL REMAINS AMERICAN. New York: Norton, 1975.
31 LETTERS AND 13 DREAMS. New York: Norton, 1977.
ROAD ENDS AT TAHOLA. Pittsburgh: Slow Loris Press, 1978.
SELECTED POEMS. New York: Norton, 1979.

BIOGRAPHY

821 Hugo, Richard. THE TRIGGERING TOWN: LECTURES AND ESSAYS ON POETRY AND WRITING. New York: Norton, 1979. 109 p.

The kinds of things Hugo says to his university writing classes, a few examples of his own work and how it came to be, and numerous autobiographical anecdotes. Hugo also mentions Roethke as his mentor and inspiration.

CRITICAL ARTICLES

822 Allen, Michael. "'Because Poems Are People': An Interview with Richard Hugo." OHIO REVIEW, 19, No. 1 (1978), 74-90.

Hugo talks about the effect of his past life on the way he is now and about writing, from the aspect of why and how people write.

823 _____. "Richard Hugo and the Poetics of Need." Dissertation, Indiana University, 1978 (DAI, 39: 4235).

In a "style marked by honest emotion and tension, Hugo shows us an America still tied to need and American men tied to an image of tough isolation, needful of human connection in order to overcome the emotional impoverishments of their ingrained, individualistic dreams."

824 Bell, Vereen M. "We Are Called Human." PARNASSUS, 6, No. 2 (1978), 143-50.

Review-essay of 31 LETTERS AND 13 DREAMS. Hugo shows us "our plain human-ness" in this book, "which makes a kind of forlorn human ecology from its themes of creation, loneliness, and community."

825 Garber, Frederick. "Fat Man at the Margin: The Poetry of Richard Hugo." IOWA REVIEW, 3, No. 4 (1972), 58-67.

"Margins are places where things change into other things, and Hugo's stereoscopic vision (one of his most brilliant repeated feats of the imagination) sees the past and the present and the point of change all together and all at once." One of Hugo's images representing this position is "a version of the ubiquitous fat man look[ing] out at the sea."

826 _____. "Large Man in the Mountains: The Recent Work of Richard Hugo." WESTERN AMERICAN LITERATURE, 10 (Fall 1975), 205-18.

On Hugo in Montana, and how THE LADY IN KICKING HORSE RESERVOIR and WHAT THOU LOVEST WELL REMAINS AMERICAN differ from his previous books when his location was near the sea.

827 Helms, Alan. "Writing Hurt: The Poetry of Richard Hugo." MODERN POETRY STUDIES, 9, No. 2 (1978), 106-18.

Though Hugo has talent, "his work is marred from its beginnings to the present." Helms cites several examples of poems that "stopped short of finished art" and tries to explain the underlying cause in Hugo's split between a poseur and a serious poet.

828 Wright, James. "Hugo: Secrets of the Inner Landscape." AMERICAN POETRY REVIEW, 2, No. 3 (1973), 13.

Wright describes the characteristic Hugo theme, subject, and diction. He suggests an affinity with Orwell, a "deeper and truer spiritual affinity than any man I know."

DAVID IGNATOW

(American; February 7, 1914--)

POEMS

POEMS. Prairie City, Ill.: Decker Press, 1948.
THE GENTLE WEIGHTLIFTER. New York: Morris Gallery, 1955.
SAY PARDON. Middletown, Conn.: Wesleyan University Press, 1961.
FIGURES OF THE HUMAN. Middletown, Conn.: Wesleyan University Press, 1964.
EARTH HARD. London: Rapp and Whiting, 1968.
RESCUE THE DEAD. Middletown, Conn.: Wesleyan University Press, 1968.
POEMS: 1934-1969. Middletown, Conn.: Wesleyan University Press, 1970.
FACING THE TREE: NEW POEMS. Boston: Atlantic-Little, Brown, 1975.
SELECTED POEMS. Middletown, Conn.: Wesleyan University Press, 1975.
THE ANIMAL IN THE BUSH: POEMS ON POETRY. Pittsburgh: Slow Loris Press, 1978.
TREAD THE DARK: NEW POEMS. Boston: Little, Brown, 1978.
SUNLIGHT: A SEQUENCE FOR MY DAUGHTER. Brockport, N.Y.: BOA Editions, 1979.

BIBLIOGRAPHY

See no. 58, pages 83-84.

BIOGRAPHY

829 Mills, Ralph J., Jr., ed. THE NOTEBOOKS OF DAVID IGNATOW. Chicago: Swallow Press, 1973. 376 p.

Ignatow's "reflections, meditations, speculations, observations, confessions, and memories" from 1934 to 1971, with gaps before 1950, amount, Mills says, to "an informal or irregular autobiography of the poet."

SPECIAL ISSUES

830 BELOIT POETRY JOURNAL, 26 (Fall 1975).

A collection of poems in tribute.

831 TENNESSEE POETRY JOURNAL, 3, No. 2 (1970), 3-48.

This special issue contains in sequence the items listed below:

Poems by Ignatow, pages 3-16. Robert Bly, "Some Thoughts on RESCUE THE DEAD," pages 17-21, revised from the NEW LEADER, 20 May 1968, discusses ideas in Ignatow's poems. Scott Chisholm, "An Interview with David Ignatow," pages 22-40 [excerpts], in New York City, 28 November 1969, asks Ignatow about being a "city poet." Linda W. Wagner, "On David Ignatow," pages 41-45, describes Ignatow's themes and techniques; reprinted in no. 296. David Verble, "Some Notes on Articles about Ignatow," page 46, lists reviews and critical comments on Ignatow.

CRITICAL ARTICLES

832 Contoski, Victor. "Time and Money: The Poetry of David Ignatow." UNIVERSITY REVIEW, 34, No. 3 (1968), 211-13.

Reflections on the kind of world Ignatow creates--a chaotic, irrational, nightmare world, pervaded by a "time-money relationship."

833 Kazin, Alfred. "The Esthetic of Humility." AMERICAN POETRY REVIEW, 3, No. 2 (1974), 14-15.

Review of THE NOTEBOOKS OF DAVID IGNATOW. Kazin finds almost unbearable the unhappiness and frustration recorded in the book, but the notes here "are the worldly shells" of poems that Ignatow has written out of "desperate sincerity, . . . sometimes unbelievable humility."

834 Lavenstein, Richard. "A Man with a Small Song." PARNASSUS, 4, No. 1 (1975), 211-22.

Review of THE NOTEBOOKS OF DAVID IGNATOW, SELECTED POEMS, and FACING THE TREE. Lavenstein considers all three of these rather dull, sometimes unpleasant, and minor: Ignatow "remains that man with a small song, too often singing in the wrong key."

835 Mazzaro, Jerome. "Circumscriptions: The Poetry of David Ignatow." SALMAGUNDI, 22-23 (Spring-Summer 1973), 164-86.

Ignatow's "small songs" amount in their totality "to something approaching a major voice." Mazzaro responds to various critical views that emphasize what is missing from Ignatow's poems by pointing out what is there. Reprinted in no. 273.

836 Swados, Harvey. "David Ignatow: The Meshuganeh Lover." AMERICAN POETRY REVIEW, 2, No. 3 (1973), 35-36.

Review of POEMS 1934-36. On Ignatow's persona and some of the personae (all meshuganehs--eccentrics) of his poems.

837 Zweig, Paul. "David Ignatow." AMERICAN POETRY REVIEW, 5, No. 1 (1976), 29.

Review of FACING THE TREE and SELECTED POEMS. Zweig explains what unifies all of Ignatow's work. His poems "are like letters to someone who has got to be made to listen."

RANDALL JARRELL

(American; May 6, 1914-October 14, 1965)

POEMS

BLOOD FOR A STRANGER. New York: Harcourt, Brace, 1942.
LITTLE FRIEND, LITTLE FRIEND. New York: Dial Press, 1945.
LOSSES. New York: Harcourt, Brace, 1948.
THE SEVEN-LEAGUE CRUTCHES. New York: Harcourt, Brace, 1951.
SELECTED POEMS. New York: Knopf, 1955.
THE WOMAN AT THE WASHINGTON ZOO: POEMS AND TRANSLATIONS. New York: Atheneum, 1960.
SELECTED POEMS. New York: Atheneum, 1964.
THE LOST WORLD: NEW POEMS. New York: Macmillan, 1965.
THE COMPLETE POEMS. New York: Farrar, Straus and Giroux, 1969; London Faber and Faber, 1971.

BIBLIOGRAPHY

838 Calhoun, Richard James. "Randall Jarrell (1914-1965)." In A BIBLIOGRAPHICAL GUIDE TO THE STUDY OF SOUTHERN LITERATURE. Ed. Louis D. Rubin, Jr. Baton Rouge: Louisiana State University Press, 1969, pp. 226-27.

Lists and very briefly annotates works about Jarrell from the fifties and sixties.

839 Gillikin, Dure Jo. "A Checklist of Criticism on Randall Jarrell 1941-1970 with an Introduction and a List of His Major Works." BULLETIN OF THE NEW YORK PUBLIC LIBRARY, 75 (April 1971), 176-94.

A brief introduction describing Jarrell's principal subjects precedes a list of primary works including translations and works edited; and secondary works, including 254 reviews itemized under the work reviewed. Other articles listed range from a newspaper column on Jarrell's death and other one-page items to studies of ten to thirty pages.

840 Kisslinger, Margaret V. "A Bibliography of Randall Jarrell." BULLETIN OF BIBLIOGRAPHY, 24, No. 10 (1966), 243-47; and 28, No. 3 (1971), 79-81.

Continues Charles M. Adams' 1958 bibliography to 1965. Kisslinger arranges primary and secondary listings together under three major groupings: Individual Poems and Books of Poetry and Criticism of Them; Essays, Addresses and Books by Jarrell and Criticism about Them; and Prose about Randall Jarrell. The 1971 number has primary items only.

See also no. 78, pages 154-55.

CRITICAL BOOKS

841 Quinn, Sister Bernetta. RANDALL JARRELL. Boston: Twayne, 1981. 172 p. Notes, ref., bibliog., index.

Quinn chooses to concentrate on a few poems rather than skim over many. In six chapters she touches most aspects of Jarrell--teacher, critic, novelist, poet--and concludes with a chapter of tributes and memories by former Greensboro students.

842 Shapiro, Karl. RANDALL JARRELL. Washington, D.C.: Library of Congress, 1967. 47 p. Bibliog.

Shapiro's lecture (17 October 1966) characterizes Jarrell's style, both of literature and life, as deriving from "a terrible conflict in his soul between his instinct for freedom and his desire for cultural asylum." Shapiro assesses Jarrell's career and place among contemporary poets. Primary bibliography of works in the Library of Congress collection.

CRITICAL ARTICLES

843 Beck, Charlotte Hudgens. "The Dramatic Mode in the Poetry of Randall Jarrell." Dissertation, University of Tennessee, 1972 (DAI, 33: 745).

After studying his matter, technique, and the critical response to his work, Beck concludes that Jarrell's best poems are dramatic.

844 Browne, Elizabeth J. "Criticism and the Artist: The Writings of Randall Jarrell." Dissertation, Loyola University of Chicago, 1973 (DAI, 34: 1895).

Jarrell is "a man of his age--a man bereft of faith, dismayed by the very successes of science and technology, discouraged by . . . the American dream." Browne studies the theme of alienation in Jarrell's verse and prose.

845 Cornelius, David K. "Jarrell's 'Death of the Ball Turret Gunner.'" EXPLICATOR, 35, No. 3 (1977), Item 3.

On Jarrell's imagery relating to the structure of a World War II B-17.

846 Damashek, Richard. "The Lost World of Randall Jarrell." Dissertation, University of Wisconsin, 1972 (DAI, 33: 4406).

Jarrell's view of life did not so much evolve or change during his career as it was deepened and refined.

847 _____. "Randall Jarrell: The Face in the Mirror." PERSPECTIVES ON CONTEMPORARY LITERATURE, 1, No. 1 (1975), 74-84.

Jarrell's poetry is the confronting of his alienation.

848 Fisher, Nancy McWhorter. "Fantasy and Reality in the Poetry of Randall Jarrell." Dissertation, University of Tennessee, 1969 (DAI, 31: 755).

The conflict between fantasy and reality running through Jarrell's poetry is a unifying theme.

849 Funkhouser, Linda Kay. "Acoustical Rhythm in Performances of Three Twentieth Century American Poems." Dissertation, St. Louis University, 1978 (DAI, 39: 1517).

Examines Jarrell's "The Death of the Ball Turret Gunner," and two other poems not by Jarrell, "through acoustical measures of duration, or rate, pause, and levels of energy in oral performance" and discovers thereby the "highest acoustical energy on 'loosed.'"

850 Gordon, Lois, and Alan Gordon. "Say Goodbye to Randall Jarrell (1914-1965)." UNIVERSITY OF HARTFORD STUDIES IN LITERATURE, 10 (1978), 122-36.

An assessment of Jarrell's career and speculations about his state of mind on the night he died.

851 Griswold, Jerome Joseph. "Mother and Child in the Poetry and Children's Books of Randall Jarrell." Dissertation, University of Connecticut, 1979 (DAI, 40: 5442).

Jarrell's major theme is the anxiety of separation in mother and child and its resolution. Griswold includes a discussion with Maurice Sendak on his illustrations for Jarrell's books.

852 Jacobson, Kent Alan. "Randall Jarrell: In Search of Authority." Dissertation, Yale University, 1975 (DAI, 36: 8059).

Jarrell's "contradictory attitudes toward authority" show his poetic voice shifting from "masculine" to "feminine."

853 Jarrell, Mary. "Ideas and Poems." PARNASSUS, 5, No. 1 (1976), 213-30.

Review of THE COMPLETE POEMS. An anecdotal account of Jarrell's ideas for poems and to some extent in poems. But for Mary Jarrell what seems most pleasing is the transformation of her ideas in his poems.

854 Rabuzzi, Kathryn Allen. "The Lost Worlds of Randall Jarrell." Dissertation, Syracuse University, 1976 (DAI, 38: 2793).

Jarrell's central theme "is a search for lost worlds." He explores in his protagonists "the gap between their idealistic phantasies and the actualities of their lives."

855 Rethinger, Alice Marie. "'Slight, Separate, and Estranged': The Child and His World in the Poetry of Randall Jarrell." Dissertation, Bowling Green State University, 1975 (DAI, 36: 909).

How the perceptions of children "serve the poet in the expression of his concern about the human condition."

856 Schwarz, John Moritz. "An Introduction to the Poems of Randall Jarrell." Dissertation, University of California, Los Angeles, 1969 (DAI, 30: 5002).

On the development of Jarrell's themes and techniques and a brief sketch, derived from this study, of his personality.

857 Selby, Thomas Norwood. "Randall Jarrell as Critic." Dissertation, University of South Carolina, 1977 (DAI, 38: 2129).

Jarrell's various kinds of criticism, educational, social, artistic, and literary, and the measure of his success.

858 Sharistanian, Janet. "The Poet as Humanitarian: Randall Jarrell's Literary Criticism as Self-Revelation." SOUTH CAROLINA REVIEW, 10, No. 1 (1977), 32-42.

Although Jarrell rarely criticized his own work, he nevertheless reveals in his criticism of others his ideas about poetry. By looking closely at numerous critical pieces, Sharistanian outlines and elaborates Jarrell's poetic credo.

859 _____. "Powerless Victims in the Poetry of Randall Jarrell." Dissertation, Brown University, 1975 (DAI, 37: 316).

"Ultimately, Jarrell's characters and speakers are powerless victims in an almost unrelentingly deterministic world."

860 Zanderer, Leo. "Randall Jarrell: About and for Children." LION AND THE UNICORN, 2, No. 1 (1978), 73-93.

Zanderer traces the motif of childhood in Jarrell's poems before looking at his stories for children. "The victories of the stories' heroes may seem small, but they are clearly an advance over the plight of the poems' protagonists."

ELIZABETH JENNINGS

(English; July 18, 1926--)

POEMS

A WAY OF LOOKING. London: Andre Deutsch, 1955; New York: Rinehart, 1956.
A SENSE OF THE WORLD. London: Andre Deutsch, 1958; New York: Rinehart, 1959.
EVERY CHANGING SHAPE. London: Andre Deutsch, 1961.
RECOVERIES. London: Andre Deutsch; Philadelphia: Dufour Editions, 1964.
THE MIND HAS MOUNTAINS. London: Macmillan; New York: St. Martin's Press, 1966.
COLLECTED POEMS. London: Macmillan; Philadelphia: Dufour Editions, 1967.
THE ANIMALS' ARRIVAL. London: Macmillan, 1969.
LUCIDITIES. London: Macmillan, 1970.
RELATIONSHIPS. London: Macmillan, 1972.
GROWING-POINTS. Manchester: Carcanet Press, 1975.
CONSEQUENTLY I REJOICE. Manchester: Carcanet Press, 1977.

CRITICAL ARTICLES

861 Clark, Leonard. "Taste and . . . ." POETRY REVIEW, 58 (Spring 1967), 52.

> Review of THE MIND HAS MOUNTAINS. These poems "for all their restraint" are nevertheless "very self-conscious." They are about Jennings' recovery from a mental breakdown. An excerpt appears in no. 72.

862 Harrison, Janet Elizabeth. "The Quiet Pursuit: Poetry of Elizabeth Jennings." Dissertation, Ohio University, 1968 (DA, 29: 1227).

> Studies each collection in chronological order through THE MIND HAS MOUNTAINS (1966), her critical works, and her relationship to "The Movement." "Her best [poems] achieve a balance of content and form."

DAVID JONES

(Welsh; November 1, 1895-October 28, 1974)

POEMS

IN PARENTHESIS. London: Faber and Faber, 1937.
THE ANATHEMATA. London: Faber and Faber, 1952.
THE FATIGUE. Cambridge: Rampant Lion Press, 1965.
THE TRIBUNE'S VISITATION. London: Fulcrum Press, 1969.
THE SLEEPING LORD AND OTHER FRAGMENTS. London: Faber and Faber, 1974.
THE KENSINGTON MASS. London: Agenda Editions, 1975.

BIBLIOGRAPHY

863 Rees, Samuel. DAVID JONES: AN ANNOTATED BIBLIOGRAPHY AND GUIDE TO RESEARCH. New York: Garland, 1977. 97 p.

An annotated list of writings about David Jones follows the primary bibliography and includes practically everything to 1976.

CRITICAL BOOKS

864 Mathias, Roland, ed. DAVID JONES: EIGHT ESSAYS ON HIS WORK AS WRITER AND ARTIST. Llandyssul, Wales: Gomer, 1976. 144 p.

Rees annotates this (no. 863), but the following list may be helpful in locating the separate entries: "David Jones: An Autobiography" and "David Jones and His Recorded Readings" by Peter Orr; "The Efficacious Word" by William Blissett; "The Present Past in THE ANATHEMATA and Roman Poems" by N. K. Sandars; "The Medieval Inspiration of David Jones" by David Blamires; "The Artist David Jones" by Arthur Giardelli; "Fragility and Force: A Theme in the Later Poems of David Jones" by Désirée Hirst; "Brut's Albion" by Jeremy Hooker; and "Bibliography of Writings by and on David Jones 1970-1975" by David Blamires.

865 Rees, Samuel. DAVID JONES. Boston: Twayne, 1978. 154 p. Bibliog., index.

An introduction to and critical assessment of Jones. Chapter 1 is biographical; 2 is philosophical and aesthetic; 3 and 4 are close readings of IN PARENTHESIS and THE ANATHEMATA; 5 is on shorter pieces; and 6 assesses Jones as a writer.

866 Summerfield, Henry. AN INTRODUCTORY GUIDE TO THE ANATHEMATA AND THE SLEEPING LORD SEQUENCE OF DAVID JONES. Victoria, B.C.: Sono Nis Press, 1979. 192 p. Bibliog.

One needs copies of the poems to use this guide. The Introduction supplies a brief overview of the poems, their language, structure, and personae. In addition to the gloss, which makes up the bulk of the work, there is a Chronology of Jones's life.

JOURNAL

867 Blamires, David, ed. THE DAVID JONES SOCIETY NEWSLETTER, 1976-- . Irregular.

Contents and policy are described in no. 863, page 19.

CRITICAL ARTICLES

868 Abercrombie, Nigel. "For the Love of David Jones (1895-1974)." MONTH, 236 (January 1975), 20-22.

A musing, reflecting commentary on "sources" and "echoes" in Jones's poems.

869 Alexander, Michael. "David Jones." AGENDA, 16, No. 2 (1978), 26-32.

Review of Jones's DYING GAUL and René Hague's COMMENTARY ON THE ANATHEMATA (1977). These are prose works, but Alexander points out what is revealed about Jones the craftsman and artist. He praises Hague's book for having the special knowledge only a close friend of Jones can give.

870 Blamires, David. "Making the Past Present." BOOKS AND BOOKMEN, 16 (September 1971), 28-31.

On THE ANATHEMATA but Blamires comments also on IN PARENTHESIS and other works. He says Jones sees the role of poet as one of preserving tradition--that is, of being a "rememberer--and shows how this belief of Jones's makes his work what it is.

871 Grant, Patrick. "Belief in Religion: The Poetry of David Jones." In his SIX MODERN AUTHORS AND PROBLEMS OF BELIEF. New York: Barnes and Noble, 1979, pp. 67-92.

In his book as a whole Grant is interested in "the interconnections between literature, science and technology," and Jones represents the problem of the artist who believes in religion. Grant compares him with Joyce and Empson and has a seven-page study of Christian imagery in THE ANATHEMATA focused by the figure of the cross.

872 Hague, René. "Myth and Mystery in the Poetry of David Jones." AGENDA, 15, Nos. 2-3 (1977), 37-79.

Explains what Jones himself means by "myth," the uses he made of myth, and how much his work can be considered "a making of myth." Hague goes into some detail about specific uses and "makings" but could not finish his essay (in hospital); he leaves two pages of notes instead for the reader to puzzle out and apply to Jones's ANATHEMATA.

873 Heath-Stubbs, John. "New Writing." POETRY REVIEW, 61 (Summer 1970), 168-70.

A commentary on "The Fatigue" and "The Tutelar of the Place" to fit THE TRIBUNE'S VISITATION into its place in Jones's work and to describe the structure and theme of the poem.

874 Hirst, Désirée. "David Jones: Poet of Obscure Delight." THE REVIEW (London), 7 (Winter 1970-71), 42-53.

Biographical details and an analysis of the language of IN PARENTHESIS and THE ANATHEMATA. Hirst likes Jones's amalgamation of diverse elements of European culture and science. The phrase in her title comes from a comment by Edwin Muir.

875 Jennings, Elizabeth. "David Jones: A Vision of War." In her SEVEN MEN OF VISION: AN APPRECIATION. New York: Barnes and Noble, 1976, pp. 151-72.

Jennings analyzes IN PARENTHESIS from the thesis of her book that the writers included illuminate life because "they have joy, . . . attained through their own suffering and their own kind of surrenders." Thus she interprets "the sense of joy--and occasionally of fear, a fear which is usually more like awe than terror--which [Jones's] work provides."

876 Keith, W. J. "'The Carpentry of Song': New Approaches to David Jones." UNIVERSITY OF TORONTO QUARTERLY, 47, No. 3 (1978), 277-82.

Review of six recent books about David Jones and THE KENSINGTON MASS. Keith praises all the books reviewed but warns that expert knowledge nothwithstanding "the poems will live by virtue of their language." He turns to Hague's COMMENTARY (see Rees, no. 865) last with the judgments that "all subsequent readers and scholars will find themselves indebted to it" and that Hague is "the perfect commentator."

877 Levy, Edward. "David Jones 'Life-Out-There' and the Limits of Love." ANGLO-WELSH REVIEW, 27, No. 61 (1978), 66-88.

Levy explains Jones's philosophy of life by contrasting the darker, pessimistic, more negative attitudes of better known poets like Larkin and Auden. He sees Jones as much more hopeful and finds this attitude embodied in his work, where he "represents a constant and eternal view of man, rooted in love of the natural world, and a love for man as a peculiar kind of creature in the natural world."

878 Li, Victor Paw Hoon. "The Inward Continuities: Aesthetics, Crisis, and THE ANATHEMATA of David Jones." M.A. thesis, University of British Columbia, Vancouver, 1975.

Relates Jones's theories of art as set forth in his writings on art to his practice, particularly in THE ANATHEMATA. Jones's central concern in his art is to demonstrate the interrelatedness of all things because in reality all things are interrelated.

879 Mathias, Roland, ed. "Three Letters." ANGLO-WELSH REVIEW, No. 61 (1978), pp. 53-65.

Mathias prints two letters to Wyn Griffith and one to Mr. Diffey along with an account of his receiving and editing them. He describes the physical appearance of the letters and points out the impossibility of reproducing Jones's idiosyncracies.

880 Orr, Peter. "Mr. Jones, Your Legs Are Crossed: A Memoir." AGENDA, 15, Nos. 2-3 (1977), 110-25.

Reminiscences of Orr's acquaintance with Jones from October 1964 to a few days before his death and also biographical notes of earlier years. Orr recounts several anecdotes about Jones's state of mind and condition of health in his last years.

881 Raine, Kathleen. "Waste Land, Holy Land." PROCEEDINGS OF THE BRITISH ACADEMY, 62 (1976), 379-97.

Warton Lecture on English Poetry, read 8 December 1976. Raine comments on Jones, pages 393-95, and sees IN PARENTHESIS as "a consecration of the most waste of all land, the battlefield." It portrays men not only "in all their poignant physical vulnerability, but also in the dignity of their confrontation."

882 Wilborn, William Francis. "Sign and Form in the Poetry of David Jones: A Study in the Poetics of Image." Dissertation, Cornell University, 1976 (DAI, 37: 7148).

Compares Jones's use of form and image with that of Eliot and Pound.

883 Wilcockson, Colin. "David Jones and 'The Break.'" AGENDA, 15, Nos. 2-3 (1977), 126-31.

Jones was concerned about the break between the useful and the beautiful, which had occurred sometime during the Industrial Revolution. To him man's difference from beasts lies in "his desire to beautify his artifacts."

DONALD JUSTICE

(American; August 12, 1925--)

POEMS

THE SUMMER ANNIVERSARIES. Middletown, Conn.: Wesleyan University Press, 1960.
A LOCAL STORM. Iowa City: Stone Wall Press, 1963.
NIGHT LIGHT. Middletown, Conn.: Wesleyan University Press, 1967.
SIXTEEN POEMS. Iowa City: Stone Wall Press, 1970.
FROM A NOTEBOOK. Iowa City: Seamark Press, 1972.
DEPARTURES. New York: Atheneum, 1973.
SELECTED POEMS. New York: Atheneum, 1979.

CRITICAL ARTICLES

884 Fussell, Paul. "Conventions and the Individual Talent." In his POETIC METER AND POETIC FORM. Rev. ed. New York: Random House, 1979, pp. 177-80.

Shows that Justice relies on conventional rhyme, meter, and stanzaic form to convey meaning in "In Bertram's Garden."

885 Johnson, Larry. "Poetry of Deflection: The Art of Donald Justice." Dissertation, University of Tennessee, 1978.

Not seen. Cited in no. 33.

886 Rewa, Michael. "'Rich Echoes Reverberating': The Power of Poetic Convention." MODERN LANGUAGE STUDIES, 9, No. 1 (1978-79), 25-32.

Responds to Paul Fussell's reading of "In Bertram's Garden." Rewa believes that Fussell, with whom he agrees essentially, has remained too "conventional" and should have extended his interpretation.

GALWAY KINNELL

(American; February 1, 1927--)

POEMS

WHAT A KINGDOM IT WAS. Boston: Houghton Mifflin, 1960.
FLOWER HERDING ON MOUNT MANADNOCK. Boston: Houghton Mifflin, 1964.
BODY RAGS. Boston: Houghton Mifflin, 1968.
FIRST POEMS: 1946-1954. Mt. Horeb, Wis.: Perishable Press, 1970.
THE BOOK OF NIGHTMARES. Boston: Houghton Mifflin, 1971.
THE SHOES OF WANDERING. Mt. Horeb, Wis.: Perishable Press, 1971.
THE AVENUE BEARING THE INITIAL OF CHRIST INTO THE NEW WORLD: POEMS 1956-1964. Boston: Houghton Mifflin, 1974.
THREE POEMS. New York: Phoenix Book Shop, 1976.
MORTAL ACTS, MORTAL WORDS. Boston: Houghton Mifflin, 1980.

CRITICAL BOOK

887 Kinnell, Galway. WALKING DOWN THE STAIRS: SELECTIONS FROM INTERVIEWS. Ann Arbor: University of Michigan Press, 1977. 127 p.

Comments on the craft of writing poems selected by Kinnell from interviews 1969-76. Some of these were published previously in fuller or longer versions, and apparently all have been edited from earlier transcripts.

CRITICAL ARTICLES

888 Dodd, Wayne, and Stanley Plumly. "The Weight That a Poem can Carry: An Interview with Galway Kinnell." OHIO REVIEW, 14, No. 1 (1972), 24-38.

Held in Athens, Ohio, 15 May 1972. Kinnell discusses structure and narrative in long poems, influences on his work, and his acquaintance with W. S. Merwin; but almost all his answers are to questions about THE BOOK OF NIGHTMARES. Reprinted in no. 887.

889 Davis, William V. "'The Rank Flavor of Blood': Galway Kinnell's 'The Bear.'" NOTES ON CONTEMPORARY LITERATURE, 7, No. 2 (1977), 4-6.

Kinnell's "Bear" prepares us for THE BOOK OF NIGHTMARES as the poem where Kinnell "merges in symbolic fashion at least, the incongruities between the sacred and the profane . . . , and, as well, sets the scene for the nightmare visions which are to follow."

890 Evans, Tania. "Galway Kinnell: An Appraisal." RACKHAM LITERARY STUDIES, 4 (1973), 91-96.

On Kinnell's development between BODY RAGS (which Evans says appeared in 1965) and THE BOOK OF NIGHTMARES (1971). Kinnell in those years made "a drastic shift in perspective." He seems to have shifted toward a greater concern for others while he has also improved his "artistic tools."

891 Fortunato, Mary Jane. "Craft Interview with Galway Kinnell." NEW YORK QUARTERLY, No. 8 (Autumn 1971), pp. 10-19.

Discusses his craft, reading poems, teaching, and contemporary poetry. Reprinted in no. 887 and THE CRAFT OF POETRY (Ed. William Packard, New York: Doubleday, 1974).

892 "Galway Kinnell: Interview with Al Poulin, Jr., and Stan Samuel Rubin." AMERICAN POETRY REVIEW, 5, No. 4 (1976), 6-7.

In Brockport, New York, November 1971. Kinnell replies to questions about his beginning as a writer, his early reading, inspiration and motive in writing, specific poems and collections of his own, long poems and sequences, and what is left to write about.

893 Gerber, Philip L., and Robert J. Gemmett, eds. "'Deeper Than Personality': A Conversation with Galway Kinnell." IOWA REVIEW, 1, No. 2 (1970), 125-33.

For SUNY Brockport WRITERS FORUM, October 1969. Kinnell explicates "How Many Nights" but begs off "The Bear," "the poem of mine which I understand least." He comments on "what is behind" some other poems and on poetry generally. Excerpts are reprinted in no. 887.

894 Hawkins, Sherman. "Galway Kinnell: Moments of Transcendence."

PRINCETON UNIVERSITY LIBRARY CHRONICLE, 25 (Autumn 1963), 56-70.

Kinnell's "representation of reality is uncompromising . . . . But the holy is incarnate in the real." Hawkins traces the influence of Frost, Yeats, and Whitman that brings Kinnell to this kind of perspective. Checklist of primary works, including his contributions to books and periodicals.

895 McKenzie, James J. "To the Roots: An Interview with Galway Kinnell." SALMAGUNDI, Nos. 22-23 (Spring-Summer 1973), 206-21.

From questions about experiences on the poetry-reading circuit and its audiences, McKenzie leads to a discussion of "audience feed-back" and its effect on a poet's writing including Kinnell's responses to critics. They talk about other poets and their influence on Kinnell. Reprinted in nos. 223 and 887.

896 Marcello, Leo Luke. "Galway Kinnell: Adamic Poet and Deep Imagist." Dissertation, Louisiana State University, 1976 (DAI, 37: 2862).

Trying "various means of transcendence," Kinnell came to "the concept of a self-redeeming persona," which he employs in THE BOOK OF NIGHTMARES. Marcello examines Kinnell's early work to show this process.

897 Mills, Ralph J., Jr. "A Reading of Galway Kinnell." IOWA REVIEW, 1, No. 1 (1970), 102-22.

Kinnell "explores relentlessly the actualities of his existence to wrest from them what significance for life he can." Reprinted in Mills's CRY OF THE HUMAN (Urbana: University of Illinois Press, 1975), pp. 134-91.

898 Molesworth, Charles. "The Rank Flavor of Blood: Galway Kinnell and American Poetry in the 1960's." WESTERN HUMANITIES REVIEW, 27, No. 3 (1973), 225-39.

Molesworth uses Kinnell as an example of the "new poetic" that originated with Charles Olson and Allen Ginsberg.

899 Reiter, Lora Kay. "The Poetry of Galway Kinnell." Dissertation, University of Kansas, 1975 (DAI, 36: 4497).

Investigates Kinnell's claim that he has come through his first period to "an avant garde" attached to "transcendental and religious meditation." Reiter believes "his statements . . . support what he is about in his poetry."

900 Taylor, Jane. "The Poetry of Galway Kinnell." PERSPECTIVE, 15, No. 3 (1968), 189-200.

Taylor points out distinctive qualities of individual poems in Kinnell's first two collections. "Perhaps the most pleasing thing about Mr. Kinnell is his simple confidence in the power and sufficiency of his perceptions: in his wholehearted commitment to what he is saying, one never finds a labored casting about for meaning and significance, nor the kind of evasive and deprecating self-scrutiny which ends in contempt for self and others."

901 Wagner, Linda W. "Spindrift: The World in a Seashell." CONCERNING POETRY, 8 (Spring 1975), 5-9.

Wagner discusses Kinnell's poem as "intimations of immortality." Reprinted in no. 296.

KENNETH KOCH

(American; February 27, 1925--)

POEMS

POEMS. New York: Tibor de Nagy Gallery, 1953.
KO; OR, A SEASON ON EARTH. New York: Grove Press, 1960.
PERMANENTLY. New York: Tiber Press, 1960.
THANK YOU AND OTHER POEMS. New York: Grove Press, 1962.
POEMS FROM 1952 AND 1953. Los Angeles: Black Sparrow Press, 1968.
SLEEPING WITH WOMEN. Los Angeles: Black Sparrow Press, 1969.
WHEN THE SUN TRIES TO GO ON. Los Angeles: Black Sparrow Press, 1969.
THE ART OF LOVE. New York: Random House, 1975.
THE BURNING MYSTERY OF ANNA IN 1951. New York: Random House, 1979.

BIBLIOGRAPHY

See no. 58, pages 85-86.

CRITICAL ARTICLES

902 See Author Index and chapter 1 of this guide for bibliographies and general reference works on poets.

MAXINE KUMIN

(American; June 6, 1925--)

POEMS

HALFWAY. New York: Holt, Rinehart and Winston, 1961.
THE PRIVILEGE. New York: Harper and Row, 1965.
THE NIGHTMARE FACTORY. New York: Harper and Row, 1970.
UP COUNTRY. Harper and Row, 1972.
HOUSE, BRIDGE, FOUNTAIN, GATE. New York: Viking Press, 1975.
THE RETRIEVAL SYSTEM. New York: Viking Press, 1978.

CRITICAL ARTICLES

903 See Author Index and chapter 1 of this guide for bibliographies and general reference works on poets.

STANLEY KUNITZ

(American; July 29, 1905--)

POEMS

INTELLECTUAL THINGS. Garden City, N.Y.: Doubleday, 1930.
PASSPORT TO THE WAR: A SELECTION OF POEMS. New York: Holt, Rinehart, and Winston, 1944.
SELECTED POEMS 1928-1958. Boston: Little, Brown, 1958.
THE TESTING TREE: POEMS. Boston: Little, Brown, 1971.
THE LINCOLN RELICS: A POEM. Port Townsend, Wash.: Graywolf Press, 1978.
THE POEMS OF STANLEY KUNITZ 1928-1978. Boston: Atlantic-Little, Brown, 1979.

BIBLIOGRAPHY

See nos. 5 and 58, pages 87-89.

CRITICAL ARTICLES

904 Boyers, Robert. "'Imagine Wrestling with an Angel': An Interview with Stanley Kunitz." SALMAGUNDI, Nos. 22-23 (Spring-Summer 1973), pp. 71-83.

Held at Skidmore College, April 1972. This talk with Kunitz constitutes a kind of literary history of the situation of poetry in the past fifty years, the changing fashions in verse and thought, the various attitudes towards poetry, and, of course, Kunitz' likes and dislikes. Reprinted in no. 223.

905 Davis, Cynthia. "An Interview with Stanley Kunitz." CONTEMPORARY LITERATURE, 15, No. 1 (1974), 1-14.

Held at Kunitz' home in New York, 9 March 1972. Kunitz gives his ideas about the nature of poetry and its interpretation, comments on other poets, and lists some of the influences on him, even negative ones: "That Eliot rhythm had an hypnotic effect."

906 ______. "Stanley Kunitz's 'The Testing Tree.'" CONCERNING POETRY, 8 (Spring 1975), 43-46.

The structure of the poem is related to the speaker's emotional states.

907 Hagstrum, Jean H. "The Poetry of Stanley Kunitz: An Introductory Essay." TRI-QUARTERLY, 1 (Spring 1959), 20-26.

Kunitz believes that modern neurosis stems from the separation of art from life in our culture. Hagstrum discusses Kunitz' themes and practices and supplies some biographical details. Reprinted in no. 258.

908 Perloff, Marjorie. "The Testing of Stanley Kunitz." IOWA REVIEW, 3, No. 1 (1972), 93-103.

In THE TESTING TREE "Kunitz has finally found a lyric mode that suits his temperament." Perloff has felt a failure or at least a lack of a personal style in earlier poems and examines several poems from this collection to exemplify his new voice.

909 Ryan, Michael. "An Interview with Stanley Kunitz." IOWA REVIEW, 5, No. 2 (1974), 76-85.

Kunitz explains what writing poetry means to him and comments on poets, art and its forms, his way of working, teaching, and popular media.

910 Weisberg, Robert. "Stanley Kunitz: The Stubborn Middle Way." MODERN POETRY STUDIES, 6, No. 1 (1975), 49-73.

Critics have damned Kunitz to obscurity by praising him as "the poet's poet." Instead, says Weisberg, he is "a still point in the turning world of recent poetry, a poet where dynamic order will remind us of what subject matter may be worth a poet's excluding."

PHILIP LARKIN

(English; August 9, 1922--)

POEMS

THE NORTH SHIP. London: Fortune Press, 1945; rev. ed., Faber and Faber, 1966.
XX POEMS. Belfast: Privately printed, 1951.
POEMS. Oxford: Fantasy Press, 1954.
THE LESS DECEIVED. Hessle, Engl.: Marvell Press, 1955.
THE WHITSUN WEDDINGS. London: Faber and Faber; New York: Random House, 1964.
HIGH WINDOWS. London: Faber and Faber; New York: Farrar, Straus, and Giroux, 1974.

CRITICAL BOOKS

911 Brownjohn, Alan. PHILIP LARKIN. Writers and Their Work, no. 247. Harlow, Engl.: Longmans for the British Council, 1975. 34 p. Bibliog.

Brief biographical section, followed by discussion of the verse in order of publication and a final section on other writings.

912 Martin, Bruce. PHILIP LARKIN. Boston: Twayne, 1978. 166 p. Bibliog.

Attempts to combine synthesis and analysis to see the broad development of Larkin's work. Chapters on his life, aesthetics, historical and social milieu, poems, prose, and reputation. Selected annotated bibliography of secondary works to about 1977.

CRITICAL ARTICLES

913 Bowen, Roger. "Death, Failure, and Survival in the Poetry of Philip Larkin." DALHOUSIE REVIEW, 58, No. 1 (1978), 79-94.

Bowen discerns in Larkin's verse two views of death: "personal death, which is seen as inevitable and unmitigated" and "death in relation to a world which perpetually renews itself." In his latest work Larkin by this latter view betokens "a quiet trust . . . in continuity," in the survival of something "beyond his individual 'extinction.'"

914 _____. "Poet in Transition: Philip Larkin's XX POEMS." IOWA REVIEW, 8, No. 1 (1977), 87-104.

These poems, between Larkin's first and second commercially published volumes, suggest "a different poetic character"; in them, after repeated failures to publish, "Larkin tries to reassess his talent." Although XX POEMS shows numerous weaknesses, "the germ of Larkin's authentic voice is there."

915 Brown, Merle. "Larkin and His Audience." IOWA REVIEW, 8, No. 4 (1977), 117-34.

Larkin's poems seem so clear as to be difficult to talk about but contain qualities that seem to be inexpressible. Brown looks closely at several poems to explain the kind of reader they need, the kinds of questions to raise and not to raise.

916 Coulette, Henri. "The Thought of HIGH WINDOWS." SOUTHERN REVIEW, 12 (Spring 1976), 438-41.

Review of HIGH WINDOWS. Praises Larkin's skill as "maker" of poems and how through that "making" he speaks "about man's condition."

917 Cox, C B. "Philip Larkin, Anti-Heroic Poet." STUDIES IN THE LITERARY IMAGINATION, 9, No. 1 (1976), 155-68.

"The influence of Hardy is most relevant to a proper understanding of the anti-heroic qualities in Larkin's poetry." And misinterpretation of this tradition in English verse is the chief cause of misunderstanding Larkin, particularly by American critics.

918 Cox, C.B., and A.E. Dyson. "Philip Larkin: 'At Grass.'" In no. 304, pages 137-41.

Old race horses put out to pasture are a pattern of man's old age, which the authors see as Larkin's reflection on "submitting to death."

919 Enright, D.J. "Down Cemetery Road." NEW STATESMAN, 67 (28 February 1964), 331-32.

Review of THE WHITSUN WEDDINGS. Larkin's "marvellous skill" is devoted to "conveying . . . a valetudinarian attitude towards life."

920 Ferguson, Peter. "Philip Larkin's XX POEMS." AGENDA, 14 (Autumn 1976), 53-62.

Ferguson believes that the few poems left uncollected from this book (thirteen are in THE LESS DECEIVED) are as good as any in the book and better than any in THE NORTH SHIP. He describes these poems in some detail and explains their place in Larkin's literary biography.

921 Fraser, G. S. "Philip Larkin: The Lyric Note and the Grand Style." In his ESSAYS ON TWENTIETH-CENTURY POETS. Totowa, N.J.: Rowman and Littlefield, 1977, pp. 243-53.

Argues for a "lyrical and romantic quality" in Larkin's verse.

922 Hamilton, Ian. "Four Conversations: Philip Larkin." LONDON MAGAZINE, 4, No. 6 (1964), 64-85.

"The Movement," the state of poetry, and Larkin's own poems all receive comment in this interview. Larkin believes he is "less likely to write a really bad poem now, but possibly equally less likely to write a really good one." Reprinted in no. 203.

923 _____. "Poetry: Philip Larkin's THE WHITSUN WEDDINGS. LONDON MAGAZINE, 4, No. 3 (May 1964), 70-74.

"Larkin has extended his range of interests . . . and seems no longer concerned to pose." Reprinted in POETRY CHRONICLE (New York: Barnes and Noble, 1973).

924 Hirschberg, Stuart. "Larkin's 'Dry-Point': Life without Illusion." NOTES ON CONTEMPORARY LITERATURE, 8, No. 1 (1978), 5-6.

Interprets the imagery of the poem on a sexual and then an artistic level, the process of the poem leading to a disillusionment which gives way itself to a newly forming illusion in the last line.

925 Hope, Francis. "Philip Larkin." ENCOUNTER, 22, No. 5 (1964), 72-74.

Review of THE WHITSUN WEDDINGS. This volume confirms Larkin's talent but "does not extend" it. Despite comparisons with Betjeman, Hope thinks Larkin more a twentieth-century Housman or Horace in his handling of themes.

926 Kelly, Philip Hogan. "Philip Larkin's Poetry: An Analysis and a Curriculum." Dissertation, Carnegie-Mellon University, 1977 (DAI, 39: 1590).

Examines the "personae" of Larkin's work in individual poems, each of which has its own, and in each volume, which Kelly believes has its own persona, "the cumulative effect of all the poems in a volume." The "curriculum" part of his title refers to his outline of a course in poetry appreciation.

927 Lampard, Donald Earl. "Philip Larkin: The Poetry of Absolute Maturity." Dissertation, University of Tennessee, 1979 (DAI, 40: 3318).

Larkin's theme is "self-knowledge, which he sets against delusion." Lampard studies this theme in the later poems, contrasting them with the earlier, in which Larkin emphasized "the pain of life."

928 Lehmann, John. "The Wain-Larkin Myth." SEWANEE REVIEW, 66 (1958), 578-87.

See Wain, below (no. 1566); not really on Larkin.

929 Lodge, David. "Philip Larkin." In his THE MODES OF MODERN WRITING: METAPHOR, METONYMY, AND THE TYPOLOGY OF MODERN LITERATURE. Ithaca, N.Y.: Cornell University Press, 1977, pp. 212-20.

On "form" in Larkin and his affinity with Wordsworth. Lodge regards him as a "metonymic" poet.

930 Moon, Kenneth. "Cosmic Perspective: A Use of Imagery in the Poetry of Philip Larkin." POETRY AUSTRALIA, No. 68 (1978), pp. 59-63.

A line from "This was your place of birth . . ." illustrates what Moon means by cosmic perspective, an image of "wind, clouds, sky, rain, night, sea, fields," intended as a distancing device. He shows the device at work in this early poem and on through Larkin's maturer verse.

931 Murphy, Richard. "The Art of Debunkery." NEW YORK REVIEW OF BOOKS, 22, No. 8 (15 May 1975), 30-33.

Review of HIGH WINDOWS. Larkin "makes poetry out of common situations in ordinary lives." He likes to debunk "any notions he thinks are unintelligible, untenable, or absurd." Murphy says he found three misprints in the American edition, "rather too many for such a short and exact work."

932 Newton, J.M. "'. . . And a More Comprehensive Soul.'" CAMBRIDGE QUARTERLY, 1 (1965), 96-101.

Review of WHITSUN WEDDINGS. Newton is not impressed by the poems: "At best, though rarely, a very pale tenderness of feeling partly modifies the effect of the cold liveliness and observation and self-anxiety." His poetry is "a limitedly personal poetry which, because the poet never struggles for any finer-than-average or even fine-as-average humanity in it, is of little or no use to anyone."

933 Oberg, Arthur. "Larkin's Lark Eggs: The Vision Is Sentimental." STAND, 18, No. 1 (1976), 21-27.

On the relative statures of Larkin and Lowell. An examination of THE WHITSUN WEDDINGS and HIGH WINDOWS shows Larkin in decline as Lowell's NOTEBOOKS showed Lowell in decline.

934 Press, John. "The Poetry of Philip Larkin." SOUTHERN REVIEW, 13, No. 1 (1977), 131-46.

Like Tennyson--and Press extends this comparison--Larkin has the technical skill to transmute everyday matter into poetry. Press describes "the range and variety of Larkin's achievement" and "the quality of his art" and concludes that he is "at once the public laureate . . . and the solitary poet of human isolation, fear, and longing." Reprinted in ESSAYS BY DIVERS HANDS, 39 (1977), 76-91.

935 ______. "W. B. Yeats, Thomas Hardy and Philip Larkin." ALIGARH JOURNAL OF ENGLISH STUDIES, 3, No. 2 (1978), 153-65.

Larkin's "youthful infatuation with Yeats" was never completely dispelled by the subsequent influence of Hardy as Larkin had thought. Though he speaks in his own voice in his later work, in some things he is "nearer in spirit to Yeats than to Hardy."

936 Reibetanz, John. "'The Whitsun Weddings': Larkin's Reinterpretation of Time and Form in Keats." CONTEMPORARY LITERATURE, 17, No. 4 (1976), 529-40.

Reibetanz contends that Larkin's echoes of "Ode on a Grecian Urn" in "The Whitsun Weddings" illuminates both poems.

937 Ricks, Christopher. "A True Poet." NEW YORK REVIEW OF BOOKS, 3, No. 11 (14 January 1965), 10-11.

Review of THE WHITSUN WEDDINGS. Ricks admires Larkin's "technical surety, imaginative delicacy, a feeling heart, and unforgettable rightness of cadence." He points out some of the influences of Hardy, affinities with Tennyson, and techniques that seem to be Larkin's own.

938 Scofield, Martin. "The Poetry of Philip Larkin." MASSACHUSETTS REVIEW, 17 (Summer 1976), 370-89.

Scofield replies to charges by critics that Larkin's verse is "low key," has "doubting prosaic and limited personae," and takes "a negative stance" by pointing out differences "between Larkin's kind of poetry and the bulk of American poetry" to show how the very qualities criticized "are raised to the condition of finely wrought art."

939 Swigg, Richard. "Descending to the Commonplace." PN REVIEW, 4, No. 2 (1977), 3-13.

Swigg sees in the popularity of Larkin the depressing fact that not only do present-day readers like it but that no better poetry is expected or desired. His comparisons are mostly with the late great moderns to support his complaint that Larkin has won his laurels by default.

940 Wain, John. "Engagement or Withdrawal? Some Notes on the Work of Philip Larkin." CRITICAL QUARTERLY, 6, No. 2 (1964), 167-68.

Larkin is simply "the best craftsman now working in English." In his elaboration of this point, Wain feels the need to denigrate other poets but manages to point out some excellences of Larkin's craftsmanship.

941 _____. "The Poetry of Philip Larkin." MALAHAT REVIEW, 39 (July 1976), 95-112.

A lecture at Oxford University, 12 March 1975. Wain interprets Larkin's use of the ordinary: We do not just "know" it, but "under-stand" it, "possess it in its fullness." From various poems he enumerates and illustrates Larkin's major themes to give some idea of his range. Reprinted in Wain's PROFESSING POETRY (New York: Viking Press, 1978), pp. 113-33.

LAURIE LEE

(English; June 26, 1914--)

POEMS

THE SUN MY MONUMENT. London: Hogarth Press, 1944.
THE BLOOM OF CANDLES. London: John Lehmann, 1947.
THE VOYAGE OF MAGELLAN [Verse Play]. London: John Lehmann, 1948.
MY MANY-COATED MAN. London: Andre Deutsch, 1955; New York: Morrow, 1961.
POEMS. Santa Monica, Calif.: Vista, 1960.

BIOGRAPHY

942 Lee, Laurie. CIDER WITH ROSIE. London: Hogarth Press, 1959; also published as THE EDGE OF DAY (New York: Morrow, 1960).

On Lee's boyhood.

943 ______. AS I WALKED OUT ONE MIDSUMMER MORNING. London: Andre Deutsch; New York: Atheneum, 1969. 250 p.

Lee's life from age 19 to 22, during which time he left home, went to Spain, went back home because of the civil war there, and then returned to Spain "with a winter of war" ahead of him.

944 ______. I CAN'T STAY LONG. London: Andre Deutsch, 1975; New York: Atheneum, 1976.

Prose pieces that are autobiographical.

944A Devas, Nicolette. "'I Hear the Owl.'" In her TWO FLAMBOYANT FATHERS. New York: William Morrow, 1967, pp. 243-54.

Comments on Lee begin on page 249. Devas describes Lee's appearance and behavior while he lodged in her house in Markham Square, London, during the war.

DENISE LEVERTOV

(American; October 24, 1923--)

POEMS

THE DOUBLE IMAGE. London: Cresset Books, 1946.
HERE AND NOW. San Francisco: City Lights Press, 1957.
OVERLAND TO THE ISLANDS. Highlands, N.C.: Jargon Books, 1958.
WITH EYES AT THE BACK OF OUR HEADS. New York: New Directions, 1959.
THE JACOB'S LADDER. New York: New Directions, 1961.
O TASTE AND SEE: NEW POEMS. New York: New Directions, 1964.
CITY PSALM Berkeley, Calif.: Oyez, 1964.
THE SORROW DANCE. New York: New Directions, 1966.
THREE POEMS. Mt. Horeb, Wis.: Perishable Press, 1968.
A TREE TELLING OF ORPHEUS Los Angeles: Black Sparrow Press, 1968.
EMBROIDERIES. Los Angeles: Black Sparrow Press, 1969.
SUMMER POEMS/1969. Berkeley, Calif.: Oyez, 1970.
RELEARNING THE ALPHABET. New York: New Directions, 1970.
TO STAY ALIVE. New York: New Directions, 1971.
FOOTPRINTS. New York: New Directions, 1972.
THE FREEING OF THE DUST. New York: New Directions, 1975.
LIFE IN THE FOREST. New York: New Directions, 1978.
COLLECTED EARLIER POEMS 1940-1960. New York: New Directions, 1979.

BIBLIOGRAPHY

945 Wilson, Robert A. A BIBLIOGRAPHY OF DENISE LEVERTOV. New York: Phoenix Book Shop, 1972. 98 p.

Descriptive primary bibliography, including translations of Levertov's work and miscellaneous items like unverified comments in Carol Bergé's VANCOUVER REPORT or two-line blurbs on dustwrappers of books. Wilson distinguishes where necessary between American and British editions.

See also no. 58, pages 95-97.

CRITICAL BOOKS

946 Wagner, Linda Welshimer. DENISE LEVERTOV. New York: Twayne, 1967. 159 p. Bibliog., index.

Chapter 1 relates Levertov's theory and practice; chapters 2 and 3 describe characteristic subjects and themes; 4 and 5 are on "technical concerns"; 6 studies her worksheets; and 7 relates her prose and poetry and ranks her among contemporary poets. Primary and annotated secondary bibliography (to 1965).

947 _____, ed. DENISE LEVERTOV: IN HER OWN PROVINCE. New York: New Directions, 1979. 158 p.

Introduction surveys Levertov's career, describes some of her principal habits of mind as they appear in her work, and indicates her major concerns. Reprinted are interviews from NEW YORK QUARTERLY and MINNESOTA REVIEW and essays and talks by Levertov. Wagner has selected essays and reviews about her from 1965 to 1975.

CRITICAL ARTICLES

948 André, Michael. "Denise Levertov: An Interview." LITTLE MAGAZINE, 5, Nos. 3-4 (1971-72), 42-55.

Levertov describes her early years, discusses her attitudes toward poetry and poets, and comments on her methods of working, on particular poems and prose pieces, and on the situation for writers now.

949 _____. "Parts Remaining of the Levertov Piece." UNMUZZLED OX, 1 (Summer 1972), 41-50.

These are presumably notes not used in André's publication of his interview. This piece has much more evaluative comment by André than the earlier one (no. 948).

950 Block, Sandra Jean. "The Archetypal Feminine in the Poetry of Denise Levertov." Dissertation, Kansas State University, 1978 (DAI, 39: 2936).

Examines Levertov's imagery and its relation to myth and archetype.

951 Bowering, George. "Denise Levertov." ANTIGONISH REVIEW, No. 7 (Autumn 1971), pp. 76-87.

Bowering contrasts Levertov to Anne Bradstreet and Emily Dickinson (and a few other poets) in pursuing his thesis that Levertov's work "is all centered on the religious stance."

952 Brent, Joanna R., et al. "Poem Opening: An Invitation to Transactive Criticism." COLLEGE ENGLISH, 40, No. 1 (1978), 2-16.

This piece is made up by contributors to a Colloquium for Psychoanalytic Criticism at SUNY-Buffalo in 1976. Here are ten different reactions to Levertov's "To a Snake," which demonstrate what is meant by "transactive criticism."

953 Burrows, E.G. "An Interview with Denise Levertov." MICHIGAN QUARTERLY REVIEW, 7, No. 4 (1968), 239-42.

Burrows asks about Levertov's activities connected with resistance to the draft and how they have affected her life. To explain her avoidance of the dangers of writing propaganda, she points out the difference between following a "party line" and espousing the cause of peace.

954 Carruth, Hayden. "Levertov." HUDSON REVIEW, 27, No. 3 (1974), 475-80.

Review of THE POET IN THE WORLD by Levertov. What Carruth likes most about these prose pieces is their "good sense and practical wisdom." He tries to relate the ideas about the role of the poet to her poems.

955 "Craft Interview with Denise Levertov." NEW YORK QUARTERLY, No. 7 (Summer 1971), pp. 8-25.

On influences, poetic practice, teaching, drug use, social protest, and translating. Reprinted in nos. 279 and 947.

956 Deren, Jane Martha. "Denise Levertov's Postmodern Poetic: A Study in Theory and Criticism." Dissertation, Temple University, 1977 (DAI, 38: 2111).

Levertov's theory of poetry and its application to practical criticism.

957 Duddy, Thomas A. "To Celebrate: A Reading of Denise Levertov." CRITICISM, 10, No. 2 (1968), 138-52.

How Levertov resolves the conflict between the imagination and the actual in her poems.

958 Gitzen, Julian. "From Reverence to Attention: The Poetry of Denise Levertov." MIDWEST QUARTERLY, 16, No. 3 (1975), 328-41.

Gitzen applies Levertov's theory of art to her poems.

959 Harris, Victoria. "The Incorporative Consciousness: Levertov's Journey

from Discretion to Unity." EXPLORATION, 4, No. 1 (1976), 33-48.

"This type of poetic consciousness encompasses both internal and external reality, integrating self, others, and nature into an organic whole." It is in O TASTE AND SEE that Levertov "approaches and at times achieves that reciprocal relationship with reality."

960 Kyle, Carol A. "Every Step an Arrival: SIX VARIATIONS and the Musical Structure of Denise Levertov's Poetry." CENTENNIAL REVIEW, 17, No. 3 (1973), 281-96.

Kyle uses musical and dance terminology and imagery to describe the structure of Levertov's work.

961 Levertov, Denise. "Origins of a Poem: A Reverence for Life." MICHIGAN QUARTERLY REVIEW, 7, No. 4 (1968), 233-38.

Levertov outlines "the attitudes and realizations" related to her poem "The Necessity." Actually these relate to her whole concept of what a poet is and does.

962 Sutton, Walter. "Denise Levertov and Emerson." NOTES ON MODERN AMERICAN LITERATURE, 1, No. 1 (1976), Item 1.

In THE POET IN THE WORLD Levertov's essays "reveal . . . the many correspondences of their ideas about organic form, the nature of poetry, and the role of the poet." Sutton also remarks Levertov's departures from Emerson.

963 Wagner, Linda W. "'Sound of Direction.'" MASSACHUSETTS REVIEW, 8, No. 1 (1967), 218-25.

Review of O TASTE AND SEE. It is the "apex of her poetry to date." Wagner compares the poems in this collection to earlier poems. Reprinted in no. 296.

964 Younkins, Ronald. "Denise Levertov and the Hasidic Tradition." DESCANT, 19 (1974), 40-48.

"A familiarity with Hasidism is a valuable aid to the understanding and appreciation of the poetry of the early 1960's, while an understanding of the decline of the Hasidic influence provides an informative perspective on the change in Levertov's work of the later 1960's." Younkins details this influence.

PHILIP LEVINE

(American; January 10, 1928--)

POEMS

ON THE EDGE. Iowa City: Stone Wall Press, 1961.
SILENT IN AMERICA: VIVAS FOR THOSE WHO FAILED. Iowa City: Shaw Avenue Press, 1965.
NOT THIS PIG. Middletown, Conn.: Wesleyan University Press, 1968.
FIVE DETROITS. Santa Barbara, Calif.: Unicorn Press, 1970.
THISTLES. London: Turret Books, 1970.
PILI'S WALL. Santa Barbara, Calif.: Unicorn Press, 1971.
RED DUST. Santa Cruz, Calif.: Kayak Press, 1971.
THEY FEED THEY LION. New York: Atheneum, 1972.
1933. New York: Atheneum, 1974.
THE NAMES OF THE LOST. New York: Atheneum, 1976.
ASHES: POEMS OLD AND NEW. New York: Atheneum, 1979.
7 YEARS FROM SOMEWHERE. New York: Atheneum, 1979.

BIBLIOGRAPHY

See no. 58, pages 99-100.

CRITICAL ARTICLES

965 "And See If the Voice Will Enter You: An Interview with Philip Levine." OHIO REVIEW, 16, No. 2 (1975), 44-63.

Recorded in Athens, Ohio, 18 October 1974. This note on Athens seems a bit puzzling since one question is "How long have you lived in California?" to which Levine replies, "I came here in '57." He discusses difficulties of writing, personal experiences in an anecdotal way, success and failure, poetry in America, Galway Kinnell, and, naturally, being a poet.

966 Bedient, Calvin. "An Interview with Philip Levine." PARNASSUS, 6, No. 2 (1978), 40-51.

In Los Angeles, January 1978. Levine comments on politics, romanticism, and poets. His advice to everyone is, "Keep trying, kid, buddy, old man."

967 Broughton, Irv. "An Interview with Philip Levine." WESTERN HUMANITIES REVIEW, 32, No. 2 (1978), 139-63.

Broughton manages to ask questions that bring out the personality of Levine, who talks about poets and poetry, but also recounts numerous illuminating personal anecdotes to Broughton.

968 Mills, Ralph J., Jr. "'The True and Earthy Prayer': Philip Levine's Poetry." AMERICAN POETRY REVIEW, 3, No. 2 (1974), 44-47.

Levine's poems show a consciousness of "an unflinching acquaintance with the harsh facts of life." Reprinted in Mills's CRY OF THE HUMAN (Urbana: University of Illinois Press, 1975), pp. 251-65.

969 Molesworth, Charles. "The Burned Essential Oil: The Poetry of Philip Levine." HOLLINS CRITIC, 12, No. 5 (December 1975), 1-15.

On Levine's development from a "gift for capturing the terminal moment, the final gesture" to "a capacity for finding the sustaining originals, the freshening sources."

970 Saleh, Dennis, and Glover Davis. "'Touch Them Because They Gave Me My Life': An Interview with Philip Levine." AMERICAN POETRY REVIEW, 1, No. 1 (1972), 35-37.

In Fresno, California, 28 November 1971. Levine describes his experiences in Spain, influences on his work from translating and from other poets, life in Fresno and Detroit, and his newest book (THEY FEED THEY LION) as "more affirmative" than his previous work.

971 Smith, Arthur. "Philip Levine Interviewed by Arthur Smith." STAND, 17, No. 4 (1976), 38-45.

A longer version appeared in PARTISAN REVIEW, 62, No. 1 (1975). Levine discusses poetry in America, various groups like Black Mountain and New York poets, individual poets like Bly, Roethke, and Merwin, and his book THEY FEED THEY LION.

972 Yenser, Stephen. "Bringing It Home." PARNASSUS, 6, No. 1 (1977), 101-17.

Philip Levine

Review of THE NAMES OF THE LOST. On realism in Levine's poems, the political aspect of the conditions Levine describes, and the relation of this book to his other collections.

JOHN LOGAN

(American; January 23, 1923--)

POEMS

CYCLE FOR MOTHER CABRINI. New York: Grove Press, 1955; rpt. Berkeley, Calif.: Cloud Marauder, 1972.
GHOSTS OF THE HEART. Chicago: University of Chicago Press, 1960.
SPRING OF THE THIEF: POEMS 1960-1962. New York: Knopf, 1963.
THE ZIG-ZAG WALK: POEMS 1963-1968. New York: Dutton, 1969.
THE ANONYMOUS LOVER. New York: Liveright, 1973.
POEM IN PROGRESS. Washington, D.C.: Dryad Press, 1975.
JOHN LOGAN/POEMS AARON SISKIND/PHOTOGRAPHS. Rochester, N.Y.: Visual Studies Workshop, 1976.
THE BRIDGE OF CHANGE: POEMS 1974-1979. Brockport, N.Y.: BOA Editions, 1980.

SPECIAL ISSUE

973 "Homage to John Logan." VOYAGES, Nos. 12-13 (1972), pp. 9-53. Photos. by Aaron Siskind, Thomas Victor, Bruce Jackson, and Robert Sund.

"John Logan on Poets and Poetry Today," pages 17-24, talks about poets' "tragic encounters." Robert Bly, "John Logan's Field of Force," pages 29-36, discusses Logan's use of language. Marvin Bell, "Logan's Teaching," pages 38-39, reminisces about a poetry writing course. Michael Rust, "Singing for the Shadow," pages 40-47, muses on Logan's having written a poem for him and on the essences of Logan's poems. The "John Logan Bibliography," pages 51-53, lists books, short stories, and articles by Logan and articles about Logan.

CRITICAL ARTICLES

974 Altieri, Charles. "Poetry as Resurrection: John Logan's Structures of

Metaphysical Solace." MODERN POETRY STUDIES, 3, No. 5 (1973), 193-224.

"Logan's ultimate task is to resurrect sentiment from sentimentality, and he achieves this by embodying in his work . . . a continual struggle between the sufferings of fallen flesh and the forces allowing momentary transcendence."

975 Bell, Marvin. "What Poetry Means: For John Logan: An Interview." TRACE, No. 43 (Autumn 1961), pp. 230-34.

The questions are meant as "mere scaffolding" to allow Logan's "humanity [to] make itself known." Logan tells us what he thinks about poetry and poets, that good critics are made by love, the difference between poetry and prose, that poets ought to be rich, there are no heretical books of "imaginative literature," and nine children give him "a distinction no other American poet has."

976 Bly, Robert [Crunk]. "The Work of John Logan." SIXTIES, No. 5 (Fall 1961), pp. 77-87.

On Logan's strangeness, metaphors, ideas, subjects, and, briefly, faults. "The thought as a whole forms a content, the main drift of which is against the generally accepted ideas, whether ideas of personality, sainthood, love, or poetry."

977 Carroll, Paul. "John Logan: Was Frau Heine a Monster? or 'Yung and Easily Freudened' in Dusseldorf and Hamburg and Berlin and Paris and New York City." MINNESOTA REVIEW, 8, No. 1 (1968), 67-84.

How "errors of fact" in Logan's poem "A Century Piece for Poor Heine" contribute to the excellences of the poem. Reprinted in Carroll's THE POEM IN ITS SKIN (Chicago: Follett; Toronto: Ryerson Press, 1968).

978 Chaplin, William H. "Identity and Spirit in the Recent Poetry of John Logan." AMERICAN POETRY REVIEW, 2, No. 3 (1973), 19-24.

Logan "places his sense of man's tragic bondage against two equally powerful resolutions: the momentary obliteration of both dread and hope that comes through identifying himself with the dying animal, and the momentary release of the soul through identification with a creating spirit that transcends human hope and dread into grace."

979 Isbell, Harold. "Growth and Change: John Logan's Poems." MODERN POETRY STUDIES, 2, No. 5 (1971), 213-23.

Logan's earlier books showed his "ability and willingness to utilize literary allusion was nearly unlimited," but in later ones "the poet speaking to us links himself to the event with a directness quite unexpected." Isbell takes us through CYCLE FOR MOTHER CABRINI to THE ZIG-ZAG WALK.

980 Mazzaro, Jerome. "Ventures into Evening: Self-Parody in the Poetry of John Logan." SALMAGUNDI, 2, No. 4 (1968), 78-95.

In all his work Logan invites us "to move from a realm of familiar social content to direct mythic confrontation," from the everyday into mystery. The "self-parody" enters "as a way of getting rid of a socially defined, materialistic ego."

ROBERT LOWELL

(American; March 1, 1917-September 13, 1977)

POEMS

LAND OF UNLIKENESS. Cummington, Mass.: Cummington Press, 1944.
LORD WEARY'S CASTLE. New York: Harcourt, Brace, 1946.
THE MILLS OF THE KAVANAUGHS. New York: Harcourt, Brace, 1951.
LIFE STUDIES. New York: Farrar, Straus and Giroux, 1959.
FOR THE UNION DEAD. Farrar, Straus and Giroux, 1964.
NEAR THE OCEAN. Farrar, Straus and Giroux, 1967.
NOTEBOOK 1967-1968. New York: Farrar, Straus and Giroux, 1969; augmented edition, 1970.
FOR LIZZIE AND HARRIET. New York: Farrar, Straus and Giroux, 1973.
HISTORY. New York: Farrar, Straus and Giroux, 1973.
THE DOLPHIN. New York: Farrar, Straus and Giroux, 1973.
SELECTED POEMS. New York: Farrar, Straus and Giroux, 1976.
DAY BY DAY. New York: Farrar, Straus and Giroux, 1977.
SELECTED POEMS. Rev. edition. New York: Farrar, Straus and Giroux, 1977.

BIBLIOGRAPHY

981 Edelstein, J.M. ROBERT LOWELL: A CHECKLIST. Detroit: Gale Research Co., 1973.

Not seen; cited in A. Poulin, CONTEMPORARY AMERICAN POETRY (3rd ed. Boston: Houghton Mifflin, 1980), page 553.

982 Mazzaro, Jerome. THE ACHIEVEMENT OF ROBERT LOWELL, 1939-1959. Detroit: University of Detroit Press, 1960. 41 p.

Primary bibliography lists individual poems as well as collections and miscellaneous items. Secondary bibliography is not annotated but lists items under individual collections where appropriate.

BIOGRAPHY

982A Hamilton, Ian. ROBERT LOWELL: A BIOGRAPHY. New York:

Random House, 1982. 480 p. Photos.

Not seen. Announced and described glowingly in THE GRIFFIN, 32 (November 1982), 3-4.

CRITICAL BOOKS

983 Cooper, Philip. THE AUTOBIOGRAPHICAL MYTH OF ROBERT LOWELL. Chapel Hill: University of North Carolina Press, 1970. 170 p.

Searches for coherence in the body of Lowell's work, emphasizing LIFE STUDIES. "Lowell's confessional mode is not other than the principle of poetry itself: the personal touches the archetypal, becoming autobiographical myth."

984 Fein, Richard J. ROBERT LOWELL. New York: Twayne, 1970. 174 p. 2nd ed. Boston: Twayne, 1979. 223 p. Bibliogs., index.

Traces development in Lowell's work, using "extra-poetic issues" but concentrating on poems. Updated 1979 edition adds a chapter on PROMETHEUS BOUND, adds a prologue and epilogue (see below nos. 1013 and 1014), revises the chapters on individual works, removes a chapter on NEAR THE OCEAN, and, now that Lowell is dead, "evaluates and concludes." Checklist of primary books, an annotated list of Lowell's prose articles, and an annotated secondary bibliography.

985 Martin, Jay. ROBERT LOWELL. University of Minnesota Pamphlets on American Writers, no. 92. Minneapolis: University of Minnesota Press, 1970. 48 p.

Biographical critical introduction to Lowell, describing the "paradoxes" of his family lineage and the influence on his poems. "Lowell's poetic manner," Martin says, "has changed drastically during the last thirty years." Reprinted in no. 73.

986 Martz, William J. THE ACHIEVEMENT OF ROBERT LOWELL: A COMPREHENSIVE SELECTION OF HIS POEMS WITH A CRITICAL INTRODUCTION Glenview, Ill.: Scott, Foresman, 1966. 86 p. Notes.

In his introduction, "Robert Lowell--'Which Way I Fly Is Hell,'" pages 1-20, Martz explains Lowell's poetic achievement measured by the figures of Satan and Prufrock--one who dares all and one who dares nothing. He analyzes several poems to elaborate his thesis. The remainder of the book is a selection of poems and five pages of notes on the poems.

987 Parkinson, Thomas, ed. ROBERT LOWELL: A COLLECTION OF CRITICAL ESSAYS. Englewood Cliffs, N.J.: Prentice-Hall, 1968. 176 p.

The critical essays and interviews in this collection are individually annotated by Fein (no. 984).

SPECIAL ISSUE

988 MODERN POETRY STUDIES, 1, No. 4 (1970).

Articles by John R. Reed, Charles Altieri, Christopher Morris, and Robert Emmet Long. See below for annotations.

CRITICAL ARTICLES

989 Altieri, Charles. "Poetry in a Prose World: Lowell's 'Life Studies.'" MODERN POETRY STUDIES, 1, No. 4 (1970), 182-99.

On "the oppositions . . . between the fictive or mythic world of imagination and the empirical world of fact."

990 Axelrod, Steven. "Baudelaire and the Poetry of Robert Lowell." TWENTIETH CENTURY LITERATURE, 17 (October 1971), 257-74.

Baudelaire as source and influence in Lowell's work, so important as to appear in nearly every collection though Axelrod singles out specific poems.

991 ______. "Lowell's THE DOLPHIN as a 'Book of Life.'" CONTEMPORARY LITERATURE, 18 (1977), 458-74.

A close reading of THE DOLPHIN, which Axelrod thinks afforded Lowell "artistic and personal renewal." It records Lowell's unconditional acceptance of "his world and himself."

992 ______. "The Meaning of Robert Lowell's IMITATIONS." In STUDIES IN LANGUAGE AND LITERATURE. Ed. Charles Nelson. Richmond: Eastern Kentucky University, 1976, pp. 41-47.

Lowell's book is a collection of individual translations of European poems but also a long poem personal to Lowell. This paradox has been the cause of critics' difficulty and their neglect of it as a sequence.

993 ______. "Private and Public Worlds in Lowell's FOR THE UNION DEAD." PERSPECTIVES ON CONTEMPORARY LITERATURE, 1, No. 1 (1975), 53-73.

"It is the first volume in which Lowell achieved the balance, or fusion, of naked private confession and eloquent public statement which we have come to think of as his characteristic voice." Reprinted in BUCKNELL REVIEW, 22, No. 2 (1976).

994 Bedford, William. "The Morality of Form in the Poetry of Robert Lowell." ARIEL: A REVIEW OF INTERNATIONAL ENGLISH LITERATURE, 9, No. 1 (1978), 3-17.

"Lowell's achievement has been to articulate a sense of moral and political confusion, and to render that confusion as a richness and complexity of immediately-felt experience, creating poetry out of chaos without imposing an artificial notion of order." Bedford thus relates form to matter and theme in poems from LIFE STUDIES, FOR THE UNION DEAD, and NEAR THE OCEAN.

995 Bell, Vereen M. "Robert Lowell 1917-1977." SEWANEE REVIEW, 86 (Winter 1978), 101-05.

An obituary essay, observing that Lowell believed "the world's humanness was what made it cherishable in the long run and gave everything its meaning."

996 Bigsby, C. W. E. "The Paradox of Revolution: Robert Lowell's THE OLD GLORY." RECHERCHES ANGLAISES ET AMERICAINES, No. 5 (Summer 1972), pp. 63-79.

Bigsby's interpretation of the three plays in THE OLD GLORY rests on his belief that Lowell searches for "the mythical dimension behind the face of history and the mask of progress" and that he "probes the paradox whereby evil is born of goodness and the redeemer stained with other blood than his own."

997 Bowles, James Bradley. "A Strategic Analysis of Robert Lowell's THE OLD GLORY" Dissertation, University of Iowa, 1976 (DAI, 37: 4710).

A study of Lowell's scripts of his trilogy to show his "plans for shaping the experiences of audiences," with a chapter on each play and a final, unifying chapter.

998 Branscomb, Jack. "Robert Lowell's Painters: Two Sources." ENGLISH LANGUAGE NOTES, 15, No. 2 (1977), 119-22.

Kenneth Clark's comments on Rembrandt and Albert P. Ryder's comments on himself are direct sources for two sonnets in HISTORY. These are useful for "understanding Lowell's methods of writing."

999 Braybrooke, Neville. "The Poetry of Robert Lowell." CATHOLIC WORLD, 198 (January 1964), 230-37.

Lowell's use of the parable of the unjust steward is "most keenly pronounced" in LAND OF UNLIKENESS. Braybrooke illustrates with "Children of Light" and more briefly with other poems both early and late. Reprinted as "Robert Lowell and the Unjust Steward: A Study of His Poetry." DALHOUSIE REVIEW, 44 (Spring 1964), 28-34.

1000 Bromwich, David. "Reading Robert Lowell." COMMENTARY, 52, No. 2 (August 1971), 78-83.

Observations on Lowell and his critics and on Lowell's books through NOTEBOOK.

1001 Brumleve, Sister Eric Marie. "Permanence and Change in the Poetry of Robert Lowell." TEXAS STUDIES IN LITERATURE AND LANGUAGE, 10, No. 1 (1968), 143-53.

The idea of permanence and change in Lowell has basically two formulations: "Unity and multiplicity with regard to reality; timeliness and time with regard to duration."

1002 Butler, Christopher. "Robert Lowell: From NOTEBOOK to THE DOLPHIN." YEARBOOK OF ENGLISH STUDIES, 8 (1978), 141-56.

Lowell's work underwent a formal change after LIFE STUDIES, leaving "thematic sequence and plot as the crucial formal ingredients." With NOTEBOOK this new manner seemed a decline; but with THE DOLPHIN Lowell, "compromising once more with literary conventions," becomes more intelligible and lays "claim to that existential authenticity which . . . underlies confessional poetry."

1003 Clary, Frank N. "'A Great Reckoning in a Little Room': Robert Lowell's Visions and Revisions." PUBLICATIONS OF THE MISSOURI PHILOLOGICAL ASSOCIATION, 2 (1977), 53-60.

Studies Lowell's compromises and innovations in writing sonnets by examining various versions of his renditions of Rimbaud's "Le Dormer Du Val" and his revisions on other poems.

1004 Clearman, Mary. "Monster Imagery in Robert Lowell's THE DOLPHIN." PUBLICATIONS OF THE MISSOURI PHILOLOGICAL ASSOCIATION, 1 (1976), 58-67.

Examines the "dominant image [of THE DOLPHIN], the ocean-dwelling monster, in the light of its appearances in the earlier, political poems."

1005 Cooper, Philip, Jr. "Lyric Ambivalence: An Essay on the Poetry of William Butler Yeats and Robert Lowell." Dissertation, University of Rochester, 1967 (DA, 28: 2241).

Studies ambivalence as a poetic principle, beginning with Yeats's play PURGATORY and applying what is learned there to Lowell's poems.

1006 Davie, Donald. "Lowell." PARNASSUS, 2, No. 1 (1973), 49-57.

Raises objections to the kind of writing exhibited in NOTEBOOK, HISTORY, THE DOLPHIN, and FOR LIZZIE AND HARRIET and then replies to these objections. "Lowell, because he has been famous for so long, has to go to desperate lengths so as not to write with his avidly interested public in mind." Reprinted in no. 307.

1007 Doyno, Victor. "Poetic Language and Transformation." STYLE, 1, No. 2 (1967), 151-57.

Considers the relationship of Lowell's poem "1790 (From the Memoirs of General Thiebault)" to the actual passage in the MEMOIRS, concentrating on his use of language.

1008 Druska, John. "Aspects of Robert Lowell: For Some, a Kind of American Yeats." COMMONWEAL, 104, No. 25 (9 December 1977), 783-88.

Sets Lowell's position among his contemporaries, points to Lowell's autobiographical center in his work, and muses on who, now that he is gone, will continue the "intellectual tradition."

1009 Eddins, Dwight. "Poet and State in the Verse of Robert Lowell." TEXAS STUDIES IN LANGUAGE AND LITERATURE, 15, No. 2 (1973), 371-86.

Eddins shows that Lowell's early concerns about political realities and the poet's role in the world continued through the poetry labeled "confessional," which label "has obscured . . . the continuity of his focus upon the state, and the complex changes of attitude which form the continuum."

1010 Elton, William. "A Note on Robert Lowell." POETRY, 71, No. 3 (December 1947), 138-40.

Lowell shows signs of promise in his LORD WEARY'S CASTLE.

1011 Estrin, Mark W. "Robert Lowell's BENITO CERENO." MODERN DRAMA, 15, No. 4 (1973), 411-26.

Estrin first interprets what Melville was about and then what Lowell has made of Melville's tale. For him, Lowell "explores . . . the racial conflict in the national experience." The play reminds us also "of the violence that has permeated so many aspects of life in America in the 60s and early 70s."

1012 Eulert, Donald. "Robert Lowell and W.C. Williams: Sterility in 'Central Park.'" ELN, 5, No. 2 (1967), 129-35.

Compares Lowell's "Central Park" with Williams' "Sunday in the Park," showing how close Lowell's method is to Williams'.

1013 Fein, Richard J. "Looking for Robert Lowell in Boston." LITERARY REVIEW, 21, No. 3 (1978), 285-303.

Used in no. 984, 2nd edition, as "Epilogue," pages 184-99, with very few changes: a paragraph added or removed and for some reason a shift from the southeast corner of Boston Common to the northeast. Fein describes a walk in Boston, musing on Lowell, his life there, his poems as prompted by streets, monuments, and edifices, and the meaning of lines now expanded or clarified. Reprinted in no. 984.

1014 ______. "Memories of Brooklyn and Robert Lowell." BALL STATE UNIVERSITY FORUM, 12, No. 4 (1971), 20-28.

Used in no. 984, 2nd edition, as "Prologue," pages 17-27, with only minor changes. Fein reminisces about his first reading of LORD WEARY'S CASTLE and his early reading of Lowell. Later reading never replaced LORD WEARY'S CASTLE as his first love. Reprinted in no. 984.

1015 Ferguson, Frances. "Appointments with Time: Robert Lowell's Poetry through the NOTEBOOKS." In no. 288, pages 15-27.

On Lowell's grappling with historical time and the effect on his verse and on his thinking.

1016 Freimarck, Vincent. "Another Holmes in Robert Lowell's 'Hawthorne.'" ENGLISH LANGUAGE NOTES, 8, No. 1 (1970), 48-49.

On the appropriateness of Lowell's borrowing from Holmes's 1884 Memorial Day address for the poem "Hawthorne."

1017 Fulton, Robin. "Lowell and Ungaretti." AGENDA, 6, Nos. 3-4 (1968), 118-23.

On Lowell's translation of Ungaretti, which Fulton thinks goes "against the grain of the original."

1018 Furia, Philip. "'IS, the Whited Monster': Lowell's Quaker Graveyard Revisited." TEXAS STUDIES IN LITERATURE AND LANGUAGE, 17, No. 4 (1976), 837-54.

For an explanation of "IS" in Lowell's poem, Furia looks

to the Book of Revelation and other sources about "leviathan," including Hobbes, Melville, Job, Jonah, and Greek mythology. He weaves all of these into his interpretation of the poem.

1019 Graham, Desmond. "The Significance of Feeling: Robert Lowell's DAY BY DAY." STAND, 19, No. 3 (1978), 66-70.

Graham summarizes Lowell's early books to focus the problem of Lowell's grandiloquent rhetoric and show us how the problem is resolved formally and simply in DAY BY DAY.

1020 Haffenden, John. "The Last Parnassian: Robert Lowell." AGENDA, 16, No. 2 (1978), 40-46.

Review of DAY BY DAY. "As heir to Leconte de Lisle and his group, the Parnassians, Lowell had adopted in HISTORY impersonal rhetoric and conventional forms against the free verse utterances that the age had licensed." His return to free verse in DAY BY DAY "represents a wilful regression to the type of free-verse expression for which he first won praise."

1021 Hampton, Kirk Richard. "A Year Runs Out in the Movies: Robert Lowell's HISTORY." Dissertation, University of California, Los Angeles, 1976 (DAI, 37: 5121).

Lowell's HISTORY is unified by its central "Issue"--man's "divisiveness" versus his "desire for unity" and by "its symbolic motifs" figured by such things as "the moon, God, women, water, breath, and . . . historical figures."

1022 Hayman, Ronald. "The Imaginative Risk: Aspects of Robert Lowell." LONDON MAGAZINE, NS 10, No. 8 (1970), 8-30.

Hayman discusses most "aspects" of Lowell, who, as Lowell said of Sylvia Plath, seems to see the exhaustion, the nervous breakdowns as all "part of the imaginative risk." Surveys Lowell's career to NOTEBOOK.

1023 Lensing, George. "'Memories of West Street and Lepke': Robert Lowell's Associative Mirror." CONCERNING POETRY, 3 (Fall 1970), 23-26.

Noticing that the "I" in a Lowell poem is frequently realized through "its association with other personae in the poem," Lensing gives attention to this technique in "Memories of West Street and Lepke" and finds the poem "more sophisticated" than commonly thought.

1024 Long, Robert Emmet. "The Theatre of Political Moralism: Lowell,

Hawthorne, and Melville." MODERN POETRY STUDIES, 1, No. 4 (1970), 207-24.

Lowell's trilogy suffers because he has written propaganda.

1025 Lunz, Elisabeth. "Robert Lowell and Wallace Stevens on Sunday Morning." UNIVERSITY REVIEW, 37, No. 4 (1971), 268-72.

The faults Lowell found with Stevens' "Sunday Morning" are "metaphysical and political," and Lowell wrote "Waking Early Sunday Morning" in response to the "errors" in it.

1026 _____. "The True and Insignificant: A Study of Robert Lowell's Nature Imagery." Dissertation, Tulane University, 1969 (DA, 30: 2537).

Lowell's nature imagery reveals his view of man. In nature he sees "the continuing order and hope of reconciliation."

1027 McCabe, Jane. "Life Changed to Landscape: The Politics of Robert Lowell's LIFE STUDIES." Dissertation, Tufts University, 1976 (DAI, 38: 1391).

The politics in Lowell's LIFE STUDIES derives from his transformation of "private experience into public meaning." His descriptions of his grandfather, for example, are critical statements "about the destructive demands of our patriarchal society." But, McCabe says, he does not seem to understand women.

1028 McKain, David W. "Poetic Diction, Nonsense and Robert Lowell." Dissertation, University of Connecticut, 1969 (DA, 30: 4993).

Studies the relationship of Lowell's diction in his early poems to the "tenets of the New Criticism."

1029 Maini, Darshan Singh. "The Rhetoric of Robert Lowell." INDIAN JOURNAL OF AMERICAN STUDIES, 7, No. 2 (1977), 1-20.

Lowell's rhetoric is "a rhetoric of vision and anti-vision structured with the force of an oppressive personality." Maini studies shifts in theme and style through the several collections and finds a diminishing skill in THE DOLPHIN in that Lowell's rhetoric seems wasted on trivia.

1030 Mazzaro, Jerome. "The Classicism of Robert Lowell's PHAEDRA." COMPARATIVE DRAMA, 7, No. 2 (1973), 87-106.

Lowell's "changes" in Racine's PHAEDRA prompt Mazzaro to assess their effects on the meaning of the play and to explore some of the meanings of the term "classicism."

1031 _____. "National and Individual Psychohistory in Robert Lowell's 'Endecott and the Red Cross.'" UNIVERSITY OF WINDSOR REVIEW, 8 (Fall 1972), 99-113.

Describes Lowell's uses of and departures from history and his sources in the play and also his revisions for the acting version. Lowell's purpose in this play "is to align the national character with his own and the past with the present."

1032 _____. "Robert Lowell's 'Benito Cereno.'" MODERN POETRY STUDIES, 4, No. 2 (1973), 129-58.

On the differences of "Benito Cereno" from the other plays in THE OLD GLORY. Mazzaro explores sources and influences that may account for these differences and also comments on the critics' reactions to the play.

1033 _____. "Robert Lowell's THE OLD GLORY: Cycle and Epicycle." WESTERN HUMANITIES REVIEW, 24, No. 4 (1970), 347-58.

Shows how Lowell attempts to have his own say about the present and the future by structuring it with Thomas Morton, Nathaniel Hawthorne, and Herman Melville.

1034 _____. "The World of Robert Lowell." Dissertation, Wayne State University, 1963 (DA, 28: 4640).

On the development of Lowell's "sensibility" from LAND OF UNLIKENESS through LIFE STUDIES.

1035 Meek, Martha George. "'Mind and Murder at the Scything Prow': Energy and Form in the Confessional Poetry of Robert Lowell." Dissertation, Syracuse University, 1977 (DAI, 38: 4831).

Meek studies the "writer's relationship to his material" in confessional poetry and the "reader's relationship to that material" and concludes that "The reader's position has become comparable to Lowell's as the victim of an energy not wholly satisfied by form."

1036 Moore, Andy J. "Frost--and Lowell--at Midnight." SOUTHERN QUARTERLY, 15, No. 3 (1977), 291-95.

Lowell manages to give us both a portrait of Robert Frost and a portrait of himself in his sonnet on Frost; but, Moore says, "the reader views two men with much in common, yet who do not seem to be able to communicate in conversation despite their desire and effort."

1037 Moore, Stephen C. "Politics and the Poetry of Robert Lowell." GEORGIA REVIEW, 27, No. 2 (1973), 220-31.

Moore traces the causes of and influences on the changes in Lowell "from the poet of the suffering self . . . to the poet of the public horror."

1038 Morris, Christopher. "The Ambivalence of Robert Lowell's 'For the Union Dead.'" MODERN POETRY STUDIES, 1, No. 4 (1970), 199-206.

"Central . . . is a pervasive emotional ambivalence which finds its most anguished expressions in the author's meditations on time."

1039 Neill, Edward. "Aspects of a Dolphinarium: Robert Lowell's Subjective Correlative." ARIEL, 6 (October 1975), 81-108.

"Later poems . . . attempt to establish a collective humaneness."

1040 O'Malley, Frank. "The Blood of Robert Lowell." RENASCENCE, 25, No. 4 (1973), 190-95; rpt. from RENASCENCE, 2, No. 1 (1949).

Lowell "is a rare, an originative, a powerful genius of poetry, who has transmuted and transformed all influences, ancient and modern, all experiences into the packed, pounding pressures of his own insight and of his own--often startling--idiom." O'Malley is an admirer of LORD WEARY'S CASTLE.

1041 Perloff, Marjorie G. "Realism and the Confessional Mode of Robert Lowell." CONTEMPORARY POETRY, 11, No. 4 (1970), 470-87.

Reminders that "confession" in poetry is a convention and that we must emphasize "poetry" rather than "confessional." Perloff demonstrates how Lowell "mythologizes" his personal life for use in his poems.

1042 Purcell, J.M. "Robert Lowell: A Non-Obituary." ANTIGONISH REVIEW, 34 (1978), 93-97.

Not seen; cited in 1978 MLA INTERNATIONAL BIBLIOGRAPHY, Item 11151.

1043 Ralph, George. "History and Prophecy in BENITO CERENO." EDUCATION THEATRE JOURNAL, 22, No. 2 (1970), 155-60.

Lowell's play is not so much concerned with racial crisis as it is in presenting "his discovery of violence as the fundamental characteristic of the formative events in our national life."

1044 Reed, John R. "Going Back: The Ironic Progress of Lowell's Poetry." MODERN POETRY STUDIES, 1, No. 4 (1970), 162-81.

"When . . . the subject matter of art is more elusive than its skills . . . then some radical revision of the ordinary procedure is necessary."

1045 Remaley, Peter P. "Epic Machinery in Robert Lowell's LORD WEARY'S CASTLE." BALL STATE UNIVERSITY FORUM, 18, No. 2 (1977), 59-64.

Remaley reinforces the judgments of critics, whom he names, struck by the "epic" quality of LORD WEARY'S CASTLE, by enumerating the epic conventions employed by Lowell.

1046 _____. "Epic Spirit in LORD WEARY'S CASTLE." Dissertation, Carnegie-Mellon University, 1972 (DAI, 33: 3667).

Argues that Lowell's book is an epic and points to the numerous epic conventions he sees there.

1047 _____. "The Quest for Grace in Robert Lowell's LORD WEARY'S CASTLE." RENASCENCE, 28, No. 3 (Spring 1976), 115-22.

Lowell's protagonist in LORD WEARY'S CASTLE is a persona designated as Exile who represents "the universal moral condition of the post-World War II man" and whose struggle is "to return spiritually to God's grace."

1048 Rollins, James Barton. "The Metaphysical Tradition in Modern American Poetry: The New Criticism and Robert Lowell." Dissertation, Duke University, 1976 (DAI, 37: 4358).

The influence of Tate and Ransom on Lowell's poetry.

1049 Ross, Mitchell S. "Robert Lowell." In his THE LITERARY POLITICIANS. Garden City, N.Y.: Doubleday, 1978, pp. 212-46.

A survey of Lowell's career by one who prefers William F. Buckley, Jr., dislikes English professors, and thinks John Kenneth Galbraith among the finest literary artists of the age. Ross's subject, though, is politics, not poetry.

1050 Schwaber, Paul. "Robert Lowell in Mid-Career." WESTERN HUMANITIES REVIEW, 25, No. 4 (1971), 348-54.

Reviews NOTEBOOK against the background of Lowell's previous work and finds it "diminished" but attractive--"For Lowell's poetry can be harrowing." Schwaber uses "NOSTALGIE DE LA BOUE" as his theme for the article.

1051 Spackman, W. M. "Professus Grandia Turget." CANTO, 1, No. 3 (1977), 135-43.

Review of SELECTED POEMS (1976) and DAY BY DAY. Spackman suggests Lowell's "endless labors" are a result of "critical indecision," that he "is spiritually trapped between [the Establishment's] invention of him and how much of this he can persuade himself is nonsense."

1052 Stone, Albert E. "A New Version of American Innocence: Robert Lowell's BENITO CERENO." NEW ENGLAND QUARTERLY, 45, No. 4 (1972), 467-83.

THE OLD GLORY, of which BENITO CERENO is the climactic play, "compresses history and personal experience into a form of 'literary power.'" Stone examines the dramatic form and poetic language of BENITO CERENO in which Lowell "expresses the complexities of the historical record in the stark simplicities of image and scene."

1053 Tillinghast, Richard. "An Introduction to Robert Lowell's Recent Poetry." Dissertation, Harvard University, 1970.

Not seen; cited in COMPREHENSIVE DISSERTATION INDEX, 1961-1972, vol. 37, page 528.

1054 Tulip, James. "The Poetic Voices of Robert Lowell." POETRY AUSTRALIA, No. 39 (1971), pp. 49-57.

Assesses Lowell's achievement by starting with Mailer's picture of Lowell in ARMIES OF THE NIGHT as one in a well saying, "Now, look up!" and goes on from there to note the various voices heard in the poems over the years. In all of them, Tulip says, "is a consistency of tone that we need to see as Augustan."

1055 Twombly, Robert G. "The Poetics of Demur: Lowell and Frost." COLLEGE ENGLISH, 38, No. 4 (1976), 373-92.

Argues that Lowell's poetry is based on "a poetics of stringent social decorum, of constraints thrown upon the reader not to respond in certain ways." And "by a gesture of demur or annoyance or of deep confidentiality the speaker enjoins his audience to strict forbearance."

1056 Tyson, Hannah Connor. "The Elegiac Poetry of Robert Lowell, 1944-1970." Dissertation, Catholic University of America, 1977 (DAI, 37: 7756).

Measures fifty poems of Lowell's "against the conventional understanding of the term 'elegy' as it is used in literary criticism" and points out some departures.

1057 Vendler, Helen. "The Difficult Grandeur of Robert Lowell." ATLANTIC, 235 (January 1975), 68-73.

Annotated in Fein (no. 984), 2nd edition. Reprinted in no. 294.

1058 ______. "Lowell's Last Poems." PARNASSUS, 6, No. 2 (1978), 75-100.

Compares DAY BY DAY to Lowell's other works. Lowell ends, Vendler says, in this book "as a writer of disarming openness" which may "spoil a reader for early Lowell."

1059 Vogler, Thomas. "Robert Lowell: Payment Gat He Nane." IOWA REVIEW, 2, No. 3 (1971), 63-95.

On parallels between Lowell and Vergil, both poets in transitional states.

1060 Yankowitz, Susan. "Lowell's BENITO CERENO: An Investigation of American Innocence." YALE/THEATRE, 2 (1968), 81-90.

Describes Lowell's necessary changes in Melville's novella in order to dramatize it. Yankowitz finds only a few but thinks these significant--changes in the ending particularly illustrate Lowell's transformation of the novella to make it "timely."

1061 Yenser, Stephen Irwin. "Circle to Circle: Structures in the Poetry of Robert Lowell." Dissertation, University of Wisconsin, 1970 (DAI, 31: 773).

Published as CIRCLE TO CIRCLE: THE POETRY OF ROBERT LOWELL by University of California Press at Berkeley, 1975; see bibliography in no. 984 for description. Yenser "traces the evolution of Lowell's concept of poetic structure" and tries to account for his "vicissitudes of style and theme." He seeks to explain what Lowell meant by saying his poems are "in a sense, one poem."

1062 Zapatka, F.E. "Moreana in the Poetry of Robert Lowell." MOREANA, No. 51 (September 1976), pp. 148-52.

Parallels between Lowell and More and Lowell's frequent mention of More and historical figures around him "suggest that More must be for Lowell far more than a remote figure in English history."

MICHAEL McCLURE

(American; October 20, 1932--)

POEMS

HYMNS TO ST. GERYON AND OTHER POEMS. San Francisco: Auerhahn Press, 1959.
DARK BROWN San Francisco: Auerhahn Press, 1961.
THE NEW BOOK/A BOOK OF TORTURE. New York: Grove Press, 1961.
GHOST TANTRAS. San Francisco: Privately printed, 1964.
THIRTEEN MAD SONNETS. Milan: East 128 Milano, 1964 [1965].
MANDALAS. San Francisco: Dave Haslewood, 1965.
HAIL THEE WHO PLAY: A POEM. Los Angeles: Black Sparrow Press, 1968; rev., Berkeley, Calif.: Sand Dollar Press, 1974.
HYMNS TO ST. GERYON AND DARK BROWN. London: Cape Goliard Press, 1969.
STAR. New York: Grove Press, 1971.
SEPTEMBER BLACKBERRIES. New York: New Directions, 1974.
JAGUAR SKIES. New York: New Directions, 1975.
ANTECHAMBER AND OTHER POEMS. New York: New Directions, 1978.

CRITICAL ARTICLES

1063 See no. 62 and Author Index.

PHYLLIS McGINLEY

(American; March 21, 1905-February 22, 1978)

POEMS

ON THE CONTRARY. Garden City, N.Y.: Doubleday, 1934.
A POCKETFUL OF WRY. New York: Duell, Sloan, and Pease, 1940.
A SHORT WALK FROM THE STATION. New York: Viking Press, 1952.
THE LOVE LETTERS OF PHYLLIS McGINLEY. New York: Viking Press, 1954.
TIMES THREE: SELECTED VERSE FROM THREE DECADES. New York: Viking Press, 1960.

BIOGRAPHY

1064 McGinley, Phyllis. SIXPENCE IN HER SHOE. New York: Macmillan, 1964. 281 p.

Essays on being a housewife, which, McGinley says, "turned into a kind of autobiography." Most of these essays appeared in LADIES HOME JOURNAL, 1960-- .

CRITICAL BOOK

1065 Wagner, Linda Welshimer. PHYLLIS McGINLEY. New York: Twayne, 1971. 128 p. Bibliogs., index.

Chapter 1 illustrates the "range of effects and of thematic concerns"; 2 defines "light verse"; 3, 4, 5, and 6 take up each work chronologically to 1960; 6 includes work after 1960 and summarizes trends and assesses McGinley's "critical position."

DAVID MELTZER

(American; February 17, 1937--)

POEMS

POEMS. San Francisco: Privately printed by Donald and Alice Schenker, n.d.
RAGAS. San Francisco: Discovery Books, 1959.
THE CLOWN. Larkspur, Calif.: Wallace Berman, 1960.
THE PROCESS. Berkeley, Calif.: Oyez Press, 1965.

BIBLIOGRAPHY

1066 Kherdian, David. A SKETCH FROM MEMORY AND DESCRIPTIVE CHECKLIST. Berkeley, Calif.: Oyez Press, 1965. 9 p.

Biographical details in the descriptive sketch. Checklist has primary items: books, broadsides, poems in periodicals and books.

JAMES MERRILL

(American; March 3, 1926--)

POEMS

THE BLACK SWAN. Athens: Icaros, 1946.
FIRST POEMS. New York: Knopf, 1951.
SHORT STORIES. Pawlet, Vt.: Banyan Press, 1954.
THE COUNTRY OF A THOUSAND YEARS OF PEACE AND OTHER POEMS. New York: Knopf, 1959; rev., New York: Atheneum, 1970.
WATER STREET. New York: Atheneum, 1962.
NIGHTS AND DAYS. New York: Atheneum, 1966.
THE FIRE SCREEN. New York: Atheneum, 1969.
BRAVING THE ELEMENTS. New York: Atheneum, 1972.
TWO POEMS: FROM THE CUPOLA AND THE SUMMER PEOPLE. London: Chatto and Windus, 1972.
THE YELLOW PAGES. Cambridge, Mass.: Temple Bar, 1974.
DIVINE COMEDIES. New York: Atheneum, 1976.
MIRABELL: BOOKS OF NUMBER. New York: Atheneum, 1978.

CRITICAL ARTICLES

1067 Eaves, Morris. "Decision and Revision in James Merrill's (Diblos) Notebook." CONTEMPORARY LITERATURE, 12, No. 2 (1971), 156-65.

A description and an analysis of Merrill's novel. Eaves emphasizes structure, made up of a novelist's diary and his working pages for a novel.

1068 Guillory, Daniel L. "The Mystique of Childhood in American Literature." TULANE STUDIES IN ENGLISH, 23 (1978), 229-47.

A brief commentary, pages 243-46, on Merrill's "Lost in Translation," an autobiographical poem concerning the memory's translation of past experiences.

1069 Kalstone, David. "Transparent Things." In no. 369, pp. 77-128.

On Merrill's style, personality, and meaning in his work. A survey of his career.

1070 Moffett, Judith. "Masked More and Less Than Ever: James Merrill's BRAVING THE ELEMENTS." HOLLINS CRITIC, 10, No. 3 (1973), 1-12.

Merrill's most prominent subject is love and his major theme the mask. Moffett focuses on BRAVING THE ELEMENTS but also applies this thesis generally to his work. "After its craftsmanship, the two most salient components of Merrill's poetry are its beauty and pain."

1071 Sheehan, Donald. "An Interview with James Merrill." CONTEMPORARY LITERATURE, 9, No. 1 (1968), 1-14.

Held in Madison, Wisconsin, 23 May 1967. Merrill and Sheehan stay close to the subject of Merrill, his work, influences, attitudes toward other writers, and way of working.

1072 Sloss, Henry. "James Merrill's THE BOOK OF EPHRAIM " SHENANDOAH, 27, No. 4 (1976), 63-91; "Part 2." SHENANDOAH, 28, No. 1 (1976), 83-110.

Sloss applies strategies for reading Merrill's poem about his enchantment by a familiar spirit, with explanatory comments and explication of details.

W.S. MERWIN

(American; September 30, 1927--)

POEMS

A MASK FOR JANUS. New Haven, Conn.: Yale University Press, 1952.
THE DANCING BEARS. New Haven, Conn.: Yale University Press, 1954.
GREEN WITH BEASTS. New York: Knopf, 1956.
THE DRUNK IN THE FURNACE. New York: Macmillan, 1960.
THE MOVING TARGET. New York: Atheneum, 1963.
THE LICE. New York: Atheneum, 1967.
ANIMAE: POEMS. San Francisco: Kayak Press, 1969.
THE CARRIER OF LADDERS. New York: Atheneum, 1970.
CHINESE FIGURES: SECOND SERIES. Mt. Horeb, Wis.: Perishable Press, 1971.
JAPANESE FIGURES. Santa Barbara, Calif.: Unicorn Press, 1971.
ASIAN FIGURES. New York: Atheneum, 1972.
WRITINGS TO AN UNFINISHED ACCOMPANIMENT. New York: Atheneum, 1973.
THE FIRST FOUR BOOKS OF POEMS. New York: Atheneum, 1975.
THE COMPASS FLOWER. New York: Atheneum, 1977.
FEATHERS FROM THE HILL. New York: Windhover Press, 1978.

CRITICAL BOOK

1073 Davis, Cheri [Cheryl Colby]. W. S. MERWIN. Boston: Twayne, 1981. 178 p. Notes, refs., bibliog., index.

Chapter 1 is on biography and milieu and also early poems; chapters 2 through 5 are on the later poems; 6 is on prose; and 7 is a summary. Davis attempts to show development and unity in Merwin's work including his translations.

CRITICAL ARTICLES

1074 Anderson, Kenneth. "The Poetry of W.S. Merwin." TWENTIETH CENTURY LITERATURE, 16, No. 4 (1970), 278-86.

Traces the evolution of Merwin's style and changing point of view from THE DANCING BEARS through THE LICE.

1075 Atlas, James. "Diminishing Returns: The Writings of W.S. Merwin." In no. 288, pages 70-81.

Noting the tendency by American poets toward an unwillingness "to risk a language that would engage our imaginative energies [and therefore] to write as if words are in danger of extinction," Atlas finds Merwin "the most ambitious and unusual proponent of this school." Atlas traces these symptoms in Merwin's verse throughout his work.

1076 Benston, Alice N. "Myth in the Poetry of W.S. Merwin." TRI-QUARTERLY, 4 (Fall 1961), 36-43.

Merwin's "conception of the poet as myth maker . . . is his aesthetic premise for poetry itself." He is thus able "to write pertinently about the contemporary world without succumbing to the fallacy of assuming that his problems are unique." Reprinted in no. 258.

1077 Breslow, Stephen P. "W.S. Merwin: An American Existentialist." Dissertation, Columbia University, 1978 (DAI, 39: 2267).

An analysis of themes in Merwin's verse.

1078 Cassity, Turner. "Dresden Milkmaids: The Pitfalls of Tradition." PARNASSUS, 5, No. 1 (1976), 295-304.

Review of THE FIRST FOUR BOOKS OF POEMS. On this collection of Merwin's first books, says Cassity, "Not to put too fine a point on it, the early poems are derivative." That is the "pitfall"; in these poems "the techniques of presentation remain naive." Cassity analyzes individual poems and emphasizes technique.

1079 Davis, Cheri Colby. "Merwin's Odysseus." CONCERNING POETRY, 8, No. 1 (1975), 25-33.

On his "Odysseus" and "Memory." A flash of memory can lead to "self-awareness."

1080 _____. "Time and Timelessness in the Poetry of W.S. Merwin." MODERN POETRY STUDIES, 6 (Winter 1975), 224-36.

Discusses first the negative or "darker" aspects of Merwin's view of time (of decline and end) and then the positive aspects ("images of timelessness"). Davis believes that Merwin has "prophetic powers, which are immense."

1081 Folsom, L. Edwin. "Approaches and Removals: W.S. Merwin's Encounter with Whitman's America." SHENANDOAH, 29, No. 3 (1978), 57-73.

In THE LICE Merwin wonders "what America is," in THE CARRIER OF LADDERS "what America was." Folsom concludes, "Merwin finds the American creation to be not a creation at all, but a destruction, an imposed obliteration that he believes will be repaid in kind."

1082 Frawley, William. "Merwin's Unpunctuated Verse." NOTES ON CONTEMPORARY LITERATURE, 7, No. 4 (1977), 2-3.

Linguistic explanation of how Merwin achieves order in a poem without using punctuation.

1083 Frost, Lucy. "The Poetry of W.S. Merwin: An Introductory Note." MEANJIN QUARTERLY, 30 (September 1971), 294-96.

Comment on five poems (included), linking them to Merwin's other work. His "sensitivity to an isolation overwhelming and inescapable has affected his style." Includes some biographical details.

1084 Gordon, Jan B. "The Dwelling of Disappearance: W.S. Merwin's THE LICE." MODERN POETRY STUDIES, 3, No. 3 (1972), 119-38.

"Merwin duplicates the actual creation of the philosophical void in which depersonalization is the final product of shared fictions of man and his creator." On Merwin's ideas about time, history, and man.

1085 Gross, Harvey. "The Writing on the Void: The Poetry of W.S. Merwin." IOWA REVIEW, 1, No. 3 (1970), 92-106.

Gross tests Merwin's poetry for "competence," meaning technical skill; but in so doing, he cannot "separate Merwin's 'method' from his subjects." Looks at poems through THE LICE.

1086 Kerman, Judith Berna. "Merwin's Journey: The Poems of W.S. Merwin as a Hero-Journey." Dissertation, SUNY, Buffalo, 1977 (DAI, 38: 5481).

Subjective analysis of the quest-myth.

1087 Kyle, Carol. "A Riddle for the New Year: Affirmation in W.S. Merwin." MODERN POETRY STUDIES, 4, No. 3 (1973), 288-303.

Kyle bases her study on THE LICE. She says Merwin's "affirmation lies in the greatest of all riddles: the paradoxical nature of the accident, the reproduction through the poetic experience of the stumbling, human activity of making mistakes that turn out to be right." Among other technical matters, Kyle is interested in Merwin's imagery.

1088 Libby, Anthony. "W. S. Merwin and the Nothing That Is." CONTEMPORARY LITERATURE, 16, No. 1 (1975), 19-40.

Once a "poet of many styles," Merwin now has a "style that focuses with obsessive frequency on the subject for which it seems to have been devised: human emptiness and cultural death." Man must become nothing to become "responsive to otherness."

1089 Lieberman, Laurence. "The Church of Ash." In no. 223, pages 256-66.

On Merwin's artistry and themes. His "artistry has steadily deepened in the anger of an uncompromising honesty that pares away falsities, layer by layer, always leaving him in a condition of final exposure, vulnerability, nakedness."

1090 McFarland, Ronald E. "W. S. Merwin's 'Home for Thanksgiving.'" CONTEMPORARY POETRY, 2, No. 2 (1977), 38-44.

Sees the poem as a transitional one having affinities with his earlier "disciplined" style and also with the later "terse, often cryptic poems."

1091 MacShane, Frank. "A Portrait of W. S. Merwin." SHENANDOAH, 21, No. 2 (1970), 3-14.

An account of the changes in Merwin's methods in contrast to recurrent themes. Merwin's poems examine the paradox that the only permanence is change.

1092 Nelson, Cary. "The Resources of Failure: W. S. Merwin's Deconstructive Career." BOUNDARY 2, 5 (Winter 1977), 573-98.

Merwin's latest poetry is "of extraordinary force, a poetry that inherits the despair of the century but gives it a prophetic new form, a form that ruthlessly deconstructs its own accomplishments." Nelson contrasts the earlier poems with this recent verse, for there we have almost "a semantic glossary to the imagery of the later work." Now, as a result of such repetition perhaps, Merwin questions even "the possibility of any kind of formal perfection."

1093 Quinn, Theodore Kinget. "W. S. Merwin: A Study in Poetry and Film." Dissertation, University of Iowa, 1972 (DAI, 33: 3665).

Studies Merwin's later verse for the possibilities of a "film-poem."

1094 Ramsey, Jarold. "The Continuities of W.S. Merwin: 'What Has Escaped Us We Bring with Us.'" MASSACHUSETTS REVIEW, 14, No. 3 (1973), 569-90.

Examines THE LICE to show the "continuities" critics have overlooked for the variety. Merwin has a "deep concern with the continuities of his life as a poet and of human life in general."

1095 Roche, Thomas P., Jr. "Green with Poems." PRINCETON UNIVERSITY LIBRARY CHRONICLE, 25, No. 1 (1963), 89-104.

"Merwin set out to become a poet." Roche describes the variety of subjects and styles of his verse and translations. Checklist of primary works, pages 94-104.

1096 Slowik, Mary Helen. "The Loss That Has Not Left This Place: The Problem of Form in the Poetry of W.S. Merwin." Dissertation, University of Iowa, 1975 (DAI, 36: 8064).

Studies "the formal changes in Merwin's poetry as they relate to a quasi-religious quest for meaning and to the qualified affirmations such a quest yields."

1097 Thompson, Ruth Fosness. "The Quest for Harmony: A Thematic Analysis of the Poetry of W.S. Merwin." Dissertation, University of Minnesota, 1977 (DAI, 38: 3505).

Despite variety of form and style, Merwin's "continual search is always for the one beginning which, through its encompassing order, will bring harmony to the chaotic world of men."

1098 Vogelsang, John. "Toward the Great Language: W.S. Merwin." MODERN POETRY STUDIES, 3, No. 3 (1972), 97-118.

Merwin wants a language that will express what is "beyond the human, the silent world and the divine." Vogelsang examines the progress of Merwin's wish from early to late poems.

1099 Watkins, Evan. "W.S. Merwin: A Critical Accompaniment." BOUNDARY 2, 4, No. 1 (1975), 187-200.

Watkins suggests a critical theory for Merwin's poetic practice.

CHRISTOPHER MIDDLETON

(English; June 10, 1926--)

POEMS

POEMS. London: Fortune Press, 1944.
NOCTURNE IN EDEN. London: Fortune Press, 1945.
THE VISION OF THE DROWNED MAN. Ditchling, Engl.: Ditchling Press, 1950.
TORSE 3. London: Longmans; New York: Harcourt, Brace, 1962.
NONSEQUENCES. London: Longmans, 1965; New York: Norton, 1966.
OUR FLOWERS AND NICE BONES. London: Fulcrum Press, 1969.
THE FOSSIL FISH: 15 MICROPOEMS. Providence: Burning Deck Press, 1970.
BRIEFCASE HISTORY: 9 POEMS. Providence: Burning Deck Press, 1972.
FRACTIONS FOR ANOTHER TELEMACHUS. Knotting, Engl.: Sceptre Press, 1974.
WILDHORSE. Knotting, Engl.: Sceptre Press, 1975.
THE LONELY SUPPERS OF W.V. BALLON. Cheadle, Engl.: Carcanet Press; Boston: Godine, 1975.
RAZZMATAZZ. Austin, Tex.: W. Thomas Taylor, 1976.
EIGHT ELEMENTARY INVENTIONS Knotting, Engl.: Sceptre Press, 1977.
PATAXANDU: PROSE POEMS. Manchester: Carcanet Press, 1977.
CARMINLENIA. Manchester: Carcanet Press, 1979.

CRITICLE ARTICLE

1100 Hamilton, Ian. "Four Conversations." LONDON MAGAZINE, 4, No. 8 (November 1964), 78-82.

> Middleton describes what he thinks modernism is by comparing European writers to Anglo-American writers. The Europeans seem to be "more forward looking." He laments the lack of a true historical sense in poets writing today, acknowledges influences, but thinks these are too many to specify, and comments on some of his poems, "Male Torso," for example, which Hamilton thinks puzzling. Reprinted in no. 203.

VASSAR MILLER

(American; July 19, 1924--)

POEMS

ADAM'S FOOTPRINT. New Orleans: New Orleans Poetry Journal, 1956.
WAGE WAR ON SILENCE. Middletown, Conn.: Wesleyan University Press, 1960.
MY BONES BEING WISER. Middletown, Conn.: Wesleyan University Press, 1963.
ONIONS AND ROSES. Middletown, Conn.: Wesleyan University Press, 1968.
IF I COULD SLEEP DEEPLY ENOUGH. New York: Liveright, 1974.
SMALL CHANGE. Houston, Tex.: Wings Press, 1977.

CRITICAL ARTICLES

1101 Fitts, Dudley. "A Varied Quintet." NEW YORK TIMES BOOK REVIEW, 26 February 1961, p. 10.

"The difficulties of her verse are as uncompromising as they are inevitable." Fitts compares Miller with Herbert and Hopkins as writers of religious verse.

1102 Friedman, Norman. "The Wesleyan Poets--IV: The In-Between Poets." CHICAGO REVIEW, 19, No. 3 (1967), 64-90.

Review of WAGE WAR ON SILENCE and MY BONES BEING WISER, pages 73-79. Friedman prefers the second book because its poems seem to have "more direct human confrontation with life" and also "more natural and passionate speech." Sometimes her technique interferes with the experience to be communicated.

1103 Levertov, Denise. "Rhythms of Speech." NEW YORK TIMES BOOK REVIEW, 21 June 1964, pp. 10, 12.

Review of MY BONES BEING WISER. Miller's poems are

"spare, taut and exact." Her "nervous intensity" in some poems recalls that of Plath.

1104 Nemerov, Howard. "Younger Poets: The Lyric Difficulty." In his POETRY AND FICTION: ESSAYS New Brunswick, N.J.: Rutgers University Press, 1963, pp. 215-25.

Review of ADAM'S FOOTPRINT, pages 222-23. Nemerov likes Miller's "hard-working vocabulary, rich, strange, accurate, beautifully paced by rhetorical and rhythmic organization, the harmonies of sentence and stanza brought into unity by the kind of freehand control which is technically the first sign of a poet." He also points out some weaknesses.

DOM MORAES

(English; July 19, 1938--)

POEMS

A BEGINNING. London: Parton Press, 1957.
POEMS. London: Eyre and Spottiswoode, 1960.
POEMS 1955-1965. New York: Macmillan, 1966.
BEDLAM ETCETERA. London: Turret Books, 1966.

BIOGRAPHY

1105 Moraes, Dom. MY SON'S FATHER: A POET'S AUTOBIOGRAPHY. London: Secker and Warburg, 1968; New York: Macmillan, 1969. 242 p.

"I have tried to produce a narrative which has the same relationship to chronology as the memory has: that is, not much." Moraes' autobiography shows "the progress of a child towards being a man." Of special interest is his acquaintance with other writers.

CRITICAL ARTICLE

1106 De Souza, Eunice. "Four Expatriate Writers." JOURNAL OF THE SCHOOL OF LANGUAGES, 4, No. 2 (1976-77), 54-60.

Not seen; cited in 1978 MLA INTERNATIONAL BIBLIOGRAPHY, Item 2776.

HOWARD NEMEROV

(American; March 1, 1920--)

POEMS

THE IMAGE AND THE LAW. New York: Henry Holt, 1947.
GUIDE TO THE RUINS. New York: Random House, 1950.
THE SALT GARDEN. Boston: Little, Brown, 1955.
MIRRORS AND WINDOWS. Chicago: University of Chicago Press, 1958.
NEW AND SELECTED POEMS Chicago: University of Chicago Press, 1960.
THE NEXT ROOM OF THE DREAM: POEMS AND TWO PLAYS. Chicago: University of Chicago Press, 1962.
THE BLUE SWALLOWS. Chicago: University of Chicago Press, 1967.
THE WINTER LIGHTNING: SELECTED POEMS. London: Rapp and Whiting, 1968.
GNOMES AND OCCASIONS. Chicago: University of Chicago Press, 1973.
THE WESTERN APPROACHES. Chicago: University of Chicago Press, 1975.
THE COLLECTED POEMS. Chicago: University of Chicago Press, 1977.

BIBLIOGRAPHY

See no. 58, pages 105-07.

BIOGRAPHY

1107 Nemerov, Howard. JOURNAL OF THE FICTIVE LIFE. New Brunswick, N.J.: Rutgers University Press, 1965. 189 p.

Nemerov probes his own psyche through "reflexions," memories, and dreams.

CRITICAL BOOK

1108 Labrie, Ross. HOWARD NEMEROV. Boston: Twayne, 1980. 159 p. Notes, bibliogs., index.

Chapters on Nemerov's aesthetics (Art is "essentially religious"), his fiction, his early poetry, and his later poetry with a final summarizing assessment of his strengths and weaknesses.

CRITICAL ARTICLES

1109 Boyers, Robert. "Howard Nemerov's True Voice of Feeling." AMERICAN POETRY REVIEW, 4, No. 3 (1975), 4-9.

Boyers exemplifies Nemerov's "false" voice with "Thirtieth Anniversary Report" in order to set forth his "true" voice, which in late poetry has had to cope with "weariness of the heart." Focus is on GNOMES AND OCCASIONS. Reprinted in no. 224.

1110 _____. "An Interview with Howard Nemerov." SALMAGUNDI, Nos. 31-32 (Fall 1975-Winter 1976), pp. 109-19.

Edited transcript of a public interview, Skidmore College, March 1975. Nemerov describes how he writes and what he has been trying; comments on Auden and other poets, on poetry and politics; and explains his views on influence and style.

1111 Frederickson, Ronald Quayle. "Rhetoric in Howard Nemerov's Poetry of Wit." Dissertation, University of Utah, 1977 (DAI, 38: 5476).

Examines Nemerov's "rhetorical strategies" in seventy-seven of his poems selected for their "persuasive" qualities.

1112 Gerstenberger, Donna. "An Interview with Howard Nemerov." TRACE, No. 35 (1960), 22-35.

From a question about the audience for modern poetry, Nemerov is moved to a discussion of universities and their effect on poets: "What is a university, anyhow, but a lot of people in a library?" He responds to questions about other poets and about obstructions to writing today.

1113 Harvey, Robert D. "A Prophet Armed: An Introduction to the Poetry of Howard Nemerov." TRI-QUARTERLY, 3, (Fall 1960), 37-42.

Nemerov can integrate "complex materials by means of a mature and powerful technical equipment of diction, imagery, and rhythm." On poems through NEW AND SELECTED POEMS. Reprinted in no. 258.

1114 "An Interview with Howard Nemerov." ISLAND, 4 (November 1966), 2-8.

Held in Nemerov's Lexington home, 2 October 1966. Nemerov answers questions about writing and subjects for writing, about beauty and significance, objectivity, teaching, and audiences. He concludes the interview with, "Ideally the poet teaches you to see, not so much to think, but to see in a thinking way."

1115 Kiehl, James M. "The Poems of Howard Nemerov: Where Loveliness Adorns Intelligible Things." SALMAGUNDI, Nos. 22-23 (1973), pp. 234-57.

Kiehl touches practically every base in his overview of the poetry: Nemerov's subjects and themes, his interest in "all that is," use of language, tone, perception of reality, variety of forms, satire, dramatics and lyrics, imagery--and withal a generous sprinkling of titles and lines. Reprinted in no. 223.

1116 Kinzie, Mary. "The Signatures of Things: On Howard Nemerov." PARNASSUS, 6, No. 1 (1977), 1-57.

Review of COLLECTED POEMS and four of Nemerov's prose books. On Nemerov's career and what he has to offer other poets as well as readers of poetry. The prose books discussed also lead Kinzie to evaluate him as a critic and commentator on poetry and its nature.

1117 Mills, William Ward. "A Critical Introduction to the Poetry of Howard Nemerov." Dissertation, Louisiana State University, 1972 (DAI, 33: 6923).

Nemerov "has been preoccupied with questions that have likewise preoccupied modern philosophers: the relation between mind and matter, the universe as unity or diversity, and the source of the beautiful."

1118 Ramsey, Paul. "To Speak, or Else to Sing." PARNASSUS, 4, No. 2 (1976), 130-38.

Review of THE WESTERN APPROACHES. Describes Nemerov's "typical style, attitude, metrical convention." Ramsey thinks this may be Nemerov's best book but points out its weaknesses as well as its strengths.

1119 Randall, Julia. "Saying the Life of Things." AMERICAN POETRY REVIEW, 5, No. 1 (1976), 46-47.

Review of THE WESTERN APPROACHES. Randall compares Nemerov and Wordsworth. They "share the plain style and the same grand epistemological theme."

1120 Stock, Robert. "The Epistemological Vision of Howard Nemerov." PARNASSUS, 2, No. 1 (1973), 156-63.

Review of GNOMES AND OCCASIONS. On the development of Nemerov's "vision" from THE SALT GARDEN to GNOMES AND OCCASIONS. His poems join objects of the world to the self, "thus bringing the world out into the open and affording us insight into the self before it shatters in meaningless multiplicity."

1121 Vance, Jane Gentry. "Stylistic and Thematic Development in the Poetry of Howard Nemerov: 'Verbs of Glass and Nouns of Stone.'" Dissertation, University of North Carolina, Chapel Hill, 1975 (DAI, 37: 1544).

Studies the evolution of his style and themes.

BINK NOLL

(American; April 15, 1927--)

POEMS

THE CENTER OF THE CIRCLE. New York: Harcourt, Brace, 1962.
THE FEAST. New York: Harcourt, Brace, 1967.

CRITICAL ARTICLE

1122 Towers, Robert. "The Poetry of Bink Noll." PRINCETON UNIVERSITY LIBRARY CHRONICLE, 25, No. 1 (1963), 107-15.

Biography and personality sketch of Noll with comment on salient characteristics of his poems. A two-page checklist of primary works follows the essay.

FRANK O'HARA

(American; June 27, 1926-July 25, 1966)

POEMS

A CITY WINTER AND OTHER POEMS New York: Tibor de Nagy Gallery, 1952.
MEDITATIONS IN AN EMERGENCY. New York: Grove Press, 1957.
HARTIGAN AND RIVERS WITH O'HARA: AN EXHIBITION OF PICTURES, WITH POEMS. New York: Tibor de Nagy Gallery, 1959.
SECOND AVENUE. New York: Totem Press-Corinth, 1960.
ODES. New York: Tiber Press, 1960; rpt. New York: Poets Press, 1969.
LUNCH POEMS. San Francisco: City Lights, 1964.
LOVE POEMS: TENTATIVE TITLE. New York: Tibor de Nagy Gallery, 1965.
IN MEMORY OF MY FEELINGS: A SELECTION OF POEMS. Ed. Bill Berkson. New York: Museum of Modern Art, 1967.
THE COLLECTED POEMS. Ed. Donald Allen. New York: Knopf, 1974.
SELECTED POEMS. Ed. Donald Allen. New York: Knopf, 1974.
POEMS RETRIEVED. Ed. Donald Allen. Bolinas, Calif.: Grey Fox Press, 1977.

BIBLIOGRAPHY

1123 Smith, Alexander, Jr. FRANK O'HARA: A COMPREHENSIVE BIBLIOGRAPHY. New York: Garland, 1979. 350 p.

> A descriptive bibliography of primary works and an annotated list of works about O'Hara. Section F, pages 201-30, includes criticism, poetry, fiction, and memoirs in chronological order to 1978.

CRITICAL BOOK

1124 Feldman, Alan. FRANK O'HARA. Boston: Twayne, 1979. 172 p. Bibliog.

Feldman organizes this book by aspects of O'Hara like language, unity, subjects and themes, aesthetic goals. He stresses "O'Hara's most significant quality--a blend of personal intensity and comic detachment."

CRITICAL ARTICLES

1125 Boone, William Bruce, Jr. "Frank O'Hara's Poems." Dissertation, University of California, Berkeley, 1976 (DAI, 38: 784).

Traces O'Hara's "idea of a self" and "the exchange relations of the ego created by O'Hara in becoming a poet." Noted by Smith (no. 1123).

1126 Feldman, Alan Grad. "The Coherent Instant: An Introduction to the Poetry of Frank O'Hara." Dissertation, SUNY, Buffalo, 1973 (DAI, 34: 1276).

On how O'Hara achieves the qualities of "immediacy and honesty" in his work.

1127 Lucie-Smith, Edward. "An Interview with Frank O'Hara." In STANDING STILL AND WALKING IN NEW YORK. Ed. Donald Allen. Bolinas, Calif.: Grey Fox Press, 1975, pp. 3-26.

Held October 1965. O'Hara talks about links between poetry and painting, the avant-garde, and poets.

1128 Mueller, Lavonne. "Frank O'Hara: Going the Full Length." WEST COAST REVIEW, 7 (October 1972), 25-29.

The qualities of an O'Hara poem are similar to those of a Jackson Pollock painting: "The picture or poem is a wager kept riding on throws of the dice. Everything can be lost at any roll. When it can no longer be lost, the picture or poem is finished."

1129 Perloff, Marjorie. "Frank O'Hara and the Aesthetics of Attention." BOUNDARY 2, 4 (1976), 779-806.

Perloff explains what O'Hara thinks is important about art, her interpretation of "Music" illustrating his technique. Copious quotations from his prose show his immense good humor.

CHARLES OLSON

(American; December 27, 1910-January 10, 1970)

POEMS

Y & X. Washington, D.C.: Black Sun Press, 1948.
LETTER FOR MELVILLE. N.p.: Privately printed, 1951.
THIS. Black Mountain, N.C.: Black Mountain College Graphics Workshop, 1952.
IN COLD HELL, IN THICKET. Mallorca: Divers Press, 1953.
THE MAXIMUS POEMS 1-10. Stuttgart: Jonathan Williams, 1953.
ANECDOTES OF THE LATE WAR. Highlands, N.C.: Jargon Press, 1955.
O'RYAN 2 4 6 8 10. San Francisco: White Rabbit Press, 1958; expanded 1965.
THE MAXIMUS POEMS. New York: Jargon-Corinth, 1960.
MAXIMUS FROM DOGTOWN I. San Francisco: Auerhahn Press, 1961.
WEST. London: Cape Goliard, 1966.
THE MAXIMUS POEMS IV, V, VI. New York: Grossman, 1968.
ARCHAEOLOGIST OF MORNING: THE COLLECTED POEMS OUTSIDE THE MAXIMUS SERIES. New York: Grossman, 1970.
THE MAXIMUS POEMS, VOLUME THREE. Ed. Charles Boer and George F. Butterick. New York: Grossman, 1975.
SPEARMINT AND ROSEMARY. Berkeley, Calif.: Turtle Island, 1975.
THE HORSES OF THE SEA. Santa Barbara, Calif.: Black Sparrow Press, 1976.

BIBLIOGRAPHY

1130 Butterick, George F., and Albert Glover. A BIBLIOGRAPHY OF WORKS BY CHARLES OLSON. New York: Phoenix Book Shop, 1967. 90 p.

Descriptive primary bibliography, including section on recordings (most of which are not available to the public) and an index of Olson's published work.

BIOGRAPHY

1131 Butterick, George F., ed. CHARLES OLSON & ROBERT CREELEY: THE COMPLETE CORRESPONDENCE. 2 vols. Santa Barbara, Calif.: Black Sparrow Press, 1980. 360 p.

These letters afford insight into both poets. Presumably there are still about twenty years of letters to be published.

1132 Glover, Albert, ed. LETTERS FOR ORIGIN, 1950-1956. New York: Grossman, 1970. 143 p.

Glover captures as much as possible in print of the original flavor of these letters to Cid Corman, editor of ORIGIN.

1133 Seelye, Catherine, ed. CHARLES OLSON & EZRA POUND: AN ENCOUNTER AT ST. ELIZABETH'S. New York: Grossman, 1975. 173 p.

Olson's reflections on Pound show us how Olson thinks.

1134 Boer, Charles. CHARLES OLSON IN CONNECTICUT. Chicago: Swallow Press, 1975. 162 p.

Biographical but not biography, Boer warns: "Here is the story of Charles Olson only as he presented himself to me, or to others, at the end of his life." Numerous passages in second person are inserted into the usual narrative third-person passages.

CRITICAL BOOKS

1135 Butterick, George F. A GUIDE TO THE MAXIMUS POEMS OF CHARLES OLSON. Berkeley: University of California Press, 1978. 880 p. Photos.

Butterick supplies notes for Olson's MAXIMUS sequence, "all three volumes . . ., page by page, line by line, identifying names . . ., foreign words and phrases, and supplying the precise sources of the many literary and historical allusions and borrowings." His introduction describes the process of collecting this material, the nature of the sequence, and Olson and his family.

1136 Byrd, Don. CHARLES OLSON'S MAXIMUS. Urbana: University of Illinois Press, 1980. 218 p.

Byrd outlines "the development of the idiosyncratic and personal image of man which appears in Olson's MAXIMUS." He says this sequence "proposes a kind of action which again allows the possibility of meaningful political life."

1137 Charters, Ann. OLSON/MELVILLE: A STUDY IN AFFINITY. Berkeley, Calif.: Oyez Press, 1968. 94 p.

Charters studies Olson's book on Melville to show Olson as poet, philosopher, prophet, and unconventional critic. She rounds off her discussion with comments on Olson's other essays on Melville and reprints excerpts from his lectures at Black Mountain College.

1138 Christensen, Paul. CHARLES OLSON: CALL HIM ISHMAEL. Austin: University of Texas Press, 1979. 260 p. Notes, list of works, index.

Christensen attempts to describe the "essential Olson," to find the unifying premise of his life and work. He inspects Olson's poetics and his relation with the Black Mountain poets as well as his poems.

1139 Paul, Sherman. OLSON'S PUSH: ORIGIN, BLACK MOUNTAIN AND RECENT AMERICAN POETRY. Baton Rouge: Louisiana State University Press, 1978. 291 p.

"His push involved . . . reconceiving the nature of the cosmos and the nature of man." Paul explores the details of various aspects of Olson's life and thought, attempting to measure his accomplishments as poet, thinker, and educator.

1140 Von Hallberg, Robert. CHARLES OLSON: THE SCHOLAR'S ART. Cambridge, Mass.: Harvard University Press, 1978. 252 p.

On Olson's poetics, philosophy, themes, background, and development. Von Hallberg's interest is in the questions raised by Olson's verse rather than in the verse itself. He calls it "expository" verse.

JOURNAL

1141 JOURNAL OF CHARLES OLSON ARCHIVES, Spring 1974-- . Biannual.

George Butterick, as editor, makes available to interested readers materials from the Olson Archives at the University of Connecticut and coordinates other primary materials and works of scholarship.

SPECIAL ISSUES

1142 "Charles Olson: From Black Mountain to Gloucester." PARNASSUS, 4, No. 2 (1976), 243-76.

This special issue contains in sequence the following items: Jonathan Williams, "Am--O," pages 243-50, reminisces and prints some previously unpublished letters by Olson. Guy Davenport, "In Gloom on Watch-House Point," pages 251-59, reviews MAXIMUS POEMS: VOLUME THREE, commenting on the personality and habits of the poet. And Paul Metcalf, "A Seismic Rift," pages 260-74, observes Olson's gradual loss of "Jeffersonian" faith from volume 1 to volume 3 of THE MAXIMUS POEMS.

1143 "A Gathering for Charles Olson." MASSACHUSETTS REVIEW, 12, No. 1 (1971), 33-68.

This special issue contains in sequence the following essays which "were part of a memorial program for Charles Olson," Wesleyan University, 18 November 1970: John Finch, "Dancer and Clerk," pages 34-40, recounts anecdotes ("clerk" here means scholar). Wilbert Snow, "A Teacher's View," pages 40-44, talks about Olson at Wesleyan working on his M.A. and after. M.L. Rosenthal, "Olson/His Poetry," pages 45-57, explains "issues that Olson gets us into." And William Aiken, "A Preface," pages 57-68, discusses the critical neglect of Olson and the main themes of his poems.

CRITICAL ARTICLES

1144 Aiken, William Minor. "Charles Olson: The Uses of the Vatic." Dissertation, Boston University Graduate School, 1977 (DAI, 37: 7746).

Aiken "combines an examination of Olson's poetics with an assessment of its varied effects on some of Olson's contemporaries": Creeley, Duncan, Synder, Levertov, and Ginsberg.

1145 Apsel, Maxine. "Moral History and Modern Irony in 'There was a Youth Whose Name Was Thomas Granger.'" MARKHAM REVIEW, 7 (1978), 76-77.

Irony applied to historical documentation transforms the account of Thomas Granger's death from sermon into folk legend.

1146 Bertholf, Robert. "On Olson, His Melville." IO, 22 (1976), 5-36.

How Olson's study of Melville affected his ideas about language and existence.

1147 Bové, Paul Anthony. "A 'New Literary History' of Modern Poetry: History and Deconstruction in the Works of Whitman, Stevens, and Olson." Dissertation, SUNY, Binghamton, 1976 (DAI, 36: 3682).

Offers a "more adequate" method of reading Olson (and Whitman and Stevens) than is afforded by "the New Criticism and the Modernist critical tradition." Olson shows "that the privileged notion of a constant 'tradition' is itself a defensive trope."

1148 Butterick, George F. Introduction, THE POST OFFICE: A MEMOIR OF HIS FATHER, by Charles Olson, Bolinas, Calif.: Grey Fox Press, 1975, pp. vii-x. Photos.

Biographical background of Olson's father and mother and also of Olson as well as the background of three autobiographical stories in the book.

1149 Charters, Ann. "I, Maximus: Charles Olson as Mythologist." MODERN POETRY STUDIES, 2, No. 2 (1971), 49-60.

To Olson "myth was always causal"; it caused something else to occur. "Causal mythology is at the center of Olson's work."

1150 Christensen, Paul Norman. "Charles Olson: Call Him Ishmael." Dissertation, University of Pennsylvania, 1975 (DAI, 36: 8056).

On Olson's rejection of modern culture and advocacy of a new awareness of reality as exemplified by his theories of verse. Also see no. 1138.

1151 Dembo, L. S. "Charles Olson and the Moral History of Cape Ann." CRITICISM, 14, No. 2 (1972), 165-74.

Dembo describes the historical views that form the basis of THE MAXIMUS POEMS. The sequence is "unified by a specific reading of the history of Gloucester and Cape Ann, a history that in its stylized consideration of men and events aims not simply at the disclosure of what happened, but at the revelation of moral truth."

1152 Dorn, Edward. "What I See in 'The Maximus Poems.'" In POETICS OF THE NEW AMERICAN POETRY. Ed. Donald M. Allen and Warren Tallman. New York: Grove Press, 1973, pp. 293-307.

Subjective analysis ("I never had a taste for analysis") of Olson's MAXIMUS, or a stream-of-consciousness commentary.

1153 Ganahl, Anna Elaine. "The Informative Act: Charles Olson's Poetics."

Dissertation, University of California, Irvine, 1978 (DAI, 38: 6132).

The basis for Olson's poetics lies in acceptance of "the confusion of multiplicity." Applied to ideas, technique, and language in his work.

1154 Kenny, Herbert. "Charles Olson: A Memoir." NEW BOSTON REVIEW, 2 (Summer 1976), 25-26.

Kenny recounts some memorable meetings with Olson during the sixties--from his first interview in 1960, more intimate visits at parties and at Kenny's home, to readings at Harvard.

1155 McPheron, William Graves, Jr. "Charles Olson: Toward Another Humanism." Dissertation, University of New Mexico, 1976 (DAI, 37: 2863).

Olson's ideas are drawn from various sciences, physical and social, to formulate a different "humanism" from that inherited from the Greeks through the Renaissance.

1156 Malanga, Gerard. "The Art of Poetry XII: Charles Olson." PARIS REVIEW, 13, No. 49 (Summer 1970), 176-204.

Held near Gloucester, Massachusetts, in Annisquam, 16 April 1970. Olson maneuvers around Malanga's prepared questions, discussing his writing, history, the world today, and Malanga's marvelous questions themselves.

1157 Merrill, Thomas F. "'The Kingfishers': Charles Olson's 'Marvelous Maneuver.'" CONTEMPORARY LITERATURE, 1, No. 4 (1976), 506-28.

Finding the poem a kind of "concentrate" of Olson before "Projective Verse" [essay 1950] appeared, Merrill first examines a number of "misreadings" and then explicates the difficulties in it. Olson managed to do in this poem what he later was able to codify in prose.

1158 Navero, William Anthony. "The Rediscovery of the Usages of the Utensils and the Services (The Emergence of Mythopoeic Post-Modern Image and the Poetics of Charles Olson)." Dissertation, SUNY, Buffalo, 1977 (DAI, 38: 1393).

Includes a close analysis of Olson's APOLLONIUS OF TYANA: A DANCE, WITH SOME WORDS FOR TWO ACTORS (1951) "as a primer on the transition from modern to post-modern form."

1159 Paul, Sherman. "In and About THE MAXIMUS POEMS." IOWA REVIEW, 6, No. 1 (1975), 118-30; concluded in IOWA REVIEW, 6, No. 3 (1975), 74-96.

The first essay is on THE MAXIMUS POEMS 1-10 and the second on 11-37. Paul reflects on meaning both general and specific, on personae, and on Olson himself as aids to seeing the coherence in the poems. He attempts to illustrate and explain what is meant by "composition by field."

1160 _____. "MAXIMUS: Volume 3 or Books VII and After." BOUNDARY 2, 5 (1977), 557-71.

Describes the earlier volumes so as to fit this installment into the sequence and show its relationship to the whole. With this new sequence "his awareness of origins is not only historical but mythical."

1161 Perloff, Marjorie G. "Charles Olson and the 'Inferior Predecessors': Projective Verse Revisited." ELH, 40, No. 2 (1973), 285-306.

Shows parallels between Olson's ideas in his essay "Projective Verse" and their "probable sources" in Pound and Williams.

1162 Philip, J.B. "Charles Olson Reconsidered." JOURNAL OF AMERICAN STUDIES, 5, No. 3 (1971), 293-305.

Answers two of Olson's early critics, Gabriel Pearson and Martin Dodsworth, by responding directly to their major objections that Olson neglects the American past and evades the responsibilities of life and of the society that confronts him. Philip illustrates his points from various selections from THE MAXIMUS POEMS.

1163 Pops, Martin L. "Melville: To Him, Olson." MODERN POETRY STUDIES, 2, No. 2 (1971), 61-96.

A study of Melville's "possession" of Olson, leading to a discussion of Olson's poetics and poems. Pops calls Olson the Marshall McLuhan of the history of verse. Reprinted in no. 223.

1164 Salerno, Joseph. "Poet as Map Maker: Charles Olson's THE MAXIMUS POEMS." Dissertation, University of Michigan, 1975 (DAI, 36: 3718).

Examines the first volume of MAXIMUS to establish a general background for the major ideas and to focus on the unity of the complete work.

1165 Smith, Philip E., II. "Descent into Polis: Charles Olson's Search for Community." MODERN POETRY STUDIES, 8, No. 1 (1977), 13-22.

Two poems to Rainer Maria Gerhardt ("To Gerhardt" and "The Death of Europe") and Olson's essay on Ernst Robert Curtius "provide an important basis for understanding the communitarian idea of 'polis' in THE MAXIMUS POEMS."

1166 Sossaman, Stephen. "Olson's Sequence: The 1960 Maximus Poems." JOHN BERRYMAN STUDIES, 3, No. 4 (1977), 70-77.

On the technical characteristics of Olson's style in THE MAXIMUS POEMS.

1167 Tallman, Warren. "Proprioception in Charles Olson's Poetry." OPEN LETTER, 3rd Series, No. 6 (Winter 1976), 159-74.

PROPRIOCEPTION, according to Olson, is "sensibility within the organism by movement of its own tissues." Tallman studies Olson's aesthetics and beliefs as blended from Whitman and Pound.

1168 Tuttle, Siri. "The Stopping of the Battle: Syntactic Deviation in 3 Poems by Charles Olson." IO, 22 (1976), 37-47.

Linguistic study as a way to clarify ambiguity.

1169 Von Hallberg, Robert. "Olson's Relation to Pound and Williams." CONTEMPORARY LITERATURE, 15, No. 1 (1974), 15-48.

Von Hallberg tends to draw lines of allegiance--allegiance to Williams "means absolute opposition to Eliot" except in diction, to Pound means against Williams. He rests his arguments about the complexity of this relationship on what Pound, Williams, and Eliot say about one another.

1170 ______. "The Scholar's Art: The Poetics and Poetry of Charles Olson." Dissertation, Stanford University, 1975 (DAI, 37: 974). See also no. 1140.

On a pedagogical poetics.

1171 Wagner, Linda. "Call Me Maximus." In no. 296, pages 152-57.

Uses Olson's ideas about Melville in CALL ME ISHMAEL to explain Maximus as the purveyor of "Olson's primary beliefs." Reprinted from TRACE, 15 (June 1967).

1172 Waldrop, Rosmarie. "Charles Olson: Process and Relationship." TWENTIETH CENTURY LITERATURE, 23, No. 4 (1977), 467-86.

Waldrop explicates Olson's essay "Projective Verse" by concentrating on context (rather than on key phrases) within the essay itself and the essay in context with his other work.

JOHN ORMOND

(Welsh; April 3, 1923--)

POEMS

INDICATIONS. London: Grey Walls Press, 1943.
REQUIEM AND CELEBRATION Llandybie, Wales: Christopher Davies, 1969.
DEFINITION OF A WATERFALL. London: Oxford University Press, 1973.

CRITICAL ARTICLES

1173 Collins, Michael J. "The Anglo-Welsh Poet John Ormond." WORLD LITERATURE TODAY, 51, No. 4 (1977), 534-37.

Brief biographical-critical introduction to Ormond. Collins analyzes "Cathedral Builders" as "a fair indication of the characteristic themes and peculiar virtues of John Ormond's poetry" and glances at several other poems. Collins especially admires his craftsmanship.

1174 Hooker, Jeremy. "The Accessible Song: A Study of John Ormond's Recent Poetry." ANGLO-WELSH REVIEW, 23, No. 51 (1974), 5-12.

John Ormond at age fifty "has emerged as a major poet" with the publication of his DEFINITION OF A WATERFALL. Hooker finds his poems "both entertaining, with no superficial difficulties to hinder understanding, and profoundly appealing." He discusses Ormond's language, subjects, and themes.

1175 Jenkins, Randall. "Poetry of John Ormond." POETRY WALES, 8, No. 1 (1972), 17-28.

A brief critical biography leads into a description of Ormond's poetry, the theme of which is a "painful awareness of mortality" and a "perplexed search for the wisdom to understand it."

1176 Norris, Leslie. Review of REQUIEM AND CELEBRATION. POETRY WALES, 5, No. 2 (1969), 47-53.

Norris places Ormond among fellow poets born in the twenties and, therefore, among those touched by the inescapable influence of Dylan Thomas. He evaluates three films made by Ormond on Vernon Watkins, Dylan Thomas, and Ceri Richards and explains that the strengths of those films--namely, honesty, sensitivity, and sense of form--are also in his poems, suggesting cause and effect.

KENNETH PATCHEN

(American; December 13, 1911-January 8, 1972)

POEMS

BEFORE THE BRAVE. New York: Random House, 1936.
FIRST WILL & TESTAMENT. Norfolk, Conn.: New Directions, 1939.
THE DARK KINGDOM. New York: Ganis and Harris, 1942.
CLOTH OF THE TEMPEST. New York and London: Harper and Brothers, 1943.
RED WINE & YELLOW HAIR. Norfolk, Conn.: New Directions, 1949.
SELECTED POEMS. Enlarged ed. New York: New Directions, 1957.
WHEN WE WERE HERE TOGETHER. New York: New Directions, 1957.
HALLELUJAH ANYWAY. New York: New Directions, 1966.
LOVE POEMS OF KENNETH PATCHEN. San Francisco: City Lights Press, 1966.
COLLECTED POEMS. New York: New Directions, 1968.
SELECTED POEMS. London: Jonathan Cape, 1968.
WONDERINGS. New York: New Directions, 1971.
IN QUEST OF CANDLELIGHTERS. New York: New Directions, 1972.
A POEM FOR CHRISTMAS. Mountain View, Calif.: Artichoke Press, 1976.

BIBLIOGRAPHY

1177 Morgan, Richard G., comp. KENNETH PATCHEN: A COMPREHENSIVE BIBLIOGRAPHY. New York: Paul Appel, 1978. 174 p.

This along with nos. 1178 and 1181 completes Patchen's bibliography up to 1978. The list of periodical articles here is arranged chronologically.

1178 See, Carolyn. "Kenneth Patchen, 1934-1958: A Partial Bibliography." BULLETIN OF BIBLIOGRAPHY, 23, No. 4 (1961), 81-84.

Primary and annotated secondary bibliography arranged chronologically. The writings about Patchen are early reviews and notices and a few essays.

CRITICAL BOOKS

1179 Detro, Gene. PATCHEN: THE LAST INTERVIEW. Capra Chapbook Series, no. 40. Afterword by Henry Miller. Santa Barbara, Calif.: Capra Press, 1976. 48 p.

Conducted in early September 1967, perhaps as late as the 15th. Patchen talks about his art and about art. The two-page afterword is an excerpt from Miller's "Patchen: Man of Anger and Light," in STAND STILL LIKE THE HUMMINGBIRD (New York: New Directions, 1962). Also published as "Homage to Kenneth Patchen," OUTSIDER, 4-5 (1968), and reprinted in no. 1180.

1180 Morgan, Richard G., ed. KENNETH PATCHEN: A COLLECTION OF ESSAYS. New York: AMS, 1977. 262 p.

Smith (no. 1181) annotates each essay separately from this book except the following: Tom Lozar, "BEFORE THE BRAVE: Portrait of Man as a Young Artist," pages 193-207, a paper read at 1976 MLA convention and, I presume the first chapter of his dissertation; and Ray Nelson, "The Moral Prose of Kenneth Patchen," pages 229-52, reprinted from STEPPENWOLF, 3 (Summer 1969), placing the novels in the tradition "that emphasizes the artist's moral responsibility." Morgan includes a brief annotated guide to secondary sources, pages 258-62.

1181 Smith, Larry R. KENNETH PATCHEN. Boston: Twayne, 1978. 195 p. Bibliogs.

Chapters on Patchen's life and his view of art and criticism, his "role of poet-prophet," specific works, and his "place in American and world literature." Primary bibliography and annotated secondary list to 1978.

CRITICAL ARTICLES

1182 Cohen, Martin Steven. "Every Child May Joy to Hear." Dissertation, SUNY, Buffalo, 1975 (DAI, 36: 1495). Bibliog.

Chapter 4 is entitled "Patchen People" and discusses his "allusions and catalogues, his typographical inventiveness, and his picture poems."

1183 Lozar, Thomas Anthony. "An Introduction to the Work of Kenneth Patchen." Dissertation, University of Toronto, 1977 (DAI, 39: 2275).

Lozar shows how a sympathetic reading of Patchen's early

work, despite its faults, can lead to a greater understanding of and thus a proper appreciation for his later work.

1184 Patchen, Miriam. "Of Human Warmth and Love: Kenneth Patchen." PEMBROKE MAGAZINE, No. 6 (1975), pp. 25-29.

Mrs. Patchen describes the development of Patchen's "painted books," how they started as a special edition of THE DARK KINGDOM to defray the expenses of publishing the regular edition and continued as the technical problems interested him. His artistic aims involved "releasing the imprisoned word forms with the help of non-verbal visual factors."

SYLVIA PLATH

(American; October 27, 1932-February 11, 1963)

POEMS

THE COLOSSUS. New York: Knopf, 1962.
ARIEL. London: Faber and Faber, 1965; New York: Harper and Row, 1965.
UNCOLLECTED POEMS. London: Turret Books, 1965.
CROSSING THE WATER: TRANSITIONAL POEMS. New York: Harper and Row, 1971.
CRYSTAL GAZER AND OTHER POEMS. London: Rainbow Press, 1971.
LYONESSE: POEMS. London: Rainbow Press, 1971.
WINTER TREES. New York: Harper and Row, 1972.
THE COLLECTED POEMS. Ed. Ted Hughes. New York: Harper and Row, 1981.

BIBLIOGRAPHY

1185 Lane, Gary, and Maria Stevens, comps. SYLVIA PLATH. Metuchen, N.J.: Scarecrow Press, 1978. 144 p. Author index.

Primary and secondary bibliography to and into 1976. Books, articles, reviews, dissertations, and bibliographies in separate unannotated lists. Chronology of publications and list of anthologies containing Plath's work.

1186 Northouse, Cameron, and Thomas P. Walsh, eds. SYLVIA PLATH AND ANNE SEXTON: A REFERENCE GUIDE. Boston: G.K. Hall, 1974. 143 p.

Chronological list of works by Plath and annotated list (arranged alphabetically within years) of books and articles about her to 1973. Separate index for Plath.

BIOGRAPHY

1187 Plath, Aurelia Schober, ed. LETTERS HOME: CORRESPONDENCE

1950-1963. New York: Harper and Row, 1975. 502 p. Photos.

Introduction gives a brief account of Aurelia and Otto Plath's background and married life. Letters begin with Sylvia's arrival at Smith and end about a week before her death. They are to friends as well as family, but most are to her mother.

CRITICAL BOOKS

1188 Barnard, Caroline King. SYLVIA PLATH. Boston: Twayne, 1978. 132 p. Bibliog., index.

By examining Plath's work chronologically, Barnard discerns "a definite movement . . . toward greater concreteness of voice and imagery." The late work, she says, affirms "the special vision to which all of her work attests."

1189 Broe, Mary Lynn. PROTEAN POETIC: THE POETRY OF SYLVIA PLATH. Columbia: University of Missouri Press, 1980. 226 p. Notes, bibliog., index.

Broe sees her task with this book as "remedial: to demythologize." Chapters on "Early Fiction and Poetry," "THE COLOSSUS," "CROSSING THE WATER," and "ARIEL and WINTER TREES: The Late Poems."

1190 Butscher, Edward, ed. SYLVIA PLATH: THE WOMAN AND THE WORK. New York: Dodd, Mead, 1977. 242 p. Notes.

A collection of seventeen articles, poems, and reminiscences. Most of the articles have been annotated by Northouse and Walsh (no. 1186) and by Barnard (no. 1188). The memoirs were commissioned for the book.

1191 Eder, Doris L. THE LIFE AND POETRY OF SYLVIA PLATH. Saratoga Springs: Empire State College, SUNY, 1974. 53 p.

A study guide with an essay and study questions.

1192 Kroll, Judith. CHAPTERS IN A MYTHOLOGY: THE POETRY OF SYLVIA PLATH. New York: Harper and Row, 1976. 303 p. Notes, bibliog., index.

On Plath's themes, images, symbols, her use of myth, and her creation of myth in her late poems. Kroll attempts to correct the misreading that followed her death. "[H]er poems would mean what they do even if she had not attempted suicide."

1193 Kyle, Barry. SYLVIA PLATH: A DRAMATIC PORTRAIT. London:

Faber and Faber, 1976. 72 p.; New York: Harper and Row, 1977. 92 p.

A biographical portrait in play form based on Plath's writings and others' commentary, first presented October 1972 by the Royal Shakespeare Company. Includes Plath's "Three Women: A Poem For Three Voices."

1194 Lane, Gary, ed. SYLVIA PLATH: NEW VIEWS ON THE POETRY. Baltimore: Johns Hopkins University, 1979. 264 p. Bibliog., index.

Lane selects thirteen essays. Represented are Calvin Bedient, J.D. McClatchy, Hugh Kenner, David Shapiro, Richard Allen Blessing, J.D. O'Hara, Sister Bernetta Quinn, Lane, Barnett Guttenberg, Marjorie Perloff, Murray M. Schwartz and Christopher Bollas, Carole Ferrier, and Jerome Mazzaro. Lane gives the gist of each essay in his introduction.

1195 Rosenblatt, Jon. SYLVIA PLATH: THE POETRY OF INITIATION. Durham: North Carolina University Press, 1979. 195 p. Notes, bibliog., index.

Rosenblatt conceives of Plath's work "as a poetry of personal process in which the central development was an initiation, a transformation of the self from a state of symbolic death to one of rebirth." He criticizes the critics, describes her structures and themes, her method and imagery, and the nature of her struggle.

1196 Uroff, Margaret Dickie. SYLVIA PLATH AND TED HUGHES. Urbana: University of Illinois Press, 1979. 235 p.

Studies the two poets together, noting the influences of each on the other, or as Uroff puts it, "In this enterprise the crucial concern must be the poetic interests they nurtured."

CRITICAL ARTICLES

1197 Annas, Pamela Jeanne. "A Disturbance in Mirrors: The Poetry of Sylvia Plath." Dissertation, Indiana University, 1977 (DAI, 37: 7126).

Plath's poetry tries to "re-define" self because her "self has already been defined . . . in a way felt by the poet to be false." Treats Plath's collections of verse and "Three Women."

1198 Ashford, Deborah. "Sylvia Plath's Poetry: A Complex of Irreconcilable Antagonisms." CONCERNING POETRY, 7, No. 1 (1974), 62-69.

Plath's "single real subject is the nature of her being."

Ashford examines the images in her poems, focusing on "Three Women." She believes Plath's "suicide was for her not a cowardly act of escape but the only honorable exercise of her freedom."

1199 Balitas, Vincent D. "A Note on Sylvia Plath's 'The Hanging Man.'" NOTES AND QUERIES, NS 22 (May 1975), 208.

The source of Plath's poem is Leonard Baskin's woodcut "The Hanged Man."

1200 _____. "On Becoming a Witch: A Reading of Sylvia Plath's 'Witch Burning.'" STUDIES IN THE HUMANITIES, 4, No. 2 (1975), 27-30.

"Plath is both wary of and intrigued by the possibilities of powerful, other-worldly women who were persecuted by the same forces that threaten her personae: men, religion, and society." Her poem is "a presentation of the speaker <u>in the process of becoming</u> a witch."

1201 _____. "Sylvia Plath, Poet." Dissertation, Indiana University of Pennsylvania, 1973 (DAI, 35: 6126).

On the development of Plath's art, her roots in the Romantic tradition, and the importance of her vision.

1202 Ballif, Gene. "Facing the Worst: A View from Minerva's Buckler." PARNASSUS, 5, No. 1 (1976), 231-60.

Review of LETTERS HOME. Ballif relates details from the letters to the poems.

1203 Barnard, Caroline King. "God's Lioness: The Poetry of Sylvia Plath." Dissertation, Brown University, 1973 (DAI, 34: 5953).

Studies the change in Plath's view of death from early to late poems.

1204 Berkenkotter, Carol Ann. "Sylvia Plath: Poet and Persona." Dissertation, University of Iowa, 1977 (DAI, 39: 275).

Examines Plath's "poetic persona as a structural element," relating her novel THE BELL JAR to ARIEL and noting in late poems changes that "reveal a shift in the poet's conception of the self."

1205 Berman, Jeffrey. "Sylvia Plath and the Art of Dying: Sylvia Plath (1932-1963)." UNIVERSITY OF HARTFORD STUDIES IN LITERATURE, 10 (1978), 137-55.

On THE BELL JAR and psychiatry.

1206 Birje-Patil, J. "The Autobiography of a Fever: The Poetry of Sylvia Plath." INDIAN JOURNAL OF AMERICAN STUDIES, 5, Nos. 1-2 (1976), 10-20.

On the dominance of the death motif in Plath's poems.

1207 Boyers, Robert. "On Sylvia Plath." SALMAGUNDI, No. 21 (Winter 1973), pp. 96-104.

Review of CROSSING THE WATER. With the appearance of this collection, poems in ARIEL may now be read in broader perspective. "The figure of the demon-lady with red hair eating men . . . is considerably attenuated."

1208 Broe, Mary Lynn. "Persona and Poetic: The Poetry of Sylvia Plath." Dissertation, University of Connecticut, 1975 (DAI, 36: 7406).

In this early version of no. 1189, Broe divides Plath's career into four stages according to "her imaginative vision" and "developing craft."

1209 Buell, Frederick. "Sylvia Plath's Traditionalism." BOUNDARY 2, 5 (Fall 1976), 195-212.

Plath's self-consciousness and self-appraisal are related to "the tradition of post-Romantic, symbolist writing."

1210 Burnham, Richard E. "Sylvia Plath's 'Lady Lazarus.'" CONTEMPORARY POETRY, 1, No. 2 (1973), 42-46.

Restores some lines to the printed version from the Spoken Arts recording of the poem and speculates why they were omitted.

1211 Capek, Mary Ellen Stagg. "'Perfection Is Terrible': The Poetry of Sylvia Plath." Dissertation, University of Wisconsin, 1973 (DAI, 34: 6629). Bibliog.

Plath's poetry is "a personal struggle for freedom." Includes bibliography of uncollected poems.

1212 Dobbs, Jeannine. "'Viciousness in the Kitchen': Sylvia Plath's Domestic Poetry." MODERN LANGUAGE STUDIES, 7, No. 2 (1977), 11-25.

On the conflict between Plath's career as poet and her career as domesticated female. "Paradoxically, it is out of her domestic relationships and experiences . . . that the majority of her most powerful, most successful work was created."

1213 Donovan, Josephine. "Sexual Politics in Sylvia Plath's Short Stories." MINNESOTA REVIEW, NRP No. 4 (Spring 1973), pp. 150-77.

In Plath's fiction, choosing five stories as representative, Donovan sees that "social roles . . . express psychic dimensions of reality."

1214 Doran, Rachel S. "Female--or Feminist: The Tension of Duality in Sylvia Plath." TRANSITION: LITERARY MAGAZINE FOR A WORLD OF CHANGE, 1, No. 2 (1977-78), 14-20.

Not seen; cited in 1977 MLA INTERNATIONAL BIBLIOGRAPHY, page 183.

1215 Efron, Arthur, ed. "Sylvia Plath's 'Tulips': A Festival." PAUNCH, No. 42-43 (December 1975), pp. 65-122.

1975 MLA ABSTRACTS, Vol. 1, pages 233-34, has an abstract of each essay in this gathering, two by Efron, and one each by Brian Caraher, Robin Reed Davis, Marjorie Perloff, and M.D. Uroff.

1216 Evans, Nancy Burr. "Looking Back Over Four Years." COLLEGE ENGLISH, 35, No. 3 (1973), 240-51.

Evans gives an account, pages 245-47, of her reading of Plath and the effect on her consciousness.

1217 Ferrier, Carole. "The Beekeeper and the Queen Bee." REFRACTORY GIRL, Spring 1973, pp. 31-36.

Traces the role of the father in his various images as "colossus, drowned man, man in black and bee-keeper." Through these, Plath exorcises or eliminates "the destructive or repressive aspects of dominating male influence."

1218 Fraser, G. S. "A Hard Nut to Crack from Sylvia Plath." CONTEMPORARY POETRY, 1 (Spring 1973), 1-12.

A reading of "The Hanged Man" from a discussion at a seminar by Fraser, who describes some of the emotional attitudes aroused in his students.

1219 Gilbert, Sandra M. "'A Fine White Flying Myth': Confessions of a Plath Addict." MASSACHUSETTS REVIEW, 19, No. 3 (1978), 585-603.

A survey of Plath's work by one who was impressed from the start and who wishes to show its positive virtues. Gilbert sees Plath's dilemma as one caught between the "exigencies of the species [woman]" and "the urgencies of her own self."

1220 Gordon, Lydia Caroline. "'From Stone to Cloud': A Critical Study of Sylvia Plath." Dissertation, University of Pennsylvania, 1975 (DAI, 36: 2820).

Images of stone in THE COLOSSUS give way to water images in CROSSING THE WATER and then to cloud images in ARIEL. "The prominent theme in the final poetry is transformation to nonphysical elements, an evanescence of identity."

1221 Guttenberg, Barnett. "Sylvia Plath, Myth, and 'The Hanging Man.'" CONTEMPORARY POETRY, 2, No. 3 (1977), 17-23.

Argues that "The Hanging Man," though originating like other poems in personal experience, has as "its thematic concern . . . the fate of the poet and of the creative spirit."

1222 Hakeem, A. "Sylvia Plath's 'Elm' and Munch's 'The Scream.'" ENGLISH STUDIES, 55, No. 6 (1974), 531-37.

Discusses parallels between the poem and the painting.

1223 Hardy, Barbara. "The Poetry of Sylvia Plath." In her THE ADVANTAGE OF LYRIC: ESSAYS ON FEELING IN POETRY. Bloomington: Indiana University Press, 1977, pp. 121-40.

Studies the complexity and depth of feelings expressed in several poems, including "Nick and the Candlestick" and other poems in THE COLOSSUS and ARIEL.

1224 Herman, Judith B. "Plath's 'Daddy' and the Myth of Tereus and Philomela." NOTES ON CONTEMPORARY LITERATURE, 7, No. 1 (1977), 9-10.

In the lines referring to the speaker's effort to talk there is an allusion to Philomela, thus heightening "the ideas of violence and victimage which are its theme."

1225 ______. "Reflections on a Kitchen Table: A Note on Sylvia Plath's 'Black Rook in Rainy Weather.'" NOTES ON CONTEMPORARY LITERATURE, 7, No. 5 (1977), 5.

Notes some parallels between the poem and Lily Briscoe's meditations on a chair and table in TO THE LIGHTHOUSE.

1226 Hobsbaum, Philip. "The Temptation of Giant Despair." HUDSON REVIEW, 25 (Winter 1972-73), 597-612.

Review of THE SAVAGE GOD by A. Alvarez. Hobsbaum disagrees with Alvarez's thesis about Plath and her suicide.

1227 Hughes, Ted. Introduction, JOHNNY PANIC AND THE BIBLE OF DREAMS, by Sylvia Plath. New York: Harper and Row, 1979, pp. 1-9.

Hughes describes Plath's writing habits relating her numerous prose pieces, particularly some of those collected in this volume. He assesses strengths and weaknesses.

1228 Kamel, Rose. "'A Self to Discover': Sylvia Plath's Bee Cycle Poems." MODERN POETRY STUDIES, 4, No. 3 (1973), 304-18.

Though less directly than other Plath poems, the bee poems do reflect the theme of "survival as destiny." The changes and shifts of personae tend to emphasize "the dialectical urgency of survival and extinction and . . . our awareness of the problematical quality of woman's existence."

1229 Kinzie, Mary. "A New Life and Other Plath Controversies." AMERICAN POETRY REVIEW, 5, No. 2 (1976), 5-8.

Review of SYLVIA PLATH: METHOD AND MADNESS (1976) by Edward Butscher and LETTERS HOME. Kinzie finds Butscher's book "unpalatable" and offensive, since he must portray a real person from incomplete evidence because husband and brother refused to contribute. She finds the letters more helpful, but "overstatement is the consistent mode of expression." Kinzie also gives her own analysis of Plath's personality.

1230 Kroll, Judith. "Chapters in a Mythology: The Poetic Vision of Sylvia Plath." Dissertation, Yale University, 1974 (DAI, 38: 806).

An early version of no. 1192.

1231 Krook, Dorothea. "Recollections of Sylvia Plath." CRITICAL QUARTERLY, 18 (Winter 1976), 5-14.

Krook knew Plath at Cambridge and later as teacher and friend; thus her recollections contribute information about Plath in the middle and late fifties. Reprinted in no. 1190, pp. 49-60.

1232 Lane, Gary Martin. "Sylvia Plath's 'The Hanging Man': A Further Note." CONTEMPORARY POETRY, 2 (Spring 1975), 40-43.

Lane relates the "blue volts" of line 2 to electroconvulsive therapy received by Plath in 1953.

1233 Levy, Laurie. "Outside the Bell Jar." OHIO REVIEW, 14 (Spring 1973), 67-73.

Reminiscences of Sylvia Plath as guest editor of MADEMOISELLE by another guest editor. Levy feels she was left out of THE BELL JAR though other women in their group of twenty are recognizable. Reprinted in no. 1190.

1234 Lindberg-Seyersted, Brita. "Notes on Three Poems by Sylvia Plath." EDDA, 74 (1974), 47-54.

"Watercolour of Grantchester Meadows" is an idyllic view punctured by the irony of real nature's indifference. "Two Campers in Cloud Country" is an effort to escape the self that may lead to a loss of self. "Daddy" is a "fiction" and not necessarily autobiographical.

1235 ______. "On Sylvia Plath's Poetry." EDDA, 72 (1972), 54-59.

Points out a need for more careful and scholarly criticism of Plath and uses that as a basis for evaluating Ingrid Melander's dissertation, "The Poetry of Sylvia Plath: A Study of Themes," University of Gothenburg, 1971 (annotated in no. 1186)

1236 McCann, Janet. "Sylvia Plath's Bee Poems." SOUTH AND WEST, 14, No. 4 (1978), 28-36.

In these Plath shows a different attitude toward her father from that of earlier poems like "Daddy." In the bee poems her father "has been sublimated into the bees; . . . they are the good/evil masculine principle."

1237 McClatchy, J.D. "Staring from Her Hood of Bone: Adjusting to Sylvia Plath." In no. 288, pages 155-56.

Tries to give a more realistic evaluation of Plath's work than the extravagant praise of earlier critics. Her suicide, McClatchy says, "led most critics to assume a greater degree of fulfilment and completion in her work than it can justly claim."

1238 McKay, D.F. "Aspects of Energy in the Poetry of Dylan Thomas and Sylvia Plath." CRITICAL QUARTERLY, 16, No. 1 (1974), 53-67.

"Both Thomas and Plath demonstrate a desire to regain the simultaneity of experience by the strategic manipulation of language: to bring together dancer, the act of dancing and the dance." Most examples are from Plath.

1239 Malmberg, Carole. "Sylvia Plath: The Unity of Desolation." DENVER QUARTERLY, 8, No. 2 (1973), 113-22.

Plath's early poems ask for the participation of a reader, betokened by the presence of "conventional poetic gestures--metrics, rhyme, and so on." But her later ones do not. Malmberg shows the process of the change.

1240 Martin, Wendy. "'God's Lioness'--Sylvia Plath, Her Prose and Poetry." WOMEN'S STUDIES, 1 (1973), 191-98.

Biographical criticism of Plath's work. Martin believes her a pioneer who wrote of her emotions without disguising them and thereby challenged the conventions of the lady-like gentility required for women writers.

1241 Meissner, William. "The Opening of the Flower: The Revelation of Suffering in Sylvia Plath's 'Tulips.'" CONTEMPORARY POETRY, 1 (Spring 1973), 13-17.

"Tulips" reveals Plath's "gloom brought about by pain and disillusionment." In the poem she is caught between the "sorrow of living" and "the torment of inevitable death."

1242 Milliner, Gladys W. "The Tragic Imperative: THE AWAKENING and THE BELL JAR." MARY WOLLSTONECRAFT NEWSLETTER, 2 (1973), 21-27.

Comparisons of the plights of the protagonists in these novels show that there has been "little change in the status of women between the Victorian age and the modern age."

1243 Mollinger, Robert N. "Sylvia Plath's 'Private Ground.'" NOTES ON CONTEMPORARY LITERATURE, 5, No. 2 (1975), 14-15.

Although this poem may seem to be about life because the speaker rescues some dying carp, it is really about death as can be seen in the imagery.

1244 _____. "A Symbolic Complex: Images of Death and Daddy in the Poetry of Sylvia Plath." DESCANT, 19, No. 2(1975), 44-52.

An analysis of the imagery relating to death behind which "lies the father." Apparently disparate images all point to death in Plath's work.

1245 Nance, Guinevara A., and Judith P. Jones. "Doing Away with Daddy: Exorcism and Sympathetic Magic in Plath's Poetry." CONCERNING POETRY, 11, No. 1 (1978), 75-81.

Some readers have considered "Daddy" a ritualistic murder,

but Plath's "methods . . . are more akin to magic . . . , a combination of exorcism and sympathetic magic that she works to dispossess herself of her own fantasies."

1246 Nguyen, Thanh-Binh. "A Stylistic Analysis of Sylvia Plath's Semantics." LANGUAGE AND STYLE, 11 (1978), 69-81.

A linguistic study of "Fever 103."

1247 Oates, Joyce Carol. "The Death Throes of Romanticism: The Poems of Sylvia Plath." SOUTHERN REVIEW, 9 (Summer 1973), 501-22.

Sylvia Plath's poems reveal an increasingly isolated and alienated person, not so different from the rest of us. Reprinted in Oates's NEW HEAVEN, NEW EARTH (New York: Vanguard, 1974), in nos. 223 and 1190. Reprinted versions have been slightly revised.

1248 Patterson, Rena Marie. "Sylvia Plath: A Study of Her Life and Art." Dissertation, SUNY, Buffalo, 1978 (DAI, 39: 282).

On the relationship of Plath's art to the women's movement. Plath confronts "issues which the women's movement subsequently analyzed."

1249 Pickard, Linda Kay Haskover. "A Stylo-Linguistic Analysis of Four American Writers." Dissertation, Texas Woman's University, 1974 (DAI, 36: 6103).

Through a transformational analysis of Hemingway, K.A. Porter, J.D. Salinger, and Sylvia Plath (THE BELL JAR), Pickard finds more differences between pre- and post-World War II writers than between men and women writers. She describes the nature of these differences.

1250 Roland, Laurin K. "Sylvia Plath's 'Lesbos': A Self Divided." CONCERNING POETRY, 9, No. 2 (1976), 61-65.

Plath's fascination with "doubles motif" in other poems points to "the theme of moral and psychological schizophrenia in 'Lesbos'" and clears up the question of the "I" and the "you," which are "two halves of the same psyche."

1251 Romano, John. "Sylvia Plath Reconsidered." COMMENTARY, 57 (April 1974), 47-52.

Attempts to defend Plath's work against the more extravagant biographical interpretations.

1252 Rosenblatt, Jon Michael. "The Poetic Development of Sylvia Plath:

A Study in Theme and Image." Dissertation, University of North Carolina, Chapel Hill, 1975 (DAI, 36: 4497).

Studies Plath's "personal symbolism, image sequences and self dramatization."

1253 _____. "Sylvia Plath: The Drama of Initiation." TWENTIETH CENTURY LITERATURE, 25 (Spring 1979), 21-36.

Plath's poems are not notes left by a suicide but rather present "the dramatic conflict between opposed external forces on the field of the poet's body and self." Rosenblatt tries to show the chief characteristics of her work.

1254 Rosenstein, Harriet Cecile. "Sylvia Plath: 1932-1952." Dissertation, Brandeis University, 1973.

Not seen; cited in no. 1185, page 102.

1255 Scheerer, Constance. "The Deathly Paradise of Sylvia Plath." ANTIOCH REVIEW, 34 (1976), 469-80.

Taking the term from Ted Hughes's comment about poems Plath had written in 1956-57, Scheerer describes the nature and paradox of the "deathly paradise" that not only "affirms death instead of life but also . . . swallows up purpose and individuality." Reprinted in no. 1190.

1256 Schvey, Henry I. "Sylvia Plath's THE BELL JAR: Bildungsroman or Case History?" DUTCH QUARTERLY REVIEW, 8 (Summer 1978), 18-37.

Not seen; cited in JOURNAL OF MODERN LITERATURE, 7, No. 4 (1979), 796.

1257 Schwartz, Murray M., and Christopher Bollas. "The Absence of the Center: Sylvia Plath and Suicide." CRITICISM, 18, No. 2 (1976), 147-72.

Title on Contents page has "of" and first page of article has "at" in title; the sense of the essay allows either. The authors "approach Plath's art as an expression of personal style, her way of being in the world, and [they] . . . view her suicide as a convergence of actions, inner and outer." It is a psychoanalytic interpretation of her life and work. Reprinted in no. 1194.

1258 Sequeira, Isaac. "From Confession to Suicide: The Poetry of Sylvia Plath." In STUDIES IN AMERICAN LITERATURE: ESSAYS IN HONOUR OF WILLIAM MULDER. Ed. Jagdish Chander and Narindar S. Pradhan. Delhi: Oxford University Press, 1976, pp. 232-42.

The very qualities that make Plath's poems a success contributed to her self-destruction.

1259 Snively, Susan Rumble. "The Language of Necessity: The Poetry of Sylvia Plath." Dissertation, Boston Graduate School, 1976 (DAI, 36: 7445).

Plath writes of a "landscape of imperfections," which "imperfections," Snively says, "derive both from the landscape's unreconstructed and irredeemable nature . . . and the mind of the poet."

1260 Spendal, R. J. "Sylvia Plath's 'Cut.'" MODERN POETRY STUDIES, 6, No. 2 (1975), 128-34.

Explains the logic and coherence of the poem. It is "a psychological drama: the displacement of an impulse toward suicide by the renewed claims of life."

1261 Stainton, Rita Tomasallo. "The Magician's Girl: Power and Vulnerability in the Poetry of Sylvia Plath." Dissertation, Rutgers University, 1975 (DAI, 36: 2828).

Traces these "contradictory emotional states--of omnipotence and of vulnerability--from the earliest college verse . . . through the brilliant and original last poems."

1262 ______. "Vision and Voice in Three Poems by Sylvia Plath." WINDLESS ORCHARD, 17 (Spring 1974), 31-36.

"The Disquieting Muse," "Facelift," and "The Tour" illustrate "the evolution of a remarkable new voice, possessed of a self-mocking, defiant, rasping edge we have come to know as the Plath of ARIEL."

1263 Stone, Carole Barbara. "Sylvia Plath's Spiritual Quest." Dissertation, Fordham University, 1976 (DAI, 37: 2882).

Although her subject is death, Plath treats "death as a means of self-generation through which she may be reborn into a new existence." On "the evolution of Plath's attitude toward death."

1264 Talbot, Norman. "Sisterhood Is Powerful: The Moon in Sylvia Plath's Poetry." NEW POETRY (Sydney), 21, No. 3 (1973), 23-36.

Talbot emphasizes the image of the moon in her work and touches on other figures of female power. The moon is one image of "female power mobilized against the male tyranny of father, husband, priest and all the other black men."

1265 Taylor, Andrew. "Sylvia Plath's Mirror and Beehive." MEANJIN, 33, No. 3 (1974), 256-65.

Taylor argues against the idea of Plath as "a suicidal poet." Her poems show that "she brings to bear on the ambiguities of her experience very great resources of courage and honesty, a penetrating self-awareness, and a coherent, unifying, and articulating imagery. These qualities are hardly the hallmarks of suicidal withdrawal."

1266 Thwaite, Anthony. "'I Have Never Been So Happy in My Life': On Sylvia Plath." ENCOUNTER, 46, No. 6 (1976), 64-67.

Review of LETTERS HOME. Thwaite seems somewhat exasperated by what this collection leaves out; but, "One positive thing the letters do is to give the lie, with circumstantial absoluteness to those who have seen Sylvia Plath as a pioneer, or founder-member of women's liberation."

1267 Uroff, M.D. "Sylvia Plath and Confessional Poetry: A Reconsideration." IOWA REVIEW, 8, No. 1 (1977), 104-15.

Challenging M.L. Rosenthal's view of Plath (in THE NEW POETS, 1967) as a confessional poet, Uroff examines "the nature of the speaker in Plath's poems, her relationship to the poet, and the extent to which the poems are confessional."

1268 _____. "Sylvia Plath on Motherhood." MIDWEST QUARTERLY, 15, No. 1 (1973), 70-90.

In her treatment of mothering and motherhood, Plath "breaks through conventional attitudes to explore her own intense and ambivalent reactions."

1269 _____. "Sylvia Plath's Women." CONCERNING POETRY, 7, No. 1 (1974), 45-56.

Uroff attempts to detach these women from Plath herself and study them as literary figures in a poetic context. "It is the women, not the men, who survive and dominate."

1270 Vendler, Helen. "An Intractable Metal." NEW YORKER, 15 February 1982, pp. 124-38.

Review of THE COLLECTED POEMS. Vendler relates various events in Plath's life to her poems, which are printed in chronological order in this edition, and enumerates her strengths and weaknesses: "The one thing that recommends Plath to us most strongly now is her ability to change her mind when she saw a new truth." "What is regrettable in Plath's work is not the domestic narrowness of her subject matter . . . but the narrowness of tone." Vendler summarizes, "She did possess--and it gives her a claim on us--a genius for the transcription in words of those wild states of feeling which in the rest of us remain so inchoate that we quail under them, speechless."

1271 Wagner, Linda. "Plath's 'Ariel': 'Auspicious Gales.'" CONCERNING POETRY, 10, No. 2 (1977), 5-7.

Attempts to correct the misreadings of "Ariel" and other poems caused by a biographical approach. Wagner believes "we must learn to read them with an insight closer to Plath's own emphasis, and to her equally personal thematic direction." Reprinted in no. 296.

HYAM PLUTZIK

(American; July 13, 1911-January 9, 1962)

POEMS

DEATH AT THE PURPLE RIM. New York: Privately published, 1941.
ASPECTS OF PROTEUS. New York: Harper and Brothers, 1949.
APPLES FROM SHINAR. Middletown, Conn.: Wesleyan University Press, 1959.
HORATIO. New York: Atheneum, 1961.

CRITICAL ARTICLES

1272 Bewley, Marius. Review of APPLES FROM SHINAR. PARTISAN REVIEW, 26, No. 4 (1959), 651-60.

Reviewed with four other poets, Plutzik comes last in a brief paragraph, page 659. Bewley says in part, "Mr. Plutzik brings a moving, elegiac note to his modification of Whitman's spiral [an image for man's ascent used earlier], so quietly effective and sensitive that it becomes more a matter of personal sensibility than of metaphysics."

1273 Dickey, James. Review of APPLES FROM SHINAR. SEWANEE REVIEW, 68, No. 4 (1960), 660-74.

Dickey gives a paragraph to Plutzik, pages 668-69; he thinks this collection "inventive, quizzical, and varied" and an advance over previous work.

1274 Dickey, William. Review of HORATIO. KENYON REVIEW, 23, No. 4 (1961), 702-09.

Dickey finds HORATIO "An original and compelling work of art," especially impressive in its narrative language--"masterly: unimpeded, fluid, various."

1275 Friedmann, Thomas. "Time for Hyam Plutzik: "A Critique and Checklist of Criticism." THOTH, 11, No. 2 (1971), 37-46.

Plutzik's subjects are time, poetry, and his Jewishness; and though critics have thought these too narrow, Friedmann says Plutzik, convinced that poetry reveals our "unperceived daily experience," manages to show them all related to man's existence. The annotated checklist has nineteen reviews, pages 45-46.

1276 Kaehele, Sharon, and Howard German. "In Pursuit of a Precious Ghost: Hyam Plutzik's HORATIO." LAUREL REVIEW, 8, No. 1 (1968), 53-64.

"Embodied in the episodes and made immediate and concrete by the texture of the poetry are Plutzik's ideas about the self, truth, and time." A critical analysis of HORATIO.

1277 Oreovicz, Frank S. "Hyam Plutzik: The Man and His Poetry." Dissertation, Pennsylvania State University, 1978 (DAI, 39: 3575).

Sketches events in Plutzik's life to establish a context for interpretation; examines his major works, using "drafts, letters, taped interviews and comments" as background material; and concludes with a study of HORATIO, "the finest expression of his art."

1278 Porter, Kenneth. Review of DEATH AT THE PURPLE RIM. NEW ENGLAND QUARTERLY, 15, No. 2 (1942), 389-90.

Porter likes the book and hopes Plutzik's verse will appear in a more public way. Very briefly, he describes the contents and Plutzik's theme and technique.

1279 Sachs, David. "Passion without Style." POETRY, 75, No. 3 (1949), 118-20.

Review of ASPECTS OF PROTEUS. Sachs tests the book for the qualities of "passion, imagination, a sense of history and of tragedy, inventiveness, and taste," all of which he took from a blurb, and finds any claims to these exaggerated.

PETER PORTER

(English; February 16, 1929--)

POEMS

ONCE BITTEN, TWICE BITTEN. London: Scorpion Press, 1961.
POEMS ANCIENT AND MODERN. New York: Walker, 1964; London: Scorpion Press, 1965.
SOLEMN ADULTERY AT BREAKFAST CREEK: AN AUSTRALIAN BALLAD. Richmond, Engl.: Keepsake Press, 1968.
WORDS WITHOUT MUSIC. Oxford: Sycamore Press, 1968.
A PORTER FOLIO: NEW POEMS. Pakefield, Engl.: Scorpion Press, 1969.
THE LAST OF ENGLAND. London: Oxford University Press, 1970.
EPIGRAMS BY MARTIAL. London: Poem-of-the-Month Club, 1971.
AFTER MARTIAL. London: Oxford University Press, 1972.
PREACHING TO THE CONVERTED. London: Oxford University Press, 1972.
A SHARE OF THE MARKET. Belfast: Ulsterman, 1973.
LIVING IN A CALM COUNTRY. London: Oxford University Press, 1975.
THE TRES RICHES HEURES. Richmond, Engl.: Keepsake Press, 1978.

CRITICAL ARTICLES

1280 Dunn, Douglas. "Moral Dandies." ENCOUNTER, 40 (March 1973), 66-67.

Review of PREACHING TO THE CONVERTED. "Porter is more than just a 'Social Poet.' He is a tragedian who can't stop laughing."

1281 Garfitt, Roger. "The Group." In no. 327, pages 49-57.

On Porter's career and his relationship with "The Group."

1282 Jaffa, Herbert C. "Expatriate Poets." In his MODERN AUSTRALIAN POETRY, 1920-1970: A GUIDE TO INFORMATION SOURCES. American Literature, English Literature, and World Literatures in English Information Guide Series, vol. 24. Detroit: Gale Research Co., 1979, pp. 199-205.

Comments on Porter are on page 202. Having been born in Brisbane, Porter is claimed by the Australians; he is "an 'Australian' poet living abroad." Jaffa points out what is Australian about Porter and what critics have said about him.

1283 Nicklin, Lenore. "Peter Porter--An Atheist Who Prays." SYDNEY MORNING HERALD, 19 July 1975, p. 11.

An interview on the occasion of Porter's return to Australia as writer in residence at Sydney University. He comments on his beliefs and his art, including autobiographical details and some comparisons of Australians with the English. When reminded of a "bleak, biting quality" in his poetry, he replies that "to be without hope" is "very Australian." When asked why religion seems a preoccupation in his work, he says that one's death "is the lynchpin of religion and of everything else. It's the prime focus of poetry."

1284 Review of POEMS ANCIENT AND MODERN. LONDON MAGAZINE, 4, No. 1 (1965), 100-101.

Reviewer praises Porter's originality of thought and language, "his ability to write seriously without being solemn." Excerpt in no. 72.

PETER REDGROVE

(English; January 2, 1932--)

POEMS

THE COLLECTOR AND OTHER POEMS. London: Routledge and Kegan Paul, 1960.
THE NATURE OF COLD WEATHER. London: Routledge and Kegan Paul, 1961.
AT THE WHITE MONUMENT. London: Routledge and Kegan Paul, 1963.
THE FORCE AND OTHER POEMS. London: Routledge and Kegan Paul, 1966.
WORK IN PROGRESS. London: Poet and Printer, 1969.
THE MOTHER, THE DAUGHTER AND THE SIGHING BRIDGE. Oxford: Sycamore Press, 1970.
DR. FAUST'S SEA-SPIRAL SPIRIT AND OTHER POEMS. London: Routledge and Kegan Paul, 1972.
SONS OF MY SKIN: SELECTED POEMS 1954-1974. London: Routledge and Kegan Paul, 1975.
FROM EVERY CHINK OF THE ARK AND OTHER NEW POEMS. London: Routledge and Kegan Paul, 1977.
THE WEDDINGS AT NETHER POWERS AND OTHER NEW POEMS. London: Routledge and Kegan Paul, 1979.

CRITICAL ARTICLES

1285 Dunn, Douglas. "Moral Dandies." ENCOUNTER, 40 (March 1973), 67-68.

Review of DR. FAUST'S SEA-SPIRAL SPIRIT. Dunn praises Redgrove's strangeness, imagery, and skill. This review includes Donald Davie (no. 616) and Peter Porter (no. 1280).

1286 Garfitt, Roger. "The Group." In no. 327, pages 57-62.

On Redgrove's career and his membership in "The Group."

1287 Hobsbaum, Philip. "The Poetry of Barbarism." In his TRADITION AND EXPERIMENT IN ENGLISH POETRY. Totawa, N.J.: Rowman and Littlefield, 1979, pp. 310-17.

"Peter Redgrove is the most imaginative and vital poet of the last thirty years." His work is a fusion of nature and man's artifices. But, Hobsbaum says, "the proportion of poetry to obsession has been worsening over the years."

1288 Rasula, Jed, and Mike Erwin. "Interview with Peter Redgrove." HUDSON REVIEW, 28 (Autumn 1975), 377-401.

Redgrove talks about himself, his beliefs, his poetic practice, and the nature of poetry.

1289 Thomas, D.M. Introduction, WORK IN PROGRESS, by Peter Redgrove. London: Poet and Printer, 1969, pp. v-vii.

Redgrove is concerned with "the point of tremulous marriage between matter and spirit," man drawn to the earth yet longing to leave it.

KENNETH REXROTH

(American; December 22, 1905-June 6, 1982)

POEMS

IN WHAT HOUR. New York: Macmillan, 1940.
THE PHOENIX AND THE TORTOISE. Norfolk, Conn.: New Directions, 1944.
THE SIGNATURE OF ALL THINGS. Norfolk, Conn.: New Directions, 1949.
THE ART OF WORLDLY WISDOM. Prairie City, Ill.: Decker Press, 1949.
THE DRAGON AND THE UNICORN. New York: New Directions, 1952.
IN DEFENSE OF THE EARTH. New York: New Directions, 1956.
THE HOMESTEAD CALLED DAMASCUS. New York: New Directions, 1963.
NATURAL NUMBERS: NEW AND SELECTED POEMS. New York: New Directions, 1963.
COLLECTED SHORTER POEMS. New York: New Directions, 1966.
COLLECTED LONGER POEMS. New York: New Directions, 1968.
THE HEART'S GARDEN, THE GARDEN'S HEART. Cambridge, Mass.: Pym Randall Press, 1968.
THE SPARK IN THE TINDER OF KNOWING. Cambridge, Mass.: Pym Randall Press, 1968.
SKY SEA BIRDS TREES EARTH HOUSE BEASTS FLOWERS. Santa Barbara, Calif.: Unicorn Press, 1970.
THE REXROTH READER. Ed. Eric Mottram. London: Jonathan Cape, 1972.
NEW POEMS. New York: New Directions, 1974.
ON FLOWER WREATH HILL. Burnaby, B.C.: Blackfish Press, 1976.
THE SILVER SWAN: POEMS WRITTEN IN KYOTO 1974-75. Port Townsend, Wash.: Copper Canyon Press, 1976.
THE MORNING STAR: POEMS AND TRANSLATIONS. New York: New Directions, 1979.

BIOGRAPHY

1290 Rexroth, Kenneth. AN AUTOBIOGRAPHICAL NOVEL. Garden City, N.Y.: Doubleday, 1966. 367 p.

Rexroth narrates his family's background and the first twenty-one years of his life. He felt that his youthful world changed, ended, with the execution of Sacco and Vanzetti in 1927 because of the subsequent division among American intellectuals.

CRITICAL BOOK

1291 Gibson, Morgan. KENNETH REXROTH. New York: Twayne, 1972. 156 p. Notes, refs., bibliog., index.

Chapter 1 is on Rexroth's "visionary esthetics in relation to his personality"; 2 on poetry of 1920 to 1940; 3 on THE PHOENIX AND THE TORTOISE and THE SIGNATURE OF ALL THINGS; 4 on BEYOND THE MOUNTAINS and THE DRAGON AND THE UNICORN; 5 on IN DEFENSE OF THE EARTH, NATURAL NUMBERS, translations and essays; 6 on THE COLLECTED SHORTER POEMS and THE COLLECTED LONGER POEMS with Morgan's assessment of Rexroth's place in poetry.

CRITICAL ARTICLES

1292 Garren, Samuel Baity. "Quest for Value: A Study of the Longer Poems of Kenneth Rexroth." Dissertation, Louisiana State University, 1976 (DAI, 37: 3623).

Evaluates Rexroth's achievement in his COLLECTED LONGER POEMS.

1293 Grigsby, Gordon K. "The Presence of Reality: The Poetry of Kenneth Rexroth." ANTIOCH REVIEW, 31, No. 3 (1971), 405-22.

Discusses the development of Rexroth's independent, personal style--working his way "through the modish [and] overcooked" to "clarity, honesty, a personal idiom."

1294 McKenzie, James, and Robert W. Lewis. "'That Rexroth--He'll Argue You into Anything': An Interview with Kenneth Rexroth." NORTH DAKOTA QUARTERLY, 44, No. 3 (1976), 7-33.

Held at Grand Forks, North Dakota, 22 March 1974. A relaxed, conversational interview, discussing American Indians, culture, art, poets in America and their knowledge of one another, and, as the tape ran out, the democratization of poetry.

1295 Odell, Ling Chung. "Kenneth Rexroth and Chinese Poetry Translation, Imitation, and Adaptation." Dissertation, University of Wisconsin, 1972 (DAI, 33: 2338).

Odell discusses the background of Rexroth's experience and assesses the merits of his translations in an effort to explain his success at working with "a tradition in many aspects very alien from the 20th century American poetry."

1296 Parkinson, Thomas. "Kenneth Rexroth, Poet." OHIO REVIEW, 17, No. 2 (1976), 54-67.

Parkinson tries to cut through the polemical treatments of Rexroth as a social critic or politician and demonstrate what he does as a poet. The concentration here is on THE PHOENIX AND THE TORTOISE as only an introduction to Rexroth, whose poetry is "diverse and rich beyond the limits of any single book."

1297 Sakurai, Emiko. "The Oriental Tradition in the Poetry of Kenneth Rexroth." Dissertation, University of Alabama, 1973 (DAI, 34: 2577).

Although the effect on Rexroth "of his contact with the Oriental tradition," both Japanese and Chinese, is considerable, Sakurai believes he "relied heavily on other people's renderings for his reconstruction rather than use the originals."

1298 Woodcock, George. "Realms beyond the Mountains: Notes on Kenneth Rexroth." ONTARIO REVIEW, 6 (1977), 39-48.

An appreciation of Rexroth rather than an analysis. He is philosopher, anarchist, and defender of culture in BEYOND THE MOUNTAINS, "Golden Section," and other works.

CHARLES REZNIKOFF

(American; August 30, 1894-January 22, 1976)

POEMS

RHYTHMS. Brooklyn: Privately printed, 1918.
RHYTHMS, II. Brooklyn: Privately printed, 1919.
POEMS. New York: S. Roth, 1920.
FIVE GROUPS OF VERSE. New York: Charles Reznikoff, 1927.
IN MEMORIAM: 1933. New York: Objectivist Press, 1934.
SEPARATE WAY. New York: Objectivist Press, 1936.
GOING TO AND FRO AND WALKING UP AND DOWN. New York: Futuro Press, 1941.
INSCRIPTIONS: 1944-1956. New York: Charles Reznikoff, 1959.
BY THE WATERS OF MANHATTAN: SELECTED VERSE. New York: New Directions, 1962.
TESTIMONY: THE UNITED STATES (1891-1900): RECITATIVE. New York: Privately printed, 1968.
BY THE WELL OF LIVING & SEEING: NEW & SELECTED POEMS, 1918-1973. Los Angeles: Black Sparrow Press, 1976.

BIBLIOGRAPHY

See no. 58.

CRITICAL BOOK

1299 Hindus, Milton. CHARLES REZNIKOFF: A CRITICAL ESSAY. Santa Barbara, Calif.: Black Sparrow Press, 1977. 70 p.

On Reznikoff's life and career, on the nature of his poetry and other writing, and on his attachment to New York City.

CRITICAL ARTICLES

1300 Alter, Robert. "Charles Reznikoff: Between Present and Past." In his DEFENSES OF THE IMAGINATION. Philadelphia: Jewish Publication Society of America, 1977, pp. 119-35.

Alter discusses Reznikoff among the "Objectivists." He concludes: "The literary enterprise of Charles Reznikoff is an instructive test case for the whole phenomenon of American Jewish writing because no one has gone farther than he in the explicit effort to be both a conscious Jewish writer and an emphatically American one."

1301 Cooney, Seamus. Introduction, BY THE WELL OF LIVING & SEEING: NEW & SELECTED POEMS 1918-1973, by Charles Reznikoff. Los Angeles: Black Sparrow Press, 1976, [pp. 15-24].

On Reznikoff's affinity to the imagists, the effect Jewishness and life in New York City had on his subjects, and the nature of his career. Cooney also mentions some of the problems of editing this volume.

1302 Dembo, L.S. "Charles Reznikoff." CONTEMPORARY LITERATURE, 10, No. 2 (1969), 193-202.

Reznikoff talks about the beginning of the objectivists and how the aims of objectivism figure in his work. He also explains his intentions in TESTIMONY. Earlier, page 157, Dembo generalizes briefly on Reznikoff and his work as an introduction to a series of interviews with objectivist poets.

1303 Feinstein, Elaine. "The Tone of a Human Voice." PN REVIEW, 5, No. 3 (1978), 31-33.

Review of BY THE WELL OF LIVING & SEEING and CHARLES REZNIKOFF by Milton Hindus. Reznikoff's "very simplicity is an essential part of his quality as a visionary poet--a visionary, determined to write what he sees without hiding or pretence." Feinstein also thinks Hindus' book very helpful.

1304 Hindus, Milton. "Poet in New York: Charles Reznikoff." NEW BOSTON REVIEW, 3 (Fall 1977), 3-4, 6.

Not seen; cited in JOURNAL OF MODERN LITERATURE, 7, No. 4 (1979), 803.

1305 Kaufman, Shirley. "Charles Reznikoff, 1894-1976: An Appreciation." MIDSTREAM, 22, No. 7 (1976), 51-56.

Kaufman discusses Reznikoff's theories related to Pound and Williams, the founding of the Objectivist Press, his poems and other writings chronologically as published, and HOLOCAUST and TESTIMONY. She also prints his last poem, "Pessimist."

1306 Roditi, Eduoard. "American Jewish Poets by the Waters of Manhattan." MIDSTREAM, 25, No. 7 (1979), 59-62.

Review of various books by Jewish writers issued by Black Sparrow Press, seven of them by or about Reznikoff. The first part of the review is an attack on Pound, an influence on Reznikoff, and then Roditi moves to an evaluation of Reznikoff's poems on Jewish themes and of his novel, THE MANNER MUSIC, which Roditi says has "the same qualities of compassion" as the poems.

1307 Zukofsky, Louis. "Sincerity and Objectification: With Special Reference to the Work of Charles Reznikoff." POETRY, 37, No. 5 (1931), 272-85.

Illustrates objectivist principles by lines from Reznikoff. "The verbal qualities of Reznikoff's shorter poems do not form mere pretty bits . . . but suggest . . . entire aspects of thought: economics, beliefs, literary analytics, etc."

ADRIENNE RICH
(American; May 16, 1929--)

POEMS

A CHANGE OF WORLD. New Haven, Conn.: Yale University Press, 1951.
THE DIAMOND CUTTERS. New York: Harper and Brothers, 1955.
SNAPSHOTS OF A DAUGHTER-IN-LAW: POEMS 1954-1962. New York: Harper and Row, 1963; rev., New York: Norton, 1967; London: Chatto and Windus, 1970.
NECESSITIES OF LIFE: POEMS 1962-1965. New York: Norton, 1966.
SELECTED POEMS. London: Chatto and Windus, Hogarth, 1967.
LEAFLETS: POEMS 1965-1968. New York: Norton, 1969; London: Chatto and Windus, 1972.
THE WILL TO CHANGE: POEMS 1968-1970. New York: Norton, 1971; London: Chatto and Windus, 1973.
DIVING INTO THE WRECK: POEMS 1971-1972. New York: Norton, 1973.
POEMS: SELECTED AND NEW, 1950-1974. New York: Norton, 1975.
TWENTY-ONE LOVE POEMS. Emeryville, Calif.: Effie's Press, 1976.
THE DREAM OF A COMMON LANGUAGE: POEMS 1974-1977. New York: Norton, 1978.

CRITICAL BOOK

1308 Gelpi, Barbara C., and Albert Gelpi, eds. ADRIENNE RICH'S POETRY. New York: Norton, 1975. 215 p. Bibliog., index of poems.

Selects poems from Rich's collections, excerpts from her talks and essays, and critical essays. Includes the critical essays listed below.

W.H. Auden, "Foreword to A CHANGE OF WORLD," pages 125-27; Rich at age twenty-one is modest and craftsmanlike, good signs for her future. Randall Jarrell, "Review of THE DIAMOND CUTTERS AND OTHER POEMS," pages 127-29; describes and evaluates two or three poems and declares Rich "a good poet who is all too good" (reprinted from YALE REVIEW, 46, No. 1 (1956), 100-103).

Albert Gelpi, "Adrienne Rich: The Poetics of Change," pages 130-48; on Rich's changes in voice and attitude (reprinted in no. 288, pages 123-43).

Robert Boyers, "On Adrienne Rich: Intelligence and Will," pages 148-60; on "the will to change" and "the variety of wills" in her verse (reprinted in nos. 223-24). Helen Vendler, "Ghostlier Demarcations, Keener Sounds," pages 160-71 (see below, no. 1323). Erica Jong, "Visionary Anger," pages 171-74; on the relationship "between poetry and patriarchy" (reprinted MS, 2, No. 1 (1973), 31-33). Wendy Martin, "From Patriarchy to the Female Principle: A Chronological Reading of Adrienne Rich's Poetry," pages 175-89; on "the evolving consciousness of the modern woman." Nancy Milford, "This Woman's Movement," pages 189-202; "I hear in her voice the nerve and swing my own lacks."

CRITICAL ARTICLES

1309 Allen, Carolyn. "Failures of Word, Uses of Silence: Djuna Barnes, Adrienne Rich, and Margaret Atwood." REGIONALISM AND THE FEMALE IMAGINATION, 4, No. 1 (1978), 1-7.

Not seen; cited in 1978 MLA INTERNATIONAL BIBLIOGRAPHY, Item 10267.

1310 Bere, Carol. "A Reading of Adrienne Rich's 'A Valediction Forbidding Mourning.'" CONCERNING POETRY, 11, No. 2 (1978), 33-38.

The themes of this poem, "the failure of language, the isolated loneliness of individuals, the paralyzing destructiveness of received ideals . . . , converge in a moving personal statement that, nevertheless, carries with it implications of our collective failures." Close-reading analysis.

1311 Brown, Rosellen. "The Notes for the Poem Are the Only Poem." PARNASSUS, 4, No. 1 (1975), 50-67.

Review of POEMS: SELECTED AND NEW, 1950-1974. "Each poem is an amazing point on the grid where individual personality and the historical moment collide."

1312 Bulkin, Elly. "An Interview with Adrienne Rich: Part One." CONDITIONS, 1 (April 1977), 50-65.

Not seen; cited in JOURNAL OF MODERN LITERATURE, 7, No. 4 (1979), 803.

1313 Chenoy, Polly Naoshir. "Dives and Descents: Thematic Strategies in the Poetry of Adrienne Rich and Ann Stanford." Dissertation, University of Utah, 1975 (DAI, 36: 2805).

Explicates poems and compares the themes of the two poets: "change" in Rich and "adaptation" in Stanford.

1314 _____. "'Writing These Words in the Woods': A Study of the Poetry of Adrienne Rich." In STUDIES IN AMERICAN LITERATURE: ESSAYS IN HONOUR OF WILLIAM MULDER. Ed. Jagdish Chander and Narindar Pradhan. Delhi: Oxford University Press, 1976, pp. 194-211.

Poems discussed express outrage at other people's lack of perspective. Chenoy places Rich in a group of revolutionary poets, addressing issues and involved "in the fight for truth and justice."

1315 Farwell, Marilyn R. "Adrienne Rich and an Organic Feminist Criticism." COLLEGE ENGLISH, 39, No. 2 (1977), 191-203.

Rich's criticism as gathered from various essays is based on "a coherent theory of feminism" and a literary theory "which attempts to relate ethics and language, text and artist, creation and relation, and ultimately art and life."

1316 Flynn, Gale. "The Radicalization of Adrienne Rich." HOLLINS CRITIC, 11, No. 4 (1974), 1-15.

Explains and enumerates the steps by which the poet has "closed the gap between her public and private selves." Flynn touches on each collection through DIVING INTO THE WRECK.

1317 Kalstone, David. "Adrienne Rich: Face to Face." In no. 369, pages 129-69.

On Rich's autobiographical style, its differences from Lowell's, and similarities to James Merrill's.

1318 _____. "Talking with Adrienne Rich." SATURDAY REVIEW, 55 (22 April 1972), 56-59.

Rich talks about the changes in her way of thinking from her first book, A CHANGE OF WORLD to THE WILL TO CHANGE; about being a woman and a poet; and about the nature and use of poetry.

1319 Morrison, Margaret. "Adrienne Rich: Poetry of 'Re-Vision.'" Dissertation, George Washington University, 1977 (DAI, 38: 2778).

In her poems of the sixties and seventies, Rich combines her urge to "re-see" everything, "to approach and re-approach what is old with fresh vision" with the urge to survive as evident in "her love of life and her love of creating."

1320 Plumly, Stanley, Wayne Dodd, and Walter Tevis. "Talking with Adrienne Rich." OHIO REVIEW, 13, No. 1 (1971), 28-46.

Held in Athens, Ohio, 9 March 1971. The subjects of discussion are the nature of poetry, the relation of actual experience to the imaginative work, oral delivery of written poems, films and poems, other poets, the future of poetry, and, inevitably, male-female roles in our society.

1321 Spiegelman, Willard. "Voice of the Survivor: The Poetry of Adrienne Rich." SOUTHWEST REVIEW, 60 (Autumn 1975), 370-88.

On unity and change in Rich's poetry over her twenty-five year career.

1322 Van Dyne, Susan R. "The Mirrored Vision of Adrienne Rich." MODERN POETRY STUDIES, 8, No. 2 (1977), 140-73.

Rich's present-day political commitment is part of a "process of shape-shifting by which this poet seeks to know herself."

1323 Vendler, Helen. "Ghostlier Demarcations, Keener Sounds." PARNASSUS, 2, No. 1 (1973), 4-33.

Vendler feels she has in Rich a poet who speaks for her and her life, whose poems are like "dispatches from the battlefield." She considers early works to show how DIVING INTO THE WRECK continues Rich's thematic concerns and advances. Reprinted in no. 1308.

1324 Whelchel, Marianne. "'Re-Forming the Crystal': The Evolution of Adrienne Rich as Feminist Poet." Dissertation, University of Connecticut, 1977 (DAI, 38: 4833).

Traces this "evolution" chronologically through Rich's poems and supplementing from her numerous prose statements.

1325 Wilner, Eleanor. "'This Accurate Dreamer': An Appreciation." AMERICAN POETRY REVIEW, 4, No. 2 (1975), 4-7.

Rich's POEMS: SELECTED AND NEW, 1950-1974 by its chronological arrangement lets us see the changes in her work over the quarter century it covers. "The measure of that change, that alchemy, is in the transformation of the central images."

1326 "Women and Honor: Some Notes on Lying." HERESIES: A FEMINIST PUBLICATION ON ART AND POLITICS, 1 (January 1977), 23-26.

Not seen; cited in JOURNAL OF MODERN LITERATURE, 7, No. 4 (1979), 804.

THEODORE ROETHKE

(American; May 25, 1908-August 1, 1963)

POEMS

OPEN HOUSE. New York: Knopf, 1941.
THE LOST SON AND OTHER POEMS. Garden City, N.Y.: Doubleday, 1948.
PRAISE TO THE END! Garden City, N.Y.: Doubleday, 1951.
THE WAKING: POEMS 1933-1953. Garden City, N.Y.: Doubleday, 1953.
WORDS FOR THE WIND: THE COLLECTED VERSE OF THEODORE ROETHKE. Garden City, N.Y.: Doubleday, 1958.
SEQUENCE, SOMETIMES METAPHYSICAL. Iowa City, Iowa: Stone Wall Press, 1963.
THE FAR FIELD. Garden City, N.Y.: Doubleday, 1964.
THE COLLECTED POEMS. Garden City, N.Y.: Doubleday, 1966.

BIBLIOGRAPHY

1327 McLeod, James Richard. THEODORE ROETHKE: A BIBLIOGRAPHY. Serif Series, no. 27. Kent, Ohio: Kent State University Press, 1973. 241 p.

Biobibliographical introduction. Descriptive primary bibliography and list of secondary materials. McLeod describes the contents or occasions when necessary but does not annotate each item. He lists reviews of critical or biographical works and also films and recordings.

1328 ______. THEODORE ROETHKE: A MANUSCRIPT CHECKLIST. Kent, Ohio: Kent State University Press, 1971. 295 p.

Descriptive list of Roethke's manuscripts, letters, and notebooks along with their locations. The largest collection is at the University of Washington; the remainder are in eighteen other "repositories" throughout the United States and one in Canada.

1329 Moul, Keith R. THEODORE ROETHKE'S CAREER: AN ANNOTATED BIBLIOGRAPHY. Boston: G. K. Hall, 1977. 254 p.

Moul's introduction discusses Roethke's "concern for the seemingly inconsequential." Moul annotates works about Roethke through 1973 but does not annotate his list of dissertations. He gives a checklist of primary works, but readers should see McLeod for full descriptions.

BIOGRAPHY

1330 Seager, Allan. THE GLASS HOUSE: THE LIFE OF THEODORE ROETHKE. New York: McGraw-Hill, 1968. 301 p.

Seager begins with the Saginaw Valley in precolonial times, continues with the history of the Roethke family, and then after establishing that background narrates Roethke's life from childhood to his death in Seattle in 1963. He describes very frankly but sympathetically Roethke's various bouts with mental illness and attempts to account for these, as he does for Roethke's creativeness, as aspects of Roethke's ambivalent personality.

CRITICAL BOOKS

1331 Blessing, Richard Allen. THEODORE ROETHKE'S DYNAMIC VISION. Bloomington: Indiana University Press, 1974. 240 p. Bibliog., notes, index.

Blessing bases his study on the material at Suzzallo Library, University of Washington, on conversations with former students, colleagues, and friends of Roethke, and on "pioneering studies" by other critics. He starts with Roethke's student days where he finds developing the vision he labels "dynamic" and then applies what he learns to an interpretation of Roethke's sequences.

1332 La Belle, Jenijoy. THE ECHOING WOOD OF THEODORE ROETHKE. Princeton: Princeton University Press, 1976. 174 p.

Roethke "defined and created in his poetry that cultural tradition in which he felt himself to be living and writing." La Belle shows how he used the tradition and furthered it in the way Eliot described in "Tradition and the Individual Talent." She has drawn on and in some cases reprinted material from her articles cited below.

1333 Parini, Jay. THEODORE ROETHKE: AN AMERICAN ROMANTIC. Amherst: University of Massachusetts Press, 1979. 203 p. Notes, index.

Parini tries "to isolate major patterns in the work, to discover the poet's mythos, and to relate his body of writing to the Romantic tradition, its proper context."

1334 Ross-Bryant, Lynn. THEODORE ROETHKE: POETRY OF THE EARTH, POET OF THE SPIRIT. Port Washington, N.Y.: Kennikat Press, 1980. 211 p. Bibliog., index.

Studies Roethke's poetry (except OPEN HOUSE) on the basis of "Roethke's vision of the rootedness of human beings in the natural world and the necessity of relationship for the life of the spirit."

1335 Sullivan, Rosemary. THEODORE ROETHKE: THE GARDEN MASTER. Seattle: University of Washington Press, 1975. 220 p. Bibliog., index.

Treats Roethke's work chronologically to show the poet's continual probing of his psyche.

1336 Williams, Harry. "THE EDGE IS WHAT I HAVE": THEODORE ROETHKE AND AFTER. Lewisburg, Pa.: Bucknell University Press, 1976. 219 p.

Williams summarizes the critical assessment of Roethke, studies his subjects and themes in the long poems, and suggests the lines of his influence on contemporary poets, using James Wright, Robert Bly, James Dickey, Sylvia Plath, and Ted Hughes as examples.

1337 Wolff, George. THEODORE ROETHKE. Boston: Twayne, 1981. 152 p. Notes, refs., bibliog., index.

Wolff attempts to describe and explain the unifying principle of Roethke's work and trace his overall development. He treats the work chronologically in five chapters to show the increasing complexity of his themes and the maturing of his thought. A sixth chapter offers a critical summing up.

CRITICAL ARTICLES

1338 Alkalay, Karen H. "Spiral Knowledge: A Study of the Collected Works of Theodore Roethke." Dissertation, University of Rochester, 1974 (DAI, 36: 1493).

Roethke's study of the self is "'layered' vision," in which every poem is a step on "a spiralic path."

1339 Bogen, Donald Howard. "Composition and the Self in Three Modern Poets." Dissertation, University of California, Berkeley, 1976 (DAI, 37: 5813).

On the discovery of the self through writing. PRAISE TO THE END is one example. The other poets are Yeats and Eliot.

1340 Bowers, Larry Neal. "Mysticism in the Poetry of Theodore Roethke." Dissertation, University of Florida, 1976 (DAI, 37: 6473).

Roethke's struggle for self-knowledge "resembles the mystic's movement toward the Absolute through the stages of awakening, purgation, illumination, dark night of the soul, and union."

1341 Brown, Dennis E. "Theodore Roethke's 'Self-World' and the Modernist Position." JOURNAL OF MODERN LITERATURE, 3, No. 5 (1974), 1239-54.

Previous assumptions about "self" in Roethke overlook "modern ideas about the nature of experience." Brown studies Roethke's work from the viewpoint of philosophers like James, Bradley, and Bergson, who "sought to establish the primary wholeness of experience."

1342 Chavkin, Allan Richard. "The Secular Imagination: The Continuity of the Secular Romantic Tradition of Wordsworth and Keats in Stevens, Faulkner, Roethke, and Bellow." Dissertation, University of Illinois, Urbana-Champaign, 1977 (DAI, 38: 6129).

Roethke's contribution to this study is "Meditations of an Old Woman." A "secular imagination" is a romanticism of Wordsworthian aspect that search[es] for an earthly affirmation in an earthly manner."

1343 Cruz, I.R. "Roethke's 'The Return.'" NOTES ON CONTEMPORARY LITERATURE, 7, No. 1 (1977), 8-9.

An inconsistency of voice in the poem confuses the identity of "I." Is it man or dog?

1344 Davis, William V. "Fishing an Old Wound: Theodore Roethke's Search for Sonship." ANTIGONISH REVIEW, No. 20 (Winter 1974), pp. 29-41.

On Roethke's attempt to come to terms with "the spectral figure of his father." Davis thinks this obsession informs his whole career and "helped him to create some of the finest poems of the century." Davis employs examples from OPEN HOUSE through THE FAR FIELD.

1345 Ely, Robert. "Roethke's 'The Waking.'" EXPLICATOR, 34 (1976), Item 54.

Identifies the speaker of the poem as "a leaf on the tree . . . reluctant to enter the rational world."

1346 Everette, Oliver. "Theodore Roethke: The Poet as Teacher." WEST COAST REVIEW, 3, No. 1 (1968), 5-11.

Everette's memories of Roethke during the fall of 1949 when he took a course from the poet at the University of Washington and of several encounters afterward.

1347 Foster, Ann Tucker. "A Field for Revelation: Mysticism in the Poetry of Theodore Roethke." Dissertation, Florida State University, 1977 (DAI, 38: 5458).

The "mystic elements" in Roethke's major sequences "in the light of [his] Notebooks and his readings in mystical literature."

1348 Galvin, Brendan James. "What the Grave Says, the Nest Denies: Burkean Strategies in Theodore Roethke's 'Lost Son' Poems." Dissertation, University of Massachusetts, 1970 (DAI, 31: 2384).

Influence of Kenneth Burke on Roethke's "Lost Son" poems.

1349 Gloege, Randall George. "Suspension of Belief in the Poetry of Theodore Roethke." Dissertation, Bowling Green State University, 1969 (DAI, 31: 757).

Roethke's poetry develops from "relatively conventional attitudes and forms" towards an "enlargement of consciousness" and open and free verse forms. "Also, the poet discovered in himself a public voice, making universal his personal vision."

1350 Haislip, John. "The Example of Theodore Roethke." NORTHWEST REVIEW, 14 (Spring 1975), 14-20.

Haislip describes the kind of advice and instruction he received from Roethke at the University of Washington in the spring of 1948.

1351 Heringman, Bernard. "Images of Meaning in the Poetry of Theodore Roethke." AEGIS, No. 2 (Fall 1973), pp. 45-57.

Classifies and elaborates images in Roethke's poems and discusses their "contributory function."

1352 Heyen, William Helmuth. "Essays on the Later Poems of Theodore Roethke." Dissertation, Ohio University, 1967 (DA, 28: 3185).

Treats in separate essays three aspects of poems from the fifties and sixties: "Roethke's 'minimals' or 'diminutives'"; Yeats's influence; and "mysticism."

1353 _____. "The Yeats Influence: Roethke's Formal Lyrics of the Fifties." JOHN BERRYMAN STUDIES, 3, No. 4 (1977), 17-63.

Not seen; cited in 1977 MLA INTERNATIONAL BIBLIOGRAPHY, page 185.

1354 Hirsch, David H. "Theodore Roethke." CONTEMPORARY LITERATURE, 19, No. 2 (1978), 243-48.

Review of La Belle's THE ECHOING WOOD and Sullivan's THE GARDEN MASTER. Hirsch does not care much for either book; "neither has anything 'new' to tell us."

1355 Hutchison, Alexander Norman. "The Context of Illumination in the Poetry of Theodore Roethke." Dissertation, Northwestern University, 1975 (DAI, 36: 4491).

Roethke's view of the relationship of self, world, and God is evidenced by "certain patterns of spiritual emergence" in his COLLECTED POEMS.

1356 La Belle, Jenijoy. "Martyr to a Motion Not His Own: Theodore Roethke's Love Poems." BALL STATE UNIVERSITY FORUM, 16, No. 2 (1975), 71-75.

La Belle sees Roethke's "borrowings" as homage paid to other poets and studies some of these influences or love relationships in WORDS FOR THE WIND.

1357 _____. "Out of the Cradle Endlessly Robbing: Whitman, Eliot, and Theodore Roethke." WALT WHITMAN REVIEW, 22, No. 2 (1976), 75-84.

MEDITATIONS OF AN OLD WOMAN, La Belle says, sounds somewhat like Eliot's FOUR QUARTETS because they have a common source in Whitman. She enumerates the details of these resemblances.

1358 _____. "Theodore Roethke and Tradition: 'The Pure Serene of Memory in One Man.'" Dissertation, University of California, San Diego, 1969 (DAI, 30: 2029).

An early treatment of the ideas presented in no. 1332.

1359 _____. "Theodore Roethke's 'The Lost Son': From Archetypes to Literary History." MODERN LANGUAGE QUARTERLY, 37 (June 1976), 179-95.

Weaves together influences on Roethke's ideas about regression which inform "The Lost Son." Jung as introduced to Roethke through Maud Bodkin's theories and Eliot's thoughts about "auditory imagination" seem to be chief. Other associations are Blake, Coleridge, and more Eliot. All these help to make up Roethke's idea of literary tradition.

1360 _____. "Theodore Roethke's Dancing Masters in 'Four for Sir John Davies.'" CONCERNING POETRY, 8 (Fall 1975), 29-35.

Dante, Davies, Shakespeare, Pope, and Yeats are the masters.

1361 Lecourt, Jean-Philippe. "Theodore Roethke: The Inner Wilderness and the Barrier of Ideology." In MYTH AND IDEOLOGY IN AMERICAN CULTURE. Ed. Régis Durand. Villeneuve-d'ascq, France: Universite de Lille III, 1976, pp. 42-64.

In desiring "to probe the mysteries of the self [the inner wilderness]," Roethke "refuse[s] to be the vehicle of ideology." His refusal "is itself the product of an age which is surfeited with it" and is itself ideological.

1362 Lenz, Frederick Philip. "The Evolution of Matter and Spirit in the Poetry of Theodore Roethke." Dissertation, SUNY, Stony Brook, 1978 (DAI, 39: 2941).

In the beginning, in OPEN HOUSE, for example, Roethke's struggle is between physical desires and spiritual aspirations; by his last poems the poet feels a union of body and soul.

1363 Lorimer, William Lund. "Ripples from a Single Stone: An Archetypal Study of Theodore Roethke's Poetry." Dissertation, University of Notre Dame, 1976 (DAI, 37: 3614).

The imagery of birth, death, and rebirth in Roethke.

1364 McDade, Gerard F. "The Primitive Vision of Theodore Roethke: A Study of Aboriginal Elements in His Poetry." Dissertation, Temple University, 1970 (DAI, 31: 1806).

On "Roethke's developing hero from the slime of the greenhouse and developmental poems to the condition of joy finally secured in the 'North American Sequence.'"

1365 Maselli, Sharon Ann. "'The Possibles We Dare': Art and Identity in the Poetry of Theodore Roethke." Dissertation, University of Arizona, 1978 (DAI, 39: 3582).

Roethke searches for identity through his art. He believed that "both artist and individual attempt to order and reshape reality, for the purpose of self-realization."

1366 Molesworth, Charles. "'Songs of a Happy Man': Theodore Roethke and Contemporary Poetry." JOHN BERRYMAN STUDIES, 2, No. 3 (1976), 32-53.

Explores various aspects of the theme "the self-as-problematic," such as structure, philosophy, image, and language in Roethke's poetry of the self. Reprinted in no. 275.

1367 Moore, Karl. "A Singer of Green: Pastoral Myth in Roethke's Poetry." Dissertation, University of Connecticut, 1978.

Not seen; cited in no. 33.

1368 Perrine, Laurence. "The Theme of Theodore Roethke's 'Interlude.'" NOTES ON MODERN AMERICAN LITERATURE, 1, (Summer 1977), Item 23.

Not seen; cited in JOURNAL OF MODERN LITERATURE, 7, No. 4 (1979), 805.

1369 Reichertz, Ronald Robert. "'Once More, the Round': An Introduction to the Poetry of Theodore Roethke." Dissertation, University of Wisconsin, 1967 (DA, 28: 4643).

Unity is achieved in Roethke's work by the "drama of the awakening and growth of human consciousness."

1370 Rodgers, Audrey T. "Dancing Mad: Theodore Roethke." In her THE UNIVERSAL DRUM: DANCE IMAGERY IN THE POETRY OF ELIOT, CRANE, ROETHKE, AND WILLIAMS. University Park: Pennsylvania State University Press, 1979, pp. 93-137.

"To trace the dance as an image in his poetry with its intricate and swift accretions of meaning is to follow the successive stages of Roethke's journey toward the discovery of the self." In addition, Rodgers is interested in form as well as theme.

1371 Schott, Penelope Scambly. "'I Am!' Says Theodore Roethke: A Reading of the Nonsense Poems." RESEARCH STUDIES, 43, No. 2 (1975), 103-12.

The nonsense makes much sense. Schott relates these poems to Roethke's other work.

1372 Slanger, George Comfort. "The Separateness of All Things: A Study of Development in the Poetry and Prose of Theodore Roethke." Dissertation, University of Washington, 1976 (DAI, 37: 2865).

Roethke's development divides into three stages: "contamination, confrontation and contemplation." These are represented by OPEN HOUSE, his next four books, and his last books. Slanger also produces evidence for his judgments from Roethke's unpublished prose.

1373 Snodgrass, W.D. "'That Anguish of Concreteness'--Theodore Roethke's Career." In his IN RADICAL PURSUIT: CRITICAL ESSAYS AND LECTURES. New York: Harper and Row, 1975, pp. 101-16.

Roethke's career is the modern "artistic revolt" in "miniature." In the end he flees "from his own experimental drive, his own voice, his freedom."

1374 Sullivan, Rosemary. "A Still Center: A Reading of Theodore Roethke's 'North American Sequence.'" TEXAS STUDIES IN LITERATURE AND LANGUAGE, 16, No. 4 (1975), 765-83.

Sullivan reads this sequence as "a penitential act of re-integration with nature. . . . Roethke sought to immerse himself in nature in order to find his personal regeneration there."

1375 Vanderwerken, D.L. "Roethke's 'Four for Sir John Davies' and 'The Dying Man.'" RESEARCH STUDIES, 41, No. 2 (1973), 125-35.

Vanderwerken shows the presence of Yeats in these poems.

1376 Williams, Harry Stanley. "Theodore Roethke's Long Poems: Animistic Archetypes in the Lyric Mode." Dissertation, University of Maryland, 1974 (DAI, 36: 897).

"The Lost Son," "Meditations of an Old Woman," and "North American Sequence" illustrate "the Roethkean mode."

1377 Wolff, George. "Syntactical and Imagistic Distortion in Roethke's Greenhouse Poems." LANGUAGE AND STYLE, 6, No. 4 (1973), 281-88.

Wolff studies the relationship of these two devices to meaning in poems from THE LOST SON AND OTHER POEMS. "Roethke's syntactical distortions gain their effect because they deviate from the norm of either 'ordinary language' or expository prose." In his images "Roethke repeatedly blocks the path to visualization by carefully controlled details."

M.L. ROSENTHAL

(American; March 14, 1917--)

POEMS

BLUE BOY ON SKATES. New York: Oxford University Press, 1964.
BEYOND POWER: NEW POEMS. New York: Oxford University Press, 1969.
THE VIEW FROM THE PEACOCK'S TAIL. New York: Oxford University Press, 1972.
SHE: A SEQUENCE OF POEMS. Brockport, N.Y.: BOA Editions, 1977.

CRITICAL ARTICLE

1378 Gall, Sally M. "'Wild with Morning': The Poetry of M.L. Rosenthal." MODERN POETRY STUDIES, 8, No. 2 (1977), 119-33.

Gall's interest is in SHE but looks at the other books for examples of Rosenthal's experiments with sequences. She focuses on his treatment of love, "the all important counter to the violence of the twentieth century."

MURIEL RUKEYSER

(American; December 15, 1913-February 12, 1980)

POEMS

THEORY OF FLIGHT. New Haven, Conn.: Yale University Press, 1935.
U.S. 1. New York: Covici-Riede, 1938.
A TURNING WIND. New York: Viking Press, 1939.
THE SOUL AND BODY OF JOHN BROWN. New York: Lee Ault and R.C. Von Ripper, 1940.
WAKE ISLAND. Garden City, N.Y.: Doubleday, 1942.
BEAST IN VIEW. Garden City, N.Y.: Doubleday, 1944.
THE GREEN WAVE. Garden City, N.Y.: Doubleday, 1948.
ELEGIES. Norfolk, Conn.: New Directions, 1949.
ORPHEUS. San Francisco: Centaur Press, 1949.
SELECTED POEMS. New York: New Directions, 1951.
BODY OF WAKING. New York: Harper and Brothers, 1958.
WATERLILY FIRE: POEMS 1935-1962. New York: Macmillan, 1962.
THE SPEED OF DARKNESS. New York: Random House, 1968.
29 POEMS. London: Rapp and Whiting, Deutsch, 1972.
BREAKING OPEN. New York: Random House, 1973.
THE GATES. New York: Random House, 1976.
THE COLLECTED POEMS. New York: McGraw-Hill, 1979.

BIBLIOGRAPHY

See no. 58, pages 119-21.

CRITICAL BOOK

1379 Kertesz, Louise. THE POETIC VISION OF MURIEL RUKEYSER. Foreword by Kenneth Rexroth. Baton Rouge: Louisiana State University Press, 1980. 412 p.

Kertesz "traces the progress of images and themes Muriel Rukeyser found compelling." After an introduction to

Rukeyser's work and its criticism and a chapter on her contemporaries at the beginning of her career, Kertesz treats her work chronologically by decades, ending with Rukeyser among present-day poets and movements.

CRITICAL ARTICLES

1380 Brinnin, J.M. "Muriel Rukeyser: The Social Poet and the Problem of Communication." POETRY, 61 (January 1943), 554-75.

Brinnin describes the kind of verse in Rukeyser's first three volumes of poetry, focusing on her language and images as these changed to meet the problems confronting the socially concerned poet.

1381 "Craft Interview with Muriel Rukeyser." NEW YORK QUARTERLY, No. 11 (Summer 1972), pp. 14-39.

On her beginnings as a writer, influences, writing habits, dry periods, teaching and writing, reading her own poems, advice to young poets, the nature of poetry, specific poems, and poetry at the present time.

1382 Novak, Estelle Gerhgoren. "The Dynamo School of Poets." CONTEMPORARY LITERATURE, 11 (Autumn 1970), 526-39.

Discusses some early Rukeyser poems published in the left-wing magazine DYNAMO in the thirties and also mentions a few other "left-wing poets."

1383 Terris, Virginia R. "Muriel Rukeyser: A Retrospective." AMERICAN POETRY REVIEW, 3, No. 3 (1974), 10-15.

An overview of Rukeyser's writing career, her influences, and themes. Terris believes that critics have concentrated on her themes of social protest and have "failed to notice that her greatest creative strengths have manifested themselves in her poems of intimate relationships and myth making."

MAY SARTON

(American; May 3, 1912--)

POEMS

ENCOUNTER IN APRIL. Boston: Houghton Mifflin, 1937.
INNER LANDSCAPE. Boston: Houghton Mifflin, 1939.
THE LION AND THE ROSE. New York: Rinehart, 1948.
THE LEAVES OF THE TREE. Mt. Vernon, Iowa: Cornell College, 1950.
THE LAND OF SILENCE AND OTHER POEMS. New York: Rinehart, 1953.
IN TIME LIKE AIR. New York: Rinehart, 1957.
CLOUD, STONE, SUN, VINE: POEMS SELECTED AND NEW. New York: Norton, 1961.
A PRIVATE MYTHOLOGY: NEW POEMS. New York: Norton, 1966.
AS DOES NEW HAMPSHIRE AND OTHER POEMS. Peterborough, N.H.: Richard R. Smith, 1967.
A GRAIN OF MUSTARD SEED: NEW POEMS. New York: Norton, 1971.
A DURABLE FIRE: NEW POEMS. New York: Norton, 1972.
COLLECTED POEMS 1930-1973. New York: Norton, 1974.

BIBLIOGRAPHY

1384 Blouin, Leonora P. MAY SARTON: A BIBLIOGRAPHY. Metuchen, N.J.: Scarecrow Press, 1978. 236 p.

> Primary and annotated secondary bibliography. Describes contents of individual collections of poems and identifies and locates poems not collected. Annotates book reviews and critical articles and books, intermixing studies of verse and fiction.

CRITICAL BOOK

1385 Sibley, Agnes. MAY SARTON. New York: Twayne, 1972. 160 p. Bibliog.

An account of Sarton's life, poetry, and fiction. Brief annotated bibliography of critical reviews. Sarton's chief gift is her describing nature so "that the reader is made keenly aware of its quality--its beauty, poignancy, harshness, gentleness."

CRITICAL ARTICLE

1386 Taylor, Henry. "Home to a Place of Exile: THE COLLECTED POEMS of May Sarton." HOLLINS CRITIC, 11, No. 3 (1974), 1-16.

Sarton edited her poems for this collection to reveal "the development of a career and of a person." Consequently some of her selections "seem less successful than others." Taylor describes the themes and concerns represented in these poems.

JAMES SCHEVILL

(American; June 10, 1920--)

POEMS

TENSIONS. Berkeley, Calif.: Bern Porter, 1947.
THE RIGHT TO GREET. Berkeley, Calif.: Bern Porter, 1955.
SELECTED POEMS, 1945-49. Berkeley, Calif.: Bern Porter, 1960.
PRIVATE DOOMS AND PUBLIC DESTINATIONS. Denver: Swallow Press, 1962.
THE STALINGRAD ELEGIES. Denver: Swallow Press, 1964.
RELEASE. Providence: Hellcoal Press, 1968.
VIOLENCE AND GLORY: POEMS 1962-1968. Chicago: Swallow Press, 1969.
THE BUDDHIST CAR AND OTHER CHARACTERS. Chicago: Swallow Press, 1973.
PURSUING ELEGY: A POEM ABOUT HAITI. Providence: Copper Beech Press, 1974.
THE MAYAN POEMS. Providence: Copper Beech Press, 1978.
FORCE OF THE EYES: A GUATEMALAN SEQUENCE. Providence: Copper Beech Press, 1979.

CRITICAL ARTICLE

1387 Robbins, Martin. "James Schevill: Poet with Music, and Playwright with a Message." VOYAGES, 3 (Winter 1970), 85-87.

Robbins describes some of Schevill's "Performance Poems," which in addition to sound sometimes have dance, Schevill's music, and even film projections. He also comments on Schevill, his poems, and life.

DELMORE SCHWARTZ

(American; December 18, 1913-July 11, 1966)

POEMS

IN DREAMS BEGIN RESPONSIBILITIES. Norfolk, Conn.: New Directions, 1938.
GENESIS I. Norfolk, Conn.: New Directions, 1943.
VAUDEVILLE FOR A PRINCESS. New York: New Directions, 1950.
SELECTED POEMS: SUMMER KNOWLEDGE. Garden City, N.Y.: Doubleday, 1959.
WHAT IS TO BE GIVEN. Ed. Douglas Dunn. Manchester: Carcanet Press, 1978.

BIOGRAPHY

1388 Atlas, James. DELMORE SCHWARTZ: THE LIFE OF AN AMERICAN POET. New York: Farrar, Straus and Giroux, 1977. 418 p. Illus., notes, index.

Atlas attempts to delineate "the true sensibility" of this many-faceted man. "It was his misfortune to be metonymous, the very embodiment of an entire generation's traumas and opinions."

CRITICAL BOOK

1389 McDougall, Richard. DELMORE SCHWARTZ. New York: Twayne, 1974. 156 p. Notes, refs., bibliog., index.

"Schwartz's obsession with exile and estrangement was accompanied by a longing for unity and communion." Chapter 1 is on Schwartz's career; 2 on his concept of alienation; 3 on his themes and concerns; 4 through 8 on his most important work with a summing up in 8.

CRITICAL ARTICLES

1390 Dike, Donald A. "A Case for Judgment: The Literary Criticism of Delmore Schwartz." TWENTIETH CENTURY LITERATURE, 24, No. 4 (1978), 492-509.

On Schwartz's characteristic tone and his inclination to make judgments in his literary criticism. Dike describes Schwartz's criteria for good literary works.

1391 _____. "The POETICS and the Criticism of Delmore Schwartz." NOTES ON MODERN AMERICAN LITERATURE, 1, No. 4 (1977), Item 27.

Dike points out several examples of Schwartz's indebtedness to Aristotle, which "everywhere exhibits and admits itself in his literary criticism."

1392 Flint, Robert W. "The Stories of Delmore Schwartz." COMMENTARY, 33 (April 1962), 336-39.

Review of THE WORLD IS A WEDDING and SUCCESSFUL LOVE. Flint believes Schwartz cared more for "presentation" in these stories than he did for "hitting the average highbrow literary taste." He likes their portrayal of New York's Jewish middle class, but in any case considers them "acts of discovery and celebration." SUCCESSFUL LOVE is less successful.

1393 Hall, Theodore Dana. "A Student of the Morning Light: A Study of the Cultural and Salvational Vision of Delmore Schwartz." Dissertation, Syracuse University, 1976 (DAI, 38: 2788).

Concentrates on Schwartz's work rather than on his biography in order to show the nature of his "literary vision of modern man and society."

1394 Hook, Sidney. "Imaginary Enemies, Real Terror." AMERICAN SCHOLAR, 47 (Summer 1978), 406-12.

Review of DELMORE SCHWARTZ: THE LIFE OF AN AMERICAN POET by James Atlas. Hook, Schwartz's teacher at New York University, recounts several anecdotes of his dealings with him and muses, as teachers do, how Schwartz's life might have gone differently if he had been treated differently when young.

1395 Howe, Irving. "Purity and Craftiness." TIMES LITERARY SUPPLEMENT, 28 April 1978, pp. 458-59.

Review of DELMORE SCHWARTZ by James Atlas and WHAT IS TO BE GIVEN. Howe summarizes Schwartz's life and the creating of the "legend" and relates an incident of his own experience with Schwartz. He lists a few stories and poems he thinks are notable, praising this edition by Douglas Dunn.

1396 Kloss, Robert J. "An Ancient and Famous Capital: Delmore Schwartz's Dream." PSYCHOANALYTIC REVIEW, 65 (1978), 475-90.

Not seen; cited in 1978 MLA INTERNATIONAL BIBLIOGRAPHY, Item 11617.

1397 Knapp, James F. "Delmore Schwartz: Poet of the Orphic Journey." SEWANEE REVIEW, 78 (Summer 1970), 506-16.

America to Schwartz is a place without magic, "where escape is easier than honesty," but is nevertheless new and "still to be defined." Schwartz's poems are his "search for a way out" of a sterile world.

1398 Levin, Harry. "Delmore's Gift." CANTO, 2, No. 1 (1978), 61-70.

Recollections of Schwartz by one who, except for physical details, does not recognize him in Bellow's HUMBOLDT'S GIFT. "Delmore's gift was his Angst, his unreassuring certainty that discomfort is a basic component of our psychological condition, his accusation levelled against all who are complacent enough to feel at home in the universe he rejected."

1399 Lyons, Bonnie. "Delmore Schwartz and the Whole Truth." STUDIES IN SHORT FICTION, 14, No. 3 (1977), 259-64.

Concentrates on THE WORLD IS A WEDDING (1948) because these stories have had little critical attention. What Lyons has to say about language and style, subject and theme in his fiction will interest the reader of Schwartz's poems for what it reveals about the way he thought and worked.

1400 Novak, Michael Paul. "The Dream as Film: Delmore Schwartz's 'In Dreams Begin Responsibilities.'" KANSAS QUARTERLY, 9, No. 2 (1977), 87-91.

An interpretation of the story only, the imagery and action of which suggest to Novak "a deterministic view of man's possibilities."

1401 Rahv, Philip. "Delmore Schwartz: The Paradox of Precocity." NEW YORK REVIEW OF BOOKS, 20 May 1971, pp. 19-22.

A close-up view of Schwartz by a friend. Rahv argues

that his "precocity" caused both his success and failure. In his criticism, however, Rahv says, we see one who "not only understood literature thoroughly but also loved it passionately." Reprinted in Rahv's ESSAYS ON LITERATURE AND POLITICS, 1932-1972 (Boston: Houghton Mifflin, 1978), pp. 85-92.

1402 Towers, Robert. "The Delmore File." NEW YORK REVIEW OF BOOKS, 23 March 1978, pp. 15-18.

Review of DELMORE SCHWARTZ by James Atlas and IN DREAMS BEGIN RESPONSIBILITIES (1978 reprint). Towers thinks these two books will probably satisfy any curiosity aroused about Schwartz by Saul Bellow's HUMBOLDT'S GIFT.

1403 Valenti, Lila Lee. "The Apprenticeship of Delmore Schwartz." TWENTIETH CENTURY LITERATURE, 20, No. 3 (1974), 201-16.

Describes "notes, drafts, manuscripts, journals, and letters" left by Schwartz and illustrates from them his "methods of composition" and "his general vision."

1404 Zucker, David. "Self and History in Delmore Schwartz's Poetry and Criticism." IOWA REVIEW, 8, No. 4 (1977), 95-103.

Zucker, as a student of Schwartz's at Syracuse from 1962 to 1966, presents his "sense of this brilliant poet and critic who had a deeply painful awareness of the contradictions of his own personality." In his criticism Schwartz tried always "to be generous to both the ideas and the particular forms that poets and poems took." As a poet Schwartz was "constantly dissolving the distinction between universal and personal history."

WINFIELD TOWNLEY SCOTT

(American; April 30, 1910-April 28, 1968)

POEMS

BIOGRAPHY FOR TRAMAN. New York: Covici Friede, 1937.
WIND THE CLOCK. Prairie City, Ill.: James Decker Press, 1941.
SWORD ON THE TABLE. Norfolk, Conn.: New Directions, 1942.
TO MARRY STRANGERS. New York: Crowell, 1945.
MR. WHITTIER AND OTHER POEMS. New York: Macmillan, 1948.
THE DARK SISTER. New York: New York University Press, 1958.
SCRIMSHAW. New York: Macmillan, 1959.
EXILES AND FABRICATIONS. Garden City, N.Y.: Doubleday, 1961.
COLLECTED POEMS, 1937-1962. New York: Macmillan, 1962.
CHANGE OF WEATHER. Garden City, N.Y.: Doubleday, 1964.
NEW AND SELECTED POEMS. Ed. George P. Elliott. Garden City, N.Y.: Doubleday, 1967.
A DIRTY HAND: THE LITERARY NOTEBOOKS OF WINFIELD TOWNLEY SCOTT. Austin: University of Texas Press, 1969.
ALPHA OMEGA. Ed. Eleanor M. Scott. Garden City, N.Y.: Doubleday, 1971.

BIOGRAPHY

1405 Donaldson, Scott. POET IN AMERICA: WINFIELD TOWNLEY SCOTT. Austin: University of Texas Press, 1972. 400 p. Bibliog.

Donaldson's theme is that America mistreats its poets and Scott is his example.

CRITICAL ARTICLE

1406 DeLeo, Phyllis C. "Sex, Art, and Death: Dominant Themes in the Poetry of Winfield Townley Scott." Dissertation, University of Connecticut, 1978 (DAI, 38: 6722).

A biographical approach in which DeLeo "examines the poems as a fusion of poetic technique and personal traumas at various stages in the poet's life and professional career."

ANNE SEXTON

(American; November 9, 1928-October 4, 1974)

POEMS

TO BEDLAM AND PART WAY BACK. Boston: Houghton Mifflin, 1960.
ALL MY PRETTY ONES. Boston: Houghton Mifflin, 1962.
SELECTED POEMS. London: Oxford University Press, 1964.
LIVE OR DIE. Boston: Houghton Mifflin, 1966.
LOVE POEMS. Boston: Houghton Mifflin, 1969.
TRANSFORMATIONS. Boston: Houghton Mifflin, 1971.
THE BOOK OF FOLLY. Boston: Houghton Mifflin, 1972.
THE DEATH NOTEBOOKS. Boston: Houghton Mifflin, 1974.
THE AWFUL ROWING TOWARD GOD. Boston: Houghton Mifflin, 1975.

BIBLIOGRAPHY

1407 Northouse, Cameron, and Thomas P. Walsh, eds. SYLVIA PLATH AND ANNE SEXTON: A REFERENCE GUIDE. Boston: G.K. Hall, 1974. 143 p. Bibliog., index.

Pages 89-125 list chronologically Sexton's writings, books, and articles about her through 1971.

BIOGRAPHY

1408 Sexton, Linda Gray, and Lois Ames, eds. ANNE SEXTON: A SELF-PORTRAIT IN LETTERS. Boston: Houghton Mifflin, 1977. 433 p. Photos., index.

From more than "50,000 pieces of paper" the editors have selected "the best and most representative . . . to present a balanced picture of Anne's life as we now understand it." In her letters are numerous references to contemporary poets as well as letters to them.

CRITICAL BOOK

1409 McClatchy, J. D., ed. ANNE SEXTON: THE ARTIST AND HER CRITICS. Bloomington: Indiana University Press, 1978. 297 p. Chronology, bibliog.

A collection of three interviews, a sample of Sexton's worksheets, eight reminiscences, some contemporary reviews, and four longer essays.

CRITICAL ARTICLES

1410 Axelrod, Rise B. "The Transforming Art of Anne Sexton." CONCERNING POETRY, 7 (Spring 1974), 6-13.

Axelrod sees in Sexton's first books an "inturning Therapeutic mode [that] analyzes the 'cracked mirror' of the self in search of the origins of dissolution" and in later poems a "more visionary mode [that] allows the resurrection of the true self and its reunification with others." Reprinted in no. 259.

1411 Boyers, Robert. "LIVE OR DIE: The Achievement of Anne Sexton." SALMAGUNDI, 2, No. 1 (1967), 61-71.

Sexton as confessional poet. "LIVE OR DIE is the culmination, indeed the crowning achievement, of the confessional mode."

1412 Cunningham, Lawrence S. "Anne Sexton: Poetry as a Form of Exorcism." AMERICAN BENEDICTINE REVIEW, 28, No. 1 (1977), 102-11.

Extends Rollo May's observation about the power of the word over "the demonic" and Peter Berger's that "language is the imposition of order upon experience" to an analysis of Sexton's poems, which Cunningham sees as a "search for belief."

1413 Fitz Gerald, Gregory. "The Choir from the Soul: A Conversation with Anne Sexton." MASSACHUSETTS REVIEW, 19, No. 1 (1978), 69-88.

Held in Weston, Massachusetts, 24 June 1974. Sexton talks about her "lack of education," influences, religion, sex, children, love, writing, and poetry.

1414 Kevles, Barbara. "The Art of Poetry XV: Anne Sexton." PARIS REVIEW, 13 (Summer 1971), 158-91.

Annotated in no. 1407; reprinted in no. 1409.

1415 McClatchy, J. D. "Anne Sexton: Somehow to Endure." CENTENNIAL REVIEW, 19 (Spring 1975), 1-36.

Endurance is the principal theme of Sexton's work, and her art rendered "a life into poems with all the intimacy and complexity of feeling and response with which that life has been endured." Includes a general discussion of confessional poetry and poems. Reprinted in no. 1409 in a somewhat expanded version.

1416 McGill, William J. "Anne Sexton and God: Preeminently a Confessional Poet." COMMONWEAL, 104, No. 10 (1977), 304-06.

Sexton's characteristic theme is the search for self and for God. McGill accounts for her suicide as a failure to find what she sought.

1417 Mood, John J. "'A Bird Full of Bones': Anne Sexton--A Visit and a Reading." CHICAGO REVIEW, 23, No. 4 and 24, No. 1 (1972), 107-23.

Mood narrates making the arrangements of the reading, meeting Sexton, the reading, and the party afterward.

1418 Perrine, Laurence. "Theme and Tone in Anne Sexton's 'To a Friend Whose Work Has Come to Triumph.'" NOTES ON CONTEMPORARY LITERATURE, 7, No. 3 (1977), 2-3.

Examines the tone of the poem as a clue to Sexton's changing the Icarus legend. Other clues are in her title and in the sonnet form.

1419 Poulin, A., Jr., ed. "A Memorial for Anne Sexton." AMERICAN POETRY REVIEW, 4, No. 3 (1975), 15-20. Photos. by Arthur Furst.

Brief comments and poems in tribute to Sexton.

1420 Pritchard, William H. "The Anne Sexton Show." HUDSON REVIEW, 31, No. 2 (1978), 387-92.

Review of ANNE SEXTON: A SELF-PORTRAIT IN LETTERS. Pritchard thinks these letters will teach us more "about the American poetry scene over the past twenty years" than they will about Sexton's poetry. He also evaluates her poetry and her views on poetry and poets.

1421 Rukeyser, Muriel. "Glitter and Wounds, Several Wildnesses." PARNASSUS, 2, No. 1 (1973), 215-22.

Review of THE BOOK OF FOLLY. This book draws on Sexton's earlier work. She has used "the early confessions and [made] a second poetry out of them." Reprinted in no. 1409.

1422 Sexton, Anne. "Worksheets [for 'Suicide Note']." NEW YORK QUARTERLY, No. 4 (Fall 1970), pp. 81-94.

Intended to illustrate "the craft and patience and labor that goes into the making of a poem."

1423 Shor, Ira. "Anne Sexton's 'For My Lover . . .': Feminism in the Classroom." COLLEGE ENGLISH, 34, No. 8 (1973), 1082-93.

An account of a class project on the poem at a community college, mostly "white Italian working-class students." Shor adds an epilogue on differences in the project the following term. Reprinted from FEMALE STUDIES, 6 (1972).

1424 Showalter, Elaine, and Carol Smith. "A Nurturing Relationship: A Conversation with Anne Sexton and Maxine Kumin, April 15, 1974." WOMEN'S STUDIES, 4 (1976), 115-36.

Reminiscences by Sexton and Kumin of their poetry workshop in Boston with John Holmes, their early friendship, and what Sexton and Kumin thought each other was like then. They discuss the women's movement and writing poems.

KARL SHAPIRO

(American; November 10, 1913--)

POEMS

POEMS. Baltimore: Waverly Press, 1935.
PERSON, PLACE, AND THING. New York: Reynall, 1942.
THE PLACE OF LOVE. Melbourne: Comment Press, 1943.
V-LETTER. New York: Reynall, 1944.
ESSAY ON RIME. New York: Reynall, 1945.
TRIAL OF A POET. New York: Reynall, 1947.
POEMS, 1940-1953. New York: Random House, 1953.
POEMS OF A JEW. New York: Random House, 1958.
THE BOURGEOIS POET. New York: Random House, 1964.
SELECTED POEMS. New York: Random House, 1968.
WHITE HAIRED LOVER. New York: Random House, 1968.
ADULT BOOKSTORE. New York: Random House, 1976.
COLLECTED POEMS 1940-1977. New York: Random House, 1978.

BIBLIOGRAPHY

1425 Bartlett, Lee. KARL SHAPIRO: A DESCRIPTIVE BIBLIOGRAPHY 1933-1977. New York: Garland, 1979. 194 p.

Primary bibliography of books, pamphlets, broadsides, contributions to periodicals and anthologies, and translations of Shapiro. Checklist of secondary materials with some annotations compiled by David Huwiler, pages 164-77. Reviews listed separately without annotations by title of book reviewed.

1426 White, William. KARL SHAPIRO: A BIBLIOGRAPHY WITH A NOTE BY KARL SHAPIRO. Detroit: Wayne State University Press, 1960. 113 p.

Superseded by no. 1425.

See also no. 58.

CRITICAL BOOK

1427 Reino, Joseph. KARL SHAPIRO. Boston: Twayne, 1981. 194 p. Notes, refs., bibliog., index.

Reino discusses three sides of Shapiro that seem to account for his literary personality: "the prize-winning poet, the exasperating literary critic, and the unabashed autobiographer." Several chapters on aspects of his poetry, two on the problems of being Jewish in America, concluding chapters on ESSAY ON RIME, BOURGEOIS POET, and Reino's summarizing evaluation.

CRITICAL ARTICLES

1428 Bradley, Sam. "Shapiro Strikes at the Establishment." UNIVERSITY OF KANSAS CITY REVIEW, 29, No. 4 (1963), 275-79.

The "establishment" is "academic poetry and T.S. Eliot." Shapiro may go "too far," but he does "demand that we rise from comfort and cultural dignity and find again what is natural and simple."

1429 Coleman, Alice. "'Doors Leap Open.'" ENGLISH JOURNAL, 53, No. 8 (1964), 631-33.

Coleman describes an experiment with high school students and Shapiro's "Auto Wreck," in which she found the responses of "advanced" and "average" students were similar. "Nearly every student in all four classes seemed to be not only absorbed and awed by this dilemma of mankind, but aware of Shapiro's purpose."

1430 Linebarger, J.M., and Shelly Angel. "The Argument of 'Auto Wreck.'" NOTES ON MODERN AMERICAN LITERATURE, 2 (1977), Item 2.

Musing on the last stanza of the poem, Linebarger and Angel conclude that Shapiro's purpose is "to capture his and our response to a horror frequently observed in American life."

JON SILKIN

(English; December 2, 1930--)

POEMS

THE PORTRAIT AND OTHER POEMS. Ilfracombe, Engl.: Stockwell Press, 1950.
THE PEACEABLE KINGDOM. London: Chatto and Windus, 1954.
THE TWO FREEDOMS. London: Chatto and Windus, 1958.
THE RE-ORDERING OF THE STONES. London: Chatto and Windus, 1961.
NATURE WITH MAN. London: Chatto and Windus, Hogarth, 1965.
POEMS NEW AND SELECTED. London: Chatto and Windus, Hogarth; Middletown, Conn.: Wesleyan University Press, 1966.
AMANA GRASS. London: Chatto and Windus, Hogarth; Middletown, Conn.: Wesleyan University Press, 1971.
KILLHOPE WHEEL. Ashington, Engl.: Midnag, 1971.
THE PRINCIPLE OF WATER. Cheadle, Engl.: Carcanet Press, 1974.
TWO IMAGES OF CONTINUING TROUBLE. Richmond, Engl.: Keepsake Press, 1976.
JERUSALEM. Knotting, Engl.: Sceptre Press, 1977.
INTO PRAISING. Sunderland, Engl.: Ceolfrith Press, 1978.
THE LAPIDARY POEMS. Knotting, Engl.: Sceptre Press, 1979.
THE PSALMS WITH THEIR SPOILS. London: Routledge and Kegan Paul, 1980.
SELECTED POEMS. London: Routledge and Kegan Paul, 1980.

CRITICAL ARTICLES

1431 Brown, Merle E. "On Jon Silkin's 'Amana Grass.'" IOWA REVIEW, 1 (Winter 1970), 115-25.

This discussion follows the printed text of the poem (pages 109-15). Brown traces Silkin's path from his first book of poems, which describes a dissolution of "the peaceable kingdom" while crying for action makes the condition bearable.

1432 ______. "Stress in Silkin's Poetry and the Healing Emptiness of America." CONTEMPORARY LITERATURE, 18 (Summer 1977), 361-90.

Studies the effects of Silkin's 1969 stay in America on his poems to PRINCIPLE OF WATER.

1433 Hecht, Anthony. "Poetry Chronicle." HUDSON REVIEW, 19, No. 2 (1966), 330-38.

Comment on Silkin is on page 335. Hecht is impressed by the "breadth and variety" of POEMS NEW AND SELECTED and is reminded of Roethke.

1434 "The Poetry of the Trenches." TIMES LITERARY SUPPLEMENT, 29 September 1972, pp. 1131-32.

Review of OUT OF BATTLE by Jon Silkin. Finds these essays flawed by Silkin's assuming that contemporary views were the views of war poets from the Romantics to those of World War I.

1435 Shivpuri, Jagdish. "Two Contemporary Poets in English: Jon Silkin and R.S. Thomas." SIDDHA (Siddharth College, India), 10 (1975), 1-25.

This is really two essays assessing first Silkin and then Thomas. The only link Shivpuri supplies is a mention of Dylan Thomas in each essay. He compares Silkin's poems to those of Isaac Rosenberg and finds in Silkin's essays on Rosenberg clues for reading Silkin. On Thomas, Shivpuri is most impressed with his Welshness and thinks he is a real-life Reverend Eli Jenkins from Dylan Thomas' UNDER MILK WOOD.

CHARLES SIMIC

(American; May 9, 1938--)

POEMS

WHAT THE GRASS SAYS. San Francisco: Kayak Press, 1967.
SOMEWHERE AMONG US A STONE IS TAKING NOTES. San Francisco: Kayak Press, 1969.
DISMANTLING THE SILENCE. New York: Braziller, 1971.
WHITE. New York: New Rivers Press, 1972.
RETURN TO A PLACE LIT BY A GLASS OF MILK. New York: Braziller, 1974.
CHARON'S COSMOLOGY. New York: Braziller, 1977.
BROOMS: SELECTED POEMS. Barry, Wales: Edge Press, 1978.
SCHOOL FOR DARK THOUGHTS. Pawlet, Vt.: Banyan Press, 1978.

CRITICAL ARTICLES

1436 Contoski, Victor. "Charles Simic: Language at the Stone's Heart." CHICAGO REVIEW, 28, No. 4 (Spring 1977), 145-57. [Note: The cover of this number states "Volume 48."]

> Because Simic tries to connect language and inanimate objects, his work presents special problems. Contoski tries to resolve some of these by tracing the gradual increase of difficulty from the early poems of WHAT THE GRASS SAYS to the later poems of RETURN TO A PLACE LIT BY A GLASS OF MILK.

1437 Shaw, Robert B. "Charles Simic: An Appreciation." NEW REPUBLIC, 24 January 1976, pp. 25-27.

> "It is the paradox of his style that his determined concentration on the most common things makes reality strange and, even when terrifying, strangely inviting." Shaw goes on to elaborate the characteristics of Simic's verse.

1438 Starbuck, George. "George Starbuck and Charles Simic: A Conversation." PLOUGHSHARES, 2, No. 3 (1975), 78-91.

Starbuck leads into a somewhat lengthy discussion on the composition of WHITE and then asks Simic his opinion of other contemporary poets.

1439 "Where the Levels Meet: An Interview with Charles Simic." OHIO REVIEW, 14, No. 2 (1973), 46-58.

Held in Athens, Ohio, 26 October 1972. Simic answers questions on his beginnings as a poet; on such various elements in his poems as the surreal, pastoral, mythic, and European; on his generation of poets; on his subjects and attitudes; on his methods; and on what he wants still to write.

LOUIS SIMPSON

(American; March 27, 1923--)

POEMS

THE ARRIVISTES: 1940-1949. New York: Fine Editions Press, 1949.
GOOD NEWS OF DEATH AND OTHER POEMS. New York: Scribner's, 1955.
A DREAM OF GOVERNORS. Middletown, Conn.: Wesleyan University Press, 1959.
AT THE END OF THE OPEN ROAD. Middletown, Conn.: Wesleyan University Press, 1963.
SELECTED POEMS. New York: Harcourt, Brace, 1965.
ADVENTURES OF THE LETTER I. New York: Harper and Row, 1971.
SEARCHING FOR THE OX. New York: Morrow, 1976.
ARMIDALE. Brockport, N.Y.: BOA Editions, 1980.

BIOGRAPHY

1440 Simpson, Louis. NORTH OF JAMAICA. New York: Harper and Row, 1972. Also published as AIR WITH ARMED MEN. London: Calder and Boyar, 1972. 285 p.

A narrative of his life from early memories in Jamaica to poetry readings against war in Vietnam.

CRITICAL BOOK

1441 Moran, Ronald. LOUIS SIMPSON. New York: Twayne, 1972. 187 p. Notes, refs., bibliog., index.

Chapter 1 is biographical. Chapters 2 through 7 are on poetry, 8 is on Simpson's novel, RIVERSIDE DRIVE, and 9 is a one-page summary of Simpson's career.

CRITICAL ARTICLES

1442 "Capturing the World as It Is: An Interview with Louis Simpson." OHIO REVIEW, 14, No. 3 (1973), 35-51.

Held in Athens, Ohio, 9 February 1973. Simpson explains the making of a book of poems as opposed to writing random poems and discusses his past writing practices and concerns, his sense of his own development and of the general tenor of present-day poetry ("a cult of sincerity"), the personae of ADVENTURES OF THE LETTER I, and, in conclusion, the difference between his work and Robert Bly's.

1443 Gray, Yohma. "The Poetry of Louis Simpson." TRI-QUARTERLY, 5 (Spring 1963), 33-39.

Simpson's is highly personal lyric poetry that "imposes order from within on chaos without, gives meaning to the apparently meaningless, suggests vantage points from which to probe experience." Reprinted in no. 258.

1444 Rompf, Kraft. "An Interview with Louis Simpson." FALCON, 7 (Spring 1976), 3-23.

Rompf keeps the interview strictly on Simpson's writing except near the end when he asks about other poets and advice for the young poet.

1445 Smith, Dave. "A Child of the World." AMERICAN POETRY REVIEW, 8, No. 1 (1979), 10-15.

Review of SEARCHING FOR THE OX. An assessment of the quality and scope of Simpson's work. To Smith, Simpson "demonstrates an engagement with the vicissitudes and antinomies of American life in the sixties and seventies that is equal to the best we have."

L.E. SISSMAN

(American; January 1, 1928-March 10, 1976)

POEMS

DYING: AN INTRODUCTION. Boston: Little, Brown, 1968.
SCATTERED RETURNS. Boston: Little, Brown, 1969.
PURSUIT OF HONOR. Boston: Little, Brown, 1971.
INNOCENT BYSTANDER: THE SCENE FROM THE 70'S. New York: Vanguard Press, 1975.
HELLO DARKNESS: THE COLLECTED POEMS OF L. E. SISSMAN. Boston: Atlantic, Little, Brown, 1978.

CRITICAL ARTICLES

1446 Pitchford, Kenneth. "Metaphor as Illness: A Meditation on Recent Poetry." NEW ENGLAND REVIEW, 1 (1978), 96-119.

In this essay Pitchford reviews three other books as well as Sissman's HELLO DARKNESS. He uses Susan Sontag's ILLNESS AS METAPHOR to compare the thinker's with the poet's treatment of the prevailing attitudes toward terminal illness. A reader of Sissman's poems enters "a terrain that dips into a nightmare world so frightening that it takes a measure of courage to follow him." Pitchford ends by defending the uses of metaphor against Sontag's thesis.

1447 Pritchard, William H. "Innocence Possessed." TIMES LITERARY SUPPLEMENT, 28 July 1978, pp. 847.

A biographical sketch and review of HELLO DARKNESS. Sissman was a Quiz Kid on the famous QUIZ KIDS radio program in the thirties and forties. In November 1965 he learned he had Hodgkin's disease. Pritchard discusses Sissman's attitude towards death and dying as expressed in his poems.

C.H. SISSON

(English; April 22, 1914--)

POEMS

VERSIONS AND PERVERSIONS OF HEINE. London: Gaberbocchus, 1955.
POEMS. Fairwarp, Engl.: Peter Russell, 1959.
THE LONDON ZOO. London: Abelard-Schuman, 1961.
NUMBERS. London: Methuen, 1965.
METAMORPHOSES. London: Methuen, 1968.
IN THE TROJAN DITCH: COLLECTED POEMS AND SELECTED TRANSLATIONS. Cheadle, Engl.: Carcanet, 1974.
THE CORRIDOR. Hitchin, Engl.: Mandeville Press, 1975.
ANCHISES: NEW POEMS. Manchester: Carcanet, 1976.

CRITICAL ARTICLES

1448 Bedient, Calvin. "Coming Out." PARNASSUS, 3, No. 2 (1975), 121-33.

Review of IN THE TROJAN DITCH. A survey of Sisson's career as represented by this volume. Bedient traces his development from the "classicism" of his early work to the "modernist" mode of his later. "Sisson joins the small number of English poets . . . who, since the mid-sixties, have been making over English poetry on non-Romantic avant-garde lines."

1449 Burney, John. "An Interview with C.H. Sisson." PARNASSUS, 6, No. 2 (1978), 167-69.

Sisson discusses the training of poets (and readers). His parting advice to would-be poets is "not [to] write more than you must. And burn some of that." Reprinted from NEW YORKSHIRE WRITING: A QUARTERLY REVIEW OF LITERATURE, No. 2 (Autumn 1977).

1450 Pilling, John. "The Strict Temperature of Classicism: C.H. Sisson." CRITICAL QUARTERLY, 21 (Autumn 1979), 73-81.

Argues that Sisson is the one modern poet whose individual works constitute an oeuvre. He has managed to maintain the classical temper by going back "to Augustan models and [has] not been seduced by other versions of classicism."

1451 Wright, David. "The Poetry of C.H. Sisson." AGENDA, 13 (Autumn 1975), 5-17.

Commentary on the life and works of Sisson, who published almost no verse until he was forty and received little recognition until he was sixty.

STEVIE SMITH

(English; September 20, 1902-March 7, 1971)

POEMS

A GOOD TIME WAS HAD BY ALL. London: Jonathan Cape, 1937.
TENDER ONLY TO ONE. London: Jonathan Cape, 1938.
MOTHER, WHAT IS MAN? London: Jonathan Cape, 1942.
HAROLD'S LEAP. London: Chapman and Hall, 1950.
NOT WAVING BUT DROWNING. London: Andre Deutsch, 1957.
SELECTED POEMS. London: Longmans; New York: New Directions, 1962.
THE FROG PRINCE AND OTHER POEMS. London: Longmans, 1966.
THE BEST BEAST. New York: Knopf, 1969.
THE SCORPION AND OTHER POEMS. London: Longmans, 1972.
THE COLLECTED POEMS. London: Allen Lane, 1975; New York: Oxford University Press, 1976.

CRITICAL ARTICLES

1452 Dick, Kay. "Stevie Smith." In her IVY AND STEVIE: IVY COMPTON-BURNETT AND STEVIE SMITH: CONVERSATIONS AND REFLECTIONS. London: Duckworth, 1971, pp. 33-60.

> The conversation with Smith was recorded in her Palmers Green home, 7 November 1970. Smith talks about her family and her work. She relates how she came to be called Stevie and other intimate details. Dick's reflections are her reminiscences and impressions of Smith.

1453 Enright, D.J. "Did Nobody Teach You?: On Stevie Smith." ENCOUNTER, 36 (June 1971), 53-57.

> Her poetry is classical in temperament and unromantic. It "is uncluttered, and hence must leave out, for instance, the reservations and modifications and clarifications. . . . But it leaves out what it could not accommodate and still be the kind of poetry it is: and that is all it leaves out."

1454 Helmling, Steven. "Delivered for a Time from Silence." PARNASSUS, 6, No. 1 (1977), 314-30.

Review of THE COLLECTED POEMS. Helmling examines and praises Smith's technical skill, humor, seriousness, stubbornness, cynicism, and irony. Her "poems have the tremendous power of taking weight off the mind. . . . Not the distractions of light verse, but real pleasure lifting real weight: that is this poet's freeing power."

1455 Simon, John. "The Poems of Stevie Smith." CANTO, 1, No. 1 (1977), 181-98.

Review of COLLECTED POEMS. After brief remarks on Smith's life and critical reception, Simon describes the characteristics of her poems which, he says, are mature from the beginning in A GOOD TIME WAS HAD BY ALL.

1456 Storey, Mark. "Why Stevie Smith Matters." CRITICAL QUARTERLY, 21, No. 2 (1979), 41-55.

Storey tries to lift the weight of Smith's reputation for eccentricity and points out the chief characteristics of her poems.

1457 "The Voice of Genteel Decay." TIMES LITERARY SUPPLEMENT, 14 July 1972, p. 820.

Reviews Smith's career and THE SCORPION, her posthumous book of poems. The reviewer is impressed by her honesty and her loyalty "to her inner life."

1458 Wade, Stephen. "Stevie Smith and the Untruth of Myth." AGENDA, 15, Nos. 2-3 (1977), 102-06.

Smith employs many variations in her use of myths but always with a turning inward, giving them an "open-ended nature." Myth "is one more great, overawing force in life that is totally unfamiliar and has to be made more familiar and therefore less daunting by means of art."

1459 Williams, Jonathan. "Much Further Out Than You Thought." PARNASSUS, 2, No. 2 (1974), 105-27.

Excerpts from an interview, 13 September 1963, are used in the essay. Williams recounts his personal acquaintance with Smith; and in the interview Smith describes her writing career, her past life, and her daily life. She also discusses her drawings and novels. Williams comments on her poems briefly and quotes excerpts from those he likes most.

WILLIAM JAY SMITH

(American; April 22, 1918--)

POEMS

POEMS. Pawlet, Vt.: Banyan Press, 1947.
CELEBRATION AT DARK. New York: Farrar, Straus, 1950.
TYPEWRITER BIRDS. New York: Caliban Press, 1954.
POEMS 1947-1957. Boston: Little, Brown, 1957.
THE TIN CAN AND OTHER POEMS. New York: Delacorte Press, 1966.
NEW AND SELECTED POEMS. New York: Delacorte Press, 1970.
VENICE IN THE FOG. Greensboro, N.C.: Unicorn Press, 1975.
JOURNEY TO THE DEAD SEA. Omaha, Nebr.: Abattoir Press, 1979.
THE TALL POETS. Winston-Salem, N.C.: Palaemon Press, 1979.

CRITICAL ARTICLES

1460 Jacobsen, Josephine. "The Dark Train and the Green Place: The Poetry of William Jay Smith." HOLLINS CRITIC, 12, No. 1 (1975), 1-14. Bibliog.

Jacobsen treats the various categories of Smith's verse from children's books to his poems concerned with death. She says his "development has always sprung from, and returned to, his basic convictions, and above all, his understanding of the spontaneous characteristics of his poetic gifts."

1461 Ritchie, Elisavietta. "An Interview with William Jay Smith." VOYAGES, 3 (Winter 1970), 89-103.

Smith describes his position as Poetry Consultant at the Library of Congress, some of his talks with audiences in the United States and around the world (especially elementary school children), his own writing, reading that has influenced him, and his experience with translating poems.

W.D. SNODGRASS

(American; January 5, 1926--)

POEMS

HEART'S NEEDLE. New York: Knopf, 1959; Hessle, Engl.: Marvell Press, 1960.
AFTER EXPERIENCE. New York: Harper and Row; London: Oxford University Press, 1968.
REMAINS [Pseud. S.S. Gardons]. Mt. Horeb, Wis.: Perishable Press, 1970.
THE FUEHRER BUNKER: A CYCLE OF POEMS IN PROGRESS. Brockport, N.Y.: BOA Editions, 1977.
IF BIRDS BUILD WITH YOUR HAIR. New York: Nadja, 1979.

CRITICAL BOOK

1462 Gaston, Paul. W.D. SNODGRASS. Boston: Twayne, 1978. 173 p. Notes, refs., bibliog., index.

Chapter 1 is on the character of "confessional poetry" and four experiences related to Snodgrass' poems; 2 and 3 on HEART'S NEEDLE; 4 on REMAINS; 5 and 6 on AFTER EXPERIENCE; 7 on THE FUEHRER BUNKER; and 8 on his translations and criticism and his development.

GARY SNYDER

(American; May 8, 1930--)

POEMS

RIPRAP. Ashland, Mass.: Origin Press, 1959.
MYTHS AND TEXTS. New York: Totem Press, 1960.
HOP, SKIP, AND JUMP. Berkeley, Calif.: Oyez, 1964.
NANOA KNOWS. San Francisco: Four Seasons Press, 1964.
RIPRAP AND COLD MOUNTAIN POEMS. San Francisco: Four Seasons Press, 1965.
SIX SECTIONS FROM MOUNTAINS AND RIVERS WITHOUT END. San Francisco: Four Seasons Press, 1965.
A RANGE OF POEMS. London: Fulcrum Press, 1966.
THREE WORLDS, THREE REALMS, SIX ROADS. Marlboro, Vt.: Griffin Press, 1966.
THE BACK COUNTRY. New York: New Directions, 1968.
THE BLUE SKY. New York: Phoenix Bookshop, 1969.
REGARDING WAVE. Iowa City: Windhover Press, 1969.
SOURS OF THE HILLS. Brooklyn: Portents, 1969.
ANASAZI. Santa Barbara, Calif.: Yes Press, 1971.
MANZANITA Bolinas, Calif.: Four Seasons Press, 1972.
TURTLE ISLAND. New York: New Directions, 1974.

CRITICAL BOOKS

1463 McCord, Howard. SOME NOTES TO GARY SNYDER'S MYTHS AND TEXTS. Berkeley, Calif.: Sand Dollar Press, 1971. 8 p.

Annotations are keyed to the Totem Press edition of MYTHS AND TEXTS. McCord identifies references--chiefly Asian and anthropological with some from American Indian lore. Others are the more familiar kinds of biblical and literary allusions and references.

1464 McNeill, Katherine. GARY SNYDER. New York: Phoenix Bookshop, forthcoming.

Not seen; cited in no. 63, page 1444. In June 1981, the publisher said it had not yet been published.

1465 Steuding, Bob. GARY SNYDER. Boston: Twayne, 1976. 189 p. Notes, refs., bibliog., index.

Chapter 1 is on Synder's life; 2 and 3 on his style and influences; 4 to 8 on his major books of poems; and 9 on his reputation and contribution to literature.

CRITICAL ARTICLES

1466 Almon, Bert. "Buddhism and Energy in the Recent Poetry of Gary Snyder." MOSAIC, 11, No. 1 (1977), 117-25.

Explains Buddhist influence on Snyder's poems.

1467 Altieri, Charles. "Gary Snyder's TURTLE ISLAND: The Problem of Reconciling the Roles of Seer and Prophet." BOUNDARY 2, 4 (Spring 1976), 761-77.

Considers Synder as seer and prophet as these appear in his verse, strong as the simple presenter of values, and weaker as the asker for action.

1468 Boozer, Jack, and Bob Yaeger. "An Interview with Gary Snyder." UNMUZZLED OX, 4, No. 3 (1978), 106-17.

Synder talks about America and poetry, what he reads and what he tries to do with his verse, and a little about psychology and sanity.

1469 Chua, Cheng Lok, and N. Sasaki. "Zen and the Title of Gary Snyder's 'Marin-An.'" NOTES ON CONTEMPORARY LITERATURE, 8, No. 3 (1978), 2-3.

The contrasts of moods and theme suggests that Snyder's title associates "the tranquillity of the Marin [California] countryside with the serenity of the Zen Buddhist's 'An' [an annex to a Zen temple that serves as a sanctuary for contemplation]."

1470 Chung, Ling. "Whose Mountain Is This? Gary Snyder's Translation of Han Shan." RENDITIONS: A CHINESE-ENGLISH TRANSLATION MAGAZINE, No. 7 (1977), pp. 93-102.

Compares Synder's rendition to the original in respect to "colloquialism, grammatical structure, metrical pattern, poetic imagery, and connotation." Snyder "has imbued the poems . . . with his own experience of the wilderness in North America." That experience, Ling Chung thinks, is different from Han Shan's in the mountains on the eastern coast of China. Nevertheless, Snyder's version is a "superior English verse."

1471 Geneson, Paul. "An Interview with Gary Snyder." OHIO REVIEW, 18, No. 3 (1977), 67-105.

A description of Snyder's home and family precedes the interview. Snyder tells about his life, influences on him, manner of working, and education: "Anthropology is probably the most intellectually exciting field in the universities."

1472 Gitzen, Julian. "Gary Snyder and the Poetry of Compassion." CRITICAL QUARTERLY, 15, No. 4 (1973), 341-57.

Gitzen analyzes Snyder's poem "Water" for its representative characteristics, compares MYTHS AND TEXTS to Eliot's work, and then concludes with a comment on compassion as "an essential ingredient of a pure land," a Buddhist dictum that Snyder implies will bring "harmony to our lives and to our natural surroundings."

1473 Goldstein, Laurence. "Wordsworth and Snyder: The Primitivist and His Problem of Self-Definition." CENTENNIAL REVIEW, 21, No. 1 (1977), 75-86.

Uses Wordsworth and Snyder to exemplify the thesis that though Romantic philosophy believes that a writer's language embodies his process of self-definition, "there resides in the Romantic poet a depressing and on occasion tragic recognition that language betrays its originating spirit." Goldstein applies this thesis to Snyder as a representative contemporary Romantic poet.

1474 Jungels, William J. "The Use of Native-American Mythologies in the Poetry of Gary Snyder." Dissertation, SUNY, Buffalo, 1973 (DAI, 34: 777).

Jungels studies Snyder's theory of myth and his "relation to neolithic culture," concentrating on MYTHS AND TEXTS.

1475 Kern, Robert. "Clearing the Ground: Gary Snyder and the Modernist Imperative." CRITICISM, 19, No. 2 (1977), 158-77.

Snyder's early poems have a broader base than "nature" or "ecological politics" as the development of his "ecological consciousness" shows. Snyder's poetics developed out of the modernist dictum, "Make it new."

1476 _____. "Recipes, Catalogues, Open Form Poetics: Gary Snyder's Archetypal Voice." CONTEMPORARY LITERATURE, 18 (1977), 173-97.

On Snyder, Whitman, and the values of open forms. Snyder has produced poems "in which form is truly a revelation of content."

1477 Leach, Thomas James, Jr. "Gary Snyder: Poet as Mythographer." Dissertation, University of North Carolina, Chapel Hill, 1974 (DAI, 36: 320).

Snyder's training in Buddhism makes him "well suited for the task of providing a cultural bridge between the East and the West."

1478 Lin, Yao-fu. "'The Mountains Are Your Mind': Orientalism in the Poetry of Gary Snyder." TAMKANG REVIEW, 6, Nos. 2-7, 1 (1975-76), 357-92.

Detailed inspection of the influence of Zen Buddhism on Snyder's view of himself and the world, touching on most of his collections of poems.

1479 Marsden, James Douglas. "Modern Echoes of Transcendentalism: Kesey, Snyder, and Other Countercultural Authors." Dissertation, Brown University, 1977 (DAI, 38: 4830).

Connects the contemporary "movement of dissension" with Emerson, Thoreau, and Whitman. Snyder and the other writers in the study "repeat and extend the earlier criticism of our society's materialism, conformity, and estrangement from nature."

1480 Okada, Roy Kazuaki. "Zen and the Poetry of Gary Snyder." Dissertation, University of Wisconsin, 1973 (DAI, 34: 6651).

Snyder's uses of Zen differ from the traditional uses of myth by Western poets. "Zen becomes part of the poet['s] consciousness."

1481 Paul, Sherman. "Noble and Simple." PARNASSUS, 3, No. 2 (1975), 217-25.

Review of TURTLE ISLAND. Paul comments at length on "I went into the Maverick Bar" as a representative poem. "And though many of the poems in this collection express equanimity and happiness, he is still . . . aware of shadows and the night."

1482 Peach, Linden. "EARTH HOUSE HOLD: A Twentieth Century Walden?" ANGLO-WELSH REVIEW, 25 (Autumn 1975), 108-14.

On the similarity of Snyder to Lawrence and Thoreau. "Civilization . . . reduces the individual life."

1483 Pickett, Becky. "Gary Snyder and Buddhism." Dissertation, University of Nebraska, 1978.

Not seen; cited in no. 33.

1484 Rothberg, Abraham. "A Passage to More Than India: The Poetry of Gary Snyder." SOUTHWEST REVIEW, 61, No. 1 (1976), 26-37.

Snyder's poems are part of the American bardic tradition, though he fails "to shape the new within the shell of the old." Rather than "creating the uniqueness and diversity he extols, Snyder lapses into a homogeneity and repetitiveness that quickly palls and often appalls." Snyder has "perhaps a dozen poems that are really fine--and of how many poets can one say that?"

JACK SPICER

(American; January 30, 1925- August 17, 1965)

POEMS

AFTER LORCA. San Francisco: White Rabbit Press, 1957.
BILLY THE KID. Stinson Beach, Calif.: Enkidu Surrogate, 1959.
THE HEADS OF THE TOWN UP TO THE AETHER. San Francisco: Auerhahn Society, 1962.
LAMENT FOR THE MAKERS. San Francisco: White Rabbit Press, 1962.
THE HOLY GRAIL. San Francisco: White Rabbit Press, 1964.
LANGUAGE. San Francisco: White Rabbit Press, 1965.
BOOK OF MAGAZINE VERSE. San Francisco: White Rabbit Press, 1966.
A BOOK OF MUSIC. Santa Barbara, Calif.: White Rabbit Press, 1969.
SOME THINGS FROM JACK. Verona, Italy: Plain Wrapper Press, 1972.
ADMONITIONS. New York: Adventures in Poetry, 1974.
THE COLLECTED BOOKS OF JACK SPICER. Los Angeles: Black Sparrow Press, 1975.

SPECIAL ISSUE

1485 BOUNDARY 2, 6, No. 1 (Fall 1977).

This special issue contains the following articles in sequence:

William V. Spanos, "Jack Spicer's Poetry of Absence: An Introduction," pages 1-3, discusses Spicer's "postmodernism." Robin Blaser and John Granger, eds., "An Exercise by Jack Spicer," pages 3-23, present a previously unpublished sequence with an editors' note describing the original manuscript. "A Plan for a Book on Tarot," pages 25-29, also edited by Blaser and Granger, suggests that Spicer's comments here are analogous to criticism of poems. Clayton Eshelman, "The Lorca Working," pages 31-49, comments on AFTER LORCA poem by poem and then compares earlier poems with later ones.

Jed Rasula, "Spicer's Orpheus and the Emancipation of Pronouns," pages 51-102, says Spicer as poet is like Orpheus--he leads his "message" in the way that Orpheus precedes

Eurydice out of Hades, always tempted to look back. Michael Davidson, "Incarnations of Jack Spicer: HEADS OF THE TOWN UP TO THE AETHER," pages 103-34, explains that Spicer's book "explores ideas of incarnation and absence as central themes." John Granger, "The Loss of the Bride in HEADS OF THE TOWN and the Reclamation of the text," pages 145-61, describes the displacement of self and the displacement of language as analogous to Dante or anyone else in hell and moves from "Homage to Creeley" to HEADS OF THE TOWN to show Spicer's way out.

Peter Riley, "The Narratives of THE HOLY GRAIL," pages 163-90, guides the reader book by book through Spicer's poem with commentary on meaning and on Spicer. Colin Christopher Stuart and John Scoggan, "The Orientation of the Parasols: Saussure, Derrida, and Spicer," pages 191-257, compare Spicer, Black Mountain poets, and the oral theory of poetry: "the tradition of the disembodied voice." James Liddy, "A Problem with Sparrows: Spicer's Last Stance," pages 259-66, examines Spicer's BOOK OF MAGAZINE VERSE and its iconoclastic theme. Stephanie A. Judy, "'The Grand Concord of What': Preliminary Thoughts on Musical Composition in Poetry," pages 267-85, explores what Poe and Spicer meant by the term "indefinite" as applied to music and poetry to discover what common ground music and poetry occupy.

CRITICAL ARTICLES

1486 Blaser, Robin. "The Practice of Outside." In THE COLLECTED BOOKS OF JACK SPICER. Ed. Robin Blaser. Los Angeles: Black Sparrow Press, 1975, pp. 270-329.

Explains the techniques, ideas, and personality of Spicer. In 1957, Blaser says, "that composing factor--the dictation, the unknown, or the outside--enters the work, and Jack begins to construct a poetry that was not lyric but narrative." The essay elaborates this thesis and traces its manifestations in Spicer's work.

1487 Feld, Ross. "Lowghost to Lowghost." PARNASSUS, 4, No. 2 (1976), 5-31.

Feld thinks Spicer is worth reading and goes through THE COLLECTED BOOKS showing why.

1488 Sadler, Frank. "The Frontier in Jack Spicer's 'Billy the Kid.'" CONCERNING POETRY, 9 (Fall 1976), 15-21.

An interpretation of "Billy the Kid" based on a close analysis of the narrator and on the theme "that a poem is the working out of its possibilities."

WILLIAM STAFFORD

(American; January 17, 1914--)

POEMS

WEST OF YOUR CITY. Los Gatos, Calif.: Talisman Press, 1961.
TRAVELING THROUGH THE DARK. New York: Harper and Row, 1963.
THE RESCUED YEAR. New York: Harper and Row, 1966.
ELEVEN UNTITLED POEMS. Mt. Horeb, Wis.: Perishable Press, 1968.
ALLEGIANCES. New York: Harper and Row, 1970.
TEMPORARY FACTS. Athens, Ohio: Duane Schneider, 1970.
SOMEDAY, MAYBE. New York: Harper and Row, 1973.
THAT OTHER ALONE: POEMS. Mt. Horeb, Wis.: Perishable Press, 1973.
GOING PLACES. Reno: West Coast Poetry Review, 1974.
STORIES THAT COULD BE TRUE: NEW AND COLLECTED POEMS. New York: Harper and Row, 1977.
ALL ABOUT LIGHT. Athens, Ohio: Croissant Press, 1978.
SMOKE'S WAY. Port Townsend, Wash.: Graywolf Press, 1978.
THINGS THAT HAPPEN WHERE THERE AREN'T ANY PEOPLE. Brockport, N.Y.: BOA Editions, 1980.

BIBLIOGRAPHY

1489 McMillan, Samuel H. "On William Stafford and His Poems: A Selected Bibliography." TENNESSEE POETRY JOURNAL, 2 (Spring 1969), 21-22.

Lists thirty-two items, mostly reviews, that appeared from 1961 to 1968.

CRITICAL BOOK

1490 Holden, Jonathan. THE MARK TO TURN: A READING OF WILLIAM STAFFORD'S POETRY. Lawrence: University Press of Kansas, 1976. 91 p. Notes, bibliog., index.

Holden describes Stafford's "patterns" and "meanings" to show the unity of his work. He concentrates on WEST OF YOUR CITY, TRAVELING THROUGH THE DARK, THE RESCUED YEAR, ALLEGIANCE, and SOMEDAY, MAYBE. Holden says, page 81n, that James Pirie has indexed, and continues to index, "everything published by or about Stafford" at the Lewis and Clark College Library.

SPECIAL ISSUE

1491 NORTHWEST REVIEW, 13, No. 3 (1973).

This special issue contains the following items in sequence: In "An Interval in a Northwest Writer's Life 1950-1973," pages 6-9, Stafford remembers his experiences at the Iowa Workshop. Facsimiles of "Journal Scribbling" appear on pages 10-25. "The Third Time the World Happens," pages 26-47, is a dialogue between Richard Hugo and Stafford, "taped in a motel room at Albany, Oregon, after a literary conference at Linn-Benton Community College, March 23, 1973." On pages 48-63 are photographs of writers and friends by William Stafford.

CRITICAL ARTICLES

1492 Coles, Robert. "William Stafford's Long Walk." AMERICAN POETRY REVIEW, 4, No. 4 (1975), 27-28.

Coles describes Stafford's view of America, "not Whitman's lyrical urging, really, but not a voice of despair, either, and certainly no inclination to disgust or self-righteous condemnation."

1493 Dickinson-Brown, Roger. "The Wise, the Dull, the Bewildered: What Happens in William Stafford." MODERN POETRY STUDIES, 6 (Spring 1975), 30-38.

Tries to explain, and also to answer, the charge by critics of dullness in Stafford's poetry.

1494 Ellsworth, Peter. "A Conversation with William Stafford." CHICAGO REVIEW, 30, No. 1 (1978), 94-100.

Ellsworth asks Stafford questions about a sense of community in his poems, about his tenure as poetry consultant to the Library of Congress, and about his views on other contemporary poets. To a question about influence, Stafford replies, "The voice I hear in my poems is my mother's voice."

1495 Gerber, Philip L., and Robert J. Gemmett, eds. "Keeping the Lines Wet: A Conversation with William Stafford." PRAIRIE SCHOONER, 44, No. 2 (1970), 123-36.

For the SUNY Brockport WRITERS FORUM, November 1969. Stafford discusses writing poetry, myth and patterns, geography as a subject, teaching the craft of poetry, and oral and written poetry.

1496 Kramer, Lawrence. "In Quiet Language." PARNASSUS, 6, No. 2 (1978), 101-17.

Review of STORIES THAT COULD BE TRUE and four collections by other poets. Kramer compares Stafford to Wendell Berry (whose CLEARING and THREE MEMORIAL POEMS are also reviewed), ending his remarks on Stafford on page 108. As suggested by his title, Kramer concentrates on Stafford's language, in which the poet has "a startling extravagance of trust," and on his "voices."

1497 Lensing, George S. "William Stafford, Mythmaker." MODERN POETRY STUDIES, 6 (Spring 1975), 1-17.

"The quest for myth, comprising both a technique and a theme, takes the reader to the heart of the poetry." Lensing ranges over Stafford's whole career as a poet.

1498 Lofsness, Cynthia. "An Interview with William Stafford." IOWA REVIEW, 3, No. 3 (1972), 92-107.

Stafford responds to questions about how he feels about writing and other writers. Lofsness asks him about particular poems of his own and things he has said or written about poetry, himself, and his relation to society.

1499 Lynch, Dennis Daley. "Journeys in Search of Oneself: The Metaphor of the Road in William Stafford's TRAVELING THROUGH THE DARK and THE RESCUED YEAR." MODERN POETRY STUDIES, 7, No. 2 (1976), 122-31.

Journeys in Stafford's two collections may be divided into journeys of remembrance, of quest, and of experience; each represents "important aspects of Stafford's world view."

1500 Pinsker, Sanford. "Finding What the World Is Trying to Be: A Conversation with William Stafford." AMERICAN POETRY REVIEW, 4, No. 4 (1975), 28-30.

On writing as a creative act, reading, and "discovery." Stafford says that poets need their "bad" poems as well as their good efforts.

1501 Sumner, D. Nathan. "The Poetry of William Stafford: Nature, Time, and Father." RESEARCH STUDIES, 36, No. 3 (1968), 187-95.

Sumner tries "to define the most characteristic elements of Stafford's work, to isolate and express in some way the fundamental motivating spirit in his poetry, and to evaluate his possible significance to the contemporary reader."

1502 Turner, Alberta T. "William Stafford and the Surprise Cliché." SOUTH CAROLINA REVIEW, 7, No. 2 (1975), 28-33.

Stafford uses clichés almost as one uses "historical or literary allusion," his changes or shifts then creating a new awareness.

1503 Wagner, Linda W. "William Stafford's Plain Style." MODERN POETRY STUDIES, 6 (Spring 1975), 19-30.

Close reading of some passages. Stafford's style is made up of "homey language and idiom, the running sentence rhythms and casual throw-away lines, the recurrence of Midwestern locations and characters." Reprinted in no. 296.

JON STALLWORTHY
(English; January 18, 1935--)

POEMS

THE ASTRONOMY OF LOVE. London: Oxford University Press, 1961.
OUT OF BOUNDS. London: Oxford University Press, 1963.
THE ALMOND TREE. London: Turret Books, 1967.
POSITIVES. Dublin: Dolmen Press, 1969.
ROOT AND BRANCH. London: Chatto and Windus, Hogarth; New York: Oxford University Press, 1969.
A DINNER OF HERBS. Exeter, Engl.: Rougemont Press, 1970.
THE APPLE BARREL: SELECTED POEMS 1956-1963. London: Oxford University Press, 1974.
HAND IN HAND. London: Chatto and Windus, Hogarth, 1974.
A FAMILIAR TREE. London: Chatto and Windus, Oxford University Press; New York: Oxford University Press, 1978.

CRITICAL ARTICLE

1504 Marten, Harry. Review of A FAMILIAR TREE. CONTEMPORARY LITERATURE, 21, No. 1 (1980), 146-58.

Marten's comments on Stallworthy are on pages 150-54. He describes the poet's journey through his family history and back as one "we follow to learn the outwardness of inner truths."

TERRY STOKES

(American; December 26, 1943--)

POEMS

LIVING AROUND OTHER PEOPLE. Kalamazoo, Mich.: Westigan Review Press, 1971.
NATURAL DISASTERS. New York: New York University Press, 1971.
CRIMES OF PASSION. New York: Knopf, 1973.
BONING THE DREAMER. New York: Knopf, 1975.

SPECIAL ISSUE

1505 MANASSAS REVIEW, 1 (Spring-Summer 1977).

Not seen; cited in JOURNAL OF MODERN LITERATURE, 7, No. 4 (1979), 882. Includes new poems and a bibliography.

CRITICAL ARTICLE

1506 Shevin, David. "Falling into Your Ear." PARNASSUS, 6, No. 1 (1977), 339-45.

Review of BONING THE DREAMER. Describes the harsh, casual, victimizing world of Stokes.

MARK STRAND

(American; April 11, 1934--)

POEMS

SLEEPING WITH ONE EYE OPEN. Iowa City: Stone Wall Press, 1964.
REASONS FOR MOVING. New York: Atheneum, 1968.
DARKER. New York: Atheneum, 1970.
ELEGY FOR MY FATHER. Iowa City: Windhover Press, 1973.
THE SERGEANTVILLE NOTEBOOK. Providence: Burning Deck Press, 1973.
THE STORY OF OUR LIVES. New York: Atheneum, 1973.
THE LATE HOUR. New York: Atheneum, 1978.

CRITICAL ARTICLES

1507 Brooks, David. "A Conversation with Mark Strand." ONTARIO REVIEW, 8 (1978), 23-33.

Strand tells about his work and the influences on it, about translating and the benefits to be derived from such an activity by a poet, and about limitations he feels are in his own poems.

1508 "A Conversation with Mark Strand." OHIO REVIEW, 13, No. 2 (1972), 54-71.

Strand talks about his early writing and what he is trying to do now, how poems work, and some of the ways he works on poems and the principles he applies, as well as discussing how he revises first drafts of poems, influences on him, and long poems by contemporary poets. Reprinted in no. 288 with some expansion and deletion.

1509 Crenner, James. "Mark Strand: DARKER." SENECA REVIEW, 2 (April 1971), 84-89.

"Where we like to think of awareness as a form of illumination, for Strand illumination is a form of darkening." Reading his poems is like standing in exceedingly bright daylight when "suddenly there is a bolt of darkness in which, for an instant, the heavy furniture and the corpse and the monster stand out clearly."

1510 French, Roberts W. "Eating Poetry: The Poetry of Mark Strand." FAR POINT, 5 (1970), 61-66.

Review of REASONS FOR MOVING and DARKER. Of the first book French says, "The unknown is brought into being; shadows are given substance and life." Of the second he says we are given "a way of seeing, a mode of vision, a stance from which to peer into the darkness."

1511 Kirby, David. "The Nature of No One." TIMES LITERARY SUPPLEMENT, 15 September 1978, p. 1009.

Review of THE MONUMENT [prose poems] and THE LATE HOUR. Strand makes "the idea of the quiet personal voice . . . the fertile ground of his thought and art." Kirby reviews Strand's career to demonstrate his assertion.

1512 Klein, Norman. "Mark Strand and Norman Klein: A Conversation." PLOUGHSHARES, 2, No. 3 (1975), 97-102.

Strand explains at some length the problems involved in writing long poems and mentions influences and poets from whom he has learned.

1513 Miklitsch, Robert. "Beginnings and Endings: Mark Strand's 'The Untelling.'" LITERARY REVIEW, 21, No. 3 (1978), 357-73.

Miklitsch notes what is unique about Strand, what sets him apart when at the same time he is representative and transitional. Strand does not just bring out collections; he "is publishing 'books of poems.'" Although emphasis is on "The Untelling," Miklitsch also talks about THE STORY OF OUR LIVES as a whole.

1514 Vine, Richard, and Robert von Hallberg. "A Conversation with Mark Strand." CHICAGO REVIEW, 28, No. 4 (1977), 130-40. [Note: cover of this issue reads volume 48.]

Strand replies to questions about influences on him, poets' attitudes toward their own poetry, other poets writing today, and the audience for poetry today.

JESSE STUART

(American; August 8, 1907--)

POEMS

HARVEST OF YOUTH. Howe, Okla.: Scroll Press, 1930.
MAN WITH A BULL-TONGUE PLOW. New York: Dutton, 1934; 2nd ed., 1959.
BEYOND DARK HILLS. New York: Dutton, 1938.
ALBUM OF DESTINY. New York: Dutton, 1944.
KENTUCKY IS MY LAND. New York: Dutton, 1952.
HOLD APRIL: NEW POEMS. New York: McGraw-Hill, 1962.
A JESSE STUART READER: STORIES AND POEMS. New York: McGraw-Hill, 1963.
SAVE EVERY LAMB. New York: McGraw-Hill, 1964.
THE WORLD OF JESSE STUART: SELECTED POEMS. New York: McGraw-Hill, 1975.

BIBLIOGRAPHY

1515 LeMaster, J.R. JESSE STUART: A REFERENCE GUIDE. Boston: G.K. Hall, 1979. 206 p.

Annotated secondary bibliography through 1977, listed chronologically by year and alphabetically within years. Books, articles, and reviews are in one continuous list.

1516 Woodbridge, Hensley C. JESSE AND JANE STUART: A BIBLIOGRAPHY. Murray, Ky.: Murray State University, 1969. 144 p.

Listed in no. 1515. A father-daughter bibliography with both primary and secondary items.

CRITICAL BOOKS

1517 LeMaster, J.R. JESSE STUART, KENTUCKY'S CHRONICLER-POET.

Memphis, Tenn.: Memphis State University Press, 1980. 218 p. Bibliog., index.

A survey of Stuart's writing career in eight chapters with such titles as "The Making of a Poet: An Overview," "The Juvenilia: An Experiment in Form and Technique," and "The Beauty of Words: A Concept of the Image." LeMaster has used material from his various articles.

1518 ______. JESSE STUART: SELECTED CRITICISM. St. Petersburg, Fla.: Valkyrie Press, 1978. 221 p.

Essays on Stuart's critics, teaching, humor, use of folklore, and stories, novels, and poems.

1519 LeMaster, J.R., and Mary Washington Clarke, eds. JESSE STUART: ESSAYS ON HIS WORK. Lexington: University Press of Kentucky, 1980. 176 p.

An updating of the 1977 edition listed in no. 1515, pages 189-90, with see entries to annotations.

HOLLIS SUMMERS

(American; June 21, 1916--)

POEMS

THE WALKS NEAR ATHENS. New York: Harper and Brothers, 1959.
SEVEN OCCASIONS. New Brunswick, N.J.: Rutgers University Press, 1964.
THE PEDDLER AND OTHER DOMESTIC MATTERS. New Brunswick, N.J.: Rutgers University Press, 1967.
SIT OPPOSITE EACH OTHER. New Brunswick, N.J.: Rutgers University Press, 1970.
START FROM HOME. New Brunswick, N.J.: Rutgers University Press, 1972.
OCCUPANT PLEASE FORWARD. New Brunswick, N.J.: Rutgers University Press, 1976.
DINOSAURS. Athens, Ohio: Rosetta Press, 1978.

CRITICAL ARTICLE

1520 Brown, Harry. "A Balanced Metaphysical." MODERN POETRY STUDIES, 7, No. 3 (1976), 252-54.

Summers' poems have "the subtlety, irony, ambiguity, elliptical quality, unusual figures of speech, and difficulty--in thought and syntax--that we often associate with Metaphysical style."

NATHANIEL TARN

(English; June 30, 1928--)

POEMS

OLD SAVAGE/YOUNG CITY. London: Cape Goliard, 1964; New York: Random House, 1965.
WHERE BABYLON ENDS. London: Cape Goliard; New York: Grossman, 1968.
THE BEAUTIFUL CONTRADICTIONS. London: Cape Goliard, 1969; New York: Random House, 1970.
A NOWHERE FOR VALLEJO: CHOICES, OCTOBER. New York: Random House, 1971; London: Cape Goliard, 1972.
LYRICS FOR THE BRIDE OF GOD: SECTION: THE ARTEMISION. Santa Barbara, Calif.: Tree Press, 1973; New York: New Directions, 1975.
THE PERSEPHONES. Santa Barbara, Calif.: Tree Press, 1974.
NARRATIVE OF THIS FALL. Los Angeles: Black Sparrow Press, 1976.
BIRDSCAPES, WITH SEASIDE. Santa Barbara, Calif.: Black Sparrow Press, 1978.

CRITICAL ARTICLES

1521 Corngold, Stanley. "Where Babylon Ends: Nathaniel Tarn's Poetic Development." BOUNDARY 2, 2, No. 4 (1975), 57-75.

His poetry is "a captivation by and progressive rejection of all forms of natural abundance."

1522 Lenfest, David S. "Notes Toward a Study of Nathaniel Tarn's THE BEAUTIFUL CONTRADICTIONS, the Poetry of Material Transmigration." BOUNDARY 2, 2, No. 4 (1975), 77-95.

On his conflict between the role as "preserver of culture" and "the immediate appeal of the world."

R.S. THOMAS

(Welsh; March 1, 1913--)

POEMS

STONES OF THE FIELD. Carmarthen, Wales: Druid Press, 1947.
AN ACRE OF LAND. Newtown, Wales: Montgomeryshire Printing, 1952.
SONG AT THE YEAR'S TURNING. London: Hart-Davis, 1955.
POETRY FOR SUPPER. London: Hart-Davis, 1958.
TARES. London: Hart-Davis, 1961.
THE BREAD OF TRUTH. London: Hart-Davis, 1963.
PIETA. London: Hart-Davis, 1966.
THE MOUNTAINS. New York: Chilmark Press, 1968 [prose poem for ten drawings by John Piper].
NOT THAT HE BROUGHT FLOWERS. London: Hart-Davis, 1968.
H'M: POEMS. London: Macmillan; New York: St. Martin's Press, 1972.
SELECTED POEMS 1946-1968. London: Hart-Davis, MacGibbon; New York: St. Martin's Press, 1973.
LABORATORIES OF THE SPIRIT. London: Macmillan, 1975; Boston: Godine, 1976.
THE WAY OF IT. Sunderland, Engl.: Ceolfrith Press, 1977.
FREQUENCIES. London: Macmillan, 1978.

SPECIAL ISSUE

1523 POETRY WALES, 7, No. 4 (Winter 1972).

This special issue contains the following items in sequence:

Articles by John Ackerman, pages 15-26; Roland Mathias, pages 27-45; John Ormond (filmscript), pages 47-57; Dafydd Elis Thomas, pages 59-66; Anthony Conran, pages 67-74; and Sam Adams, pages 75-81; reviews by R. George Thomas, pages 82-88, and Jeremy Hooker, pages 89-93, both on H'M; Randall Jenkins, pages 93-108, on Thomas' prose; Ioan Bowen Rees, pages 109-112, on THE MOUNTAINS; and Glyn Tegai Hughes, pages 112-15, on a German dissertation by Gisela Chan Man Fong; letters from Leslie

Norris (a negative view of Thomas), pages 118-21, and from Harri Webb (a favorable view in contrast to a negative view of Dylan Thomas), pages 121-23. See below for annotations of articles.

CRITICAL ARTICLES

1524 Ackerman, John. "Man & Nature in the Poetry of R. S. Thomas." POETRY WALES, 7, No. 4 (1972), 15-26.

Nature's influence on man as a central theme exemplifies Thomas' honest and complex response to the reality of life. Ackerman traces this theme from SONG AT THE YEAR'S TURNING to NOT THAT HE BROUGHT FLOWERS.

1525 Adams, Sam. "A Note on Four Poems." POETRY WALES, 7, No. 4 (1972), 75-81.

Analyzes four poems wherein "the poet observes the priest": "Service," "In Church," "Kneeling," and "They." These are similar not only in a point of view which shifts from without to within but also in form and development and "the concepts and attitudes of the poet."

1526 Bedient, Calvin. "On R. S. Thomas." CRITICAL QUARTERLY, 14, No. 3 (1972), 253-68.

Among other gifts, Bedient is impressed with Thomas' gift for metaphor.

1527 Conran, Anthony. "R. S. Thomas & the Anglo-Welsh Crisis." POETRY WALES, 7, No. 4 (1972), 67-74.

R. S. Thomas speaks for the middle-class Welsh, a sense of the term "Anglo-Welsh" as an "ersatz substitute for Welsh, very much a poor relation of the older language." Thomas gave these people, Conran says, "self respect."

1528 Cox, C. B., and A. E. Dyson. "R. S. Thomas: 'A Blackbird Singing.'" In no. 304, pages 133-36.

The blackbird illustrates a characteristic ambivalence in Thomas' work, a blending of opposites that increases awareness.

1529 Dyson, A. E. "The Poetry of R. S. Thomas." CRITICAL QUARTERLY, 20, No. 2 (1978), 5-31.

Isolates and examines the essential characteristics of Thomas' verse by looking closely at several poems, "Pieta," for example, and poems from SONG AT THE YEAR'S TURNING. He explores the relationship of Thomas' "religious sensibility" to his art, bringing the study up to LABORATORIES OF THE SPIRIT.

1530 Herman, Vimala. "Negativity and Language in the Religious Poetry of R.S. Thomas." ELH, 45, No. 4 (1978), 710-31.

Thomas' attitude toward God in his poetry, "a Dark God, basically unknowable, silent," creates what Herman calls the "negative moment" in his religious poems and explains the characteristic effects of his work.

1531 Knapp, James F. "The Poetry of R. S. Thomas." TWENTIETH CENTURY LITERATURE, 17, No. 1 (1971), 1-9.

Knapp focuses on Thomas' harsh view of Welsh farmers and the poet's responsibility as seer and truth-teller.

1532 Mathias, Roland. "Philosophy and Religion in the Poetry of R.S. Thomas." POETRY WALES, 7, No. 4 (1972), 27-45.

Traces the development of such subjects as philosophy and religion in Thomas' work from STONES OF THE FIELD to later volumes. A turn in Thomas' thinking takes place in "The Minister."

1533 Merchant, W. Moelwyn. "Since 1950: R.S. Thomas." CRITICAL QUARTERLY, 2, No. 4 (1960), 341-51.

The poems in POETRY FOR SUPPER mark a change from Thomas' earlier poems. Merchant finds them wider in emotional range even on the same subjects: more deeply ironic and compassionate. "Above all R.S. Thomas has become more explicit in statement; while he forces no acceptable conclusion, makes no assumption of dogma, the credal implications always present in his work are now less allusive in statement."

1534 Ormond, John. "R.S. Thomas: Priest and Poet." POETRY WALES, 7, No. 4 (1972), 47-57.

"A transcript of John Ormond's film for B.B.C. Television, broadcast on April 2nd, 1972; introduced by Sam Adams." In his introductory note Adams describes the landscape shown in the film and points out that "the visual element is subordinated to the spoken word." Thomas speaks for himself, and Adams "marvels at the frankness" of this usually reticent poet, who tells of his experiences in rural Wales.

1535 Price, Cecil. "The Poetry of R.S. Thomas." WELSH ANVIL, 4 (1952), 82-86.

In Thomas' first two volumes Price finds poems "that communicate both joy and a keen perception. We derive the one from his songs, the other from his studies of the hill farmer." Price describes Thomas' language, subjects, themes, and characteristic point of view.

1536 Savill, H.J. "The Iago Prytherch Poems of R.S. Thomas." ANGLO-WELSH REVIEW, 20 (Autumn 1971), 143-54.

Looks at Thomas' conception of the character Iago Prytherch through twenty years of the poet's verse.

1537 Shivpuri, Jagdish. "Two Contemporary Poets in English: Jon Silkin and R.S. Thomas." SIDDHA (Siddharth College, India), 10 (1975), 1-25.

Two separate essays. The second, on Thomas, shows Shivpuri impressed with his Welshness and his being a vicar in interpreting the poems. Shivpuri's idea of a Welsh vicar is the Reverend Eli Jenkins, a very sweet man, in UNDER MILK WOOD.

1538 Smith, Dorothy Anita. "R.S. Thomas: The Poet as Querulous." Dissertation, St. John's University, 1970 (DAI, 31: 2940).

Smith studies Thomas' poems through 1968 "as products of his quarrels with himself as he works out his attitudes toward conditions of life in Wales, his microcosm."

1539 Thomas, Dafydd Elis. "The Image of Wales in R.S. Thomas's Poetry." POETRY WALES, 7, No. 4 (1972), 59-66.

The term "Image" in the essay has to do with Wales as a nation. Thomas' view is "despair laden"; he sees a "dead or dying Wales." Some contrast with the views of other poets is made in order to show that frequently the same image can lead to opposite meanings or even carry "positive and negative elements in the Welsh situation."

1540 Thomas, R. George. "Humanus Sum: A Second Look at R.S. Thomas." ANGLO-WELSH REVIEW, 18 (1970), 55-62.

A summarizing look at Thomas' poetic career, reseeing poems from various volumes through NOT THAT HE BROUGHT FLOWERS.

1541 _____. "The Poetry of R.S. Thomas." REVIEW OF ENGLISH LITERATURE, 3, No. 4 (1962), 85-95.

Thomas had to "exorcise the preacher from his verse before he could write in any way at all as a parson." A chronological study of Thomas' poems, arguing that a change of tone begins and gains strength by the invention of a poetic alter ego, the character Iago Prytherch.

1542 _____. "R.S. Thomas." In ANDREW YOUNG [and] R.S. THOMAS. Writers and Their Work, no. 166. London: Longmans, Green, 1964, pp. 27-41. Bibliog.

Thomas' poetry changed in 1952 from accusatory and pulpiteering to a kind that expresses sympathy and charity for man and suggests a hard-won knowledge of shared community.

CHARLES TOMLINSON

(English; January 8, 1927--)

POEMS

RELATIONS AND CONTRARIES. Aldington, Engl.: Hand and Flower Press, 1951.
THE NECKLACE. Oxford: Fantasy Press, 1955; rev., London: Oxford University Press, 1966.
SEEING IS BELIEVING. New York: McDowell Obolonsky, 1958; London: Oxford University Press, 1960.
A PEOPLED LANDSCAPE. London: Oxford University Press, 1963.
POEMS: A SELECTION. London: Oxford University Press, 1964.
AMERICAN SCENES. London: Oxford University Press, 1966.
THE MATTACHINES. Cerillos, N. Mex.: San Marcos Press, 1968.
AMERICA WEST SOUTHWEST. Cerillos, N. Mex.: San Marcos Press, 1969.
THE WAY OF A WORLD. London: Oxford University Press, 1969.
WORDS AND IMAGES. London: Covent Garden Press, 1972.
WRITTEN ON WATER. London: Oxford University Press, 1972.
THE WAY IN AND OTHER POEMS. London: Oxford University Press, 1974.
SELECTED POEMS 1951-1974. London: Oxford University Press, 1978.
THE SHAFT. London: Oxford University Press, 1978.

CRITICAL ARTICLES

1543 "Charles Tomlinson at 50: A Celebration." PN REVIEW, 5, No. 1 (1977), 33-50.

A brief tribute by Michael Schmidt, praising Tomlinson's achievement, page 33. An interview by Schmidt, pages 35-40, in which Tomlinson does his own summing up. In "Fifteen Ways of Looking at Tomlinson" other brief tributes are given, one in Italian. Graphics by Tomlinson appear throughout the section.

1544 Edwards, Michael. "Charles Tomlinson: Notes on Tradition and Impersonality." CRITICAL QUARTERLY, 15, No. 2 (1973), 133-44.

Edwards looks at RENGA, a long poem in four languages, the English translation by Tomlinson; WORDS AND IMAGES, selections from his graphics and twelve poems; and WRITTEN ON WATER, a collection of his verse. Together, these three books offer Edwards an opportunity to assess Tomlinson's work and reexamine "one's sense of tradition and impersonality."

1545 ______. "The Poetry of Charles Tomlinson." AGENDA, 9 (Spring-Summer 1971), 126-41.

Assessment of Tomlinson's verse through THE WAY OF A WORLD. His verse "is a negotiation with space and time . . ., a continually repeated attempt, by meeting an uncontrollable world of spatial complexity and temporal flux, to create a dwelling for human imagination and for human passion." Occasional notes on affinities and influences.

1546 Gitzen, Julian. "Charles Tomlinson and the Plenitude of Fact." CRITICAL QUARTERLY, 13, No. 4 (1971), 355-62.

"Pointing to inflexible natural laws and to processes beyond our control, [Tomlinson] argues against the premise that the natural world is the plaything of man and concludes that we are shaped by our surroundings." From THE NECKLACE through THE WAY OF A WORLD.

1547 Grogan, Ruth. "Charles Tomlinson: Poet as Painter." CRITICAL QUARTERLY, 19, No. 4 (1977), 71-77.

Poet and painter are "antithetical" in Tomlinson. Grogan's thesis is "that the process of painting seemed to release energies which in unprecedented ways trouble the poetry as well." She examines WORD AND IMAGES and IN BLACK AND WHITE, this latter a book of graphics accompanied by prose meditations and essays.

1548 ______. "Charles Tomlinson: The Way of His World." CONTEMPORARY LITERATURE, 19, No. 4 (1978), 472-96.

A survey of Tomlinson's career. "Tomlinson's poems and groups of poems have been engaged over the years in a kind of dialogue with themselves and others, an invigoration and clarification of a distinctive idiom." Grogan examines imagery and themes.

1549 Gross, Michael. "The Meditative Eye of Charles Tomlinson." HOLLINS CRITIC, 15, No. 2 (1978), 1-18.

Gross discusses Tomlinson's subjects, techniques, and influences and also evaluates his poems. "The poems not only see, they are about the difficult and creative act of seeing. This in turn leads him to investigate the paradox of a dual allegiance to the shaping imagination and to the splendors of the unshaped world."

1550 Lee, L.L. "Charles Tomlinson as American Un-American." CONTEMPORARY POETRY, 2, No. 2 (1977), 11-15.

On American and English characteristics of Tomlinson's verse. "Tomlinson's poetry . . . derive[s] a good deal of its power from the tension between the American and English poles of his value and aesthetic systems."

1551 Mariani, Paul. "Tomlinson's Use of the Williams Triad." CONTEMPORARY LITERATURE, 18 (Summer 1977), 405-15.

The influence of W.C. Williams on Tomlinson's verse technique.

1552 Rasula, Jed, and Mike Erwin. "An Interview with Charles Tomlinson." CONTEMPORARY LITERATURE, 16, No. 4 (1975), 405-16.

Conducted by correspondence, January 1974. Tomlinson responds to questions about his published statements on the nature of poetry, specific lines in his poems, his intentions and meanings in these poems, and his sense of an audience.

1553 Saunders, William Savacool. "Reaching Beyond Desire: Charles Tomlinson's Poetry of Otherness." Dissertation, University of Iowa, 1975 (DAI, 36: 8052).

Studies Tomlinson's poetic development and the characteristics of his verse.

1554 Spears, Monroe K. "Shapes and Surfaces: David Jones, with a Glance at Charles Tomlinson." CONTEMPORARY LITERATURE, 12, No. 4 (1971), 402-19.

This essay is annotated in no. 863, page 62, since it is on Jones. Spears's glance at Tomlinson is very cursory, a frame for his analysis of Jones. "Both Jones and Tomlinson are convinced that the poet must be fully aware of the modern world; but they are equally convinced that he need not surrender to violence or despair."

1555 Weatherhead, A.K. "Charles Tomlinson: With Respect to Flux." IOWA REVIEW, 7, No. 4 (1976), 120-33.

Weatherhead pursues the ambivalent answers in Tomlinson's verse to questions like "whether there is form in reality, whether form in a scene is part of the act of perception, or whether it belongs not to reality but to the alien 'order of discourse,' in a word whether in the literary act form is discovered or imposed."

LEWIS TURCO

(American; May 2, 1934--)

POEMS

DAY AFTER HISTORY. Arlington, Va.: Samisdat, 1956.
FIRST POEMS. Francestown, N.H.: Golden Quill Press, 1960.
THE SKETCHES OF LEWIS TURCO AND LIVEVIL: A MASK. Cleveland: American Weave Press, 1962.
AWAKEN, BELLS FALLING: POEMS 1959-1967. Columbia: University of Missouri Press, 1968.
THE INHABITANT. Northampton, Mass.: Despa Press, 1970.
POCOANGELINI: A FANTOGRAPHY. Northampton, Mass.: Despa Press, 1971.
THE WEED GARDEN. Orangeburg, S.C.: Peaceweed Press, 1973.
A CAGE OF CREATURES. Potsdam, N.Y.: Banjo Press, 1978.
THE COMPLEAT MELANCHOLICK. Madison, Wis.: Bieler Press, 1979.

BIBLIOGRAPHY

1556 "Lewis Turco: A Bibliography of His Works and of Criticism of Them." In F.W. CRUMB MEMORIAL LIBRARY BIBLIOGRAPHIES IN CONTEMPORARY POETRY. Potsdam, N.Y.: SUNY, Potsdam, 1972, pp. 57-68.

Lists books, periodical publications, poems in anthologies, reviews of some works, and critical essays about Turco. Includes periodical publication of individual poems later appearing in single volume collections.

CRITICAL ARTICLES

1557 Fitz Gerald, Gregory, and William Heyen. "The Poetry of Lewis Turco: An Interview." COSTERUS, OS 9 (1973), 239-51.

For SUNY Brockport WRITERS FORUM, 22 February 1968. Turco comments on politics in poems and on techniques of poetry in an anecdotal way.

1558 Heyen, William. "The Progress of Lewis Turco." MODERN POETRY STUDIES, 2, No. 3 (1971), 115-24.

Each collection of Turco's makes an advance over the previous one. THE INHABITANT, for example, is a volume "Turco has been heading toward for a long time."

1559 McLean, David, ed. "Craft and Vision: An Interview with Lewis Turco." DE KALB LITERARY ARTS JOURNAL, 4, No. 4 (1970), 1-14.

At Potsdam's Spring Poetry Festival, April 1969; Turco gives his views on "tendencies" now in modern poetry. He sums up with what William Knott, one of the interviewers, felt was a reflection of the theme in their conversation, after a list of Turco's favorite poets: "Most of them are not in vast favor at the moment as are the Emersonians and pop-Emersonians; yet they speak to me because they are poets who know how to write and are not just people who think they have 'soul.'"

1560 Waggoner, Hyatt. "The 'Formalism' of Lewis Turco: Fluting and Fifing with Frosted Fingers." CONCERNING POETRY, 2 (Fall 1969), 50-58.

"Turco as poet has tended to preserve and rework Modernist attitudes in our post-Modernist period, and Turco as critic has . . . taken on the role of valiant defender of the timeless verities of the poet's art against all those who promote confusion by putting first what is properly secondary, for instance by writing 'confessional' poetry or striking a 'prophetic' stance." Emerson, Waggoner says, has "saved" Turco.

DAVID WAGONER

(American; June 5, 1926--)

POEMS

DRY SUN, DRY WIND. Bloomington: Indiana University Press, 1953.
A PLACE TO STAND. Bloomington: Indiana University Press, 1958.
POEMS. Portland, Oreg.: Portland Art Museum, 1959.
THE NESTING GROUND. Bloomington: Indiana University Press, 1963.
STAYING ALIVE. Bloomington: Indiana University Press, 1966.
NEW AND SELECTED POEMS. Bloomington: Indiana University Press, 1969.
WORKING AGAINST TIME. London: Rapp and Whiting, 1970.
RIVERBED. Bloomington: Indiana University Press, 1972.
A GUIDE TO DUNGENESS SPIT. Port Townsend, Wash.: Graywolf Press, 1975.
COLLECTED POEMS 1956-1976. Bloomington: Indiana University Press, 1976.
TRAVELLING LIGHT. Port Townsend, Wash.: Graywolf Press, 1976.
WHO SHALL BE THE SUN? POEMS BASED ON THE LORE, LEGENDS, AND MYTHS OF NORTHWEST COAST AND PLATEAU INDIANS. Bloomington: Indiana University Press, 1978.
IN BROKEN COUNTRY. Boston: Little, Brown, 1979.

CRITICAL ARTICLES

1561 Boyers, Robert. "The Poetry of David Wagoner." KENYON REVIEW, 32, No. 1 (1970), 176-81.

Review of NEW AND SELECTED POEMS. Assesses the strengths and weaknesses of Wagoner as illustrated by poems in this collection, which includes many early poems. His poetry, Boyers concludes, "is a poetry of consolation, that genuinely lifts the spirit that greets it."

1562 Cording, Robert Kenneth. "A New Lyricism: David Wagoner and the Instructional Voice." Dissertation, Boston College, 1976 (DAI, 37: 4352).

Wagoner's instructional technique unifies his central concerns and offers poets a way to speak to a skeptical audience.

1563 Pinsker, Sanford. "On David Wagoner." SALMAGUNDI, 22-33 (Spring Summer 1973), 306-14.

The consistent satisfaction given by Wagoner's poems is partly achieved by "that dual allegiance to craft and continual surprise which makes a developing body of poetry possible" and partly by "an ongoing love affair with the world." Reprinted in no. 223.

JOHN WAIN

(English; March 14, 1925--)

POEMS

A WORD CARVED ON A SILL. London: Routledge and Kegan Paul; New York: St. Martin's Press, 1956.
WEEP BEFORE GOD. London: Macmillan; New York: St. Martin's Press, 1961.
WILDTRACK. London: Macmillan; New York: Viking Press, 1965.
LETTERS TO FIVE ARTISTS. London: Macmillan, 1969; New York: Viking Press, 1970.
THE SHAPE OF FENG. London: Covent Garden Press, 1972.
FENG. London: Macmillan; New York: Viking Press, 1975.

BIBLIOGRAPHY

1564 Salwak, Dale, ed. JOHN BRAINE AND JOHN WAIN: A REFERENCE GUIDE. Boston: G.K. Hall, 1980. 195 p. Index.

Wain's section is on pages 61 to 171; items are listed by year from 1953 to 1977 and alphabetically within each year. All secondary items are fully annotated.

BIOGRAPHY

1564A Wain, John. SPRIGHTLY RUNNING: PART OF AN AUTOBIOGRAPHY. London: Macmillan, 1962; New York: St. Martin's Press, 1963. 264 p.

Wain's view of his first thirty-five years--at least from the time he could notice "the dwindling countryside" to the summer of 1960.

CRITICAL ARTICLES

1565 Cox, C.B., and A.E. Dyson. "John Wain: 'On the Death of a Murderer.'" In no. 304, pages 153-60.

"The poem . . . is organised in terms of its meaning": that "because we are tainted we should not seek revenge, but a return to civilised values."

1566 Lehmann, John. "The Wain-Larkin Myth: A Reply to John Wain." SEWANEE REVIEW, 66, No. 4 (1958), 578-87.

Examines Wain's argument that a "violent poetic revolution (in two stages)" has "produced a major poet in the person of Mr. Larkin" and finds that argument wanting. It is Wain's view of the poetic revolution that Lehmann challenges, however; he stops short of assessing Larkin's rank among poets.

DIANE WAKOSKI

(American; August 3, 1937--)

POEMS

COINS AND COFFINS. New York: Hawk's Well Press, 1962.
DISCREPANCIES AND APPARITIONS. Garden City, N.Y.: Doubleday, 1966.
THE GEORGE WASHINGTON POEMS. New York: Riverrun Press, 1967.
GREED: PARTS I & II. Los Angeles: Black Sparrow Press, 1967.
THE DIAMOND MERCHANT. Cambridge, Mass.: Sans Souci Press, 1968.
INSIDE THE BLOOD FACTORY. Garden City, N.Y.: Doubleday, 1968.
GREED: PARTS III & IV. Los Angeles: Black Sparrow Press, 1969.
THE MOON HAS A COMPLICATED GEOGRAPHY. Palo Alto, Calif.: Adda Tala Press, 1969.
GREED: PARTS V-VII. Los Angeles: Black Sparrow Press, 1970.
THE MAGELLANIC CLOUDS. Los Angeles: Black Sparrow Press, 1970.
THE MOTORCYCLE BETRAYAL POEMS. New York: Simon and Schuster, 1971.
SMUDGING. Los Angeles: Black Sparrow Press, 1972.
GREED: PARTS VIII, IX, XI. Los Angeles: Black Sparrow Press, 1973.
TRILOGY: COINS AND COFFINS, DISCREPANCIES AND APPARITIONS, THE GEORGE WASHINGTON POEMS. Garden City, N.Y.: Doubleday, 1974.
WAITING FOR THE KING OF SPAIN. Santa Barbara, Calif.: Black Sparrow Press, 1976.
THE MAN WHO SHOOK HANDS. Garden City, N.Y.: Doubleday, 1978.

See a more detailed listing in no. 62, page 1591.

CRITICAL ARTICLES

1567 Fortunato, Mary Jane, and Marc Tretin. "Craft Interview with Diane Wakoski." NEW YORK QUARTERLY, No. 17 (1975), pp. 19-39.

Wakoski describes her beginnings as a student in Thom Gunn's poetry workshop, methods of writing, ideas on the nature of poetry, and the complexities involved in writing and teaching.

1568 Gerber, Philip L., and Robert J. Gemmett, eds. "A Terrible War: A Conversation with Diane Wakoski." FAR POINT, 4 (1970), 44-54.

For SUNY Brockport WRITERS FORUM, 30 October and 1 November 1968. Wakoski discusses her own poetic practices and her ideas about the nature of poets, poetry, and life.

1569 Healy, Claire. "An Interview with Diane Wakoski." CONTEMPORARY LITERATURE, 18 (1977), 1-19.

A brief introduction summarizes Wakoski's main responses during the interview. Healy observes, "One of the best things I have heard about you is that you were a landlady." She asks Wakoski such questions as "Are women writers more visceral than male writers? Do you think that being a misfit is an American phenomenon? What last comment would you like to make about your life as a poet?"

1570 Jeffrey, Phillis Jane Rienstra. "Diane Wakoski: An Expressive Voice in Contemporary American Poetry." Dissertation, University of Texas, Austin, 1976 (DAI, 37: 7405).

On the relationship of oral performance to Wakoski's poetry.

1571 Smith, Larry. "A Conversation with Diane Wakoski." CHICAGO REVIEW, 29, No. 1 (1977), 115-25.

Wakoski explains her feelings about feminism as a movement, other poets, and reviewers. She says satire will be the mode in the new age.

ROBERT PENN WARREN

(American; April 24, 1905--)

POEMS

THIRTY-SIX POEMS. New York: Alcestis Press, 1936.
ELEVEN POEMS ON THE SAME THEME. Norfolk, Conn.: New Directions, 1942.
SELECTED POEMS 1923-1943. New York: Harcourt, Brace: London: Fortune Press, 1944.
BROTHER TO DRAGONS. New York: Random House, 1953; rev. ed., 1979.
PROMISES: POEMS 1954-1956. New York: Random House, 1957.
YOU, EMPERORS, AND OTHERS: POEMS 1957-1960. New York: Random House, 1960.
SELECTED POEMS: NEW AND OLD 1923-1966. New York: Random House, 1966.
INCARNATIONS. New York: Random House, 1968; London: W.H. Allen, 1970.
AUDUBON: A VISION. New York: Random House, 1969.
OR ELSE--POEM/POEMS 1968-1974. New York: Random House, 1974.
SELECTED POEMS: 1923-1975. New York: Random House; London: Secker and Warburg, 1976.
NOW AND THEN: POEMS 1976-1978. New York: Random House, 1978.

BIBLIOGRAPHY

1572 Grimshaw, James A., Jr., ed. ROBERT PENN WARREN: A DESCRIPTIVE BIBLIOGRAPHY 1922-79. Charlottesville: University Press of Virginia, 1981. xxiii, 494 p. Index.

Primary bibliography is fully descriptive. Items in secondary bibliography are not annotated, but the contents of complete books and special journal issues are listed.

1572A Nakadate, Neil. ROBERT PENN WARREN: A REFERENCE GUIDE. Boston: G.K. Hall, 1977. 396 p. Indexes.

Lists and annotates writings about Warren from 1925 to 1975 with a checklist of dissertations and theses. Index includes subject entries as well as author and title entries. One may look up a title of a poem, for example, and find a list of critical comments.

1573 "Robert Penn Warren." In no. 78, pages 197-202.

Lists a hundred and thirty items, only two of which are not in no. 1572A. Entries are listed alphabetically by author.

CRITICAL BOOKS

1574 Clark, William Bedford, ed. CRITICAL ESSAYS ON ROBERT PENN WARREN. Boston: G.K. Hall, 1981. 239 p.

In his introduction Clark surveys the critical opinion of Warren, beginning with Warren as a member of the Fugitive Group and continuing to the present. Among the essays reprinted by Clark are nos. 1582, 1583, and 1585, listed below. Other essays are on Warren's prose works. Richard G. Law's "Notes on the Revised Version of BROTHER TO DRAGONS" (pp. 210-15), written especially for this volume, argues that this new version justifies our ranking Warren among "the major poetic voices of the century."

1574A Justus, James H. THE ACHIEVEMENT OF ROBERT PENN WARREN. Baton Rouge: Louisiana State University Press, 1982. 400 p.

Not seen; advertisement from the publisher calls it "the first comprehensive survey of Warren's complete canon, including the poetry of 1980."

1575 Strandberg, Victor. THE POETIC VISION OF ROBERT PENN WARREN. Lexington: University Press of Kentucky, 1977. 292 p. Notes, indexes.

Strandberg summarizes the criticism on Warren, explores his major themes, and traces his development.

1576 Walker, Marshall. ROBERT PENN WARREN: A VISION EARNED. New York: Barnes and Noble, 1979. 279 p. Appendix.

Walker presents a literary biography with emphasis on Warren the creative writer rather than the critic and teacher. He treats both fiction and poetry. An appendix reprints an interview Walker began with Warren in 1969 but extended over the years with subsequent conversations. It is also reprinted, but without Walker's notes, in no. 1577, pages 173-95.

1577 Watkins, Floyd C., and John T. Hiers. ROBERT PENN WARREN TALKING: INTERVIEWS 1950-1978. New York: Random House, 1980. 318 p.

Eighteen talks and interviews, which the editors believe paint a portrait of Warren. In addition to Warren's statements about himself are talks with Harvey Breit, Ralph Ellison and Eugene Walter, Frank Gado, William Kennedy, C. Vann Woodward, Richard B. Sale, Ruth Fisher, Edwin Newman, Marshall Walker, Bill Moyers, Benjamin DeMott, Peter Stitt, John Baker, and Dick Cavett. Other interviewers are anonymous.

CRITICAL ARTICLES

1578 Bartsch, Friedemann Karl. "The Redemptive Vision: Robert Penn Warren and Spiritual Autobiography." Dissertation, Indiana University, 1977 (DAI, 38: 2117).

Studies guilt and innocence in Warren's fiction as it relates to an archetypal pattern of fall and redemption. Considers BROTHER TO DRAGONS but emphasis is on ALL THE KING'S MEN.

1579 Burnes, Ann Patricia. "Mannerist Mythopoesis: A Reading of Warren's BROTHER TO DRAGONS." Dissertation, St. Louis University, 1978 (DAI, 39: 1560).

Explains the nature of the mannerist style and illustrates its use for literary interpretation with BROTHER TO DRAGONS as example.

1580 Chambers, Robert Hunter III. "Robert Penn Warren: His Growth as a Writer." Dissertation, Brown University, 1969 (DAI, 31: 381).

Attempts to show the relationship (and thus the unity) of Warren's work in various genres to modify the view "through the rather restricting lens of the specific genre study."

1581 Clark, William Bedford. "'Canaan's Grander Counterfeit': Jefferson and America in A BROTHER TO DRAGONS." RENASCENCE, 30, No. 4 (1978), 171-78.

A BROTHER TO DRAGONS shows us not only Jefferson's personality and character but also the "significance of the American experience as a whole." The contradictions in Jefferson and in the American dream may receive "fuller exploration of their implications" in a literary work than in a study of history.

1582 _____. "A Meditation on Folk History: The Dramatic Structure of Robert Penn Warren's THE BALLAD OF BILLIE POTTS." AMERICAN LITERATURE, 49, No. 4 (1978), 635-45.

Clark justifies the structure as an "obvious outgrowth of one of [Warren's] most characteristic preoccupations as a writer--an overwhelming need to come to terms with the significance of the past." Reprinted in no. 1574, pp. 151-59.

1583 Clements, A. L. "Sacramental Vision: The Poetry of Robert Penn Warren." SOUTH ATLANTIC BULLETIN, 43, No. 4 (1978), 47-65.

Sees in Warren's work a "triune theme of self, time, and moral responsibility." Clements surveys Warren's poetic career and shows it developing toward the defining of joy as "a sacramental vision." Reprinted in no. 1574, pp. 216-33.

1584 Dooley, Dennis Michael. "This Collocation of Memories: The Poetic Strategy of Robert Penn Warren." Dissertation, Vanderbilt University, 1970 (DAI, 31: 1268).

Studies the way the "growing complexity" of Warren's themes affects his formal strategies in poems published from 1936 to 1957.

1585 Law, Richard G. "BROTHER TO DRAGONS: The Fact of Violence vs. the Possibility of Love." AMERICAN LITERATURE, 49, No. 4 (1978), 560-79.

Close-reading analysis to show the book as "an inquiry into the nature of love." Warren questions the meaning of the ax murder, the motive for which is love, by "a consideration of what love is or what it might be." Law explores characterization, imagery, and structure. Reprinted in no. 1574, pp. 193-209.

1586 Lubarsky, Richard Jared. "The Instructive Fact of History: A Study of Robert Penn Warren's A BROTHER TO DRAGONS." Dissertation, University of Pennsylvania, 1976 (DAI, 37: 7130).

Sees the poem as central to Warren's work and a summarizing statement of his fictional themes. It marks a "major shift in sensibility" and explains his turn to an almost different career in later work.

1587 Mariani, Paul. "Vespers: Robert Penn Warren at Seventy." PARNASSUS, 4, No. 1 (1975), 176-88.

Review of OR ELSE and DEMOCRACY AND POETRY by Warren. Mariani assesses and summarizes Warren's career and primary concerns, but focuses on the two books under review and what he finds to praise there.

1588 Nakadate, Neil. "Voices of Community: The Function of Colloquy in Robert Penn Warren's BROTHER TO DRAGONS." TENNESSEE STUDIES IN LITERATURE, 21 (1976), 114-24.

In examining the form of the poem, the verse colloquium, Nakadate shows "that while one voice is sufficient to cite the facts, several are needed to frame their context and reveal their implications--and ultimately to accept the knowledge they offer."

1589 Plumly, Stanley. "Warren Selected: An American Poetry, 1923-75." OHIO REVIEW, 18, No. 1 (1977), 37-48.

What may be the last collection of Warren's poems "represents American poetry, as a history, better than any other comparable collection of our period." Plumly believes Warren "has become our great poet." He describes Warren's apparent intentions in each of his collections of verse.

1590 Rotella, Guy Louis. "'Mediation of the Heart': The Tragic Theme in the Poetry of Robert Penn Warren." Dissertation, Boston College, 1976 (DAI, 37: 1553).

Close-reading analyses of poems from THIRTY-SIX POEMS through OR ELSE to show the unity which derives from "a tragic vision of man."

1591 ______. "Robert Penn Warren's YOU, EMPERORS, AND OTHERS." DESCANT, 21, No. 4 (1977), 36-48.

YOU, EMPERORS, AND OTHERS is a key volume in the development of Warren's tragic view of man, a view that sees "man as an inextricable complex of evil and good, limitation and urge for perfection." Rotella looks backward and forward from this collection in tracing out Warren's theme.

1592 Rubin, Louis D., Jr. "Robert Penn Warren: Love and Knowledge." In his THE WARY FUGITIVES: FOUR POETS AND THE SOUTH. Baton Rouge: Louisiana State University Press, 1978, pp. 327-61.

On Warren's career from his association with the "Fugitives" to the verse sequence AUDUBON: A VISION, including a section on Warren's fiction.

1593 Stitt, Peter. "Robert Penn Warren, the Poet." SOUTHERN REVIEW, 12, No. 2 (Spring 1976), 261-76.

Stitt believes that Warren has not been properly recognized as "the dean of living American poets," perhaps because of his versatility in other intellectual areas. To demonstrate Warren's preeminence, he points out the excellences of INCARNATIONS, AUDUBON, and OR ELSE and compares them with the work of other contemporary poets.

1594 Tjenos, William. "The Poetry of Robert Penn Warren: The Art to Transfigure." SOUTHERN LITERARY JOURNAL, 9, No. 1 (1976), 3-12.

Tjenos explores the concept of a past interpreted and re-interpreted by the present. "For Warren, consciousness should not only be broadened and enriched by the present, it should be continually reformed by it." Tjenos uses "Homage to Emerson" as an illustration.

1595 Wilkie, Everette C., Jr. "Robert Penn Warren's Literary Award." AMERICAN NOTES & QUERIES, 16, No. 9 (1978), 140.

Corrects an error in CONTEMPORARY AUTHORS, volumes 13-14, page 836, which attributes Warren's award to the University of Southern California.

1596 Woods, Linda Lentz. "The Language of Robert Penn Warren's Poetry." Dissertation, Emory University, 1969 (DAI, 30: 2049).

Relates Warren's "language" to his ideas of human existence.

1597 Wyatt, David M. "Robert Penn Warren: The Critic as Artist." VIRGINIA QUARTERLY REVIEW, 53, No. 3 (1977), 475-87.

Wyatt describes the effects of the "critic's desire to know" on the artist's "will to present," treating both Warren's fiction and poetry.

THEODORE WEISS

(American; December 16, 1916--)

POEMS

THE CATCH. New York: Twayne, 1951.
OUTLANDERS. New York: Macmillan, 1960.
GUNSIGHT. New York: New York University Press, 1962.
THE MEDIUM. New York: Macmillan, 1965.
THE LAST DAY AND THE FIRST. New York: Macmillan, 1968.
THE WORLD BEFORE US: POEMS 1950-1970. New York: Macmillan, 1970.
FIREWEEDS. New York: Macmillan, 1976.
VIEWS AND SPECTACLES: SELECTED POEMS. London: Chatto and Windus, 1978. Also published as VIEWS AND SPECTACLES: NEW POEMS AND SELECTED SHORTER ONES. New York: Macmillan, 1979.

CRITICAL ARTICLES

1598 Gibbons, Reginald. "The Cure: Theodore Weiss's Poetry." MODERN POETRY STUDIES, 9, No. 1 (1978), 18-33.

A survey of Weiss's poetic career. Gibbons says the "dense texture" of Weiss's poems "often turns out to be the substance." He shows the consistency of Weiss's methods from THE CATCH to FIREWEEDS.

1599 Pocalyko, Michael. "A 'Gunsight' Approach: The American Dream." CONTEMPORARY POETRY, 2, No. 2 (1978), 45-55.

Sees the narrator's predicament and the narrative in GUNSIGHT as a metaphor of America in quest of its dream.

LEW WELCH

(American; August 16,1926--)

POEMS

WOBBLY ROCK. San Francisco: Auerhahn Press, 1960.
HERMIT POEMS. San Francisco: Four Seasons Press, 1965.
ON OUT. Berkeley, Calif.: Oyez Press, 1965.
REDWOOD HAIKU AND OTHER POEMS. San Francisco: Cranium Press, 1972.
RING OF BONE: COLLECTED POEMS 1950-1971. Bolinas, Calif.: Grey Fox Press, 1973.
SELECTED POEMS. Bolinas, Calif.: Grey Fox Press, 1976.

BIOGRAPHY

1600 Welch, Lew. HOW I WORK AS A POET AND OTHER ESSAYS/PLAYS/STORIES. Bolinas, Calif.: Grey Fox Press, 1973. 139 p.

Welch talks about himself and others.

CRITICAL ARTICLES

See Author Index.

PHILIP WHALEN

(American; October 20, 1923--)

POEMS

SELF-PORTRAIT FROM ANOTHER DIRECTION. San Francisco: Auerhahn Press, 1959.

LIKE I SAY. New York: Totem Press, Corinth Books, 1960.

ON BEAR'S HEAD. New York: Harcourt, Brace; Eugene, Oreg.: Coyote Press, 1969.

SEVERANCE PAY. San Francisco: Four Seasons Press, 1970.

SCENES OF LIFE AT THE CAPITAL. Bolinas, Calif.: Grey Fox Press, 1971.

THE KINDNESS OF STRANGERS: POEMS 1969-1974. Bolinas, Calif.: Four Seasons Press, 1975.

DECOMPRESSIONS: SELECTED POEMS. Bolinas, Calif.: Grey Fox Press, 1977.

CRITICAL ARTICLE

1601 Kherdian, David. "Philip Whalen." In no. 373, pages 73-92.

Biographical sketch, criticism, and checklist.

RICHARD WILBUR

(American; March 1, 1921--)

POEMS

THE BEAUTIFUL CHANGES AND OTHER POEMS. New York: Harcourt, Brace, 1947.
CEREMONY AND OTHER POEMS. New York: Harcourt, Brace, 1950.
THINGS OF THIS WORLD: POEMS. New York: Harcourt, Brace, 1956.
POEMS 1943-56. London: Faber and Faber, 1957.
ADVICE TO A PROPHET AND OTHER POEMS. New York: Harcourt, Brace, 1961.
THE POEMS OF RICHARD WILBUR. New York: Harcourt, Brace, 1963.
WALKING TO SLEEP: NEW POEMS AND TRANSLATIONS. New York: Harcourt, Brace, 1969; London: Faber and Faber, 1971.
DIGGING FOR CHINA. Garden City, N.Y.: Doubleday, 1970.
THE MIND-READER: NEW POEMS. New York: Harcourt, Brace, 1976; London: Faber and Faber, 1977.

BIBLIOGRAPHY

1602 Dinneen, Marcia B. "Richard Wilbur: A Bibliography of Secondary Sources." BULLETIN OF BIBLIOGRAPHY, 37, No. 1 (1980), 16-22.

Annotated bibliography of works about Wilbur from 1967 to 1978. Earlier writings may be found in no. 1603.

1603 Field, John P. RICHARD WILBUR: A BIBLIOGRAPHICAL CHECKLIST. Kent, Ohio: Kent State University Press, 1971. 86 p.

Writings by and about Wilbur to 1969, not annotated. Lists about ninety articles on Wilbur.

CRITICAL BOOK

1604 Hill, Donald. RICHARD WILBUR. New York: Twayne, 1967. 192 p.

Discusses in order of publication Wilbur's books of poems through ADVICE TO A PROPHET and finds an evenness of style and technique throughout with some experimentation in this last book. Hill's Selected Bibliography lists reviews of Wilbur's work and adds annotations for eleven comments found in books and articles.

CRITICAL ARTICLES

1605 Gerber, Philip L., and Robert L. Gemmett, eds. "The Window of Art: A Conversation with Richard Wilbur." MODERN POETRY STUDIES, 1, No. 2 (1970), 56-67.

For WRITERS FORUM, SUNY, Brockport, 12 March 1969. On poetic theory and practice, present-day responsiveness to poetry in America, public issues in poetry, and Wilbur's writing habits.

1606 High, Ellesa Clay, and Helen McCloy Ellison. "The Art of Poetry: Richard Wilbur." PARIS REVIEW, 19 (Winter 1977), 68-105.

Interview held in Cummington, Massachusetts, March 1977. On Wilbur's career as poet and teacher and the relationship of the two; on his relation to other poets (Poe, Frost, Lowell); on his responses to reviewers and critics; and on his writing practices. A second interview by Peter Stitt follows, page 86, held in Louisville, Kentucky. Stitt asks him about being personal in poems, "female poets," long poems, influences, and the "advantages to being a poet."

1607 Michelson, Bruce F. "Richard Wilbur: The Quarrel with Poe." SOUTHERN REVIEW, 14, No. 2 (April 1978), 245-61.

Michelson relates Wilbur the scholar and critic of Poe to Wilbur the poet and shows the pervasiveness of Poe in Wilbur's work.

1608 Taylor, David W. "End-Words in Richard Wilbur's Poems." PUBLICATIONS OF THE ARKANSAS PHILOLOGICAL ASSOCIATION, 4, No. 3 (1978), 25-32.

On a hint from a friend, Taylor studied the end-words in numerous Wilbur poems and became convinced that "there is an intentional lining up of a poem's end-words to form a loosely syntactical and gnomic poem; or . . . Wilbur places the important descriptive elements and action words at the end of lines" to form an unintentional summary of the poem.

1609 Woodard, Charles R. "'Happiest Intellection': The Mind of Richard Wilbur." NOTES ON MODERN AMERICAN LITERATURE, 2 (Winter 1977), Item 7.

Not seen, cited in JOURNAL OF MODERN LITERATURE, 7, No. 4 (1979), 838.

1610 ______. "Richard Wilbur's Critical Condition." CONTEMPORARY POETRY, 2, No. 2 (1977), 16-24.

Summarizes the chief critical "complaints" against Wilbur's poetry and tries to answer them.

JOHN WOODS

(American; July 12, 1926--)

POEMS

THE DEATHS AT PARAGON, INDIANA. Bloomington: Indiana University Press, 1955.
ON THE MORNING OF COLOR. Bloomington: Indiana University Press, 1961.
THE CUTTING EDGE. Bloomington: Indiana University Press, 1966.
KEEPING OUT OF TROUBLE. Bloomington: Indiana University Press, 1968.
THE KNEES OF WIDOWS. Kalamazoo, Mich.: Westigan Review Press, 1971.
BONE FLICKER. La Crosse, Wis.: Juniper Press, 1972.
TURNING TO LOOK BACK: POEMS 1955-1970. Bloomington: Indiana University Press, 1972.
STRIKING THE EARTH. Bloomington: Indiana University Press, 1976.
THIRTY YEARS ON THE FORCE. La Crosse, Wis.: Juniper Press, 1978.
THE NIGHT OF THE GAME. Bloomington, Ind.: Raintree Press, 1982.
THE VALLEY OF MINOR ANIMALS. Port Townsend, Wash.: Dragon Gate Press, 1982.

CRITICAL ARTICLES

1611 Etter, David. Review of TURNING TO LOOK BACK. CHICAGO REVIEW, 24 (Winter 1972), 147-49.

Praises Woods's language. Etter thinks Woods the "best poet writing in America today."

1612 Smith, Dave. "Fifty Years, Mrs. Carter: The Poetry of John Woods." MIDWEST QUARTERLY, 17, No. 4 (1976), 410-31.

Smith describes and evaluates Woods's development from THE DEATHS AT PARAGON, INDIANA to STRIKING THE EARTH. Woods's work has been a search for "the truth of the self."

CHARLES WRIGHT

(American; August 25, 1935--)

POEMS

THE GRAVE OF THE RIGHT HAND. Middletown, Conn.: Wesleyan University Press, 1970.
HARD FREIGHT. Middletown, Conn.: Wesleyan University Press, 1973.
BLOODLINES. Middletown, Conn.: Wesleyan University Press, 1975.
CHINA TRACE. Middletown, Conn.: Wesleyan University Press, 1977.
WRIGHT: A PROFILE. Iowa City: Grilled Flowers Press, 1979.

CRITICAL ARTICLE

1613 "Charles Wright at Oberlin." FIELD, 17 (Fall 1977), 46-85.

Edited transcript of a week (November 1976) Wright spent as resident in Oberlin's creative writing program: two evening seminars answering general and specific questions chiefly about BLOODLINES and CHINA TRACE. Wright gives an autobiographical introduction.

DAVID WRIGHT

(English; February 23, 1920--)

POEMS

POEMS. London: Editions Poetry London, 1949.
MORAL STORIES. St. Ives, Engl.: Latin Press, 1952.
MONOLOGUE OF A DEAF MAN. London: Andre Deutsch, 1958.
ADAM AT EVENING. London: Hodder and Stoughton, 1965.
NERVE ENDS. London Hodder and Stoughton, 1969.
A SOUTH AFRICAN ALBUM. Cape Town: David Philip, 1976.
TO THE GODS THE SHADES. Manchester: Carcanet Press, 1976.
A VIEW OF THE NORTH. Ashington, Engl.: Midnag, 1976.

BIOGRAPHY

1614 Wright, David. DEAFNESS: A PERSONAL ACCOUNT. New York: Stein and Day, 1969. 213 p.

Wright describes the auditory limits of his world in an anecdotal way and the details of everyday life that were part of his growing up. The autobiography stops with chapter 7 after Wright left Oxford because, he says, "My life . . . had less and less to do with deafness and deafness less and less to do with my life." It continues, however, with personal descriptions of the deaf person's, and particularly the deaf poet's, manner of life.

CRITICAL ARTICLES

1615 Poole, Richard. Review of TO THE GODS THE SHADES. POETRY WALES, 12, No. 4 (1977), 145-50.

Poole admires in Wright's verse "the livingness with which tradition can speak in it, speaking easily and naturally in contemporary English." He singles out "Moon" for special qualities--its sounds, images, rhythm, and mystery.

1616 Sisson, C.H. "Reading in Depth." TIMES LITERARY SUPPLEMENT, 25 February 1977, p. 210.

In Wright's TO THE GODS THE SHADES "to dip almost anywhere is, for anyone who has what is called an ear, to find the life of the language close to speech, but nourished by the surest and most unpretentious of English traditions." Reprinted in Sisson's AVOIDANCE OF LITERATURE (Manchester: Carcanet Press, 1978).

JAMES WRIGHT

(American; December 13, 1927-March 25, 1980)

POEMS

THE GREEN WALL. New Haven, Conn.: Yale University Press, 1957.
SAINT JUDAS. Middletown, Conn.: Wesleyan University Press, 1959.
THE BRANCH WILL NOT BREAK. Middletown, Conn.: Wesleyan University Press, 1963.
SHALL WE GATHER AT THE RIVER. Middletown, Conn.: Wesleyan University Press, 1968; London: Rapp and Whiting, 1969.
COLLECTED POEMS. Middletown, Conn.: Wesleyan University Press, 1971.
TWO CITIZENS. New York: Farrar, Straus and Giroux, 1973.
MOMENTS OF THE ITALIAN SUMMER. Washington, D.C.: Dryad Press, 1976.
TO A BLOSSOMING PEAR TREE. New York: Farrar, Straus and Giroux, 1977; London: Faber and Faber, 1979.

BIBLIOGRAPHY

1617 McMaster, Belle M. "James Arlington Wright: A Checklist." BULLETIN OF BIBLIOGRAPHY, 31, No. 2 (1974), 71-82, 88.

Primary bibliography introduced by a brief biographical sketch. Lists Wright's books, poems in periodicals and anthologies, translations, review articles, and recordings through June 1973.

CRITICAL ARTICLES

1618 André, Michael. "An Interview with James Wright." UNMUZZLED OX, 1 (February 1972), 2-18.

Discussion of Wright's poems and influences on them, his poetic acquaintances, feelings about the United States and Canada, benefits received from translating, and the neglect of poets and poetry.

1619 Coles, Robert. "James Wright: One of Those Messengers." AMERICAN POETRY REVIEW, 2, No. 4 (1973), 36-37.

On Wright's universality: "he is so close to just about every American that it hurts to read him."

1620 DeFrees, Madeline. "James Wright's Early Poems: A Study in 'Convulsive' Form." MODERN POETRY STUDIES, 2, No. 6 (1972), 241-51.

Defines Wright's "deep limiting form," illustrating with "A Fit against the Country" from THE GREEN WALL and brief comments on other poems.

1621 Ditsky, John. "James Wright Collected: Alterations on the Monument." MODERN POETRY STUDIES, 2, No. 6 (1972), 252-59.

Describes the changes in form and voice in Wright's poems as selected from original volumes for COLLECTED POEMS. "Something there is in James Wright which does not allow him ever to let go completely, and . . . natural reverence for necessary formality" sets him apart; "it is the 'pure clear word' that Wright celebrates."

1622 Dodd, Wayne. "That Same Bodily Curve of the Spirit." OHIO REVIEW, 18, 2 (1977), 59-62.

Review of MOMENTS OF THE ITALIAN SUMMER. Compares and contrasts this volume with Wright's other poems. The difference in these poems seems to be in the setting, which Wright here observes from outside. "In the body and spirit of America, Wright's spirit finds body--and tongue."

1623 Dougherty, David C. "James Wright: The Murderer's Grave in the New Northwest." OLD NORTHWEST, 2, No. 1 (1976), 45-54.

What Wright has to say about self-knowledge is in his poems about his "ancestors." Dougherty uses "At the Executed Murderer's Grave" to develop his thesis and other poems to illustrate Wright's maturing view of his homeland.

1624 ______. "The Skeptical Poetry of James Wright." CONTEMPORARY POETRY, 2, No. 2 (1977), 4-10.

Because of "a general mistrust of the poet's motives and craft" Wright "has consistently been dissatisfied with his own poems." This "dissatisfaction has led him to new experiments and new attempts to create form."

1625 Hamod, Sam. "Floating in a Hammock: James Wright." CONTEMPORARY POETRY, 2, No. 3 (1977), 62-65.

A running commentary on Wright's poem "Lying in a Hammock at William Duffy's Farm in Pine Island, Minnesota" from title to last line with an interpretive note as conclusion.

1626 Matthews, William. "The Continuity of James Wright's Poems." OHIO REVIEW, 18, No. 2 (1977), 44-57.

Discusses the language of Wright's poems and its relation to his themes and his development as a poet.

1627 Molesworth, Charles. "James Wright and the Dissolving Self." SALMAGUNDI, Nos. 22-23 (Spring-Summer 1973), pp. 222-33.

The problem, which James Wright and other contemporary poets must confront, is that a "lyric poem, as it approaches song as one of its aesthetic limits, threatens to dissolve the self in which it originates." Molesworth explores Wright's various attacks on the problem of controlling emotion in his poems. Reprinted in no. 223.

1628 Robinett, Emma Jane. "'No Place to Go But Home': The Poetry of James A. Wright." Dissertation, University of Notre Dame, 1976 (DAI, 37: 1553).

Traces thematic and technical changes in Wright's poems from THE GREEN WALL through SHALL WE GATHER AT THE RIVER.

1629 Saunders, William S. "Indignation Born of Love: James Wright's Ohio Poems." OLD NORTHWEST, 4, No. 4 (1978), 353-69.

Wright and other poets learned from Robert Bly "to enter their own Minnesotas, their own felt worlds, without fear of dismissal." Saunders traces Wright's treatment of Midwestern people in order to show his poetic development.

1630 Spendal, R.J. "Wright's 'Lying in a Hammock at William Duffy's Farm in Pine Island, Minnesota.'" EXPLICATOR, 34, No. 9 (1976), Item 64.

The central conflict of the poem is "in the opposition between an impulse to change and failure or inability to do so."

1631 Stitt, Peter A. "The Poetry of James Wright." MINNESOTA REVIEW, NRP No. 2 (Spring 1972), pp. 13-32.

On the development of Wright's style which, Stitt says, "is like reading a history of the best contemporary American poetry." Stitt's examples are chronological as they appear in COLLECTED POEMS.

1632 Taylor, Richard Lawrence. "Roots and Wings: The Poetry of James Wright." Dissertation, University of Kentucky, 1974 (DAI, 36: 1512).

On the influence of Robert Bly's "critical theory" in Wright's poetry.

1633 Yenser, Stephen. "Open Secrets." PARNASSUS, 6, No. 2 (1978), 125-42.

Review of MOMENTS OF THE ITALIAN SUMMER and TO A BLOSSOMING PEAR TREE. Wright's later poems record a struggle between his imagination ("adventurousness, his extravagance") and order (his desire "to keep the work in hand moving constantly to some end that will seem appointed"). Yenser illustrates his thesis with poems from these two collections.

LOUIS ZUKOFSKY

(American; January 23, 1904-May 12, 1978)

POEMS

SOME TIME. Stuttgart, Germany: Jonathan Williams, 1956.
"A" 1-12. Ashland, N.C.: Origin Press, 1959.
ALL: THE COLLECTED SHORT POEMS 1956-1964, 1966. New York: Norton, 1971.
"A" 13-21. London: Jonathan Cape, 1969.
"A" 24. New York: Grossman, 1972.
"A" [Complete version]. Berkeley: University of California Press, 1978.

BIOGRAPHY

1634 Zukofsky, Celia, and Louis, Zukofsky. LOUIS ZUKOFSKY: AUTOBIOGRAPHY. New York: Grossman, 1970. 63 p.

Some of Zukofsky's poems set to music, interspersed with very brief autobiographical notes.

CRITICAL BOOK

1635 Terrell, Carroll F., ed. LOUIS ZUKOFSKY: MAN AND POET. Orono, Maine: National Poetry Foundation, [1979]. 449 p.

New and reprinted pieces on the life and work of Zukofsky. Includes about half the essays from PAIDEUMA, 7, No. 3 (Winter 1978), a special Zukofsky number, and several from MAPS, No. 5 (1973), another Zukofsky issue. Secondary bibliography elaborately annotated by Terrell and Winifred Hayek. Seven essays on "The Man," seven on "The Poet," four on "The Thinker," and three on "The Translator."

CRITICAL ARTICLES

1636 Cox, Kenneth. "Louis Zukofsky." AGENDA, 16, No. 2 (1978), 11-13.

An appreciative statement about Zukofsky's life and work.

1637 Webb, Timothy. "With the Zukofskys on Helicon Hill." ARIEL, 2 (April 1971), 59-64.

Webb praises the intentions of Louis and Celia Zukofsky to enliven Catullus in their free and creative translation but thinks it "largely a failure." Their efforts to pun on the Latin and refresh its meaning lead instead to obscurities.

AUTHOR INDEX

This index includes all authors and editors of books and articles cited in this guide. Individual poets are also indexed. Alphabetization is letter by letter and numbers refer to entry numbers.

A

B

C

D

G

H

L

M

N

Q

R

S

Y

TITLE INDEX

This index includes all titles in the general section of the guide and those titles in the individual poets section that do not mention the poets or their work. Alphabetization is letter by letter and numbers refer to entry numbers. Titles of books appear in upper case and titles of articles appear in upper and lower case, no quotation marks.

A

B

C

D

E

F

G

H

I

J

K

L

M

N

O

P

T

U

V

W

Y